AUSTRALIAN MARKETING: CRITICAL ESSAYS, READINGS AND CASES

AUSTRALIAN MARKETING: CRITICAL ESSAYS, READINGS AND CASES

PETER GRAHAM
EDITOR

PRENTICE HALL

New York London Toronto Sydney Tokyo Singapore

© 1993 by Prentice Hall of Australia Pty Ltd

All rights reserved. No part of this publication may be reproduced, stored in a retrieval system, or transmitted in any form or by any means, electronic, mechanical, photocopying, recording, or otherwise, without written permission of the publisher.

Acquisitions Editor: Michael Page
Production Editors: Fiona Marcar & Katie Millar
Cover design: The Modern Art Production Group, Prahran, Vic.
Typeset by Keyboard Wizards, Allambie Heights, NSW

Printed in Australia by McPhersons Printing Group

1 2 3 4 5 97 96 95 94 93

ISBN 0 7248 0060 3

National Library of Australia
Cataloguing-in-Publication Data

Australian marketing.

  Includes index.
  ISBN 0 7248 0600 3.

  1. Marketing – Australia. I. Graham, Peter.

658.800994

Prentice Hall, Inc., *Englewood Cliffs, New Jersey*
Prentice Hall Canada, Inc., *Toronto*
Prentice Hall Hispanoamericana, SA, *Mexico*
Prentice Hall of India Private Ltd, *New Delhi*
Prentice Hall International, Inc., *London*
Prentice Hall of Japan, Inc., *Tokyo*
Prentice Hall of Southeast Asia Pty Ltd, *Singapore*
Editora Prentice Hall do Brasil Ltda, *Rio de Janeiro*

PRENTICE HALL

A division of Simon & Schuster

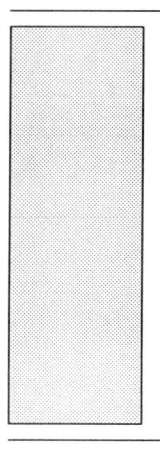

CONTENTS

Preface ix
List of Contributors xi
Acknowledgment xiii

PART A: The Process Of Studying Marketing 1
Case study references, by Peter Graham 3
The talk that informs: Tips on how to prepare an oral marketing report,
   by Terry Gatfield 4
A guide to essay writing, by Paul McCarthy and the Foundation Year
   Teaching Team, Faculty of Commerce and Administration,
   Griffith University 10
Legal aspects of marketing in Australia, by Peter M. McDermott 20

PART B: Readings and Cases 29
1. Understanding Marketing 31
   Introduction 32
   Readings: 1. Beyond competition to sur/petition, by Edward de Bono 33
               2. From woeful to wonderful: A step-by-step approach,
                  by Michael Kiely 40
   Cases: 1. Marketers: The endangered species, by Paul Shea 45
               2. Thomas Toy Company Limited, by Michael Harker 49
               3. Do you have what it takes! Specific courage—
                  Training experiences for students, by John Jackson 51
               4. How switched on are you? by John Clayton 58

2. Analysing the Market 61
   Introduction 62
   Readings: 3. Segmentation, by Neil Shoebridge 63
               4. How green was my market, by George Camakaris 64

vi CONTENTS

  Cases: 5. A lot of bullshit in the market research industry,
              by David James   67
            6. Fine Music Network, by Noela Cerutti, Peter Graham,
              Felicity Neary and Gary Thorpe   70
            7. The Australian nursery industry, by Peter Graham and
              Debra Harker   73

3. **Developing the Marketing Mix   87**
  Introduction   88
  Readings: 5. Ho hum or let's go outdoor? by Richard Luke   89
             6. Feisty Foodland on expansion trail, by Tim Treadgold   93
             7. When the highest price is right, by Ken Roberts   95
  Cases: 8. Oldies under the microscope, by St George TAFE   98
             9. The Queensland grocery industry, by Alan Dowsett,
               Peter Graham and Robert Young   100
            10. Garden centre retailing in Australia, by Peter Graham   109

4. **Applications of Marketing   119**
  Introduction   120
  Readings: 8. Deeds, not words, says Japanese guru,
               by Robert Gottliebsen   121
             9. US airline makes itself at home away from home,
               by Neil Shoebridge   124
  Cases: 11. Non-profit organisations take on new discipline,
               by David James   128
            12. The globalisation of Fosters, by Alan Kilgore and
               Terry Alchin   132
            13. Marketing Drug Arm Brisbane, by Terry Gatfield   146

5. **Designing Competitive Marketing Strategy   152**
  Introduction   153
  Readings: 10. How do you know they're satisfied? by Robert Orth   154
            11. Statistics reveal major move in supermarkets,
               by Bernard Holt   158
            12. How a steady job turned into a frantic scramble,
               by David James   160
            13. CUB gets the Tooheys blues, by Neil Shoebridge   165
  Cases: 14. The Australian financial services industry,
               by Michael Harker   171
            15. St George Bank, by Michael Harker   176

6. **Implementing Marketing   187**
  Introduction   188
  Readings: 14. The Gold Coast's mid-life crisis, by Andrew Stewart   189
            15. Where Brian Quinn went wrong, by Robert Gottliebsen   194
            16. Fosters faces a familiar foe, by Matthew Stevens   199
            17. Fast food frenzy, by Neil Shoebridge   203

Cases: 16. Marketing of the Queensland Art Gallery, by Peter Graham, Neal Hogg, Nicole Licastro and Danielle McEwan 211
17. Marketing the non-profit way, by Terry Gatfield 217

7. **Marketing and Society** 223
   Introduction 224
   Readings: 18. Is there more to ethical marketing than marketing ethics? by Mike Brennan 225
   19. Fear and loathing can sell anything, by Graham Haines 234
   20. How to protect trade secrets, by Margaret Lyons 237
   21. Consumers ain't what they used to be, by Tony Wheeler 240
   Cases: 18. The Quit Club, by Peter Graham and Debra Harker 246
   19. Ethics and international business, by Daniel W. Skubik 251

PART C: Selected Australian Statistics 259

Introduction and sources of selected statistics, by Peter Graham and Debra Harker 261
How quickly will advertising expenditure bounce back? by Bernard Holt 264
The top 200 advertisers 267
The top 10 Australian-owned agencies 273
A selection of Australia's top 300 advertising agencies 274
Australian advertising agencies, fastest rising incomes, 1990–91 275
Australian advertising agencies, fastest falling incomes, 1990–91 276
God is in the details, by Deane Russell 276
Australian Bureau of Statistics: Information sheet 280
The Australian All Ordinaries Index Companies Handbook 1990–91 283

Part D: Critical Essays 291

Competitive strategy: A critique of Porter's analysis, by John Forster 293
Marketing, strategic management and models of strategy formation, by Michael Browne 310
Marketing's domain: A critical review of the development of the marketing concept, by Peter Graham 330
Most service quality research is wrong, by Chuck Chakrapani 341
How manipulanda and discriminanda can builda your branda, by Stan Glaser, Michael Halliday and Ross Cameron 344

Company Index 349
Subject Index 353

PREFACE

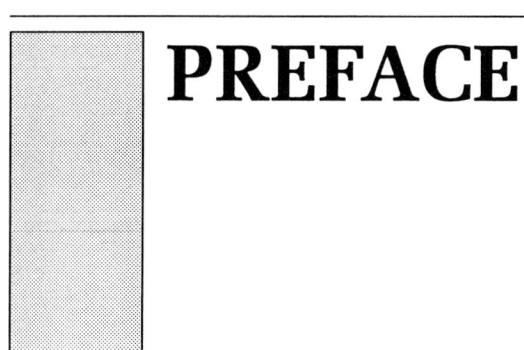

This text is designed to replace *Insights Into Australian Marketing*, published by Prentice Hall Australia 1990. The bulk of the new text comprises, as before, readings and cases to supplement any standard introductory marketing text. However, it should be made clear that neither the readings nor, more particularly, the cases are of the traditional structure that contain all or most of the material necessary for case analysis. Rather they are structured to provide a description or introduction to an area of interest in order to stimulate tutorial discussion or the search for additional material to answer in a formal written way the questions posed.

In addition to the readings and cases, the text contains a rewritten and updated section on Australian statistics and sources, and a new section on the Process of Studying Marketing. For more advanced students there is the totally new section containing a series of essays that critique some significant aspects of marketing.

It is no accident that Part B-7, Marketing and Society, is one of the largest sections of the book. The excesses of the Australian business community in the 1980s need to be addressed in the 1990s. Our society is unlikely to tolerate a perceived absence of any sense of ethics or morality. Hence the readings and cases in this conceptually difficult, but practically so important, an area.

Your feedback from my last two efforts have been incorporated in this text. For example, some very short and some extended cases. I encourage you to let me have feedback on this text either directly or through the Publishers.

Peter Graham
August 1993

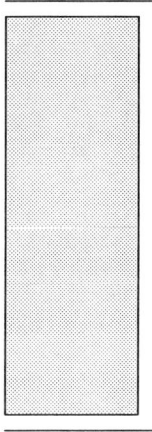

LIST OF CONTRIBUTORS

Peter Graham is a Senior Lecturer at Griffith University in Queensland

Terry Gatfield is an Associate Lecturer at Griffith University in Queensland

Paul McCarthy is a Lecturer at Griffith University in Queensland

Peter McDermott is a Senior Lecturer in Law at the University of Queensland

Edward de Bono is a world-renowned author and contributor to *Marketing Magazine*

Michael Kiely is Editor of *Marketing Magazine*

Paul Shea is a contributor to *Marketing Magazine*

Michael Harker is Lecturer at Griffith University in Queensland

John Jackson is a Lecturer at the University of Central Queensland

John Clayton is a contributor to *Marketing Magazine*

Neil Shoebridge is a contributor to *Business Review Weekly*

George Camakaris is a contributor to *Marketing Magazine*

David James is a contributor to *Marketing Magazine*

Noela Cerutti, Felicity Neary and Gary Thorpe are graduates of Griffith University in Queensland

Debra Harker is a Researcher with Griffith University in Queensland

Richard Luke is a contributor to *Marketing Magazine*

Tim Treadgold is a contributor to *Business Review Weekly*

Ken Roberts is a contributor to *Marketing Magazine*

Alan Dowsett and Robert Young are graduates of Griffith University in Queensland

xii LIST OF CONTRIBUTORS

Robert Gottliebsen is Editorial Director of *Business Review Weekly*

Alan Kilgore and **Terry Alchin** are Lecturers at the University of Western Sydney

Robert Orth is a contributor to *Marketing Magazine*

Bernard Holt is the Principal of CEASA (Commercial Economic Advisory Service of Australia) and a regular contributor to *Marketing Magazine*

Andrew Stewart is a contributor to *Business Review Weekly*

Matthew Stevens is a contributor to *Business Review Weekly*

Neal Hogg, **Nicole Licastro** and **Danielle McEwan** are graduates of Griffith University in Queensland

Mike Brennan is a Senior Lecturer at Massey University in New Zealand and also Editor of the *Marketing Bulletin*

Graham Haines is a contributor to *Marketing Magazine*

Margaret Lyons is a contributor to *Business Review Weekly*

Tony Wheeler is a contributor to *Marketing Magazine*

Daniel W. Skubik is a Lecturer at Griffith University in Queensland

Deane Russell is Director of Marketing and Public Relations for the Australian Bureau of Statistics

John Forster is a Senior Lecturer at Griffith University in Queensland

Michael Browne is a Research Fellow at Queensland University of Technology

Dr Chuck Chakrapani is President of Standard Research Systems Inc., Consultant to AMR:Quantum and Editor-in-Chief of the *Canadian Journal of Marketing Research*. He has also contributed a series of articles to *Marketing Magazine*

Dr Stan Glaser is Associate Professor at Macquarie University

Dr Michael Halliday is Head of the School of Marketing at University of Technology, Sydney

Dr Ross Cameron is Director, Marketing Major, at University of Western Sydney–Hawkesbury

Dr Norman Chorn is a contributor to *Marketing Magazine*

Howard Manning, **Kerry Waters** and **Christine Coe** are graduates of Griffith University in Queensland

David B. Wolfe is an American Consultant and Lecturer and also contributes to *Marketing Magazine*

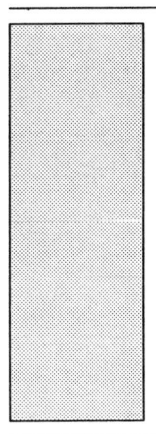

ACKNOWLEDGMENT

This textbook was compiled while the editor was on research attachment to the Graduate School of Management at the University of Queensland. The editor is appreciative of the facilities and support of the Graduate School of Management.

PART A

THE PROCESS OF STUDYING MARKETING

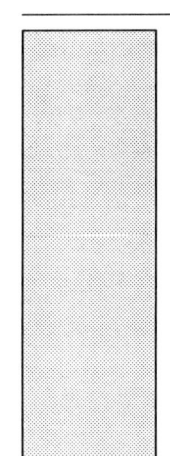

Case study references, by Peter Graham

The talk that informs: Tips on how to prepare an oral marketing report, by Terry Gatfield

A guide to essay writing, by Paul McCarthy and the Foundation Year Teaching Team, Faculty of Commerce and Administration, Griffith University

Legal aspects of marketing in Australia, by Peter McDermott

Case study references

Rather than include an article on 'how to do a case study', students will find the following reference list helpful. Different cases require different methodological approaches, for example some require financial analysis whilst others may require qualitative insights. The following list of references will be of help to students:

Balan, P. (1990), *Creating Achievable Marketing Plans*, Polyglot Enterprises, South Australia.

Bonoma, T. V. (1984), 'Questions and Answers about Case Learning', in *Managing Marketing: Text, Cases and Readings*, Macmillan, London, pp. xiii–xvii.

Bonoma, T. V. and Kosnik, T. J. (1990), 'Learning with Cases', in *Marketing Management: Text and Cases*, Irwin, pp. 24–39.

Dalrymple, D. J., Parsons, L. J. and Jeannet, J-P. (1992), 'Introduction To The Case Method' in *Cases in Marketing Management*, Wiley, pp. 2–7.

Hubbard, G. (1990), 'Analysing a Case', in P. Graham (ed.), *Insights Into Australian Marketing: Readings and Cases*, Prentice Hall, Australia, pp. 32–41.

Lehman, D. R. and Winer, R. S. (1991), *Analysis for Marketing Planning*, (2nd edn), Irwin, Australia.

Luck, D. J., Ferrell, O. C. and Lucas, G. H. Jnr. (1989), *Marketing Strategy and Plans*, (3rd edn), Prentice Hall, Englewood Cliffs, New Jersey.

McDonald, M. H. B. (1989), *Marketing Plans—How to Prepare Them: How to Use Them*, Heinemann Professional Publishing, Oxford.

Parslow, J. (1990), 'How to Make Sense of Marketing', in P. Graham (ed.), *Insights Into Australian Marketing: Readings and Cases*, Prentice Hall, pp. 1–31.

Parslow, J. (1990), 'Mastering Case Analysis', in McColl-Kennedy, J., Yau, O. and Hardman, R. (eds), *Australian Marketing: A Casebook*, Harper & Row (Australasia), pp. xxv–xxxvii.

The talk that informs: Tips on how to prepare an oral marketing report

by Terry Gatfield

"I am a poor man, your Majesty", the Mad Hatter began, in a trembling voice, "—and I hadn't begun my tea—not above a week or so—and what with the bread-and-butter getting so thin—and the twinkling of the tea—"

"The twinkling of the what?" said the King.

"It began with the tea", the Hatter replied.

And so on-and-on the Mad Hatter continued his defence in a confused stupor. The only relief was from the equally frustrating March Hare who offered but little sanity to the occasion.

Finally, in miserable exhaustion the Hatter dropped his tea cup and bread-and-butter and went down on one knee. "I am a poor man, your Majesty."

"No," said the King, "You are a very poor speaker".

Lewis Carroll, *Alice's Adventures in Wonderland*

Perhaps the King in Lewis Carroll's story was able to perceive the difference between a fool and a person who has wisdom and understanding, but unfortunately can't deliver the goods. Will you be as fortunate in meeting such a sympathetic person in the future in presenting your oral reports and ideas?

Being able to present a quality oral report in marketing is an essential part of the marketers' tool kit. The following paper consists of a structure and few ideas which you may desire to incorporate in presenting an oral report on a marketing topic. This paper has been designed to assist you in gaining clarity and strength for your presentation.

With the advent of computers we have generally substituted quality of information for quantity. Providing masses of printout data and spreadsheets to a board of management or group is no guarantee that information is being absorbed or even effectively communicated. Numerical data seems to have strong communication value only to those who have a strong left-brain orientation, to use Roger Sperry's typology. But for those who have a strong right-brain orientation, generally those individuals who think perceptually, globally and intuitively, you must go well beyond concrete and numerical data.

The presentation of the 'talk to inform' demands a special style, very different to the 'short talk to get action', the 'talk to convince' and the 'impromptu talk'. It may be considered that the 'talk to inform' is the hardest to master as it relies on your having not only a detailed knowledge of your subject but also a critical understanding of your audience and their level of comprehension. In addition, the 'talk to inform' is generally longer than the other three types and thus requires a greater variety of stimulus in presentation techniques.

This paper has nine basic parts: planning the journey, navigational aids, timing the journey, journey speed, showing the signposts, describing the landscape, colouring the landscape, getting visual and what to do on arrival.

Planning the journey

You are the executive of a guided tour company. Your task is to take your delegates on a strange and unfamiliar journey down a long road which they have not travelled before. Your first task is to clearly, but briefly, inform your fellow travellers where you intend to take them. Then you start them on the journey path and at suitable intervals stop to explain what they are to see and how that supports the purpose of the journey. Next you take them further on, stopping again and repeating the process. This continues until you reach the destination and at this point you turn your audience around, and facing up the road, you explain the journey taken. Finally you highlight other routes that may be taken by others to achieve a similar destination.

All journeys can be seen as a set of different stages directed to some final destination. Likewise any subject can be broken down and arranged in a logical sequence. Most subjects have a clear logical sequence, such as the historical development of certain concepts, or the component parts of a theoretical model. Every talk *must* have a sequential structure which is arranged logically with a central focal point. The arrangement and priorities are up to you but, if possible, start with the point which is of greatest interest to your audience. The detail you bring to each stage will depend on its relative importance and be governed by time constraints.

Navigational aids—nerves and notes

You must have both notes and nerves on your journey—don't leave home without them.

Nerves, or fear, is an essential part of your presentation. Never start a talk without nerves. If you don't have nerves there is a high chance that your presentation will be boring, lifeless and of little interest to your audience.

Nerves are your body's way of preparing you to meet unusual challenges. Dale Carnegie says: 'When you notice your pulse beating faster and your respiration speeding up, don't become alarmed. Your body is getting ready for action. If these physical preparations are held within limits, you will be capable of thinking faster, talking more fluently, and generally speaking with greater intensity than under normal circumstances'.

Try to be like the duck—on the surface it is calm and relaxed but under the surface it is paddling furiously, controlling its speed and direction towards a specific destination.

Journey notes are essential. But never, never read from a fully composed script although you may occasionally read from a written quotation of another author. Three of the greatest dangers of reading from a text are that eye contact is lost, you will not be able to continuously gauge audience reaction to which you may need to adjust, and finally if you ever lose your way in the text it is very hard to return to it (and very embarrassing). The alternatives to a written text are palm cards or highlighted brief notes arranged sequentially. Both the palm cards and highlighted text methods demand an in-depth knowledge of your subject *and* rehearsal for your audiences journey.

Time your journey

Don't try to take your audience on a detailed 3000 year archaeological tour of the Holy Lands in twenty minutes. Structure and reduce your talk to fit the time available, never the other way around. Clarity and structure are far more important than trying to elaborate on the maximum number of points you could make. A well-structured talk should centre around only one main topic and, dependent on time, be limited to between three and five sub-topics, all of which should support the main topic.

If you understand your subject well the greatest problem you may face is not, 'How is it possible to address an audience for as long as ten to 20 minutes?' but, 'how is it possible to condense the material into a digestible form in such a short space of time?'. You must ruthlessly axe out all material that does not support the logic and clarity of your argument no matter how interesting, stimulating or even funny it may be. Your objective is to inform, not impress nor entertain.

If you go over time, ask politely for a short extension and mention your remaining points briefly, while trying not to reduce your conclusions. The conclusions should contain a powerful summary of your journey.

The speed of the journey

Your general duty is to go as fast as the slowest member of your tour. If it is possible, select the slowest learner by reading their body language; gauge their comprehension and adjust your speed to that person.

A Formula One Grand Prix drive may be exhilarating but the journey is likely to be meaningless. Don't get confused between a high speed, high-powered thrill and a deep inner experience of leading your fellow travellers on a rich, and rewarding, slow discovery.

Showing the signposts

Some of your tour party will have difficulty keeping up with you, you must help them along the journey you want them to take. You can do this by plainly mentioning, as you go along the road, that you are taking up one point then another. Here are a few ideas:

- 'My first point is this . . .'
- 'My second point is . . .'
- 'My theme is . . .'
- 'Specifically I would like to . . .'
- 'Further . . .'
- 'Finally . . .'
- 'There are three principles that . . .'
- 'Firstly . . .'
- 'Secondly . . .'
- 'Thirdly . . .'

If that seems too simplistic then listen to some of the great speakers and you will find most of them use this technique.

Describing the landscape

In the recent film, 'Driving Miss Daisy', the rich millionairess said obstinately over a point of dispute with her chauffeur Hope: 'How would you know, you are old and you can't see properly'. The old man replied philosophically: 'How would you know Miss Daisy, for you to know that you have gota' get into my head and look through my eyes'.

Your duty is to get your fellow travellers to see things as beautifully and clearly as you see them. This is especially true when dealing with complex and abstract issues. In dealing with complex issues and ideas your audience will need help on the journey to appreciate the richness that you see very clearly. In these situations always compare the familiar with the unknown for your travellers. For example, suppose you are discussing one of chemistry's contributions to industry—a catalyst. It is a substance that causes changes to occur in other substances without changing itself. That is easy to understand if you are a scientist, but could this be better for a non-technical audience? A catalyst is like a little boy in a school yard, tripping, punching, upsetting, poking all the other kids but never being touched by a blow from anyone else. Never anticipate your travellers can see the value and the beauty of your subject unless you help them by describing the landscape in the language they know.

Colouring the landscape— Selecting your paints and brushes

Your words are your paints and brushes: use them wisely as an artist to paint the picture of your journey. But use them simply as Aristotle recommends: 'Think as the wise men do, but speak as the common people do'. If you must use a technical term, don't use it glibly until you have explained it so that everybody on your tour knows what it means. This is especially true of your 'keystone' words.

8 PART A

A famous lecturer was asked the formula for success in public speaking. 'Well', he said, 'in promulgating your esoteric cognitions and articulating superficial, sentimental and psychological observations, beware of platitudinous ponderosity. Let your extemporaneous decantations and unpremeditated expiations have intelligibility and veracious vivacity without rodomontade and thrasonical bombast. Sedulously avoid all polysyllabic profundity, pusillanimous vacuity, pestiferous profanity and similar transgressions. Or, 'he concluded smilingly, 'talk simply, naturally, and above all, don't use big words!'

Remember, your objective is to inform *not* to impress or to confuse. Always substitute complexities with simplicities. If your language choice fails to give your audience a clear understandable picture of the journey and the final destination then change your paints and brushes.

Getting visual

The chinese proverb is well known, 'A picture is worth a thousand words'. The experts tell us that of the total information we receive, 10% comes from hearing, 80% from seeing and 10% from the combined remaining senses. If you want your audience to be accurately *informed* and kept stimulated on the journey you are taking then you must develop a good visual-audio mix.

This section briefly introduces three important factors in visuals: the first is the effective use of visual aids, the second is body language and finally dress.

If you use visual aids such as charts or diagrams make certain they are very large, clear and that they do *not* contain too much information. Avoid reading from a projector screen, from the overhead projector (OHP) or wall charts as you will lose important eye contact. If you use exhibits to illustrate your talk think about these suggestions:

1. Keep the exhibit out of sight until you are ready to use it and when you have finished with it put it away.
2. Make certain the exhibit is large enough.
3. Never pass an exhibit around whilst you are talking.
4. One exhibit that moves is worth ten that don't.
5. Never stare or talk to the exhibit.

If you are intending to use detailed handouts never give them out until the end of the talk unless you are using them as brief illustrations to explain complex relationships.

Regarding body language, be conscious of a sloppy stand, use plenty of movement, provide maximum eye contact and use sufficient hand and body gestures. Avoid some of the obvious errors, such as folding your arms in front, clasping your hands together and placing them behind your head. Try and avoid standing behind a lectern or desk as these act as barriers between you and the audience.

With respect to dress, the first, and for some the last, sentence that your audience will read is your dress. It must be appropriate to the occasion. Appropriate dress will give you increased confidence and assured audience acceptance.

Destination arrival

You have taken your audience on a journey and have successfully reached your destination. The journey is not yet complete. You still have three short tasks to undertake: the review, alternatives and question time.

Review your journey by showing the completed map which states where you started, the route that you have taken and the place where you have landed. The review is critical and frequently overlooked, but it is the glue that should finally bind your talk together.

Secondly, you should consider sharing with your travellers the idea that the route that you have taken is not the only one and there are others that could be considered. This is especially true in the social science disciplines such as marketing. Therefore, explain a few alternative routes that could have been undertaken. This section can be brief but it is not wise generally to omit.

At the conclusion of your talk leave an appropriate time for questions. When your talk is completed never forget to thank the audience for their time and participation.

Conclusion

The 'talk to inform' is an exercise in marketing. You are the product, the promotion and the channel. You must design and tailor it all to your target needs, and you must place it in the right setting with the right timing promoting it with expertise. The brilliance of your ideas and research can only be judged on the quality of your presentation.

Spencer Tracy, the great Hollywood actor, once said in response to a question from a young boy who asked him what goes into being a great success, 'Son, it's 95% luck and 5% skill and effort'. As a timely warning he added, 'But please never ever try it without the 5%'. For your presentation it is likely to be 5% luck and 95% skill but please never ever try it without the 95%.

The most important thing to do is to practise and learn by doing. If you desire to do some further reading you will find some excellent books on the market. Mentioned below are just a few to get you started.

References

Bradley, B. E. (1991), *Fundamentals of Speech Communication*, WCB, Dubuque, Iowa.

Carnegie, D. (1962), *The Quick and Easy Way to Effective Speaking*, Morrison & Gibb, New York.

Mears, A. J. (1982), *The Right Way to Speak in Public*, Paperfronts, Kingswood, Surrey, UK.

Pease, A. (1985), *Body Language*, Camel Publishing Co, Sydney.

Snell, F. (1981), *How to Stand Up and Speak Well in Business*, Simon & Shuster, New York.

☐ A guide to essay writing
by Paul McCarthy and the Foundation Year Teaching Team, Faculty of Commerce and Administration, Griffith University

Introduction

A large part of your assessment in a university course is through *essays*. An academic essay is structured as an argument. This means that you cannot just list facts or points, rather you must *use* these as essential parts of an overall argument. An academic essay also requires you to produce reasons/evidence for any arguments you make. This form of assessment is normally chosen because it allows you to come to grips with complex ideas and concepts and to display your knowledge of them. An essay thus both displays and extends your analytical skills.

Most students will find it difficult to write an essay. If you feel confident in your ability just skim through this guide to check you have the techniques required for a university-level essay. If you don't know how to write an essay, read through the guide carefully. Keep it by you as you prepare for, and write, an essay. Remember, though, that this is just one recipe for 'How to Write'—find the method that works for you.

So, what is expected of you in an essay? The essay must:

1. *Focus* on the topic (i.e. answer the question).
2. *Display knowledge* of the area covered by the topic.
3. Present a *reasoned argument* in answer to the topic.
4. Be *competently presented*.

Focusing on the topic

Choose a topic you are interested in *early* (you are normally given a choice of topic).

Understanding the topic

Analyse the topic to find out what the question is asking:

(a) Look for *how* the question is to be handled. Usually you will be asked to analyse (i.e. to give a detailed examination in order to draw out the essential features). This means you will have to draw a *conclusion* based on the *evidence* of a *critical assessment* (discussion of merits) of the various *theories/explanations*. The following words all mean you will have to *analyse* (i.e. do more than merely make assertions—you must support your claims with good evidence and valid reasoning):

- Analyse
- Assess
- Compare
- Contrast
- Criticise
- Review
- Discuss
- Evaluate
- To what extent do you agree . . .
- Examine

(b) Underline key terms and concepts.
(c) Look at the relationships the question makes between the terms and concepts.
(d) Look to see how many parts there are to the question. If there is more than one, number the parts.

Now you should have some idea of the requirements of the topic. If you're not happy check with your tutor or the lecturer concerned.

Remember: You can disagree to any extent with the statement/question and lectures or the reading material as long as you present evidence and arguments for your point of view and give evidence of your understanding of the positions you disagree with. Essays are (or should be) exercises of scholarship. This means that you must develop a respect for *evidence* and a willingness to acknowledge well-reasoned and convincing arguments.

Finding the right approach to the topic

(a) Listen to the relevant lecture(s). Most introductory topics will be tied very closely to the lecture material. Do not write an essay before the relevant lectures have been heard.
(b) You may like to re-listen to the relevant lecture(s). Most universities provide lecture tapes in the audio-visual section of the library.
(c) Pay particular attention to tutorial preparation for this topic. Ask questions at the tutorial(s). Present ideas and see how they are received.
(d) Sit back comfortably and *read* some of the *recommended* readings. Don't take notes now—you are just getting a *feel* for the *area*.

Now you should know something about the topic.

Acquiring detailed knowledge of the area covered by the topic

(a) *Sources*:

- Lectures
- Tutorials
- Recommended reading

Note: You *must* read some of the recommended readings. Discuss (agree or disagree with) them in your essay.

12 *PART A*

There are often problems with getting recommended reading. Minimise this by:

  (i) Booking the reading—see librarians about this. 'Wealthy' students might find it easier to skim through the reading and photocopy relevant sections.
  (ii) Start the reading early.
  (iii) Use other libraries in your area.

Your reading lists may specify both books and journal articles, but you may want to consult other sources. You *must* include at least some of the recommended reading.

Be careful of relying on textbooks. They can give a useful introduction but they need to be supplemented with other, more specific material. Journal articles are often very helpful for this and they are readily available.

(b) *Note taking*

  (i) Make headings of key areas you will have to cover. You will add to these as you go on. To do this, go back to the question and *think* about the lectures, tutorials and the material you have already read.
  (ii) Use a preliminary reading of some of the more general work to gain an overall view of the problem.
  (iii) Skim through a reading, consulting your headings to find out what sections you should read.
  (iv) Read through the relevant sections *without* taking notes. This is so you will know where the author is going. It saves a great deal of time to find this out.
  (v) Go back, reread, take notes. Make sure you understand before you take final notes. Be sure you are clear when the writers are expressing their *own* views and when they are describing other people's views with which they may agree or disagree. Try to distinguish between fact and opinion; between views based on evidence and conclusions independent of evidence. You may need to write it out and reread it a few times before you feel you understand—take the time to do this. When making notes:
  - pick out the main points of the author's argument;
  - use point form or make summaries;
  - use your *own words* (this means you are learning, already writing your essay and avoiding plagiarism);
  - put notes under your headings (you're already organising your essay);
  - use only one side of the paper (then you can shuffle notes);
  - put relevant page numbers of the reading on the side (easy for referring back to, easy for essay referencing);
  - copy down all reference details for bibliography;
  - write down a *few* relevant quotations. Put them in *quotation marks* so you don't plagiarise.
  (vi) Add your own comments in a different colour. This means you're thinking, learning, organising.

Remember: Do not write everything down. If it is particularly good—photocopy.

Writing the essay

Remember: University essays require analysis and argument. We are not looking for 'correct' answers. There is no one 'line' for you to follow. We are concerned with how well you make your case. Whether we agree or disagree with you does not matter.

Drawing up a plan

(a) Reread question.
(b) Take a break—one day at least. *Think* while you drive, wash up or mow the lawn, of how you will answer the question. It's amazing how much work your mind does when it's away from pen and paper. Try to think of a *way* of answering the question that makes sense to you.
(c) Go back to the question. Reread your notes.
(d) Jot down an *outline* (no details) of your answer to the question (no more than ten sentences). As you know university essays require an argument. The answer to the question *is* your argument. It will have to be backed up by evidence and reason. Essays that just give facts with *no* argument are not acceptable.
(e) Draw up a *plan* for presenting this answer in a reasoned manner. The plan shows the *main points* and the *connections* you want to make between them. Look at it and ask yourself:

- *Is it complete?* Does it display knowledge of the area? (i.e. are the key points included?) Are the key debates included?
- *Is it logical?* Does it show a reasoned answer? (i.e. are there connections?)

(f) Go back to your notes and *fit* them into your plan. If your notes are under headings on separate pages you will just have to shuffle them around. You will have to leave out some of your information. Select in terms of relevance to the topic.
(g) The first draft of an essay is usually pretty grim. You should aim to do two or three drafts, allowing for revising, polishing and rewriting. In redrafting don't forget to check *style* and correctness of expression.

General structure

Remember: Your essay must be in the form of an argument which answers the question.
    You must have:

(a) An *introduction* where you:

- *Define* key terms and concepts.
- Give an *outline* of your answer (your argument).
- Indicate the *order* of your argument.

This will take up to a page in a shorter essay, up to two pages in a longer essay. Do not *overstate* your intentions (i.e. do not make excessive claims) in the introduction as this undermines your essay in the end.

(b) *The body*. This is where you:

   (i) *Display your knowledge* of the area covered by the topic.
   So give lots of *relevant evidence* for the *points* you are making. The marker will be marking you on what you display you know. You will have to include ideas and information from your sources and you will have to *reference* them. Remember, if there are important arguments *against* your position or case, deal with them honestly. Give those who disagree with you a fair go in your work. Do not suppress their views or distort them. The arguments or counter-claims of others should be met (if possible) by better arguments or by pointing out flaws in their reasoning. Where you cannot fully meet an objection to your viewpoint then say so.
   Remember: Make sure each *paragraph* is focused on one point or an *aspect* of one point. The first sentence of each paragraph is often used to show what the paragraph is about. Subsequent sentences expand/explain/provide evidence for the lead sentence.

   (ii) *Show your ability* to present a reasoned argument.
   This is achieved by *linking* your *points*, (i.e linking your paragraphs). Paragraphs are *linked* through the *ideas* being *logically connected* . . . so —make use of words which provide this connection:

   - therefore
   - hence
   - whereas
   - however
   - in addition
   - furthermore
   - on the other hand
   - consequently
   - as well as
   - first, second, etc.
   - moreover
   - because . . .

   —use the last sentence of a paragraph to provide the link between that paragraph and the next.
   In summary: Do *not* merely list points or facts without showing their connections to each other and to the topic.

(c) *The conclusion*, where you:

   (i) *Sum up* your answer in brief and show how it relates to your intentions as stated in the introduction. Check that you have accomplished *what* you stated in the introduction.
   (ii) Point out any interesting *implications*. (This takes about half to one page at the most).

(d) *Bibliography*. Provide a listing of:

   (i) All the books and articles *cited* in your essay (*a reference list*)

   or if you choose (or if the lecturer requires)

   (ii) All the books and articles consulted but not cited *and* those cited (a bibliography).

   Reference lists/bibliographies should be in alphabetical order by the surname of the authors—see section 'Reference list'.

Finding it hard to write

We all find it hard to write. Here are some hints to cope with this.

1. Have you made a *plan*? If not, go back and do this.
2. Don't expect your first draft to be perfect—leave blanks, poor wording, mistakes, etc. and fix up later.
3. Have a break, go for a walk.
4. Start on *any* paragraph, for example the one that has the most manageable information.
5. Leave writing the introduction until the end.
6. Put your notes away and write from what you know. Reorganise after.
7. Talk your essay into a tape—transcribe it, then you can start redrafting.
8. Jot down short notes to yourself of things to include—these can be worked up into paragraphs later.

Remember: For a good essay your first draft is only that. Leave it for a while then reread, reorganise, correct, etc.

Common faults

These are some of the faults we frequently find when marking essays:

1. *Lack of a good introduction.* Sometimes introductions are *too long*, contain *irrelevant* information, contain *detailed* information or are even totally *absent*!
2. *Opinions which are unsupported by evidence*—any assertion (opinion) without evidence is virtually worthless.
3. *Unrelated facts/ideas/points.* Some essays read like a collection of the pieces of a jigsaw puzzle. The separate pieces *if* put together correctly would make a good essay—if not connected then it makes nothing.
4. *The question is not answered*—either the whole of the question or some part of the question is ignored.
5. *Lack of a conclusion.*
6. *Stylistic faults*—especially 'wordiness', for example 'In order to answer this question it is necessary first'. Use direct phrasing, for example 'The first . . . '
7. *Plagiarism* (direct quote or paraphrasing without referencing). If this is found the section which is plagiarised *cannot* count as your essay. (See section 'How to fail easily').

Presenting your work competently

Headings

The use of headings should be sparing. It is not necessary to divide the text into dozens of small subsections, each with its own heading.

Many headings can be replaced by introductory sentences. When divisions and subdivisions are needed, the headings must be set out in a consistent style and should be centred on the page. Thus the first section of the assignment should begin with the following:

1. INTRODUCTION

Minor headings should be underlined and at the left hand side of the page. The sequence of these minor headings should be noted as follows:

1. <u>Earlier Theories</u>

If further subdivision cannot be avoided the following should be used:

- Lower case alphabetic characters: (a), (b), ...
- Lower case Roman numerals: (i), (ii), ...

Tables

The following heading format is acceptable:

TABLE 4
GROWTH RATES OF VALUE ADDED IN
AUSTRALIAN SECONDARY INDUSTRIES
(Percentages)

Column and row headings within tables should be headed with ordinary type, not underlined.

Charts and figures

Chart should be used where empirically derived data are depicted. *Figure* should be used where abstract arguments are illustrated. Arabic numerals should be used with *Chart* and *Figure*.

Footnotes

Footnotes are to add comments, explanations, examples, allusions to the differing views of other authors and similar material which is relevant to the arguments but would interrupt its flow if included in the main text.

Footnotes should be kept to a minimum and not used for citation of sources. All footnote numbers should be placed consecutively throughout and listed at the end of the assignment, that is, footnotes; appendices; references; selected bibliography (if any).

Referencing

As Clanchy and Ballard (1981, p. 117) claim:

> In an academic essay whenever you are:
> - quoting the exact words of another author;
> - closely summarising a passage from another writer; and/or
> - using an idea or material which is directly based on the work of another writer,

then you must identify and acknowledge your source in a systematic style of referencing.

So in an essay at this stage of your degree programme you will probably find yourself referencing a lot.

Use a *consistent* form of *referencing*. Here is the *Harvard* system.

(a) *Quoting, (i.e. using exact words)*

   (i) Quotations of *less than 20 words* should be included in the text within quotation marks, with the referencing as follows:

   Clegg (1975, p. 22) claims that for Dahl, 'Power must be specific and deployed. A prior capacity is no power at all'.

   or

   Early writers on power such as Dahl saw power as 'specific and deployed. A prior capacity [was] no power at all' (Clegg 1975, p. 22).

   Note *format* of referencing:

   - Author in text—   (1975   ,   p. 22)
                              (date of
                              publication   comma   page)
   - Author not in text—
     (Clegg   1975   ,   p. 22)
     (Author's   date of
     surname   publication   comma   page)

   (ii) Quotations of *more than 20 words*:

   - indent;
   - use single line spacing;
   - reference as before;
   - do *not* use quotation marks.

   For example, as Clegg (1975, p. 54) has pointed out:

   > where thought is constrained within narrowly defined notions of tradition, untouched by conceptualisation in dialogue with either everyday life, or other traditions, then one would expect it merely to reiterate the tradition.

   hence in order to understand how the concept of . . .

   (iii) If, in order to fit into your sentence, you have to *add* or *delete* something you must indicate this:

   - Additions — use square brackets [ ]
   - Deletions — use dots
                 — three dots for part of a sentence deleted . . .
                 — four dots if a sentence or more is deleted . . . .

Remember:
1. Be selective in quotations.
2. Avoid long quotations.
3. Quotations should not make up more than one fifth of your essay.

(b) *Referencing when closely summarising a passage or using an idea*

- Reference—same format as above.
- Do not use quotation marks.

For example: Clegg (1975, p. 22) pointed out that Dahl's theory of power was built on the basis that it did not refer to the capacity to do something *but* the actual doing of something.

A complication: If you are referring to an idea (etc.) which was referred to by another author, use the following format:

It was argued by Wittgenstein (cited in Clegg, 1975, p. 8) that . . .

Reference list

A *reference list* is a FULL LIST of ALL the books/articles you have REFERRED to in your essay and NO OTHERS. A complete *bibliography* includes all books consulted as well (check with the course convenor for the preferred mode of presentation).

Arrange reference list in ALPHABETICAL ORDER by surname of author, (except sometimes when you have a Government publication).

If there is more than one publication by the same author arrange these in ORDER of DATE OF PUBLICATION.

(a) *Format for referencing books*

Hunt, S. D., (1991),　　Modern Marketing Theory, South-Western Publishing Co., Cincinnati, Ohio.
(Surname　Date of　　Title—underlined　　Publisher　　　　　　　　　Place)
　　　　　Publication

(b) *Format for referencing articles*

   (i)　*Article in journal*

   Hirschman, E.　(1987),　'People as Products: Analysis of a Complex Marketing Exchange',
   (Surname　　　Date　　Title of article in inverted commas
   Journal of Marketing,　Vol. 51,　　No.1,　　pp. 98–108.
   Name of journal　　　Volume　　Number　　Page reference)
   underlined

   (ii)　*Article in edited volume*

   Roberto, E. (1991), 'Applying a Marketing Model in the Public Sector', in C. O'Faircheallaigh, P. Graham and J. Warburton (eds), Service Delivery and Public Sector Marketing, Macmillan, pp. 79–97.

(c) *Format for government publications*

Commonwealth of Australia,	(1986),	Office of Epac,
(Government	Date	Department Division or Agency

Technology and Innovation,	
Title underlined	

Council Paper No 19,	Australian Government Publishing Service	Canberra.
Series (if any)	Publisher	Place of Publication.)

There are other complications—if you come across them then ask your tutor.

Presentation

1. Have a *front page* giving:

   - Your name
   - Student number
   - The full title of the essay
   - Tutor's name
   - Assignment number/type (e.g. Essay 1)

2. Hand essays in at Faculty Office by *due date*.
3. Make sure your essay is correct in terms of spelling, grammar and punctuation. In particular, check that you have not used sexist language, that is language which uses a masculine form to refer to males and females, for example:

   - do *not* use: The manager . . . he often finds the financial data incomprehensible and out of date . . .;
   - instead say: A *manager* often finds . . . (that is, find a gender *neutral* term);
   - or say: The *managers* . . . *they* often find . . .(that is, *pluralise*);
   - or say: The worker . . . *he or she* often finds . . . (that is, use *both* pronouns. This should be avoided, if possible).

4. Make your assignment *readable*. Preferably *type* (double line spacing) or use a *very clear* writing style (also double line spacing).
5. Always leave a *wide margin* (3 cm) so there is space for comments.
6. Keep a *copy*.
7. Number your pages in order.
8. Use a staple(s) in the left hand corner of the essay/paper.

How to fail easily

Plagiarism

Plagiarism is using the ideas or the actual words of another without referencing them (applies to copying essays from other students as well as copying ideas, etc. from books). *It is academic theft.* It may seem to be an easy method to gain results but it must be stressed that plagiarism is *very easy to spot*. Recognition can occur in a number of ways, for example:

(a) If an essay is copied from one by a student on another course or from another year of the same course: Titles, reading, lists, the course content and approach in

general do differ substantially. Such essays are clearly not the product of the right course.
(b) If it is copied from another student on the same course: Essays are often double marked or redistributed for marking by other members of staff. An essay that arouses suspicion (by being of a style or content quite different from other works by the same student) may be passed around to see if anyone recognises it.
(c) If it is copied from a book: The effect is clear. Very few undergraduates can write like a book (and if they can they don't need to copy). If minor changes are made the results are often highfaluting nonsense. Markers are widely read people.

It is not worth the risk.

So:
1. If in doubt, *reference*.
2. When you are note taking do so in your *own words*, except for quotations appropriately indicated.

Reference
Clanchy, J. and Ballard, B. (1982), *Essay Writing for Students*, Longman, Melbourne.

Legal aspects of marketing in Australia

by Peter M. McDermott

Introduction

Professor Coase has discussed the justification for the intervention of the State in the legal system. In market-places of a restricted nature, such as commodity exchanges and stock exchanges, which often operate from the same building, enforcement of the rules of that market-place is relatively easy. Withdrawal of trading privileges is a powerful sanction which is sufficiently severe to compel most traders to observe the rules of that market-place. When the physical facilities of a market-place are scattered and owned by a vast number of people with differing interests, as is the case with retailing and wholesaling, the establishment and administration of a private legal system would be very difficult. Those operating in retailing and wholesale markets have to depend, therefore, on the legal system of the State (Coase 1988, p. 10).

The purpose of this article is to outline some of the important legal aspects of marketing. The article is not intended to make every person engaged in marketing their own lawyer, but rather to enable such persons to appreciate when they should obtain legal advice. It is important to appreciate that every report of a legal decision may not be a precedent that may be applied in all situations. A case must be decided on its own peculiar facts. It may have concerned the laws of another State or

Territory. Even if it was decided in the relevant State or Territory in question, it may have been effectively overruled by a later case or statute. The provision of legal advice is a complex matter upon which professional advice must be sought.

Sources of marketing law

There are two important sources of marketing law in Australia:

(i) common law; and
(ii) statute law.

Common law

Common law is essentially the body of law which consists of the decisions of the courts. A decision of an English or Commonwealth court may be relied upon as a precedent in an Australian court where there are no relevant differences in statute law. To ascertain a relevant precedent will necessitate a search in a law library. The law of contract is largely based upon the common law although consumer-oriented statutes are often now important.

Statute law

Statute law which is relevant to a person engaged in marketing will be either:

(a) Commonwealth (or Federal) legislation which has been passed by the Commonwealth Parliament, Canberra (e.g. *Trade Practices Act* 1974); or
(b) State or Territory legislation which has been passed by the Parliament of a State or Territory (e.g. *Fair Trading Act, Credit Act*).

Commonwealth legislation has application over the whole of Australia, whereas State or Territory legislation relates to the particular State or Territory. However, since 1986 the legislative powers of the Parliament of a State include full power to make laws for the peace, order and good government of the State that have extra-territorial operation: see *Australia Act* 1986, s. 2(1). Hence laws may vary between the States, although there is some degree of uniformity in regard to fair trading laws.

Another source of law is municipal or local government law. Municipal law will vary in each municipality and is not as accessible as State or Federal Acts of Parliament. In some cases municipal ordinances or by-laws are only to be found in Government Gazettes which are not conveniently indexed. Municipal law is generally relevant in areas such as town planning, for example consent to use premises for a certain purpose. Enquiries, preferably in writing, should be directed to the appropriate municipality before a marketing business is commenced or purchased.

Contract law

It is important to appreciate that marketing activity will invariably involve a contractual obligation. Hence the general principles of contract law will govern such issues as whether or not there is a contract in existence, or in other words was there a formation of a contract. The issue may arise as to what are the terms of the contract bearing in mind that there is a necessity that any such terms be certain and so capable of enforcement. In a particular case there may be a factor which tends to defeat contractual liability such as mistake, misrepresentation, and illegality.

The general law of contract will govern such matters as whether or not a contract has been performed by a party in accordance with the contract, and the remedies available to an aggrieved party where there is a breach of contract. Generally speaking a party will only be entitled to sue for damages for a breach of contract, unless the breach is sufficiently serious to go to the root of the contract in which circumstances rescission will be permitted.

Engrafted on to the general law, principles of contract are the statutory remedies provided in the *Trade Practices Act* for misrepresentation. A similar measure is in force in the Australian Capital Territory: see *Law Reform (Misrepresentation) Ordinance* 1977.

Tort law

An area of law that has rapidly evolved this century is the law of tort. Broadly speaking this subject can be divided into the intentional torts (whereby a person deliberately harms the person or chattels of somebody) and the law of negligence. From the perspective of a person engaged in marketing, the intentional tort that is likely to arise is the tort of false imprisonment whereby a trader detains a customer who it is alleged is guilty of shoplifting, or does not open a bag at an inspection point at a checkout in the supermarket. In these circumstances, advice should be sought as to what appropriate procedures should be adopted. Generally speaking a trader should not authorise any employee to arrest a customer, if necessary this should be left to the police who have special powers of arrest.

The law of negligence is an area of law that is rapidly changing. It includes the law of products liability whereby a manufacturer may be liable to an ultimate consumer for a defect in a product which is caused by the negligence of the manufacturer. The law of negligence may impose liability for a negligent or reckless statement made to a consumer who relies upon that statement. The law of negligence is invoked when a trader is liable for an injury caused by an unsafe shop, or a worker sues for an injury carried by an unsafe working environment. This is a matter upon which a trader should be guided by professional advice.

Sale of Goods Act

In England in 1893 the law relating to the sale of goods was regulated by the *Sale of Goods Act*, a codifying measure, which essentially reflected the general principles of mercantile law. Legislation has been passed in each State and Territory which essentially is a copy of the English Act. Hence, apart from minor matters, the law in Australia, England and New Zealand is highly uniform: see Sutton, K. C. T., *Sales and Consumer Law in Australia and New Zealand*, (1983) p. 3.

The various statutes define a contract of sale of goods as:

a contract whereby the seller transfers or agrees to transfer the property in goods to the buyer for a money consideration called the price.

(*Sale of Goods Act* 1923 (NSW), s. 6)

From this definition it can be seen that for there to be a contract of sale, the contract must relate to goods, and there must be a money consideration called the price.

Written memorandum

In New South Wales and most other jurisdictions (apart from Queensland and the Australian Capital Territory) a contract for the sale of goods of the value of $20 or more must be evidenced in writing. Such anachronistic provisions as to the requirement of a written memorandum have been repealed in New Zealand and England.

The question of whether or not a party has contractual capacity to enter into a contract of sale of goods is a matter which is governed by the general law of contract. Difficulties occur when a contract is entered into with an infant or a person who is intoxicated or otherwise lacks mental capacity.

Capacity

Most problems occur with infants. An infant is liable for the purchase of necessaries. In some States there has been statutory reform. For instance, in New South Wales an infant will be liable for a contract which is beneficial to the minor: see, *Minors (Property and Contracts) Act* 1970 (NSW). Where a contract for the sale of goods has been entered into with a minor, a trader has a number of possibilities. The trader may obtain an indemnity from the parent, or better still enter into the contract with the parent rather than the infant.

Price

The price of goods may be fixed in the contract or may be fixed in a manner thereby agreed, or may be determined by the course of dealing between the parties (NSW s. 13). An agreement can be made to sell goods at a price to be fixed by the valuation of a third party.

Implied warranties and conditions

A contract for the sale of goods will incorporate various implied conditions and warranties in the absence of any contrary intention of the parties. The *Sale of Goods Act* provides that a contract of sale will contain an implied condition that the seller has title to sell the goods, and implied warranties for quiet possession and freedom from undisclosed incumbrances. There is also an implied condition as to the quality or fitness for the purpose that the goods were purchased where the buyer expressly or by implication makes known the purpose. Where there is a sale of goods by sample there are implied conditions that the bulk shall correspond with the sample in quality, that the buyer shall have a reasonable opportunity of comparing the bulk with the sample, and that the goods shall be free from any defect rendering them unmerchantable.

The *Sale of Goods Act* sets out rules for when the property in goods passes to a purchaser. The relevance of the time when property rests with the purchaser is that the responsibility for the goods will generally pass upon the transfer of ownership. This can occur before the goods are in fact delivered to the purchaser. For example, if specific goods ready for delivery are sold under an unconditional contract, the property belongs to the purchaser as soon as the contract is made. There are other instances where the Act deals with the transfer of ownership.

To warn a purchaser to insure expensive goods, it is recommended that some appropriate provision should be made in a contract for the sale of goods.

Nemo dat quod non habet

The general principle of law is that a person cannot confer a greater title to goods than they already have. That is why a thief cannot sell goods that he has stolen. There are exceptions to this principle such as sales in market overt (which is not a universal principle in Australia), sales under a voidable title, and sales by mercantile agents under the *Factors Act*.

Apart from the usual contractual remedies that are available to a seller for the recovery of the price, an unpaid seller can exercise certain proprietary remedies over goods. An unpaid seller is entitled to retain goods under a seller's lien. The seller can also exercise a right of stoppage *in transitu*, where a seller becomes aware that a buyer is insolvent.

A buyer may bring an action for the non-delivery of the goods. The buyer can reject goods where there is a breach of condition. Where there is a breach of a warranty by the seller, the buyer can sue the seller for damages.

Trade Practices Act

The most important statute which affects the market place in Australia is the *Trade Practices Act* 1974 which is a Federal statute. Because of constitutional limitations which apply to the Commonwealth Parliament, the operation of the *Trade Practices Act* is mainly confined to corporations. A number of provisions of the Act are specifically expressed to apply to corporations (e.g. s. 65d), but the Act, in reliance on the full extent of constitutional power of the Commonwealth Parliament, also extends to interstate and overseas trade, the use of postal, telegraphic or telephonic services, radio and television broadcasting, where a supplier is a natural person (see, s.6). The external affairs power also enables the Act to apply to an individual where there is misleading conduct in relation to which the Industrial Property Convention applies (see, s. 55).

Part V of the *Trade Practices Act* which is entitled 'Consumer Protection' regulates dealings with consumers. Part V of the *Trade Practices Act* is divided into the following Divisions:

Division 1: Unfair practices.
Division 1A: Product safety and product information.
Division 2: Conditions and warranties in consumer transactions.
Division 2A: Actions against manufacturers and importers of goods.
Division 3: Miscellaneous.
Division 4: Enforcement and remedies.

Unfair practices (Division 1)

Division 1 of Part V of the *Trade Practices Act 1974* relates to unfair practices. The Act makes unlawful the following conduct by a corporation in trade or commerce:

- Misleading or deceptive conduct (s. 52).
- Unconscionable conduct (s. 52a).
- False or misleading representations (s. 53).
- False representations and other misleading or offensive conduct in relation to land (s. 53a).
- Misleading conduct in relation to employment (s. 53b).
- Cash price to be stated in certain circumstances (s. 53c).
- Offering gifts and prizes (s. 54).
- Misleading conduct of which the Industrial Property Convention applies (s. 55).
- Misleading conduct in relation to services (s. 55a).
- Bait advertising (s. 56).
- Referral selling (s. 57).
- Accepting payment without intending or being able to supply as ordered (s. 58).
- Misleading representations about certain business activities (s. 59).
- Harassment and coercion (s. 60).
- Pyramid selling (s. 61).
- Unsolicited credit cards (s. 63a).
- Assertion of right to payment for unsolicited goods or services, or for making an entry in a directory (s. 64).
- Liability of recipient of unsolicited goods (s. 65).

The most important provision of Part V of the *Trade Practices Act* is section 52 of the Act which provides:

> A corporation shall not, in trade or commerce, engage in conduct that is misleading or deceptive or is likely to mislead or deceive. (subsection (1))

At the outset it is apparent that the operation of this section is confined to acts which are in 'trade or commerce' thus encompassing activity which would concern a person engaged in marketing. Another matter that should be appreciated is that section 52 of the Act is not merely a consumer protection measure; that is to say the section does not only apply to conduct which is directed to consumers, such as purchasers of goods at a shop. Rather the section applies to all conduct of a corporation that is trade or commerce (such as misleading advertising in the media), and a commercial competitor, rather than a consumer, may bring an action to restrain such advertising. Indeed most reported decisions involving section 52 of the Act concern litigation between commercial competitors.

Product safety and product information (Division 1A)

Division 1A of Part V of the *Trade Practices Act* contains comprehensive provisions designed to protect the public from dangerous goods (ss. 65B–65U). The minister may publish a warning notice in the *Gazette* which states that goods may cause injury to any person (s.65B). The minister may also by a notice published in the *Gazette* prescribe a product safety standard or impose a permanent ban on the goods (s. 65C). From the point of view of a person in the market-place the crucial provision in Division 1A is section 65C of the Act which provides that a corporation shall not, in trade or commerce, supply goods that are intended to be used, or are of a kind likely to be used, by a consumer if the goods are of a kind:

- in respect of which there is a prescribed consumer product safety standard and which do not comply with that standard;

    or

- in respect of which there is a notice in force declaring the goods to be unsafe goods and imposing a permanent ban of the goods.

Where a consumer has been supplied with goods in contravention of s. 65C, suffers loss or damage because of a defect in the goods, that person is deemed to have suffered the loss or damage by the supplying of the goods, (s. 65C(8) and (9)). A consumer therefore has an effective right of action against the seller of the goods even though the seller is not the manufacturer. The term 'supply' when used in relation to goods, includes the supply (including re-supply) by way of sale, exchange, lease, hire or hire-purchase (see definition of 'supply', s. 4). The Division also includes provisions to provide for the compulsory product recall for goods (s. 65F), and applies to the supply of goods to which a recall is in force (s. 65G).

Conditions and warranties in consumer transactions (Division 2)

Division 2 of Part V of the *Trade Practices Act* provides for various conditions and warranties to be implied in a consumer contract. These conditions and warranties cannot be included or modified (see s. 68). The Act implies a condition as to title of goods, implies a warranty that the consumer will enjoy quiet possession of goods, and implies a warranty that the goods are free from a charge or encumbrance (s. 69). The Act also implies conditions that the goods will correspond to the description (s. 70), as to the quality or fitness of goods (s. 71), and that the goods correspond with a sample (s. 72). Where the purchase of goods is financed by a linked credit provider both the linked credit provider and the supplier of goods are jointly and severely liable to the consumer for the amount of loss and damage sustained by the consumer (s. 73).

Actions against manufacturers and importers of goods (Division 2A)

Division 2A of Part V of the *Trade Practices Act* imposes liability upon manufacturers and importers of goods. This Division was inserted pursuant to recommendations of the Swanson Committee in 1976 which pointed out the injustice of persons other than the manufacturer being liable for a breach of the statutory standard imposed by the *Trade Practices Act* merely because the consumer has no contractual nexus with the manufacturer.

Fair Trading Act

The *Fair Trading Acts* of the States mirror the consumer protection provisions of Part V of the *Trade Practices Act*. It was earlier pointed out that the Commonwealth Parliament in passing the *Trade Practices Act* mainly relied upon the constitutional head of power to pass laws in relation to corporations, although other heads of power were relied upon (e.g. postal and telegraph power etc.). The purpose of the *Fair Trading Acts* is essentially to enable a trade practices action to be brought against an individual as well as a corporation. Although there is scope under the *Trade Practices Act* for imposing liability upon an individual who has an association with a corporation, the passing of the *Fair Trading Acts* has the consequence that where the conduct of a natural person, who has no connection with a corporation, has caused damage to a plaintiff, that plaintiff would have a right of action under the *Fair Trading Act*.

Bailment

A bailment occurs when one person (the bailee) is entrusted with the goods of another person (the bailor). Essentially a bailee is under a duty to take reasonable care of such a chattel. A bailment will occur when a customer deposits a watch with a jeweller for repair, or a person leaves his car with a garage for servicing. In these types of case a bailee would be under a duty to take appropriate measures to safeguard the chattel. A bailee would also in some cases be able to limit their liability by an appropriate inclusion value provided that the clause was brought to the attention of the bailor. Because of the responsibilities of a bailee, difficulties were caused by customers not collecting goods left in a shop for dry cleaning or repair. In the various states statutes have been passed specifying under what conditions such goods may be lawfully disposed of by a shopkeeper.

References

Coase, R. H. (1988), *The Firm, the Market and the Law*, University of Chicago Press, Chicago.
Sale of Goods Act 1923 (NSW)
Sutton, K. C. T. (1983), *Sales and Consumer Law in Australia and New Zealand*, (3rd edn), Law Book Company, North Ryde, NSW.
Trade Practices Act 1974

PART B

READINGS AND CASES (SECTIONS 1–7)

1. UNDERSTANDING MARKETING

Introduction 32

Readings
1. Beyond competition to sur/petition, by Edward de Bono 33
2. From woeful to wonderful: A step-by-step approach, by Michael Kiely 40

Cases
1. Marketers: The endangered species, by Paul Shea 45
2. Thomas Toy Company Limited, by Michael Harker 49
3. Do you have what it takes! Specific courage— Training experiences for students, by John Jackson 51
4. How switched on are you? by John Clayton 58

Introduction

Section one in this part of the book introduces the student to the concept of 'marketing'. Presenting the 'big picture', the section covers the discipline, process and environment that surrounds marketing. Four cases and two readings have been selected in this section to demonstrate what marketing is, why we need it and how it works.

The four cases are complemented by two readings. Edward de Bono, famous for the concept of lateral thinking, applies his talents to marketing with impressive results. His thoughts can be read in 'Beyond competition to sur/petition'. Students may find his ideas an interesting contrast when studying more traditional forms of marketing, as highlighted in the Thomas Toy Company case study.

The parallel between sport and business is brought to our attention in Michael Kiely's reading 'From woeful to wonderful'. The article demonstrates how the Australian Rugby Union team benefited from the use of marketing techniques in order to win the 1991 World Cup.

'Marketers: the endangered species' examines another facet of marketing; 'new marketing'. Paul Shea discusses the move from marketing to new marketing, or as it is more popularly known, 'total quality management'. Many companies from many industries, both product and service industries, are now applying TQM with varying degrees of success. TQM is practised worldwide and, as Paul Shea says: 'Marketing is the satisfaction of clients' needs and wants in either the private or public sectors. TQM is therefore a (new) way of doing marketing'. Students are invited to critically review this case material.

The Thomas Toy case study contains most of the basic elements of marketing and John Jackson's 'Courageous marketing' is a down-to-earth look at what can be achieved through being brave. 'How switched on are you?' is a short competition to ascertain how much about marketing is already known. Whilst these cases are useful to begin a course in marketing, they are also useful as a conclusion to review what has been learned.

Reading 1—Beyond competition to sur/petition

by Edward de Bono

Edward de Bono introduces the concept of sur/petition—beyond competition—a new way to think about marketing.

The notion of competition is a dangerous and seductive trap that limits and restricts business thinking. Anyone involved in running a business needs to move beyond competition to *sur/petition*.

Competition is a fashionable concept vigorously pushed by such gurus as Michael Porter of the Harvard Business School. But any business school has to be about ten years behind the times in its thinking in order to be credible. This is true because its ideas have to be immediately acceptable; since there is a considerable time lag, the ideas of the future are not instantly acceptable. Therefore, such concepts do not necessarily enhance a school's reputation.

We all know about the global market-place and that in order to survive you must be competitive. You must be able to compete with the Japanese, the Germans, and the Taiwanese. If you cannot compete, you do not survive. So what is wrong with competition? The paradox is that you cannot truly be competitive if you seek to be competitive.

The key word here is *survive*. It is, of course, perfectly true that you must be competitive in order to survive. Giant retailers like Sears have to cut their costs considerably to be able to survive against other retailers such as Wal-Mart with its advanced computer systems and high sales per square foot. If your costs and values are out of line, you may cease to survive. But any organisation that plans just to survive will sooner or later find itself out of business. Only those organisations that plan for success will survive, while those that plan only to survive will fail. So competition is important as part of the 'baseline' for survival.

Picture an exotic garden outside Manila in the Philippines. A scented summer evening provides the perfect setting for a gourmet banquet for the Chevalier de Tastevins. Flaming torches are set among the bushes. Costumed waiters carry in the first dish of shellfish on their heads. Then follows clear soup in large earthenware bowls. Everyone, myself included, starts to spoon up the soup. It is very clear soup indeed. In fact it is not soup at all. It is plain water served in rather large finger bowls for rinsing the fingers after the shellfish dish. The mistake is understandable. Water is necessary for soup—but soup has to be more than water. In the same way there are many things that are necessary, but not sufficient, for business to survive (e.g. cost control), just like water for the soup. Competition is one of the things that is necessary for business to survive, but it is not sufficient. A serious mistake that many executives make is to believe that competition is the key to success. Competition is merely part of the baseline of survival. Success requires going beyond competition to sur/petition.

There is a serious overcapacity of about 25% in European car production. At one time I was giving a seminar for the British marketing department of Ford, the biggest

Ford operation outside of Detroit. We were discussing competition in the European market. I suggested Ford should buy up a company called National Car Parks (NCP), which owned most of the car parks in city centres throughout the United Kingdom. If NCP became a Ford company, a notice could be placed at the entrance to all city centre car parks indicating that only Ford cars could use them. A car, I argued, is no longer just a lump of engineering. If your neighbour boasts that his lump of engineering is better than your lump of engineering, you can point out that you can park in the city and he cannot. The ability to park is very much part of the 'integrated' value of a car if you have to drive in a city. So is the ability to resell the car, have it serviced and have it insured. I have been told, for instance, that it is impossible to insure a Mercedes or a BMW if you live in the Bronx in New York. It does not matter how good the engineering may be; if you cannot insure a car, you will probably not buy it.

Ford did not take up my idea. They said that, as an engineering company, it was not their business to buy up car parks. In the future, some entrepreneurs probably will buy up or build car parks and then get the Koreans to make private-label cars for them. They will sell, park, insure, and resell cars. Manufacturing will only be a service to this profit centre, and the manufacturing margins will be squeezed.

In the United States, car sales have been in decline for some time. There has been a five-year slide from sales of 16.3 million in 1986 to about 13.5 million in 1991. As everyone knows, the classic competitive response has been to slash prices and offer cash rebates. Surprisingly, competitors do the same. You may succeed in shifting sales forward in time, but then buyers get used to the rebates and wait for them before buying again.

The suggestion that Ford should have bought up the city centre car parks is an example of what I call sur/petition.

The word *com-petition* comes from the Latin and means 'seeking together'. It means 'choosing to run in the same race'. We could spell it as (com)petition to illustrate that all competitors are in the same race. The word *sur/petition* means 'seeking above'. Instead of choosing to run in the same race, competitors choose their own race. The slash in the new word sur/petition is there to indicate the notion of seeking above, just as 2/3 indicates two over three.

In addition, sur/petition is about creating *value monopolies*. Some ways of achieving a monopoly are illegal but value monopolies are not. For survival you need competition, but for success you need sur/petition and the creation of value monopolies. Instead of running the same race you create your own race. Instead of seeking 'together' you set out to seek 'above'. How do you create value monopolies? They are driven by concepts and concepts are in turn driven by serious creativity. In order to understand value monopolies you must realise that there have been three phases of business:

1. The first phase was simply based on making available a product or service. It was production driven.
2. The second phase was based on competition, because a lot of people were now providing the same goods and services.

3. The third phase, which we are now just entering, is based on integrated values. No longer do we live in a world of simple values where a car is just a piece of engineering.

A good example of integrated values comes from Ron Barbaro, one-time head of the Prudential Insurance Company in Canada. Using some of my techniques of lateral thinking (serious creativity), he came up with the idea of *living benefits*. This is a significant change in the very traditional business of life insurance, which has been unchanged for 120 years.

With traditional life insurance, the benefits are paid out after your death to your family or other beneficiaries. Ron Barbaro's concept was to have 75% of the benefits paid out immediately if a policy holder was diagnosed as having a potentially fatal illness (such as cancer or AIDS). This meant that the money was now available for extra care or medical attention. The concept was immensely successful and was one of the reasons Ron Barbaro was soon promoted to head of Prudential in the United States.

This is an excellent example of integrated values because it integrates life insurance into the lives and values of people. There are single people, people who divorce and split up, children who grow up and become self-supporting, and many others. For some of them, many of the original purposes of life insurance are gone. At the same time there are factors like AIDS and the expense of medical care that create new purposes. Barbaro created a simple concept change. Life insurance is traditionally seen as related to death; his concept emphasised life, and he had the courage and drive to see the concept through.

The business community least happy with concepts is in the United States. There is an impatience with concepts and an urgent desire to be given 'hands-on' tools. Americans want to be doing rather than thinking.

For a long time the United States was a pioneer society, and in such a society action is indeed more rewarding than thinking. The great energy and lack of inhibitions in America also favour action. Today, however, the world is more crowded. Unthinking action is not going to be rewarded. On the other hand, a concept change may be rewarded very handsomely. A new concept is the best and cheapest way of getting added value out of existing resources.

Up to now, however, our approach to concept development has been very haphazard. There has been the 'me-too' approach in which we wait for someone else to develop the concept and then we jump in with a similar copy of it. In addition, we have assumed that as intelligent, able people we will come up with the needed concepts when necessary. This attitude to concepts is not good enough today. In the future we are going to have to take concepts so seriously that we shall be setting up specific 'concept research and development' departments for the intellectual engineering that needs to take place. General Motors is said to spend about $5 billion a year on technical research and development, and Du Pont spends about $1.2 billion. Today, however, concepts are even more important than technology, and we shall have to take their development very seriously indeed.

Business schools have always taught students about how to analyse information and how to make decisions. What concepts are going to be derived from information analysis? By itself the analysis of information can never yield the concepts that are hidden in the information. What alternatives are available for decision making? Analysis can only yield some of the alternatives; the rest must be produced by creative design.

Unfortunately, the approach to creativity in the United States has been very weak. There is the mistaken notion that we are all basically creative, and it is only necessary to remove our inhibitions and fears of being ridiculous in order to release this innate creativity. That is why American creative methods have been crazy and off-the-wall.

We now know that the brain is not designed to be creative and that in order to be creative we have to use some methods that are 'not natural'. We must begin to develop systematic methods of serious creativity.

Concepts are about value. Sur/petition is also about value. It has always seemed strange to me that, although we deal so much with values, we do not have a specific word to describe the creation and formation of values. The new word that I propose in this book is *valufacture*, which I define as 'the creation and formation of values'.

Many people in business feel that we have entered the age of contraction. There have been two ages of expansion. The first age of expansion was driven by marketing. Marketing was going to create needs and open up markets. Marketing was the main competitive tool for taking market share from others. The second age of expansion was driven by 'gobble growth'. You gobbled up other organisations in order to increase market share. During this period there were all sorts of rationalisations about market synergies and critical survival size (often provided by investment bankers who liked the fat fees involved).

The present mood is for consolidation. Acquisitions have to be digested. Corporate executives are looking inward. There is cost-cutting and slimming. There is a laying off of people. There is divestment of unprofitable businesses everywhere. As part of this looking inward, there is an emphasis on cost-cutting, cost control, and quality management. All these things are important and necessary, but they are not enough. You take aspirin when you have a headache, but you cannot survive on a steady diet of aspirin.

The purpose of consolidation, contraction, quality, and all the rest is to provide a firm baseline for venture. In the end you have to provide values that customers want. Having the best quality product at the lowest price is no good if that product does not offer significant value.

There is a serious danger that the current emphasis on 'housekeeping' may divert attention from the very essence of a business, which is to provide saleable value. The essence of a business can be summed up in the following four 'C' words:

- Competence: the quality, efficiency, effectiveness, and accomplishment of what you are supposed to be doing.
- Control: the cost control, strategy, and knowledge of what is going on.
- Care: care for the customer, for the work force, which is ultimately your most precious resource, and for the community (e.g. environmental concerns).
- Creativity: the soul of the business. Without creativity you have a body with no soul. Creativity provides the value that is the whole purpose of any business.

Is there anything wrong with the fundamentals of efficiency, problem solving, analysis of information and competition? These fundamentals were developed in the early days of business and, though still valid, there is a need to examine them more critically.

In the early days of business, the economic baseline was rising. It was only necessary to keep your place on this rising baseline and all would be well. The two things necessary to keep your place were efficiency and problem solving. Efficiency in the use of capital, people, energy, and resources could keep you on the rising baseline. If a problem arose, then you solved it and returned to the baseline. The process is not unlike that of a family bringing up a child. There is shelter, care, and nutrition. If the child falls ill you call in the problem solver, the doctor. The child is cured and goes on to grow into a healthy adult. Growth is the natural state of affairs. Today, the baseline is flat and may even be declining. There is a global market-place with overproduction of goods and services. All the efficiency and problem solving in the world may only keep you efficiently on the declining baseline.

Businesses often feel that, since they have a lot of market muscle and such a dominant position, maintenance will be enough. In recent years, however, even mighty IBM found that market domination was not enough if you fell behind on concepts. IBM fell behind on the concept of 'connectivity' and has suffered as a result. IBM has also suffered from lower-priced clones when the mystique of computers wore off and there was no longer a need for reassurance from the solidity of Big Blue.

Efficiency is the ratio between input and output. It asks: What is the best output that I can get for the resources that I put in? For this required output, what is the minimum of resources that I must put in? If we think in terms of efficiency, we have to think in terms of input/output ratios. Efficiency means productivity. Efficiency means no waste. Efficiency means getting the best out of our efforts, energy and resources. What can possibly be wrong about that?

To begin with, efficiency does not look at the customer. The American auto industry removed all extras in order to give the customer the lower-priced car. This is a form of efficiency. The Japanese built up their 30% of the American car market by piling on extras as part of the basic car price. This was not the working of the efficiency concept, but the working of another concept—effectiveness. The Japanese reach efficiency in a different way than American businesses, through the route of effectiveness. The main difference is that efficiency is a ratio and effectiveness is not.

Effectiveness means that you determine exactly what you want to do. Then you use all the resources necessary to do it effectively. If you do not have enough resources to do everything, then you make a list of things you want to do and go down that list using full resources for each item. When you have used up all your available resources, you stop. Contrast this with *efficiency*, in which you divide all available resources among all the things you want to do. If effectiveness means having five people paint one lamppost, efficiency means having five people paint five lampposts, even though the paint job might not be very good.

So the first stage in effectiveness is fulfilling the objective fully—whatever the cost in resources. The second stage is to turn to the effectiveness of the process itself. How can the process be made more effective? At this point the process is improved.

That is why there are far fewer parts in a Toyota than in a car from General Motors. The fewer parts make the assembly process more effective. The end result of the whole process may seem to Western eyes to be efficiency, but it has been achieved by the double application of effectiveness, first to the output and then to the production process itself.

The principal efficiency question is, what are the minimum resources that I can use to get this output? The effectiveness question is, how can the process be made more effective? Effectiveness is not a ratio. The end point is fixed, and it is a matter of steadily improving the process of getting there.

Efficiency is measurable at one point in time. While efficiency has to be measurable, what may happen in the future cannot be measured. So it is left out of any efficiency equation. You design a suspension system for the bumps it encounters right now, not for all the possible bumps it might encounter in the future. Efficiency has always got to look backward and historically. It seeks to maximise what is now being done and what is now known. When the future turns out not to be exactly as predicted, which is usually the case, efficiency may actually have gotten us into trouble. Very efficient businesses are often very brittle.

Efficiency is often the enemy of flexibility, and in today's business world, flexibility is becoming more important. Flexibility, in fact, has been the key to the extraordinary economic development of Hong Kong, Taiwan, Singapore and Korea. Instead of working towards being the most efficient bicycle producer in the world, a business must instead have a bicycle-making capacity. But if there is a downturn in bicycles, then that same business must switch part of its production to health equipment or prams or whatever is in demand.

Too often, when we work toward efficiency, we forget about flexibility. The most dangerous saying in American business, that almost by itself has been responsible for the decline in United States basic industry, is 'If it isn't broken, don't fix it'. It was meant to indicate that business should focus its thinking on problems and not worry about other matters—and that was precisely its danger. Businesses were busy attacking and fixing their problems, and when they had fixed them they were back to where they were before. Meanwhile their competitors were making changes at points that were not problems. They were busy changing the process itself, not just fixing problems in the existing process.

The Western notion of improvement is to point out faults, defects and weaknesses, and then set about putting them right. If we remove all faults, we believe, then the job has been done. Contrast this with the Japanese culture. They do not understand argument, but prefer parallel thinking. When it comes to improvement, they are also concerned with removing obvious faults. The Japanese then go on to say, 'This is perfect—so now let us make it better'. This is perhaps the single most significant difference between Western industrial thinking and Japanese industrial thinking. The result is the Japanese habit of continuous improvement; of improving things even when there are no faults at all. Today the West is busily trying to capture this habit with the current fashion for total quality management.

Problem solving is usually urgent and has to take priority over other sorts of thinking. It is possible, however, to fill your life with so many urgent matters that there is no time left to think about truly important matters.

The third fundamental of traditional business thinking is to collect information and then make decisions by analysing information. There was a time when executives were very short of information. Any improvement in information, therefore, would immediately improve the quality of the decisions that had to be made. In a sense, the information itself made the decisions. Today, however, we have computers that give us much more information and the ability to handle it. If a decision only requires more information, then that decision can be made directly by the computer without the need for human intervention.

At first, increasing information leads to better decisions, but after a while more and more information has less and less effect. There even comes a time when further information makes it difficult to sort out important information from the rest. There is confusion and information overload. Yet, as most data processing (DP) departments will confirm, executives faced with difficult decisions simply ask for more and more information in the hope that somehow the new information will do their thinking for them.

The traditional view of competitors is that they are enemies. This can be a very limiting view. One day the different Japanese food companies got together and decided that it did not make sense for each of them to have a half-empty truck making a delivery to a supermarket. They decided to share their transportation to the supermarkets. As a result there was an 80% saving in delivery costs.

The Japanese are extremely good at distinguishing areas where competition is necessary from areas where it is wasteful. For instance, there is intense competition between the auto companies in Japan—much fiercer than in the United States. They blitz each other with model changes, price shifts and anything else they can think of. Yet at lunch, in the automakers club, they sit down every day to discuss mutual problems. When they leave the premises, they are competitors.

Basic research, for example, is an area in which competitors can get together. Indeed there are already two consortiums in the United States in which manufacturers of semiconductors have come together to co-operate on basic research. In the securities industry there is often overcapacity in data processing, and this too could be shared with competitors.

If you have an antique shop and someone sets up another antique shop near you, should you not be concerned about this competition? Not at all. The more antique shops, the more the area will be visited by antique buyers. Similarly, one hotel does not make a resort, but several competing hotels will increase business for all of them by providing a critical mass for infrastructure development, travel agent consciousness and other endeavours. When Kodak ventured into the instant camera business a few years ago, analysts marked down Polaroid stock. But in fact Polaroid's sales increased because Kodak now had to advertise instant cameras.

The traditional view of competitors as enemies may not always be correct. The key is to decide in which areas they are actually beneficial and in which areas they are rivals. It is not so much a win/lose situation but a win/win/lose situation.

Classical competition still works. The danger, however, is when our thinking is limited to this classic view of competition. Competition at its basic level is necessary for survival. A business cannot afford to be left behind. But this is not enough. There is also a need to move forward, and this is where sur/petition comes in.

This is an excellent example of sur/petition: A few years ago, Du Pont developed a carpet fibre that would resist stains (Du Pont makes fibres but not carpets). This new fibre was offered to the carpet mills, but they were not very interested. Du Pont then launched an advertising campaign directed at the general public. Because the Stainmaster carpet was such an excellent example of integrated value, the demand from the public was such that the mills were forced to make the carpets, along with increased profits. Within three years Stainmaster carpets had something like 70% of the carpet market. Interior designers were recommending light-coloured carpets, but such carpets were easily wrecked by stains. People living in smaller apartments did not have any special place for feeding youngsters, so carpet stains were likely to happen. Buying carpets became not just a matter of better colours, longer wear or cheaper prices as in classic competition. The value of Stainmaster carpets clearly is an integral part of the lifestyle of the buyers.

Reproduced with permission from *Marketing*, June 1992, pp. 9–71.

Questions

1. How is competition different to sur/petition?
2. How do De Bono's ideas on marketing vary from more traditional thinking?

Reading 2—From woeful to wonderful: A step-by-step approach

by Michael Kiely

OK. By now they've slashed your budget and retrenched everyone they can. Those remaining suffer low morale. But still upstairs want you to do the job. Business has become a war of attrition, a long slog with no end in sight. Now, more than ever before, you need to get 110% out of everyone working on your team.

Marketing magazine draws the parallel between sport and the marketing business to find ways to get more from the people on your team. In marketing, as in top level sports, you have a team which strives to defeat other teams by strategies, tactics and personal effort to achieve the final goal—success in the market-place, measured by the scoreboard.

There are lessons for marketing team managers in the way the Australian Rugby Union (ARU), under the guidance of coach Bob Dwyer, transformed the national team from a deflated rabble, often called the 'woeful Wallabies', into the world's undisputed best, taking the World Cup in open contest against teams from 16 nations from Europe, Asia/Pacific and the Americas.

They managed it not by bravado, charisma and hollow hype, but via a methodical management process that can be applied to managing your team. Commentators in the world's strongest rugby nations declared that the ARU have revolutionised the management of the game and that every major nation will now adopt this technique.

'By a special alchemy that can be observed but not explained, the almost woeful Wallabies of the early part of the 1990 season transformed themselves into the wonderful Wallabies, the world champions of Rugby in 1991', wrote Spiro Zavos who followed the team's fortunes throughout the six-Test match crusade. 'The team personnel was not much different in the two seasons, but the team *was*. It was a team that had no weaknesses and a number of the gifted players were at the peak of their powers.' Zavos observed that ten of the test side would qualify for the best-ever Wallaby side in the modern era—so Dwyer had chosen the talent. But a champion team will always beat a team of champions.

How did he create a machine-like team that was able to maintain its nerve six minutes before the bell in the quarter final, when Ireland went three points ahead, and coolly engineer an incursion into the Irish end of the field, take the ball from the resulting scrum and score in the corner after a backline movement of Ella-like magic? To win by one point when the alternative—defeat—meant the end of their long, hard, self-sacrificing campaign which had started four years before.

Bob Dwyer is an electrical engineer by training and is now co-shareholder in the promotional division of a human resources company, ASK Solutions. His company ASK Promotional Solutions specialises in event planning and management and corporate entertainment packages. He sees every large task—like winning world cups or launching big campaigns—as a series of small, logical steps which must be planned in advance and executed on time.

'We decide where we want to get to, a goal to focus on, then we put that aside. There's no need to keep your mind on the end goal because that can cause problems; your confidence can waiver and people start thinking "It's so far away, what if we don't make it?"' he says. 'Instead we concentrate on the steps and say "We will make it if we achieve these smaller goals one by one".'

He cites the case of swimmer John Nabor who, watching the Olympic finals, set himself the goal of a gold medal in the next Olympics. Although his best time was well behind that of the new champion, and would be even further behind what would be needed in four years' time, he calculated exactly the difference he would need to make up, then broke it into smaller increments to be made up at each training session. These goals turned out to be so minuscule, he was easily able to reduce his times by then. He won the gold medal.

Once the task had been sliced up, the first step in the 'special alchemy that can be observed, but not explained' was in setting up a structure that would allow the team to win. In 1988 when Dwyer became the national coach he found no organisational structures for managing and developing the team. The brilliant Alan Jones had coached the team to the Rugby Grand Slam triumph in 1984 simply by sheer personal effort.

'I'm a long-term man. I want a structure that will push us along forever', says Dwyer. Since he took over coaching Randwick and instituted a structured approach to playing the game and developing players, the team has not failed to make a grand final and in most years win it.

'We haven't tried to attract good players to the club', he says. 'More than any other club, most players have risen through the ranks from the colts team. The emphasis is on creating a personal development programme that is followed throughout the organisation so that everyone knows where they are and what they can aspire to.'

This structured approach dictated the selection of the World Cup squad. Here Dwyer broke with tradition by rejecting many of the players presented to him by the State sides. He had devised a basic principle which was to guide the team through the campaign to eventual victory, one which can be readily transferred to business. It determined the type of person he wanted on the team. 'When selecting players, I have a perception of the level of performance that is necessary to achieve the goal and won't rest until I find the people who can produce that level of performance. I've said to the players, "If you aspire to be the best scrum half in Australia and therefore get in the team, I'm not interested in having you. But if you aspire to be the best scrum half you can possibly be and therefore get in the team, I'm very keen to have you".'

Where it was tradition that the Australian test team was selected from players already representing their States, Dwyer's selectors went hunting outside, even among second-grade players, to find the ore for that special alchemy. Daly, Kearns, Nasser, Little, Horan, McKenzie and Ofahengaue all came into the Australian team from their State's B team or the Juniors. Or in Kearn's case from a second-grade club side. Such a break with tradition did not sit comfortably with some in the organisation, but Dwyer's guiding principle of ideal performance dictated his reactions: 'The decision to dump people who will never make the high ideal could result in people wanting to dump the coach. But if retaining the job is your main aim, you're the same as the guy who wants to be the best scrum half in Australia. I'd be trying to prove I was the best coach in the country and therefore they should keep me. But I didn't want to prove that. I wanted to prove that we were the best team in the world. You can't do that without taking risks'.

As in business, a good team manager must be a good surgeon.

The process of selection took the form of a comprehensive three page report on the players' on-field performance and off-field attitude—much the same as an executive search procedure. Dwyer, and the four or five others who worked very hard to transfer the woefuls into the wonderfuls, scoured the scene for potential until the right mix was located.

Next came motivation. Dwyer's is a 'softly, softly' approach. 'Motivation is about creating an atmosphere whereby players can develop to their potential, that places no limits on them', he says. In the last few years, and more so in this last crucial lead-up year, the focus was on educating the players about what was available to them, how to use it and what benefits they would get from it. Whereas the State training camps are commando-style physical endurance tests, the national camps were 80% educational.

'In their education, we start with the basics of human physiology: These are the energy systems that apply to your body. This is what is applicable to our game. This is how you work this system. These are the fuels, and so on. As their knowledge develops, they become more interested and start to ask questions. They become more confident in using the consultant available.'

For the first time in the ARU's history, the team had a full complement of experts: a dietitian, a fitness trainer, strength trainers, a sports psychologist—all of them PhDs in sports physiology or human movement. This logistical and expert support was to rise to a crescendo during the weeks when the final battles were fought on the playing fields of England, Ireland, Wales and France.

The next step towards motivation was to get the players to understand the real game was not on the scoreboard. It was in achieving the ideal performance level. The score is not always a reflection of which was the better side. And in the long term, a series of wins can disguise fundamental flaws which will trap the team into failure when the real test arrives. By means of refocusing the players' attention on the process of transformation that was taking place, Dwyer was able to get them to see past the scoreboard to an ideal performance which could carry them to the top. Playing good rugby rather than playing to win matches.

David Kirk, the captain of the All Black side which won the previous World Cup in 1987, wrote during the 1991 campaign that scoring points is a by-product of playing good rugby and the Australian team understood that, which is why he predicted they would win, defeating the legendary Cup holders and traditional rivals New Zealand.

For the 1991 Wallabies, confidence and motivation were based on more than simply knowledge. There was constant refinement of basic skills 'so that when techniques and procedures are presented to use, we have the skills to carry them out'. There was also Bob Dwyer's demand that they become a tougher, more physical side. 'I'm an aggressive rugby person. I'm into belting the other person.' He called on one of the world's most feared tacklers, former Rugby League Test player Terry Randall, to devise a series of exercises to indoctrinate the Wallabies in the techniques of the offensive tackle. This proved crucial as the Australians' defensive line was unbreachable throughout the second halves of both the Semi-Final and Final when they were unable to gain much ball possession.

Most of all Dwyer demanded commitment. Players were invited to leave the squad early in the process if they could not put in the levels of commitment. 'I told them I would tolerate only three focuses: employment or study, family, and Rugby. Rugby could never be lower then third.' He also demanded that he wanted players who would be good reserves because some of the squad would never get to play. 'I didn't want people who would be good players but not good reserves. I needed people who would bust their arse and work hard and not get a game, but still be a good team member. I told them if that idea did not appeal to them, I was not interested in them.' Two players withdrew from the squad. Finally there was the campaign management itself. On the tour the 24-man touring squad was the best-supported in the competition. Apart from a coach, manager and two assistant coaches, it had a physiotherapist, a doctor, a sports physiologist, a dietitian and two national selectors all looking after the team welfare—to give them the space in which to excel.

Three experts from the Australian Institute of Sport spent hours watching and collecting videotapes of the opposing sides, analysing their weaknesses and likely moves, gathering other intelligence and passing the information back to the Wallaby management for tactical development. Dossiers were compiled on every opponent. There was also a media manager to stage daily press conferences and to coordinate the final press campaign which shamed England into playing an open, running game. The openness of the Australians with the media—while other teams, notably the

Kiwis, were surly and hostile—and the team's readiness to join in the carnival spirit of the event helped make them crowd favourites and created a strong supporters' group out of fans from many nations. In one incident, the reserves stood out in front of the crowd and took part in the Mexican wave, something the English and New Zealanders would think beneath their dignity. For Australia, it was good PR. They made the game, and the team, more accessible to the people. Large crowds would gather at Wallaby training sessions during the World Cup campaign and cheer at the number and complexity of backline moves. The team was stunned to hear the large crowd applauding after even the warm up drills. After the victory, the *New Zealand Herald* conceded the Wallabies were 'the best organised, most talented and enterprising international side in Rugby at the moment'.

The London *Independent* said that while the spectators will remember the dazzling play, 'for our coaches the lesson is far more profound: how to adopt and adapt the Wallabies outstanding array of tactical options right from the specifics of individual moves for individual circumstances to the more general knowledge of what to do and how to do it in any given situation'.

While he concedes that being part of a human resources company helped develop and reinforce his ideas for managing the team, it was Bob Dwyer the electrical engineer who put the pieces in place. 'My single best feature as a coach is that I understand cause and effect—the basic things that effect results. You need a keen eye for cause. If you understand your game or your job, you will look for the causes: what did we do wrong, what did we do right.'

The result of Dwyer's stubborn pursuit of the ideal of playing good rugby was not simply a scoreline of 12:6 at full time in the Final. Australia's campaign in the World Cup put the code in the box seat for development in Australia, where it has always been a minority sport. Many followers of the other codes were surprised at the excitement a rugby match could generate. The ARU now has the opportunity to win crowds and build its game beyond the parochial, clannish code it has been, as a direct result of this pursuit of an ideal.

'The Australian team gained the approval of the press and the crowds because it was the team that had this excitement, that wanted to do things you don't normally see done', says Dwyer. 'If you're playing at the highest level, we should see players doing things that we cannot do, that we as mere mortals can't aspire to'.

The Dwyer approach to team building takes mere mortals with unlimited potential and gives them the opportunity to rise to the top. Successful business is merely this style of rugby, played in suits.

Reproduced with permission from *Marketing*, February 1992, pp. 9–11.

Questions

1. Do you think Michael Kiely's parallel between sport and business is valid? Why?
2. How do you think Edward de Bono might approach coaching a sporting team?

Case 1—Marketers: The endangered species

by Paul Shea

The marketing executive's place in the operation is now threatened by the quality assurance operative who will take greater control of the customer relationship, according to Paul Shea.

By the end of the 1990s, the face of services marketing will be unrecognisable due to one factor—quality! The way to cut costs and increase sales of services in the decade of the 90s is quality not technology or marketing. Unless marketers seize the quality initiative they will become little more than an appendage of operations, human resources or the quality department, a sort of broad-skilled graphic arts department. The world is ready for 'new marketing'.

This 'new marketing' is referred to generically as total quality management (TQM) and grew out of quality control in manufacturing which aims to increase customer satisfaction and reduce costs through better quality and zero defects. TQM is a *management system* for achieving continuous improvement in client satisfaction. Marketing is the satisfaction of clients' needs and wants in either the private or public sectors. TQM is therefore a (new) way of doing marketing.

There are many factors which determine service client satisfaction, many of them traditionally outside the control of marketing. The objective of the original manufacturing TQM is to minimise production variations and achieve zero manufacturing defects. The objective of services TQM is to manage service process variations in such a way as to achieve zero defections/client losses or to put it another way—to maximise client loyalty and value, a concept well understood by direct marketers.

There are many benefits from introducing TQM to service organisations. The main ones are:

1. Client satisfaction and perception of value.
2. Client loyalty/retention.
3. A sustainable competitive advantage.

Other benefits include:

1. Increased market penetration.
2. Premium pricing.
3. Lower costs especially for recovery from service breakdowns.
4. Process confidence.
5. Focus for staff motivation.
6. Focus for award restructuring.
7. Frustrating competition.

As an indication of the importance with which companies such as IBM regard the potential for quality, John Akers, chairman and chief executive officer (CEO) is Chairman of the US National Quality Month in 1991.

Marketing as we knew it in the 1970s and 1980s is a hangover from the production era 'We make it! You sell it!' or in the service version 'We have it (services and facilities)! You promote it!' The quality revolution began in Japan in the 1950s and is now belatedly sweeping US manufacturing due to the former's marketing successes in a wide variety of product categories. The notion is only now taking hold in the US services sector and will eventually include the public sector as well. The American Marketing Association, for example, held its first ever services marketing conference as recently as 1981. The venerable American Society for Quality Control with over 80 000 members has only now in May 1991 established a service quality division. However, this trend will strengthen as all mature western economies continue the shift from manufacturing to service-based employment. The maturing post-war baby boomers of the 1950s, in addition, will expect and be prepared and able to pay for better services in a wide range of industries during the 1990s.

Marketing is already losing out in four key areas:

1. the failure to deliver service through traditional means with new approaches to client satisfaction such as TQM emerging;
2. client service technologies displacing traditional marketing communications options such as electronic media;
3. non-traditional organisational structures and concepts such as matrix organisations, empowerment and self-managing teams; and
4. the growing status of employees as 'internal clients' and the importance of culture development and evaluation, internal incentives and motivation programmes, and internal organisational and staff surveys.

Of these, the first one is the most immediate and obvious threat.

Marketers are rapidly losing the service quality initiative to human resources types. If this continues, the marketing director in the service organisation will eventually be reduced to a glorified type of brand manager. This is not scaremongering. There are numerous examples from many service industries and organisations where the principles of TQM have been applied in whole or in part with demonstrated success. British Airways, SAS, Australian Airlines and Compass Airlines are all examples. The image fast food industry (McDonald's, KFC, Wendys etc.) has practised and refined TQM for 30 years to the point that they express it as an acronym which they call 'the success model'. Called QVSP (quality/value/service/perception), it is a generic model for applying TQM to any kind of service organisation in either the private or public sectors. The Australian Air Force, CSIRO, Wollongong City Council, the Gas & Fuel Corp. of Victoria, the Sydney Water Board and the Australian Taxation Office are all implementing TQM. Probably the best recent example of the power of even partial implementation of TQM principles combined with image marketing is Woolworths. Woolworths has focused both on the customers' needs and staff needs and packaged its offer in a highly visual and believable promotional campaign 'The Fresh Food People' supported with a major internal staff training effort.

What should the survival conscious marketer do? The answer is partly a matter of honing, refocusing, and re-aiming traditional marketing skills; however, new skills must be developed in technology, relationship marketing, process delivery effectiveness and self-managing organisational dynamics. Traditional marketing skills include client understanding, new services development, and research and measurement.

The most important client understanding skill in TQM is the ability to interpret what clients mean by 'quality' and communicate this to the service process designers so that client satisfaction is delivered at an acceptable cost. Quality tools to achieve this include flowcharting, blueprinting, Pareto analysis and quality function deployment.

The marketer has a key role in identifying clients' wants and then managing their expectations through marketing communications processes so that their expectations are met or exceeded. The golden rule is 'under promise and over deliver'. The reverse means client dissatisfaction and defection. Banks, for example, have discovered the perfectionist trap—the more service you give clients, the more they take it for granted and expect still better service.

Expectations and client appreciation have to be managed through appropriate expectations strategies such as positioning. The Woolworths case is an excellent example. Their positioning of 'Fresh Food People' is a food quality/natural positioning which synergises a clever pricing strategy (the margins on fresh foods are much higher than dry goods). Coles has taken a quite different cost/price/technology approach.

Some client examples will help to illustrate the concept of 'service quality expectation setting'. The Wintergarden shopping food court in Brisbane has a positioning 'Tastes-on-the-Go'. 'Tastes' says 'expect a variety of foods' and 'on-the-Go' says 'expect fast service but no comfortable seating'. The Australian Protective Service is the physical security service of the Commonwealth Government. Their chosen positioning is 'When Security Really Matters'. The expectation says: 'Security is like anything else. You get what you pay for. If you want cheap security, then it's at your own risk'. A prestige vehicle smash repairer wanted to claim that his workmanship was 'better than Porsche'. This quality guarantee/expectation positioning chosen to indicate workmanship quality was 'Our Challenge: Factory-Quality or Better!'

The traditional market research approach to services development is essentially too slow and prone to ambiguity for today's market needs. The Japanese often prefer the client observation approach to formalised research techniques. Quality improvement teams will often come up with new services or improvements without the help of the marketers and their laborious, costly and dated research.

Research does however have a major role to play in service quality measurement. TQM is about continuous improvement in service quality and client satisfaction which means continuous measurement. Concepts such as service quality and satisfaction are not simple to measure which is why they have tended to be neglected in the development of corporate information systems, especially in the public sector.

It can and must be done. The giant US communications corporation AT&T has a market research director with the title 'Director, MR & Customer Satisfaction Measurement'. Australia Post has recently let a $2 million per annum contract for a new external mail audit programme. The largest single marketing research project ever conducted at 3M in the United States will be carried out in 1991 involving 10 000 interviews to measure customer service against expectations and competition.

In addition to updating traditional marketing skills, the 'new services marketer' must develop new skills in technology, relationship marketing, service process delivery effectiveness and self-managing organisational dynamics. At the recent COMDEX computing trade show (the largest in the US), new technology available to marketers included multimedia, analysis and statistics, decision support, utilities, networks, graphic interfaces, document management and imaging and portable computers.

Apart from the demonstrated ineffectiveness of traditional methods of improving service quality, there are a range of technological developments which are undermining the marketer's traditional role of the en masse client communicator. Videotex, Smart Cards, Voice Response, 008 Inwats telephone services, VideOcarts, Computer Disks and EDI are only some of the emerging client communication technologies not traditionally under the control of the marketer.

The plus side of the technology coin is that it enables cost efficient communication with clients on virtually an individualised basis and over time as the client proceeds through their needs/wants life cycle. San Antonio-based financial services direct marketer USAA, for example, markets its products and services to US military personnel and their dependents through a sensitive relationship marketing programme they call 'life events marketing'. The process can be applied to any customer group.

However, it is in the fields of service delivery processes and quality organisation dynamics that the marketer must learn new skills and techniques. The staff after all are your best (and cheapest) marketing resource. In service process delivery effectiveness, service and manufacturing TQM come closest together, although you can't simply transpose manufacturing TQM into the service context. The TQM service delivery imperative says: The service delivery process must be capable of consistently delivering a core service quality (Q) via a service transaction (S) which is in accordance with the client's expectation or perception (P) and results in the reinforcing of value (V). This is the generic services success model (QVSP) referred to in connection with the fast food industry. The core service quality (Q) in the case of the fast food industry is 'the consistency of the food'; for a bus service it is 'buses which come on time (or a little late, but never early) with an expected frequency'. A bus timetable is a simple example of service expectation setting.

The marketer has to become much more involved in the actual service transaction because of the hot links between expectation setting and the eventual client perception of value which results from the client's experience(s) and which determine loyalty and repeat or increased business.

The marketer's role in the service quality movement is to determine Q, to measure S, to set P and reinforce V within a goal driven managerial structure such as TQM. The principle is the same for either private or public sectors.

Perhaps the biggest adjustment that marketers will face is in the area of human resources skills. There will be major changes operating relationships with cross-functional skill sharing between operations, human resources, and marketing and flatter flexible matrix-programme type organisational structures rather than the traditional control pyramid. The process has already begun. Quality teams which are empowered and self-managing will assume more traditional marketing roles (such as new services development and improvement). There will be fundamental changes to the roles of 'new manager' and the ways in which information is shared within the organisation. When the service value-adding roles of internal and other support staff become more widely recognised, the marketer will be required to develop better internal marketing programmes and apply incentive and motivational techniques which were previously the province of the sales team. The 'new services marketer' has to be a cross between a PR consultant, a brand manager, a social researcher, an information systems expert and a football coach. Like it or not, the 'new services marketer' has to become tuned into the practices and principles of modern human resources management and organisational development.

Here is a statement from the August 1991 issue of *Quality Progress*, the magazine of the American Society for Quality Control (the one with the 83 000 members): 'Down-to-earth advice for professionals managing total quality: Keep in close contact with the marketing and advertising people. Insist on being part of the design team for advertising campaigns. Ask to examine the data supporting advertising claims and send up red flags when necessary. Consider yourself the personal representative of the customer'.

The ball is currently in the marketer's court, but for much longer?

Reproduced with permission from *Marketing*, January 1992, pp. 16–20.

Questions

1. Play devil's advocate and expose what could be considered the myths of TQM, particularly that:
   —TQM improves customer focus;
   —TQM improves overall organisational performance; and
   —TQM institutionalises innovation and self-renewal.
2. Draw up a checklist of situations where you see TQM as being appropriate and a list of situations where it may be inappropriate.

Case 2—Thomas Toy Company Limited

by Michael Harker

In the early 1980s the Thomas Toy Co. Ltd was enjoying considerable success in the toy business, with its two main lines of construction sets and train sets. In recent years however, it has suffered numerous disappointments, both in the market-place and in its profit and loss account. With the largest sales since the early 1980s of $14.9

million, the company suffered its fourth consecutive annual loss in 1991. A short analysis of this time period indicates possible causes of this unsatisfactory situation.

In 1984 the company was taken over and the sales staff increased by 50% while a new general sales manager and director of international sales were appointed. It was expected that this action would result in an improvement in sales and an increase in the small profit of $20 000 in 1983. However, 1984 showed a loss of $280 000 and sales dropped from $11.6 million to $10.9 million. In an attempt to improve the position, extra effort was put into the preparation of the 1989 Christmas line. To its line of toys were added 50 new items and, at the same time, the range of the line was expanded to include preschool children and girls as well as boys. Supermarkets, a relatively new distribution channel for the company, received many goods on a sale-or-return basis as an incentive for greater push at the point of purchase. Contrary to expectations, sales fell to $10.7 million and a loss of $570 000 was experienced. The return of enormous quantities of unsold toys from the supermarkets was one of the causes of the reversal of expectations. The outcome of this was that most of the top management were dismissed and a switch was made from inside salesmen to manufacturer's representatives as an economy measure. A drastic cut was also made in factory personnel and departments.

For the 1990 Christmas season, 20 new toys were added to the line and that year saw sales increase to $11.4 million; and losses decreased to $190 000. By 1991, it seemed as if the Thomas Company might be on its way to a profitable year. The company spent $1 million on late afternoon TV advertising, and $300 000 on animated point-of-sale displays which were given to dealers free of charge. Sales did climb to $14.9 million after the 1991 Christmas season; however losses mounted to $290 000. The immediate cause of this appeared to be the large returns of car racing sets which were thought of by the trade as being of poor quality, poorly engineered, badly packed and too highly priced. Other complaints regarding Thomas' products were the downgrading of the Thomas Construction sets, and other toys in quality, packaging and price. Moreover dealers claimed poor timing in the release of Thomas' toys, citing the example of missing the peak demand for many items by introducing them on Christmas Eve 1991, obviously too late in the selling season to capture a favourable proportion of the trade.

Questions

1. Indicate what you feel are the main problems of the Thomas Toy Co., and rank these in order of importance.
2. You have just been appointed managing director. What would you do? List your solutions in order of importance.

Case 3—Do you have what it takes! Specific courage—Training experiences for students

by John Jackson

'You've either got it or you haven't!' This expression is frequently used in conversation, whether people are talking about intelligence, common sense, sex appeal, beauty, money, charisma, panache or even courage. Have you ever considered yourself to be simply not courageous? Have you ever wondered whether you 'have what it takes' to thrive, or survive, in our so-called dog-eat-dog business world? And finally, have you ever said to yourself that hopefully your student days will (automatically) prepare you for such a world? Then please participate actively in this case; it could transform you and your education. It has even been said that 'everything goes to prove that our well-being or "better-being" is going to depend more and more on our conscious and modest search for courage' (Servan-Schreiber 1987, p. 139). Note that we are not talking about being argumentative, macho, a bully or showing bravado. What we, and you, want is genuine creative, intellectual, moral and 'stickability' courage, isn't it? But can you 'get it' if you feel you haven't already got it?

Commenting on successive clinical trials in which people who were 'distressed and often disabled by intense fear' behaved bravely, fear expert Rachman makes the point that 'perhaps we should talk about courageous acts rather than courageous actors'. In other words, even though some people are clearly more inclined to be brave habitually, courage can be learned and improved upon by everyone (Maddi & Kobasa 1984). It is quite natural to 'have butterflies in your stomach', quite natural to over-predict your level of fear (Rachman 1990, p. 225), and quite natural to become more courageous if you work at it (Rachman 1990, p. 295). Maddi and Kobasa very encouragingly state that 'our experience indicates that programmes for increasing hardiness can be offered in business settings with dramatic success'.

My fascination with this topic came about as a result of a number of coincidences. Some years back I was directly involved in a new venture in which I lost some money. In hindsight it struck me that most, though not all, of our problems would not have occurred if we had been more courageous in our assessments of market research and the market-place. To increase the revenues in our 'what if' spreadsheets, we modified the product—an interactive laser-disc entertainment booth—to include a number of additions which made it predominantly a promotional product with the entertainment attraction component providing a more minor revenue stream. We also failed to enhance the physical sensation of movement for the child which we knew was essential for maximising customer satisfaction. In doing so we negated a great deal of the earlier consumer research on the product. Despite feeling uneasy about this, we perhaps lacked the courage to hold back the project because the returns looked much more acceptable on paper and the eight trial booths were doing so well in their honeymoon period. The joy of entrepreneuring distorted our priorities. More significantly, I believe, courageous entrepreneurship unfortunately took precedence over courageous marketing. In academic terms, the benefits for the entertainment buyer (who was the key to not only the coin income but also the attractiveness of the booths as a promotional medium for advertisement buyers) were largely sacrificed. There were obviously many other considerations and issues in this case but a serious deficiency in courageous marketing was an important one.

This personal experience consolidated for me an observation that most of us have probably made when examining the literature on product and business failures: namely, that failures seem to frequently reveal key errors in marketing which someone in the organisation should have anticipated and objected to *courageously*. If one studies such failures as the Ford Edsel, Xerox Computers, Harley Davidson's early defence of the motorcycle market, Zap flavoured milk, Swan Gold, the South African butter fiasco, the Beechams/Yankelovitch case and many more it can be seen that companies well staffed with professionally trained marketers did not prevent major errors in marketing theory. Someone in their marketing departments must surely have noticed the erroneous assumptions or decisions yet failed to overturn them or object to them sufficiently to have them reversed.

Lack of awareness of the errors, or belief that they were not in fact errors, explains only a proportion of these. For example, Ford did not consumer test its final designs, its number of model versions, the Edsel name and other vital marketing decisions. Zap UHT flavoured milk arbitrarily chose the 15–24 target market because it wanted to be in that lucrative beverage market even though pre-teens and their mothers would have been a more sensible hypothesis. Swan Gold ignored their own research on why Australian women drink beer, and the South African Butter Board reasoned that it could remove its butter mountain by raising butter prices to pay for substantial advertising, irrespective of competitor reaction and elementary economic theory. Surely someone in Coca-Cola's enormous marketing department should have had the *courage* to point out that the sample used to test consumer reaction to 'New Coke' was not similar to those who were brand loyal to the traditionally formulated brand? Someone in these organisations failed 'to stand up and be counted' when each of these projects veered away from marketing principles. Professionally trained marketers in these cases would have had the knowledge but not the commitment and courage.

Similarly, if we examine some of the better known success stories, such as Post-it Notes, the Ford Mustang, Trivial Pursuit and the video cassette, one notices in every case examples of considerable courage against substantial impediments. Are we confident that we are helping in the development of courageous marketing abilities when the usual difficulties arise and the pressure to ignore marketing fundamentals seems overwhelming?

Interestingly, while academic sources are largely silent on the role of courage in the market-place, other business authors and executive folklore are not so silent. This is to a certain extent understandable in that the topic in question is academically an imprecise concept that doesn't readily lend itself to scientific investigation. A notable exception is the award-winning research of Hamel and Prahalad (1989, p. 76) in which they conclude that 'in studying organisations that had surrendered (global leadership), we invariably found senior managers who, for whatever reason, lacked the courage to commit their companies to heroic goals'. Hopefully this reason should not exclude it from training programmes. The business community is unequivocal about the importance of courageous marketing in business. The Centre for Strategic Leaders in Queensland, for example, has ranked courage as one of the eight crucial qualities of all strategic leaders (1991, p. 4). Webber's (1991) survey of heroes as seen by seven groups from school students to senior executives ranked courage and leadership as the only two consistent attributes across all groups.

Here are a few notable comments from the business community.

William Bernbach of Doyle Dane Bernbach Advertising:
> Those who are going to be in business tomorrow are those who understand that the future, as always, belongs to the brave.

Robert Townsend of Avis (US):
> Things get done in our society because of a man or woman with conviction.

Sir Peter Abeles of TNT and Ansett:
> Audacity applies to every business . . . When you start to know too much about what one shouldn't do then you become very self-restrictive.

Richard Foster, Director of McKinseys, on initiating major technological change:
> The CEO must be someone with the conviction to insist that the company abandon its technology and skill base when everything in classic economic terms is going well; someone with a thick skin to endure the criticism that will come when the first steps towards new products and processes inevitably go astray or prove disappointing . . . Only a few have the courage to change and have led their companies through technological discontinuities.

Barry Jones, Federal Minister for Science, Customs and Small Business:
> The most important issue in Australian politics today is how to bring Australia up-to-date, to come to grips with the social and political significances of the technical revolution sweeping the Western World . . . We are not very tough. We give up easily.

John Keil, vice-president of Dancer Fitzgerald Sample Advertising Agency:
> The three ingredients that lead to creative success are talent, time and courage . . . sometimes referred to as guts. The courage to pursue the unusual; the courage to take risks; the courage to fail; the courage to keep going when the prospects look the blackest. Because, without this courage, everything you've worked for can fall short.

If we accept that courageous marketing is a valuable attribute of a business graduate, how extensive is the problem facing the 'typical' marketer? In other words, what are the areas of greatest danger and thus those requiring the greatest degree of courage? It could then be argued that some sort of training or practice should be undertaken within each of these areas. I would include the following 18 areas as the most important (these are not mutually exclusive):

54   PART B

1. The high failure rate of new products.
2. Exposing ghost/illusionary markets—that is, ghost potential, consumption, demand, products, customers and opportunities.
3. The strategic execution of nostalgic 'dogs' within the portfolio.
4. Predicting and averting liquidation/bankruptcy.
5. Inadequate attention to the differences between the simplicity of the marketing concept and the difficulty of implementing it.
6. Incomplete and dangerously inadequate marketing and business plans.
7. Business and marketing plans written solely as promotional documents to investors rather than clinically objective management guides.
8. Problems and dangers arising from marketing's frequent lack of line power in many organisations. This includes the need to be courageously persuasive in accounting-orientated, production-orientated, entrepreneur-orientated and sales-orientated organisations. My personal experience is that many accountants, entrepreneurs, production people and sales specialists are unable or unwilling to grasp the subject or take it seriously and will honestly concede this when pressed at the appropriate time. This magnifies the requirement for courage.
9. Ethical dilemmas regarding exploitation of customers, suppliers or employees in a predominantly amoral business and educational culture.
10. The courage to be creative in a predominantly 'left-brain' and resistant-to-change environment.
11. The cut and thrust of competitive combat and the need to appraise objectively and comprehensively one's competitors' brands and strengths.
12. Distinguishing between assertiveness and unacceptable aggression, especially for female marketers.
13. Distinguishing between excessive and appropriate politeness, especially for East Asian and South Pacific students.
14. Human frailities (such as ego-pride, stupidity, greed, resistance to change) that prevent the marketer from learning from others, changing one's opinion, and modifying a decision proactively rather than reactively. Defence mechanisms involving hostile gestures and words are also non-courageous activity in the marketing arena.
15. Tenaciously pursuing a well-chosen, robust strategy despite various tactical errors and minor environmental changes.
16. The demanding requirements of 'new product/venture championship' in terms of devotion, dedication and 'deviousness'.
17. For recent graduates, the problem of overcoming a deferential, overly polite student role habit and an impractical 'egg-head' image in a down-to-earth anti-intellectual business world.
18. For prospective graduates, the possibility of unemployment like so many other people in a turbulent world.

It is worthwhile to add to this list of the greatest dangers faced by marketers a further list of the greatest dangers faced within business education itself. Bill Edwards of the Queensland University of Technology colourfully identifies a number of ailments affecting business education (1990, p. 13), of which the following have serious implications for courage-training.

1. *Opportuniphobia*—an obsession with problems and problem-solving techniques at the expense of finding, recognising and implementing opportunities.
2. *Conceptualitis*—an excessive focus on 'head knowledge' often to the exclusion of a 'grass roots feel' for business.
3. *Paralysis traditionalis*—an over-orientation towards traditional academic respectability at the expense of 'generating a useful product'.
4. *Megalopapervirus*—an excessive fascination with paper numbers, paper entrepreneurs, and paper jobs.
5. *Disjunctivitis*—where business and other education is seen or presented as a series of unintegrated, disjointed experiences rather than 'putting it all together'.
6. *Personophobia*—a reluctance or fear of 'accepting the challenge of achieving business-essential personal development of students . . . rather than a retreat into arms-length academia'.

One further list is required, that of the most widely expressed fears in the workplace generally. Ryan and Oestreich (1991, pp. 4–5) identify these as:

1. Having one's credibility questioned.
2. Being left out of decision making.
3. Being criticised in front of others.
4. Not getting the information necessary to succeed.
5. Having a key assignment given to someone else.
6. Having disagreements which might lead to damaged relationships that matter.
7. Getting stuck in a dead-end job.
8. Not getting deserved recognition.
9. Not being seen as a team player when that is important.
10. Having one's suggestions misinterpreted as criticisms.
11. Having one's poor levels of performance found out.
12. Getting fired.

The hazards of a career in marketing, marketing education and business generally, are certainly extensive. As May Sarton once said: 'One must think like a hero to behave like a merely decent human being'. But is there danger pay? Union safety standards and protection? Rachman in *Fear and Courage* (1978) concludes that: 'Training for courage plays an important part in preparing people to undertake dangerous jobs'.

Is there training available in courageous marketing? An examination of a variety of marketing texts and casebooks reveals references to commitment, dedication, and overcoming resistance to change but without a specific focus on the subject in general, or training practice in particular. Assertiveness courses are designed primarily for disadvantaged social groups, not tailored to the needs of professional groups such as marketers. In fact, Robin Hogarth of the Centre for Decision Research in Chicago, concludes that:

> It is a curious fact that although most professionally trained persons have both followed courses and received on-the-job training concerning the

subject matter of their expertise, almost none have given serious thought, or received instruction concerning conceptual skills and in particular the intuitive processes they use to manipulate their substantive knowledge.

I would include here the process of practising courageous marketing.

To help you answer the case question, consider what some of the leading experts in the field have found through formal research and industrial experience. But please remember that courage also requires you to: (i) not devalue your own experiences: (ii) not defer to experts just because they are experts; and (iii) not reject the advice of experts because your ego feels uncomfortable:

- Maddi and Kobasa (1984, pp. 31, 32, 59): 'Personality hardiness . . . is a factor of resilience, activeness, self-reliance and zest for living . . . People who have a vigorous sense of commitment, control and challenge tend to react to stressful events with transformational rather than regressive coping . . . (Specific) interactions need to be:

    1. supportive in the sense of gratifying not only needs but also capabilities;
    2. conducive to the experience of mastery through performance of tasks of moderate difficulty; and
    3. varied, with encouragement to construe this as richness.'

- Servan-Schreiber (1987, pp. 72, 73, 91): 'If I am honest with myself, I shall see that the chief resistances (to courage) are laziness and fear . . . The essential function of courage . . . is to concretise . . . Only courage permits desire, will and decision to be enacted in reality . . . The greater my dynamism the easier it is to mobilise my emotional resources. When we are in good affective form we are less subject to fears, more inclined to optimism, attitudes which are thought to spark courage . . . Everything that gives me a feeling of greater mastery over my own life increases confidence in my ability to deal with unexpected or delicate situations.'

- Charles Watson (1992, p. 56): 'A careful analysis of the happiest people shows they have succeeded in forgetting themselves because they are all consumed in the service of something truly worthwhile . . . (they) struggle boldly in the service of something greater having genuine merit'.

- Dorothy Rowe (1987, pp. 381–382): 'In weakness we feel fear . . . If we value ourselves we are not impressed by the claims to power that other people make. If we value ourselves we see ourselves as being as valuable as other people . . . If we value ourselves we accept helpful advice, but we do not accept destructive criticism, or allow ourselves to be belittled, or insulted, or deprived, punished or injured'.

Saligman, M. E. (1988) in Rachman (1990, p. 313) 'proposes that optimism promotes courage. He goes further and postulates that optimism is a pre-condition for courage.' Other examples of this relationship have been found in studies by Rachman himself. In essence Rachman tells us:

1. Controllability and predictability—including both competence and self-confidence—have been scientifically shown to be key ingredients in the absence of fear (and presumably the presence of courage) (p. 10).

2. Military experiments and surveys have consistently shown courageous behaviour whenever the training is as realistic to battle conditions as is possible (p. 61).
3. These military studies have also indicated, though with less evidence so far, that people should be encouraged to be permissive, that is, to talk about and accept as normal, their own fears in the face of actual danger (p. 61).
4. It was also observed that people who were given socially responsible tasks to carry out experienced a noticeable growth of courage. It was not until recently that we acquired substantive evidence that 'modelling' and 'required helpfulness' did consistently breed courage (p. 240).
5. It has also been shown that group membership and morale—'not letting the side down'—is conducive to courageous behaviour (p. 243).
6. The need to avoid disapproval or ridicule enhanced instances of courage (p. 243).
7. The sight of a living courageous model is more effective than hearing about one (p. 78).
8. Compton MacKenzie traces the motivating source of moral courage to self-respect, feelings of compassion, and the social abstraction of a pursuit of justice and truth (p. 246).
9. In the early stages of courage training, success is far more likely if the person's motivation is raised appropriately. This should assist perseverance even in the face of subjective apprehension (p. 248).
10. One element of (courage) training, the gradual and graduated practice of the dangerous tasks likely to be encountered, seems to be of particular importance (p. 248).

One final comment is worth making. Although students (and others) are accustomed to observing courage exhibited within groups and organisations, courage is actually a personal attribute. As Garrison Keillor (1989, p. 13) wrote: 'Virtue can only be said to be possessed by individuals. God's grace is not dispensed at group rates. Good luck—and take courage'.

Questions

1. What do you think could be done to encourage courageous marketing in your programme?
2. What kind of situations would you like to see organised to pursue this idea?

References

Duncan, T. (1989), 'Success Secrets—The BRW Tapes', *Business Review Weekly*.
Edwards, W. (1990), 'Ailments Affecting Business Education', *QBIZ*, Winter.
Foster, R. (1987), *Innovation: The Attacker's Advantage*, Macmillan, London.
Hamel, G. and Prahalad, C. K. (1989), 'Strategic Intent', *Harvard Business Review*, May–June.
Hogarth, R. (1980), *Judgment and Choice*, Wiley, Chichester.
Jones, B. (1988), 'We're Quitters', in *Better Small Business*, No. 2, Small Business Development Corporation.

Keil, J. (1985), *The Creative Mystique*, Wiley, New York.
Keillor, G. (1989), 'Toasting the Flag', *New York Times*, July 2.
Maddi, S. and Kobasa, S. (1984), *The Hardy Executive*, Dow Jones Irwin, Homewood, Illinois.
QDEVET and Price Waterhouse Urwick (1991), *Manager as Creative Leader*, Centre for Strategic Leaders, Brisbane.
Rachman, S. J. (1978), *Fear and Courage*, Freeman & Co. San Francisco.
Rachman, S. J. (1990), *Fear and Courage*, (2nd edn), Freeman & Co., New York.
Rapp, S. and Collins, T. (1978), *Maximarketing*, McGraw-Hill, New York, foreword by William Bernbach.
Rowe, D. (1989), *Beyond Fear*, Fontana Collins, London.
Ryan, K. and Oestreich, D. (1991), *Driving Fear out of the Workplace*, Jossey-Bass Publishers, San Francisco.
Servan-Schreider, J-L. (1987), *The Return of Courage*, Addison-Wesley, Massachusetts.
Townsend, R. (1970), *Up The Organisation*, Michael Joseph, London.
Watson, C. E. (1992), 'The Meaning of Service in Business', *Business Horizons*, January–February.
Webber, R. A. (1991), *Becoming a Courageous Manager*, Prentice Hall, New Jersey.

Case 4—How switched on are you?

by John Clayton

Every marketer, old or young, new or experienced, should be on the ball.

This is a short competition designed to cover a number of major areas which are impacting modern marketing. Alert marketers should be able to answer them easily.

	A	B	C
1. What word best describes our external environment?	Hectic	Chaotic	Turbulent
2. A vision statement is:	Useful	Waste of time	Critical
3. How many steps in a marketing plan?	9	12	It depends
4. Changing the corporate culture begins where?	Shop floor workers	The CEO	Personnel Manager
5. Who is the key person in any organisation?	The Customer	The Boss	The Marketing Consultant
6. Who popularised the value chain?	Madam Lash	Michael Porter	Peter Drucker

7. What percentage of all errors are due to the process, not the staff?	25%	50%	85%
8. What does JIT mean?	Just in Time	Japanese Inform. Technology	Juran's Indust. Tachometer
9. Is service marketing different to product marketing?	Yes	No	Don't Know
10. What percentage is spent planning a campaign to running it?	30/70	50/50	60/40

Reproduced with permission from *Marketing*, June 1992, p. 67.

2. ANALYSING THE MARKET

Introduction 62

Readings
3. Segmentation, by Neil Shoebridge 63
4. How green was my market, by George Camakaris 64

Cases
5. A lot of bullshit in the market research industry, by David James 67
6. Fine Music Network, by Noela Cerutti, Peter Graham, Felicity Neary and Gary Thorpe 70
7. The Australian nursery industry, by Peter Graham and Debra Harker 73

Introduction

Section two in this part of the book examines the process of analysing markets. It looks in detail at the importance, and nature, of marketing research and information in preparing marketing plans. Consumer behaviour and organisational markets and behaviour are also examined, together with measuring and forecasting demand.

The section comprises two readings and three case studies. 'Segmentation' by Neil Shoebridge looks at the theory and practice of the concept. David James' 'A lot of bullshit in the market research industry' takes a slightly cynical view of the market research industry but acts as a forum for research industry leaders to air their views. George Camakaris reveals the latest trends in eco-consumerism in the reading, 'How green was my market'.

The two other case studies in this section cover corporate promotion and segmentation. In 'Fine Music Network', the authors give a detailed account of the problems of corporate promotion in a segment of the public broadcasting sector. In 'The Australian nursery industry' Peter Graham and Debra Harker have written a detailed case study based on the findings of a research report. The study looks at the consumer, buyer behaviour and attitudes in the nursery industry.

Reading 3—Segmentation

by Neil Shoebridge

Marketers like to categorise consumers. Organising the population into neat, homogeneous groups makes it easier to pitch specific products or services at specific people, either existing or prospective customers. The categorising process takes many forms. People can be grouped in demographic, attitudinal, economic or social clusters. A product can be pitched at 25 to 39-year-old housewives, 40-plus blue-collar workers or 18 to 24-year-old women.

Yet beyond the popular categories such as empty-nesters (retired people with plenty of money to spend) and the new poor (30 to 45-year-olds with no money to spend) there are many smaller groups of consumers that are often overlooked by the marketing community. None of these categories represent mass markets, but in an era of fragmenting consumer tastes and attitudes, maybe they are worth considering.

Angry retired people:
The property slump has squeezed the income of retired people who sank their superannuation payments into property trusts. Guess what? These retired people are mad as hell. Their dreams of a comfortable, secure retirement have evaporated. Far from the free-spending, adventurous retirees painted by some researchers, they are cautious and frugal. They do not respond well to marketing programs that urge them to spend, spend, spend in retirement. Their sense of security and dignity has been eroded and they are far from happy.

Yuppies in hiding:
Don't be fooled. The 1987 sharemarket crash and the recession didn't kill the yuppies; it simply drove them underground. Walk through Neutral Bay or Toorak on any Saturday morning and you will see hordes of yuppies in mufti. They still have money, but they know not to flash it around in the sober, responsible 1990s. The Lacoste T-shirts have been packed away and replaced by Ralph Lauren shirts (the logo is smaller). They drink Dom Perignon at home and Yellowglen in public. They holiday in Europe, but hide the holiday snaps when they get home.

Heart attack candidates:
Kerry Packer's heart attack last year briefly focused attention on this group of consumers. Typically, they are middle-aged men who work too hard, play too hard, smoke too much and drink too much. Fear of death or disability weighs heavily on their minds and is increasingly leading them to change their unhealthy lifestyles. They are embracing exercise machines, fat-free food products, vitamins and weight-loss classes. Some marketers have twigged to the emergence of this new group of consumers. Sanitarium Health Food Company, for example, is using a middle-aged businessman to promote its *So Good* soy drink and *Weetbix* breakfast cereal.

Vegetarians:
The bad press red meat copped in the 1970s and 1980s has abated in the 1990s, thanks to the aggressive marketing campaigns mounted by the meat industry and the adoption of more moderate eating habits. But vegetarians are still alive and well and, according to some researchers, growing in number. Few food marketers have

launched vegetarian lines. Where are the meatless frozen dinners, the meat-free supermarket sections and the vegetarian fast food menus?

Late-night TV watchers:

The advent of people meters, the new electronic gadgets that measure TV audiences, has revealed a big group of people who sit up late, glued to their TV sets. TV networks are starting to respond, introducing programmes such as 'Late Night with Steve Vizard' and 'Lateline'. Most advertisers and agencies still believe late-night TV is a wasteland of insomniacs and shiftworkers who don't really pay attention to what they are watching. At the moment, late-night TV advertising rates are still cheap. They won't be for much longer.

Disgruntled urbanites:

Life in the city is pretty grim, right? Why not buy four or five hectares in the country and create a rural nirvana. Along the way, the former city dwellers spend big sums on four-wheel drives, outdoor furniture, moleskins, Akubra hats and posthole diggers. One hitch: all too often, rural heaven turns into rural hell and the disgruntled urbanites return home.

Reproduced with permission from *BRW*, Australia's leading business magazine, 3 April, 1992, p. 77.

Questions

1. Who benefits from segmentation? Why?
2. Why is segmentation used by marketers?
3. How do the segments described by Neil Shoebridge differ from those in the case study, 'The Australian nursery industry'?

Reading 4—How green was my market

by George Camakaris

Concern about the environment is playing an increasingly important role in the lives of Australians, but if marketers are to respond to these concerns, they need facts rather than hearsay. They need to be able to pick the trends so they can be in a position to respond quickly to changes in behaviour, even to pre-empt them.

How important is the environment really? Who cares? What do they care most about? Does concern about the environment affect their purchasing behaviour? How is that concern changing over time? Does it wax and wane with media publicity issues? What do people expect government to do about the environment? Will people still put the environment ahead of jobs during a recession? These are some of the questions answered by *How green are we? An environmental monitor of community views* prepared by AMR Quantum Market Research.

Begun in November 1990, the study is an ongoing survey designed to monitor changes in awareness of environmental issues and in resulting attitudes and behaviour, and includes key demographic and socio-economic information. Each survey is administered over a six-month period to a sample of randomly selected households in Melbourne, Sydney and Perth. Sample sizes were 1100 for the July 1991 survey and 1458 for the February 1992 survey.

The most recent survey revealed that while the environment continued to rate as the third most important issue to Australians, concern with unemployment has become overwhelming. Nevertheless, 37% still mention the environment as one of the main issues facing Australia. Yet two-thirds of Australians are unfamiliar with the concept of sustainable development, despite the media publicity given to the subject in 1991. Those who are familiar with the concept appear to understand it well and strongly support this approach to economic development. Those most likely to be concerned are women, people aged under 30, and those in white-collar jobs. Melbourne people expressed less concern about the environment than Sydney or Perth residents, a reflection perhaps of the poorer economic conditions in that city.

Local environmental problems such as air and water pollution are the environmental issues most often nominated as a concern, although the latter has receded in the public mind, especially in Sydney, where government measures are seen to be addressing this problem. But it is the major global problems—the greenhouse effect, the hole in the ozone layer, destruction of rainforests—that are nominated as the issues of greatest concern, especially among the young.

People do believe that they can do a lot to improve some environmental problems. Some 40% believe they can improve the situation with respect to litter, the excessive use of energy, the dumping and disposal of household wastes, and the use of CFCs. The sense of empowerment is strongest among those in charge of basic household purchasing decisions (many of whom are women), and this group is also more likely to practise environmentally sensitive behaviour in all areas on a regular basis. But in the last six months there has been a loss of confidence in the individual's ability to affect product packaging, even among grocery buyers. Under 25% of all people surveyed believe they can do much to influence the vast majority of environmental issues, and a third believe they have no power to affect things positively, suggesting Australians as a whole have yet to realise the potential influence the householder can have in respect of environmental issues.

Over two-thirds continue to support the introduction of government legislation to control the dumping or disposal of toxic wastes, the destruction of forests, the pollution of the water supply and lakes and rivers, and drift-net fishing. People under 30, those with tertiary education and Sydney residents are most likely to support government intervention. Men are more likely to support intervention on global issues, while women support a stronger line on issues such as rainforest destruction, endangered species and toxic waste disposal. The government was seen as having an important educative role on issues such as the greenhouse effect, the excessive use of energy, the ozone layer, litter, packaging and the disposal of household waste.

To track shifts in significant attitudes, the population was segmented into four groups—*dark green*, *pale green*, *grey* and *black*—according to their response to a number of environmental factors. These include attitudes towards environmental movement, a belief in active participation in achieving solutions, the need for action in Australia by individuals and government, the willingness to pay more for environmentally friendly products, confidence in government commitment to the environment, and the need for greater guidance in environmental behaviour. While there were some shifts over the last six months in the constituent populations of these four groups (away from *dark green*), there was little change in the degree of their concern about the environment, apart from the *blacks* who showed a quite significant decrease in concern.

Dark greens are predominantly female, in their twenties and tertiary educated. This group continues to display a genuine concern for the environment and to be conscious of environmental considerations in their household purchasing. However, even they appear to be paying more attention to their budgets than they did six months ago, weighing cost above the environment in some purchase decisions. They show increased support for the government taking a proactive role forcing individuals to change their behaviour.

Pale greens represent the largest group of consumers, with slightly more females than males. This group acknowledges that the environment is an issue of great concern and to some extent they have modified their behaviour to reflect this. They are becoming more willing to take the environment into account in their purchase behaviour although they continue to be reluctant to pay more for environmentally friendly products.

Greys are mostly male, white collar and over 30. This group acknowledges environmental concerns but believes that the Australian community lacks real direction as to what to do to positively influence environmental trends. While still supporting more government action in educating and assisting householders, they appear to be moving towards an understanding that environmental problems are not necessarily beyond the control of the individual.

Blacks are predominantly male, blue collar, with 11 years schooling or less and mostly Melbourne-based. This group continues to deny environmental problems and considers them overrated. They absolve themselves from responsibility by believing that the issues are either out of control or beyond their control.

During 1991 they moved further away from an acknowledgment of personal responsibility, regarding it increasingly as the responsibility of government and industry. This group continues to be the most resistant to behavioural change. For more information on this monitor call (02) 957 1744 or (03) 699 5688.

Reproduced with permission from *Marketing*, May 1992, pp. 29–32.

Questions

1. What limitations do you think the AMR Quantum Market Research Study has?
2(a). The researchers have used the data collected to segment their consumers. Do you think the segments are valid?
2(b). Are the segments reliable?
3. What further research would you recommend?

Case 5—A lot of bullshit in the market research industry

by David James

These are the words of a leading practitioner. David James reports on the research industry. A cult favourite among business how-to books in recent years is the centuries-old Japanese samurai manual *The Art of War*, by Sun Tsu.

Successful principles of organisation and conflict strategy were kept hidden by the Japanese for centuries, which is not surprising as secrecy was one of its main tenets. The tactical importance of intelligence was a key principle, superior knowledge of the opposition being the crucial factor in gaining the upper hand.

Traditionally marketers have approached intelligence gathering by placing great importance on what was most threatening to them and of most interest to senior management, namely the competition. But customers are now the masters being served, so gaining intelligence about them has been elevated in importance.

Marketing research has come to a watershed in Australia in the current climate, with some companies experiencing buoyant growth, yet most experiencing cutbacks and some sinking without a trace. Things are not much different overseas.

'It doesn't much matter whether one is in Australia or the UK, it's a regrettable fact of life that the market research budget is an easy target for management seeking to cut costs', says Jonathon Shingleton, chairman of the large UK firm Business Planning & Research Limited. 'Stringencies mean reduced research budgets, cancelled projects, increased levels of tendering and pressure on research agencies' margins. Those clients who are commissioning research must think it is their lucky day!'

Mr Shingleton pointed out to this year's well attended Market Research Society Conference that the UK's economy is demonstrably worse than Australia's, and those agencies showing the best chances of survival are the very large and the very small: 'I think senior management has a pretty dim view of our profession and its relevance,' he said, echoing the view of many Australian research companies.

Although working in the rapidly growing sector of brand and advertising tracking, Frank Simper, director of Stochastic Research agrees. 'There is a lot of bullshit in the market research industry—lots of promises and price-cutting to win clients. As an industry our biggest issue is coming to grips with what our own market-place needs. Educating marketers who take a superficial view of research or allow the shysters to run a few figures up a flagpole and see who notices. Taking an interest in our own industry rather than order-taking research or sitting around complaining about the lack of funds.'

Contributing to the evolving situation in the research trade is the new breed of more educated, computer literate marketers familiar with the complexity and diversity of any market-place. In-house research departments and activities are flourishing, with agencies taking a more distant 'advisory' role.

Geo-demographic mapping is one hot-tech item fascinating the research industry and marketers alike, according to vendor Mr Bruce Graham. Essentially another of the emerging computer graphic presentation tools, geo-dg mapping presents overlaid information in several 'dimensions'. It's nearly impossible to explain some of the sophisticated types of figures and results that can be generated, so such techniques weren't a consideration previously. In the old days it was two dimensional—like the x and y co-ordinates used on graphs, whereas now you can see normal demographics on one level, geographic information on another level then overlay your customer data on yet another, narrowing your focus closely.'

Techno-faddists in the industry support other developments, such as computerised recording of site-collected information and more sophisticated monitoring of psychological and physiological responses to target stimuli, good for a giggle by the Luddites since its origins in the 1950s.

Telephone interviewing is another growing phenomenon, with proponents claiming better target selection techniques, less intrusive gathering, easier and more accurate recording of results and, importantly, cost-effectiveness.

New qualitative approaches are finding wider acceptance though, such as non-verbal devices said to expose consumer preferences. Participants may be asked to sort through a series of photographs of faces and decide which one is most likely to buy life insurance or drink Coke. Hypothetical questioning can also remove the stigma and preconditioning of subjects, although some critics question the relevance or objectivity of results.

Qualitative researchers report growing difficulty with interviewees, who are becoming more savvy to marketing techniques and what they think is a reaction or attitude more expected of them than their actual belief or perception. This is heightened by a shortage of 'virgins' and an excess of 'groupies', referring respectively to people who have not been questioned or conditioned to the process and those who enjoy research and participate too often. Groupies get a buzz or feeling of power and privilege from their participation in round table discussions, and adopt unrealistic or even false attitudes, throwing the best researchers off by giving them what they are expecting to hear. No central database of respondents has yet been established by the industry to keep tabs on these matters, so it remains in the domain of each practitioner's professionalism and responsibility.

Problems with recruitment and sampling can be overcome by adhering to industry standards, according to Spike Cramphorne, chairman of the Interviewer Quality Control Scheme. More than 40 research companies have already undertaken to participate in the IQCS scheme, which sets standards of selection, training, survey methodology and interview technique. 'Most of the new technologies apply to data gathering techniques, which mid-size companies do not necessarily concentrate on,' says David Barmer, managing director of Brian Sweeney Research. 'Our benefit is that we are a mid-size agency so can put equal emphasis on both qual and quant, which means that we are in a position to combine the two in a single study.'

Quite often research companies do little more than send printouts of figures to their clients, which some clients are happy with and that's all they want to pay for. Larger or more diligent agencies invariably try to write a report which is as interpretive as possible in terms of the marketing implications of the results discovered. 'Research is becoming an increasingly accepted tool, particularly as we are getting more 'qualified' marketers from courses and degrees, where they are learning about market research and where it can help,' Mr Barmer says.

Sweeney also produce a regular and widely respected sports industry survey of 1500 Australians, looking at the sports they participate in, watch on TV and attend as spectators. This results in a profile about the followers of 45 different sports, examining things like attitude about sponsorship, sponsor awareness and advertising.

Tracking results of sponsorships and other marketing efforts is the lifeblood of the industry, making its practitioners sometimes even more expert than clients. Research industry leader Elizabeth Dangar, for example, has outlasted many marketing clients on one particular product so is occasionally called in to brief them on their own company's previous activities and results. 'Most marketers don't appreciate how much they already know about their market-place,' she says. 'It's no accident that advertising agencies can do some of their best work in a competitive pitch—no big research budgets are available so they have to use their own resources, observe and hypothesise.'

Researchers will not usually complain that their budget is too large, but they invariably seek a more involved and better briefing. Some clients are worried that the more involved a briefing is then the less objective (or even legitimate) the result. One of Australia's biggest users of research disagrees. John Clark, marketing services manager of Unilever's L&K Rexona, briefs agencies small and large as well as possible, believing that 'knowing where their marketer's head is at will enable an agency to interpret the consumer response in a more valid way for the marketer. Everyone knows that occasionally there are ads that a client will really want to succeed in testing due to various internal pressures, which in turn really only puts pressure on the researcher, but in general researchers give the best possible consultancy advice and are as objective as they can be.'

L&K Rexona was pleased with an intensive research effort recently which resulted in a surprising success—the Omo and Drive environmental packaging campaign. 'Without market research I don't think we would have gotten the balance right between performance, economy and the environment in our positioning of those products. We found that care of the environment was not enough, and that consumers still place a high value on the brand and its value,' Mr Clark said. Signals are not always read so well, and millions have been wasted on new product launches that tested with green lights flashing.

Clients describe one of the more usual misleading results of research as the entertainment value of advertising, which is noticed, amuses and even impinges, but neither positions a brand nor motivates its purchase. Pre-testing results tend to point back to the fundamental marketing principles of getting a clear exposition of your product benefit.

Research results suffer an ignominious end. Like most decent novels, they make terrific reading and are sometimes quite informative, and then they make great bookends on the shelf.

Reproduced with permission from *Marketing*, December/January 1992, pp. 48–50.

Questions

1. Summarise the respective roles of the company's marketing executive and its advertising agency.
2. You are responsible for implementing a system for measuring customer satisfaction in a financial service industry. What techniques are available to you and what are their advantages and disadvantages?

☐ Case 6—Fine Music Network

by Noela Cerutti, Peter Graham, Felicity Neary and Gary Thorpe

Radio broadcasting in Australia has three sectors: commercial, national (ABC and SBS) and public. The public sector stations are mainly volunteer, operated with a few paid staff. The three fine music stations that make up the proposed Fine Music Network (FMN) are part of the expanding public broadcasting sector, now numbering up to 100 licensed stations. The public sector contains three categories of stations; 'E' class or educational stations, 'C' class or community access type, and 'S' class or special interest stations. The FMN is made up of 'S' class stations.

These fine music stations obtain their funding from several sources, including public subscriptions and donations, and by providing technical services to other communications industries, such as renting tower space to two-way radio companies. Sponsorship of programmes is growing in importance as a source of funding.

Sponsorship on public radio is strictly controlled by the Australian Broadcasting Tribunal. The regulations provide that the on-air sponsorship announcements can include the name of the sponsor, the nature of their business, and an address and telephone number. These announcements cannot contain advertising jingles or corporate slogans. Proposals in the new Broadcast Bill to go to Parliament in 1992 and propose a widening in what is allowed in the form of 'promotional advertising'.

One of the problems faced by the FMN stations in attracting revenue from 'sponsorship', is that many large companies refer such proposals or requests to the sponsorship manager. These requests are then evaluated against others submitted by sporting, social and charitable organisations. Often the fine music stations are not deemed worthy causes. However, if the proposal was seen as more of an advertising opportunity, it would be referred to the company's advertising agency, and measured against their usual 'reach' standards. Hence the FMN is turning from the use of the term 'corporate sponsorship' or 'advertising', and is adopting the term 'corporate promotions' in an attempt to enhance its revenue-raising programmes.

This case study examines the development of a marketing plan for the Fine Music Network—a new radio broadcasting network consisting of three public, fine music stations; 2MBS-FM in Sydney, 3MBS-FM in Melbourne and 4MBS-FM in Brisbane. Through the Fine Music Network (FMN), the stations hope to attract funding from companies interested in promotions to cover the east coast capital cities.

The FMN has been established from three previously independent stations, and is designed to attract the larger corporations, by satisfying their need for a broader-based promotional strategy. The FMN has also adapted their existing sponsorship strategies to cater for the potential client's need to reach a wider audience. The audience profile is as follows:

1. Audience size—500 000 weekly.
2. 99% of the audience is over 21 years of age:

Under 21	1%
21–35	15%
36–50	32.5%
51–65	38%
Over 65	13.5%

3. 73% of the audience are in professional, business or government positions:

Professional	49%
Business and Govt	24%
Trades	2.5%
Rural & Misc.	1.5%
Home Managers	8%
Retired	13%
Students	2%

4. The majority of the audience is in the 'high disposable income' category.

The establishment of the FMN, consisting of the three fine music stations in Sydney, Brisbane and Melbourne, presents a new means of providing corporate promotions to clients. Through the FMN, corporations and advertising agencies are offered the opportunity to reach this market. This is achieved through the Corporate Promotions Package offered by the FMN. The market segment targeted is not readily accessible through any other radio broadcaster in these cities, including the other fine music station, ABC-FM, which does not carry any corporate promotion.

The FMN Corporate Promotions Package provides the potential client with:

- exclusive programme 'sponsorship';
- linked on-air and printed promotion;
- association with a prestige service (fine music);
- an association with 'the arts'.

The key customers being targeted are:

- corporations requiring 'corporate image promotion', on a major capital city basis;
- advertising agencies seeking means of reaching the particular target market offered by FMN;
- public relations (PR) firms looking for a new means of improving an organisation's public image.

There is no other network within the broadcasting sector, which offers a similar service. However, other arts organisations, such as the Symphony Orchestras and the

Opera or Ballet companies, might present the clients with the opportunity to reach a similar, although much smaller, audience. Also, sporting and charitable organisations may be competitors for the sponsorship dollars from these corporations.

The three stations have operated separately since their establishment—2MBS and 3MBS in 1976 and 4MBS in 1979. Each has adopted similar approaches toward corporate sponsorship at a local level, and have developed management expertise in each station. With the establishment of the FMN, and the Corporate Promotions Package, the three stations plan to combine their resources to meet their objective of increasing the amount of funding raised from the corporate sector. By offering the potential clients the opportunity of a campaign targeting the three east coast capital cities, the FMN aims to attract larger national companies and thus increase its revenue. The campaign could be aimed at an exclusive target market segment—the total audience of the FMN. This could give the FMN a distinct competitive advantage over other similar organisations who have a more 'local' focus, when seeking corporate funding.

The opportunity exists to take advantage of the loosening of the guidelines affecting sponsorship on public radio stations, contained in the proposed new Broadcast Bill. This will enable more details to be contained in on-air promotions. Presently, only the nature of the business, its address and phone number are permitted, but not corporate slogans or jingles.

Currently, funding is provided by a combination of audience subscription and government grants. There are also a small number of corporate sponsors. The present revenue levels from sponsorship are:

- 4MBS—$20 000
- 2MBS—$15 000
- 3MBS—$15 000

The FMN's corporate objective is to increase the funding raised through the corporate sector, and thus gain some independence from the government grants system. The marketing objective seeks to quantify this through setting realistic financial goals and a time frame for achieving these. The number of new clients required to achieve these goals is based on the pricing of the Corporate Promotions Package at $17 500 p.a.:

- Year 1—$52 500, discounted to $50 000—a total of three new corporate clients for the year.
- Year 2—$87 500, discounted to $75 000—a total of five corporate clients for the year.
- Year 3—$122 500, discounted to $110 000—a total of seven corporate clients for the year.

The revenue raised is to be divided equally among the FMN stations.

The strategy adopted can be described as a *focus differentiation strategy*. The focus is through targeting the large corporations, ad agencies and PR firms, rather than trying to attract a broader range of clients. The FMN is differentiated through its uniqueness in their competitive environment—no other broadcaster offers such a package to the clients. The only other broadcaster likely to react to the FMN approach is SBS (television and radio), who reach a different audience. The FMN will stress the focus of its programmes being on 'fine music', 24 hours a day, compared to SBS's predominantly ethnic programming content.

Question

You are faced with the task of having to promote the FMNs concept of 'corporate promotion' as distinct from advertising. The concept needs to appear different from sponsorship, in order to avoid competition with sporting and other charitable organisations. The FMN has to be actively promoted as a network, as the perception of the stations as being only 'local' organisations needs to be overcome, in order to attract the national companies being sought as clients. Prepare an appropriate plan based on the 4Ps (product, price, place and promotion) and prepare a marketing budget for the first year.

Case 7—The Australian nursery industry

by Peter Graham and Debra Harker

Introduction

In 1990 the Horticultural Research and Development Corporation, the research arm of the Australian Horticultural Industries, commissioned a research study to gain a comprehensive picture of the national nursery industry from the perspective of: (a) consumers and potential consumers of nursery products; and (b) retailers of nursery products. The report was entitled, 'National Consumer and Retailer Study of Nursery Industry Opportunities 1991' and we gratefully acknowledge the assistance of the Corporation in the production of this case and also Case 10.

This benchmark study covered a number of issues and all relevant target groups. A range of research techniques were used, drawing from qualitative and quantitative methods, to deal effectively with diverse issues. This comprehensive research forms the basis of two case studies. This first case deals with 'the consumer'. The second case study, covering 'the retailer' is titled, 'Garden centre retailing in Australia' and can be found in section three.

An overview—The market

Nursery owners consider the weather to be a far greater risk to their livelihoods than recession. When times get tough and money is short, people stay at home, and when they stay at home, they garden. However, extreme weather conditions can adversely affect the nursery industry. A wet spring can assume disaster proportions and customers stay away in droves. Similarly, prolonged dry periods can also be bad for business as gardeners tend to put off a major planting, waiting for rain.

The gross value of production of nursery crops in Australia is put at between $400 million and $500 million a year. Some estimates, which include landscape work and products other than plants sold in nurseries, value the industry as high as $2 billion annually.

There is some discrepancy in the number of nursery outlets. The Nursery Industry Association of Australia (NIAA) reports the number of registered nurseries as 20 000. The discrepancy, however, lies in the definition of a nursery outlet. Other estimates put the number at 30 000 but this includes hardware stores and chain stores that sell plants. This higher figure would indicate that the nursery industry employs some 300 000 people nationwide. Most nurseries are small businesses, employing only one to three people. Looking at both production and retail nurseries, only around 60 could be called large businesses which turn over more than $2 million a year.

From nurseries to garden centres

One in four households shop at a retail nursery to buy plants at least once a month. Today retail nurseries are more often called garden centres. Following overseas trends, especially in the UK, garden centres have got bigger and become more regionalised. Most no longer grow the plants they sell. Facilities offered are also changing and mirroring overseas trends. The larger nurseries have set up coffee shops, display gardens and some offer child-care facilities. Buying a plant has become an event.

A green industry

The rise of the modern garden centre reflects changes in the way plants are grown and distributed. The revolution started when plastic pots and soil-free potting mixes were introduced. These two factors changed plant growing and marketing. Today plants are grown with the aid of automation and computerisation in a controlled environment. To a great extent the nursery industry is dependent on plastics and chemicals.

The nursery industry deals in green plants. On the surface it appears to be environmentally friendly. However, the way most plants are produced, the industry is far from green. Growers use chemical fertilisers and pesticides and depend on plastics, wood chips and fossil panel to produce their 'green' product. An increasing number of chemicals are also banned from use both in the nursery and in the home garden. So far the environmentalists have left the industry alone and no one is pointing the finger, although the recent scare linking potting mix to Legionnaire's disease may be enough to focus attention on the industry.

Other issues involve water and plastics. The problem with water is to find enough of it and to dispose of it once it has been used. In Europe, growers are obliged to contain and treat all run-off on their properties.

The consumer—General characteristics

The sample for the consumer study was a representative random geographic sample of Sydney, Melbourne, Brisbane, Adelaide, Perth, Hobart and Darwin. In total, 1407 households were represented in the sample. The results are based on scientific random sampling principles and can be regarded as an accurate reflection of consumer demand for retail nursery products.

Across the seven capital cities, the research found that 77% of households have mainly outdoor plants, 15% have mainly indoor plants, 8% have bedding plants and 4% of households have no plants at all. Hence, most households have plants of some type.

There are major differences in types of gardens for different socio-demographic segments, notably:

- younger households who are more likely to have indoor plants;
- residents of Sydney and Melbourne who are more likely to have indoor plants;
- lower socio-economic groups who are more likely to have indoor plants.

The research found around one in four households (23%) purchase plants at least once per month, 31% purchase at least once every six months, 10% at least yearly, 22% less often than yearly and 13% never purchase.

For those households which have indoor gardens, over half (58%) have some type of specialised garden. Native bush gardens (28%) are the most common, followed by vegetable gardens (19%).

Garden development

The two most common household gardens are:

- an established garden, with both mature and young plants (36%); and
- fully established, with mostly mature plants (33%).

New gardens and gardens currently being renovated only account for 6% of all gardens.

Some differences were noted across the seven cities in the stage of current garden development. These differences may represent specific opportunities for the nursery industry.

Table B2.1 *Current stage of garden development*

Base: Total sample (N = 1407)	%
Established, with both mature and young plants	36
Fully established, with mostly mature plants	33
Not very established, with mostly young plants	8
New garden, with young plants only	3
Currently renovating garden	3
Don't have an outdoor garden	16

Source: HRDC 1990

Buyer behaviour

The research results indicate the most active purchasers are those who have an established garden, with both mature and young plants. Although fewer in number, those who have newly established gardens (with mostly young plants) and those renovating their gardens are also active purchasers.

By volume of shoppers, the most frequent visitors to nurseries and garden centres (and who purchase plants at least monthly) are people who have established gardens, with both mature and young plants. Around three in ten consumers in this segment purchase plants or visit nurseries monthly. This segment draws equally from all age and sex groups in all cities, but is more likely to be a white collar or professional household. They have an interest in the environment . . . one in five donate to the green movement, and are also strongly represented in horticultural clubs . . . 50% of club members belong to this segment.

Almost one in two in this segment have a favourite nursery and would usually spend $30.00 each time they shop at retail nurseries. In fact, most people have a favourite nursery. For instance, 45% of those who have established gardens, with both mature and young plants, have a favourite nursery, as do 48% of those who have a new garden, with mostly young plants. Also 34% of those who have fully established gardens, with mostly mature plants, have a favourite nursery.

Attitudes towards gardening

Overview

As the research has shown already, nearly everyone (96%) has plants, and most (77%) have an outdoor garden. Even many flat/home unit dwellers have outdoor plants of some type (40%). The research found most people (56%) enjoy gardening, while an additional 14% 'absolutely love gardening'. On the other hand, 26% see gardening as a chore and 3% greatly detest doing it. The chart below illustrates the four basic attitudes towards gardening.

Group characteristics

Each of the four main attitudinal groups has distinct features and draws strongly from different groups of people. For instance:

1. Those who 'absolutely love gardening and nothing else competes' (14%):
   —two in five (41%) purchase plants at least monthly;
   —usually have a favourite nursery for purchase;
   —most are over 40 years (67%);
   —most are not in the workforce (57%);
   —more likely to be female (57%) than male (43%);
   —keen viewers of the ABC (46% watch daily);
   —16% are members of or donate to environmental groups;
   —7% are members of a horticultural or garden club.
2. Those who 'enjoy gardening but other activities compete' (56%):
   —almost three in four (72%) purchase plants less often than once a month;
   —usually have a favourite nursery for purchase;

—most are under 40 years (53%);
—most are in employment (63%);
—more likely to be female (55%) than male (45%);
—daily viewers of the ABC (40%);
—one in five (21%) are members of or donate to environmental groups;
—only 3% are members of a horticultural or garden club.
2. Those who claim 'gardening is a chore' (26%):
—almost three in five (60%) purchase plants less often than once a month, with 25% claiming they never purchase;
—most are under 40 years (61%);
—more likely to be male (59%) than female (41%);
—only 3% are members of or donate to environmental groups.
3. Those who 'absolutely detest gardening and refuse to do it' (3%):
—60% claim they never purchase plants;
—most are under 40 years (75%), with most aged 18–24 years (49%);
—more likely to be male (56%) than female (44%).

Leisure activities which compete with gardening

The research shows that only a small proportion (14%) of the population 'absolutely love gardening' and claim it is their main leisure activity. To understand which leisure activities compete with gardening for most people a list of other activities was presented. Respondents were asked to rank each activity on a scale of 1 ('not enjoyable at all') to 10 ('very enjoyable'). Table B2.2, below, shows the position of gardening and visiting nurseries in relation to the other stated activities.

Table B2.2 *Competing leisure activities*

Base: Total Sample (N = 1407)	Very enjoyable %	Not very enjoyable %
Countryside visits	28	5
BBQ/parties at home	23	10
Hobbies	22	6
Playing sport	19	24
Relaxing in garden	17	7
Beach	17	15
Entertaining at home	14	6
Watching live sport	13	24
Visiting parks/nature reserves	12	9
Watching TV sport	11	22
Gardening	10	10
Theatre	9	19
Movies	9	16
Visiting nurseries	7	16

Source: HRDC 1990

Activities which compete tend to differ between avid gardeners and those less enthusiastic. Avid gardeners tend to like activities centred around the home and their garden. These people like to enjoy the fruits of their labours, either with friends or other family members. Activities enjoyed by the avid gardener include barbecues, entertaining at home or just relaxing in the garden.

Purchase behaviour and nursery visit behaviour

Buying incidence

Across the seven capital cities, 23% of all householders claim they buy plants at least once a month. A further 19% buy plants at least once every three months. Overall, only 13% of the population do not buy plants at any time. Frequency of plant purchasing does vary to some extent across the cities with greater frequency noted in Brisbane, Hobart, Adelaide and Perth, than other cities.

Average expenditure

The research also found that $11.00 to $20.00 is usually spent at each nursery or garden centre visit. Purchases below $11.00 and up to $55.00 were also common.

Motivations for purchase

A range of reasons was explored to discover motivations for purchase. For those who buy plants at least once a year, the most common reasons were:

- to improve appearance of the home or garden (40%); and
- aesthetic appeal (32%).

Purchasing plants as a gift for someone accounted for 7% of purchases. In fact, gift buying was stronger amongst less frequent buyers (14%).

The exploratory research also found similar reasons. For example, in regard to indoor plants, consumers said: 'I love having plants. More plants in my unit makes it look less like a unit'. 'They make the home look more comfortable.'

Indoor plants are also seen as adding to the interior design of the home: 'Plants are interior decoration, helping to break up the contours of light and space.'

Outdoor plants are enjoyed for the way they enhance the appearance of the home. People also believe they help to create a different environment. For instance, many people said: 'Trees and shrubs give a feeling of the bush. They help you to forget that you live in the suburbs.'

For most people, plants were seen as pleasant and relaxing: a form of escapism. These views are stronger amongst avid gardeners, who have a more personal opinion. It was not uncommon for them to say 'I find having a nice garden lets people know I'm approachable. It helps them to know they can come to me if help is needed.'

Generally, specific plants are not seen to be in or out of fashion, though people believe different varieties become popular from one year to another.

Nursery visiting behaviour

Large groups of people (29%) visit nurseries at least once a month. Only 11% of the sample never visit nurseries, as table B2.3 shows.

Cumulatively, half of those interviewed (50%) visited a nursery or garden centre every one to three months, or more often. Those who have a more active interest in gardening are the more frequent visitors to nurseries. For instance, more than one in two (54%) who 'absolutely love gardening' are more likely to visit within once every one to three months. The most frequent visitors to retail nurseries are aged 25 to 54, while the least likely visitors are under 25. However, visitors to retail nurseries are drawn from all walks of life, with no specific socio-economic group forming a distinct shopper profile.

For those who do not go or seldom go to retail nurseries (that is do not visit at least once a year), two reasons predominate: 'It doesn't interest me' and 'I don't have a garden and have no need to go', followed by 'someone else in the household goes so I don't need to go'.

Preference for retail nurseries

The research also found quite clearly that for those consumers who purchase plants at least once a year, retail nurseries are the preferred place of purchase for almost three in four consumers. Within all consumer segments, retail nurseries were the preferred choice for plant purchases, with 'good range and variety' and the perception that 'plants are healthier and better quality' as major consumer benefits. Knowledge, trust and quality of advice were also important. Yet for garden accessories, all of these benefits became less relevant except for price. Cheaper price was the driving force for non-nursery purchases of garden accessories. Even those who 'absolutely love gardening' or 'enjoy gardening' choose hardware stores and K mart before nurseries when choosing garden accessories.

Table B2.3 *Frequency of nursery visits*

(N = 1407)	
Once a week	4%
Once a fortnight	8%
Once a month	17%
1-3 months	21%
3-12 months	24%
Less often	16%
Never	11%

Source: HRDC 1990

Despite the competitive influence of non-nursery locations for garden accessories purchase, most people are happy with the performance of retail nurseries. In fact, most people could not offer any suggestions for improvement, except for greater range and variety (21%) and cheaper prices (29%).

The exploratory research also identified positive perceptions towards nurseries. Even those who do not frequent nurseries regularly are not negative towards them. When talking about purchasing plants, nurseries are foremost in terms of quality, service and advice. When plants are purchased from a nursery, people are confident the plants have been looked after properly and therefore, the plants have a greater chance of surviving. The same confidence is not expressed about plants purchased from supermarkets or department stores.

Green consumerism and its effects on changing purchase behaviour

Consumer concern about the environment has been a major issue in marketing consumer products and services since 1987. Nursery plants and products are also being affected by green consumerism and in a quite positive way, in that most people feel that buying plants will help the environment. The research also found around 18% of the population have changed their gardening behaviour because of their concern about the environment.

The main ways in which these 18% have changed their behaviour include:

- not using toxic sprays (47%);
- use organic sprays (28%);
- plant more trees/shrubs (24%);
- use natural compost (22%);
- use less water (15%).

A change in gardening behaviour is also more pronounced amongst certain groups of people:

- those who purchase plants (and visit nurseries) monthly;
- those who 'absolutely love gardening';
- 25 to 54-year-olds; and
- male gardeners.

Major consumer influences relevant to the nursery industry

TV (and to a lesser extent, radio) gardening programmes are important influences for people who buy plants or garden accessories regularly, that is at least once a year. Spouses, relatives and friends are also important communication influences about plants and garden accessories. Newspaper and magazine articles about gardening are also influential, as are nursery staff.

Table B2.4 Major influences when choosing plants or garden accessories

Base: Purchased within 12 months*	
TV garden programme	35%
Spouse	31%
Newspaper/magazine	30%
Friends/relatives	27%
No one	20%
Nursery staff	15%
Radio gardening programme	9%

*Multiple response

Source: HRDC 1990

Not surprisingly, the importance of these influences is stronger amongst people who have an active involvement with gardening or purchase plants more often.

What emerges quite clearly from the findings is the importance of TV gardening programmes and newspaper/magazine articles for those people who have a strong desire for gardening as a leisure activity. Even those who have a favourable attitude to gardening (i.e. 'enjoy gardening') receive a lot of their influences from these two sources.

Other important findings are:

- men are also strongly influenced by their wives in plant and garden accessory purchasing;
- younger buyers (e.g. 18–24 years) rely heavily on friends and relatives for advice; and
- radio gardening programmes have a stronger influence on older consumers (55+ years).

Consumer attitudes towards nurseries and gardening

General perceptions

The exploratory consumer research found that gardening means different things to different people. For some (particularly avid gardeners), gardening is synonymous with serenity and escapism: 'I find it's like a form of meditation—it's a release. I can totally get away from my work and worries.' For others, gardening means hard work and a lot of time and effort: 'There is more to life than gardening.' Others say: 'It's not my life, but I do like to do it.'

For many people gardening is purely hard work. The association with leisure does not enter the minds of non-avid gardeners, who would do many other chores before attempting the garden. They believe gardening requires a lot of time and hard work.

Typically these people know very little about plants and the gardening process. Some do, however, realise that perhaps less effort would be required if they knew more about gardening. There appears to be an opportunity amongst this segment to increase their gardening activity, and hence purchase nursery products, through further education.

The exploratory research also found many people are not confident about plants and gardening. They are not confident in knowing what plants to buy at a garden centre or even how to seek advice from nursery staff. It appears gardening activity may be increased through public education programmes.

A typical comment made was: 'I just don't have enough knowledge about plants. It's hard work, but it wouldn't be if I knew more.'

There is a particularly strong perception held by these consumers that a good garden requires a lot of time and energy. A common excuse for lack of garden activity is the adage: 'I just don't have enough time!'

At the opposite end of the continuum are those who gain a great deal of pleasure from gardening. For these consumers it is very gratifying and therapeutic: 'It's a good therapy—being with nature—the trees.' 'It can be therapeutic, especially seeing the rewards of what you've done.' These people see gardening as a leisure activity, not a chore.

Many confident gardeners felt that when shopping at retail nurseries they know exactly what plant they should buy. On the other hand, they are also strong impulse buyers of new varieties or attractive plants, even though their main reason for shopping could be for quite a different plant or product.

Positive and negative attitudes

A series of questions was developed from the exploratory research phase which covered the range of views and opinions expressed by consumers. The national study aimed to measure the size of the positive and negative attitudes held in order to discover opportunities for the nursery industry.

It is clear that many positive attitudes are held about nurseries and gardening. Particularly important is the benefit that the nursery industry can have for the environment. Consumer trust for nursery retailer staff and desire for quality plants and products is also strong. Impulse purchasing and desire for new ideas and plants are also important.

Behavioural and attitudinal segmentation of consumers

Consumer's attitudes towards retail nursery

The research findings were also analysed using multi-variate statistical procedures (factor analysis). Five underlying attitudes emerged. Each of these five measures is a composite response to two or more items illustrated in this section. Such multiple-item factors yield more reliable, stable measurements of peoples' attitudes and behaviour than do responses to single items or questions.

The five underlying attitudes households have about plants and gardening were:

- Attitude 1: I enjoy buying plants (and going to nurseries) but I'm not confident.
- Attitude 2: More nursery signage and more information labels on plants is essential.
- Attitude 3: It is essential for plant quality and staff knowledge to be of high standard.
- Attitude 4: Plants look good and help the environment.
- Attitude 5: I buy plants on impulse, but would like to know more about gardening

Consumer segmentation

More intensive analysis (cluster analysis) was also undertaken on the range of behavioural and attitudinal measures in the consumer study. The objective of this segmentation was to provide more identification of broad marketing opportunities for the nursery industry. Four key market segments were identified:

- Segment 1: Conservative and confident gardeners who are not particularly active in purchasing plants—23% of the population.
- Segment 2: Experienced gardeners who are actively seeking new plants and gardening ideas—26%.
- Segment 3: Consumers new to gardening and looking for new plants and gardening ideas, but who are not confident in gardening—32%.
- Segment 4: Consumers who have little interest in gardening or purchasing plants—19%.

The segments are expanded in detail below.

Segment 1: Conservative and confident gardeners who are not particularly active in purchasing plants

Twenty-three per cent of the population fall into this segment. This segment is characterised by being relatively old (many of its members are over 40 years). They are frequent viewers of the ABC and are heavy readers of newspapers (65% read newspapers daily) and magazines (51% read magazines weekly). Men and women comprise this segment relatively equally.

Half of this segment does not participate in the labour force. It has the highest percentage (22%) of people who 'absolutely love gardening' and regard gardening and browsing at nurseries as relaxation. However, this is the only segment who equally prefer hardware stores, supermarkets, variety stores and nurseries for purchasing plants. They usually spend $11.00–$20.00 when purchasing plants and gardening accessories, and they are not impulse buyers. Interestingly, they have demonstrated the strongest consumer response to purchasing more environmentally friendly nursery products. Generally, they feel confident in selecting plants for purchase, but are dissatisfied with nursery signage and the quality of plant label information.

Segment 2: Experienced gardeners who are actively seeking new plants and gardening ideas

Twenty-six per cent of the population fall into this segment. This segment is also relatively older (with many of its members aged over 40 years). They are also heavy readers of newspapers and magazines and viewers of the ABC. Women slightly outnumber men in this segment. Many activities compete, but two in three people in this segment enjoy gardening. In other words, the segment does not comprise as many avid gardeners as Segment 1. Nevertheless, they are strong buyers of plants (over one in three buy plants at least once a month) and they usually spend between $21.00–$50.00 each time. In fact, they have the highest average value of purchase amongst the four consumer segments.

They are always looking for new plants and garden ideas, and feel confident when selecting plants. They are strong impulse buyers and satisfied with nursery signage and label information.

Segment 3: Consumers new to gardening and looking for new plants and gardening ideas, but who are not confident in gardening

Thirty-two per cent of the population fall into this segment. While many (57%) of its members enjoy gardening, around one in three (30%) rate gardening as a chore. Nevertheless, this segment has the second highest proportion of frequent purchasers of plants (25% buy at least once a month) and spend an average of $11.00–$20.00 each time.

They are strong impulse buyers and are always looking for new plants or garden ideas. Yet they do not feel confident in selecting plants and express a view that they would be more interested in gardening if they knew more about it. They are also very dissatisfied with nursery signage and the quality of information on labels.

Segment 4: Consumers who have little interest in gardening or purchasing plants

Nineteen per cent of the population fit into this segment and two in three are under 40 years of age. They have the highest level of workforce participation and representation from professional and white-collar occupations. Most (59%) have an active dislike of gardening and over one in three never purchase plants. Over two in three say that they do not feel confident in selecting plants. Despite many in this segment having little interest in gardening, four in ten do say that they would be more interested in plants if they knew more about them.

Customer service expectations

Overview

The general view is the service from nurseries is friendly and much different from a supermarket, where service is perceived to be non-existent. What is liked most by con-sumers is the lack of pressure to buy or 'hard sell' approach by nurserymen. Most claim nurserymen walk with them, give advice where appropriate, and then leave them alone to browse. Later the nurseryman may come back to assist in the final purchase.

Many people find nurserymen very helpful, saying: 'For them (nurserymen) it is not just a job, it's more a passion ... they're more personal and helpful.' On the other hand some people also expressed frustration regarding the lack of help from nurserymen. These people demand greater service through extra attention to their needs. People who lack knowledge are most likely to demand greater assistance in buying nursery products.

Consumers were asked to indicate the importance to them of the different elements of customer service that could be provided by retail nurseries. Table B2.5 shows the types of customer service elements rated very important to customers, which should be the focus of nursery retailers. Four elements clearly stand out as key customer demands:

- good service;
- helpful staff;
- friendly staff; and
- knowledgeable staff.

Table B2.5 *Consumer needs from nurseries (N = 1407)*

	% rating as 'very important'
Knowledgeable staff	52
Good service	46
Variety of products	38
Helpful staff	38
Friendly staff	36
Easy parking	34
Common plant name (not botanical)	28
Good signage	27
Good plant presentation	25
Personal attention	23
Guaranteed return	18
Industry recognition	17
Free delivery	12
Playgrounds	6
Self-service	5
Refreshments	3

Source: HRDC 1990

Questions

1(a). Why is segmentation useful for any organisation?

1(b). Give a name to each of the four segments. In naming the segments you will find it helpful to read 'Segmentation' by Neil Shoebridge and 'How green was my market' by George Camakaris which are both in this section of the book.

References

Kotler, R. A., Chandler, P., Gibbs, R. and McColl, R. (1989), *Marketing in Australia*, (2nd edn), Prentice Hall, New Jersey.

Pride, W. M. and Ferrell, O. C. (1987), Marketing: *Basic Concepts and Decisions*, (5th edn), Houghton Miffin, Boston.

Tull, D. S. and Hawkins, D. I. (1990), *Marketing Research: Measurement and Method*, (5th edn), Macmillan, New York.

3. DEVELOPING THE MARKETING MIX

Introduction 88

Readings
5. Ho hum or let's go outdoor? by Richard Luke 89
6. Feisty Foodland on expansion trail, by Tim Treadgold 93
7. When the highest price is right, by Ken Roberts 95

Cases
8. Oldies under the microscope, by St George TAFE 98
9. The Queensland grocery industry, by Alan Dowsett, Peter Graham and Robert Young 100
10. Garden centre retailing in Australia, by Peter Graham 109

Introduction

Section three in this part of the book looks at different aspects of the marketing mix and the impact of their integration. The section covers new product development, pricing strategies and the role of communication in the marketing mix.

Three readings and three case studies have been selected to focus the student on this important section. Richard Luke's 'Ho hum or let's go outdoor?' looks at the popularity of outdoor advertising as part of the marketing mix and 'When the highest price is right', by Ken Roberts, examines pricing strategy and dwells upon the implications of premium pricing.

In 'Feisty Foodland on the expansion trail', Tim Treadgold looks at the retail industry in Australia and especially Foodland's meteoric rise. This reading complements Dowsett, Graham and Young's case study on 'The Queensland grocery industry'. This case gives students an analysis of chain stores and Independent Grocery Retailers in Queensland and introduces them to a 'strengths, weaknesses, opportunities and threats' analysis and 'competitive position assessment'.

The case about 'Oldies under the microscope' gives students the chance to develop a strategy for selling to the growing over-fifty market. The final case in this section, 'Garden centre retailing in Australia', is by the Editor, and is the follow-up case study to 'The Australian nursery industry' in section two. The case concentrates on the supplier side of the equation providing analyses of demand, products, strategies and a profile of the industry.

Reading 5—Ho hum or let's go outdoor?

by Richard Luke

Although outdoor advertising scores very low on marketing magazine reader interest surveys, many big names are spending their money there.

Stung by constant criticism and desperate for greater market share, the outdoor advertising industry is bombarding Australian marketing and product managers with 'proof' that it is a measurable medium. The move is a backlash against mainstream electronic and print advertising interests who have argued for many years that outdoor will always remain a peripheral player when it comes to promoting a product or service. Statistically, that would appear the case: Australian outdoor advertising turns over $285 million a year out of an estimated $5 billion national mainstream advertising market.

This 5% market share is divided up among 30 players, whose promotional enticements include billboards, neon signs, supersites, shopping mall trolleys, taxi cab backs, inflight advertising, sky-writing, bulletins, spectaculars, car stickers and blimps. The Outdoor Advertising Association of Australia chief executive, Brian Gates, claims each of these 'enticers' has developed much greater research and statistical clout to convince marketers that outdoor has as much right to be taken seriously as the star mainstream vehicles of radio, newspapers and TV. Like many longstanding players in Australian outdoor, he believes this greater measurability should silence many critics over the last 30 years who have simply declared billboards, neon signs and their like a pox on advertising.

One of the most famous broadsides was written by advertising guru David Olgilvy in *On Advertising*: 'Billboards represent less than 2% of advertising in the US. I cannot believe that the free-enterprise system would be irreparably damaged if they were abolished. Who is in favour of them? Only the people who want to make money.' Reminded of this quote at his Melbourne headquarters, Nettlefold Outdoor Advertising managing director, David Nettlefold, still recoils: 'It is part of a conspiracy by both mainstream advertising interests and bureaucrats to undermine the outdoor medium. Unfortunately, the vendetta is still as strong as ever in 1992.' Flicking through some recent international magazines and periodicals, Mr Nettlefold cites the following headlines as proof of his assertion: 'Outdoor feels drought'; 'Regulate outdoors ads: poll'; 'Outdoors faces its flaws'; and 'Some bad news for outdoor'. He is particularly savage on local government authorities who seem to have choked the industry in red tape: 'Having spent 32 years in the industry, I have witnessed—particularly over the last 15 years—a very definite planned movement against outdoor advertising. Those perusing the skylines of Australia will notice a declining light pattern, rather than an expanding one. The flashing or animated neon sign is now almost as extinct as the Tasmanian tiger, courtesy of the bureaucracy and its associated, ill-informed planners.'

Mr Nettlefold says history proves the overall acceptance of outdoor advertising in Australia: 'Two examples that come to mind are the public outcry that led to reinstalling Victoria's now famous "skipping girl" sign, and the enormous press coverage and lobby pressure to retain the old Allen Sweets sign, now languishing in a government store somewhere.' Despite the heavy criticism, the revamped image of outdoor advertising is being noticed. *Ad News* in a recent editorial piece—'Medium comes of age'—observed: 'While outdoor doesn't lend itself to tight, quantifiable audience measurement in quite the same way that, for example, television does, outdoor companies have set about improving the data on sites and providing sound means of determining the worth of buys.'

Not surprisingly, the front-runner in providing greater measurability for clients is Australian Posters 3-M, which boasts a 55% market share, well ahead of nearest rivals Nettlefold, Outdoor Network Australia, Pearl and Dean, and Claude Neon. Following its well-publicised, pioneering move last year to commission AGB McNair to provide an extensive research base to prove to clients that outdoor does work, the market leader has been busy in other areas. Recently—in conjunction with a national advertiser—it commissioned a qualitative study on consumer attitudes to outdoor.

The 27-page report, compiled by Quantum Market Research, details the strategic role the poster medium plays in an overall communications campaign, following a series of interviews with consumers in Sydney and Melbourne, where 65% of the overall market resides. It concludes that the image of posters is a positive one, with most participants believing that posters disguised—if not enhanced—the drab parts of the city landscape. It also concludes that posters are applicable to a full gamut of products and services—but rarely did consumers feel that they could be successful as a single medium for new products because they were supplements to the more aggressive medium of television.

The creative approach used was found to be the number one factor in getting consumers to respond to a poster, particularly if any of the following elements were involved:

- *are unusual*, breaking through the familiar clutter;
- use *bold visuals* that grab attention; and
- have a level of *intrigue*—something beyond the obvious, something more to look for.

Australian Posters 3-M—which grades sites according to their reach and frequency under its revamped research system—is enjoying a boom in national advertising business because the results from such surveys are shaking up traditional corporate perceptions of the outdoor medium. Since November last year, it has boosted national turnover from 3% to 16% of total business, scoring $6.3 million sales in the process based on 24 campaigns that have involved such clients as Foster's ($680 000), CCA ($600 000), Pickfords ($500 000), Telecom ($480 000), Fluffy ($400 000), Michelin ($380 000) and Holeproof ($350 000). At the bottom of the list are Australian Made ($150 000), 100% Juice ($124 000), Lever & Kitchen ($130 000) and Adidas ($80 000). The $80 000 to $680 000 difference in outlay by Foster's and Adidas for their national poster campaigns provides marketers with a fair assessment of typical charges in outdoor.

Australian Posters 3-M general manager—advertising services group, Rick Salomone, is looking forward to 1992 with relish: 'Just give me 20 minutes with a marketing or product manager and—armed with the data we have extracted from better research and greater accountability—I believe I can convince him or her that outdoor is the most powerful medium for reinforcing product identification and image.' Equally confident that next year will see more and more critics finally bow to the measurable impact of outdoor is Brendan Cook, managing director of Outdoor Network Australia, Australia's largest independent media sales trolleys: 'The outdoor industry has fighting gloves on and is delivering some knock-out blows to traditional critics who whinge about lack of measurability and accountability. Take just one example: The introduction of the advertising and information system moving posters by Televidcom at Sydney's Darling Harbour, which takes the theories of outdoor advertising combined with advanced computer technology to deliver an advanced medium. The system challenges traditional advertising at the Darling Harbour shopping centre by:

- monitoring location throughout the centre, not just in one or two locations;
- using a minimum advertising frequency of one 15-second ad every 12 minutes of trading hours;
- reaching 200 000 people a week for only $150 outlay;
- employing full colour ad production with stylised animation for an average $650; and
- computer-linking all advertising for date/time corrected updates via phone modem.

Advertisers currently using the system include Tooheys, Kodak, Art Gallery of NSW, State Transit, Sydney Aquarium, Jetabout Tours, Mikes Bar, Columbia Sports Store, American Express Travel Centres and Darling Harbour Amusements.

The recent launch of Pearl and Dean's new division PosterAds is another triumph for the greater measurability provided by the outdoor medium. Sydney-based PosterAds has been awarded an exclusive licence by the State Rail Authority to operate all its poster advertising business. 'The seven year agreement is worth $52 million in revenue for the SRA,' says PosterAds national sales manager, Nick McFarlane. First-class research work helped Pearl and Dean with the contract against a hot field of competitors. 'We are committed to research and will continually monitor the effectiveness of campaigns for advertisers,' says Mr McFarlane. 'The rail audience is definable and measurable making it possible to quantify the value added by PosterAds. Mass market exposure will be achieved by roadside panels and those in public areas of rail stations. This audience is a bonus above the researched rail audience.'

Mr McFarlane says advertisers using PosterAds outdoor medium will be furnished with such insights as:

- On an average weekday there are more than 900 000 trips made, and the audience is skewed toward slightly more male than female (53.2%).
- 70% of these are 16 to 44 years old, that is predominantly the economically active sectors of the population.

- Income profile is high with 13% of travellers earning at least $40 000 p.a., 36% at least $28 000 and a total 71% at least $15 000.
- Work related and shopping trips add up to 80% of all journeys.
- The majority of commuters are frequent travellers with 83% making at least one journey a week and 71% making four or more journeys a week.
- Frequent travel produces multiple exposures to the advertising messages and builds high awareness in relatively short periods.

Telecom Australia's Payphone Advertising service is a new niche market in outdoor which also claims to be a most effective, measurable media for advertisers. We want to change the thinking of many marketers who often have the attitude: 'We' ll see what we have left in the pocket and spend it on outdoor advertising',' says Payphone Advertising marketing concept manager, Sidney Buchbinder. 'That to me, at least, is insulting to a medium that can now back its claims about measurability.'

Payphone Advertising—which allows you to advertise inside a phone booth 24 hours a day, 365 days a year—has no shortage of statistics to back its claims about superior value. 'More than 300 million calls are made each year from Australia's network of public telephones. Each Payphone Advertising zone, comprising an average of 20 booths, gives you a guaranteed minimum of 200 000 calls annually,' says Mr Buchbinder. 'We estimate that the average length of a call is four minutes, providing a uniquely captive viewer for your message. The advertising panel is placed in a tamper-proof frame, set behind 4mm of toughened plated glass and Telecom contract cleaning services ensure thorough cleaning of each booth at least once a fortnight.' Payphone Advertising has now added an LCD screen in Australia's 10 000 public Payphone booths which allows a 30-second illuminated advertising message to be shown 20 000 times a booth in one week.

At airports, corporate high-flyers such as BHP, FAI, Prudential and Diners Club are finding value for their dollar in the new 'airport channel' video concept marketed by Charlton Media. Businessmen watch high quality programmes on a range of commercial, sporting, recreational and cultural subjects that they might normally view on such television programmes as '60 Minutes', 'Business Sunday', 'Robbo's World' and 'Year 2000'. Costs for advertising are only a fraction of what advertisers would normally expect to fork out for promoting their products and services on these programmes, claims Charlton Media managing director, Jeremy Charlton.

In the area of outdoor technology a significant recent mover has been Metromedia Technologies which uses an advanced, computer-generated painting technique to produce high pictorial gigantic advertising display faces. 'Who wants to hand paint 250 national billboards? The time and money involved is often outrageous,' says Metromedia Technologies sales director Mike Nettlefold. 'Our 100% faithful reproduction means that advertisers can have magazine-quality reproduction on billboards. Beyond this, multiples are produced at the punch of a button and sign faces are no longer subject to the individual interpretation of a hand-painter.'

The cost of the service for an average supersite or superpanel is about $4500. They are being employed by such household names as Nissan, Ford, Mazda, Holden,

Phillip Morris, Tooheys, and Coca-Cola. An average three-month campaign would cost about $200 000.

To launch an outdoor advertising campaign, Coates Signco managing director, Allan Coates, advises marketers to go direct to the sign company involved rather than through an advertising agency: 'One key reason for this is that they must ensure that their sign harmonises with the various council codes likely to be involved: You could spend a lot of money with an advertising agency—be presented with an effective creative design theme—only to find out that all this good work doesn't harmonise with local government rules, particularly if your measurements are out-of-kilter.'

Like his industry counterparts, Mr Coates agrees that the ability to measure results from the outdoor medium is the industry's biggest challenge: 'In our case, the best reported sales increase from one of our clients—a major fast food outlet—is 29% in the immediate period after a signage programme was put in place. We have also had a reported 25% sales boost from another client in the fast food industry using our new illuminated information/menu board system which allows pricing to be altered quickly and easily.'

Mr Coates says an essential factor in the success of any signage advertising programme is the fact that the sign itself must be simple and can be read easily at a distance: 'This principle has worked well for many of our clients including McDonald's, Caltex, Kentucky Fried Chicken, BP, Ampol and Pizza Hut.' Seems to be stating the obvious, but isn't that what outdoor is all about?

Reproduced with permission from *Marketing*, December, January 1992, pp. 41–46.

Questions

1. Outdoor advertising is the 'niche market' of the promotions industry. Discuss.
2. Do you think that some products or services are particularly suited to outdoor advertising? What products/services and what type of outdoor advertising?

Reading 6—Feisty Foodland on expansion trail

by Tim Treadgold

In just over two years, Foodland Associated has grown from a sleepy, Perth-based, grocer-controlled co-operative into Australia's fifth-biggest retailing and wholesaling group. During the next few years it will be looking for third spot and the chance to challenge the big two, Coles Myer and Woolworths.

The recent $125 million purchase of New Zealand's Countdown supermarket chain and the J. Rattray wholesale business was the group's fourth significant corporate deal in less than a year. Previous moves included the purchase for $10 million of a 30% stake in the electrical and furniture retailer Vox Ltd, a failed $133 million take-over bid for the big Adelaide-based grocery wholesaler Independent Holdings Ltd and a $30 million take-over bid for the R & I Property Trust in Perth, which is still current.

Five years ago Foodland's sales were less than $500 million. Now it controls almost $3 billion a year of wholesale and retail sales through its traditional grocery distribution business to 290 franchise customers and 500 other retailers, its 49% interest in the Action supermarket chain in Western Australia, the Vox stake and the New Zealand chain. In seven years the company's share of the WA grocery market has grown from 32% to 55% and profits have risen from $3.1 million to $13 million. Investors have been richly rewarded. The share price has almost tripled in a year and institutions have scrambled for stock.

Foodland's managing director, David Fawcett, 47, a former senior manager with Coles, has an intimate knowledge of the grocery and retailing industry, backed by an impressive grasp of fund-raising and efficient use of the sharemarket. But he also has critics who say the company has done too much too quickly, and that its new market, 4000 kilometres and four flying hours away, is too far from home.

'Our growth has been made easier through unusual circumstances in the past few years,' Fawcett says. 'Woolworths was in trouble, then the merged Coles and Myer operations hit problems. Coles Myer had to concentrate on fixing problems in Myer and, with Woolworths in difficulty, opportunities opened, allowing Foodland to take market share from both of them.' Foodland and its assorted interests have about 5.5% of the national retail market. Included in plans to lift that percentage is a possible merger of Vox's electrical and furniture interests with Action's food business.

Fawcett believes in the old retailing maxim of 'get big, get small or get out'. He also believes that any retailer with only one line of business is vulnerable to competitors and market swings. 'It would be great to create a major new retailer in Australia, a sort of mini Coles Myer,' he says.

Institutions have been big backers of Fawcett and Foodland. In the past two months they have subscribed more than $70 million for new shares to help pay for the New Zealand expansion, the Vox purchase and the Independent Holdings bid. The company now has 63 million shares on issue, trading around $4.15, which gives Foodland a market capitalisation of more than $260 million, compared with $180 million six months ago and about $70 million during most of last year. The share placements have sharply eroded the percentage stake of the big Sydney food group Davids Holdings, down from 15% to about 11%. It and the two other major shareholders, the NRMA in Sydney and Bankers Trust Australia, have about 25% between them.

Fawcett defends the group's rapid growth and diverse take-over targets. Independent Holdings in Adelaide was stalked for months as a natural, cross-border expansion that would provide a beachhead for further moves east. The R & I Property Trust is an expansion of an existing property trust that owns a string of regional and rural shopping centres. The Vox purchase provided extra buying power and the $10 million outlay now has a market value of $35 million. The New Zealand move was 'too good to refuse'—a bargain that flowed from the cash-starved Magnum Corporation.

But Fawcett has some history to overcome. Few Perth retailers succeed with expansion out of their markets. Maurice Walsh in the 1970s, and Alistair Norwood and Tony Barlow in the 1980s tried to crack east coast clothing markets but had limited success. In one swoop, Foodland has not only crossed the Nullarbor but the Tasman as well. 'Distance is very much a state of mind,' Fawcett says, adding that Foodland now had a west coast and a far easterly position (New Zealand) and will eventually fill in the middle.

He says Foodland's growth is carefully planned. The company looks for targets that give earnings a share, have good management and can be developed to create additional value within the group. 'It is pointless to make an acquisition for the sake of a take-over,' he says. 'We will now spend some time digesting the New Zealand move.'

That will not stop him looking at opportunities, especially in liquor and general merchandise. Of interest could be distribution for Swan Brewery. Last year Foodland bought a wine and spirit distribution business, Johnson Harper, from Swan. 'We already have trucks going to shops and restaurants that one of Swan's trucks visits later in the day,' Fawcett says.

> Reproduced with permission from *BRW*, Australia's leading business magazine, 15 May, 1992, p. 40.

Questions

1. Bearing in mind the theoretical concept of the 'wheel of retailing', what do you think of David Fawcett's comment: 'It would be great to create a major new retailer in Australia, a sort of mini Coles Myer.'
2. How would you describe Foodland, and Fawcett's, growth strategy?
3. What barriers to entry exist in the grocery industry?

Note: Students may find it useful to read the case on 'The Queensland Grocery Industry' before discussing these questions.

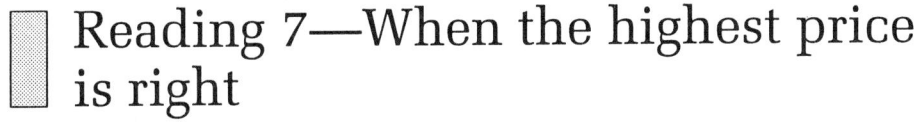

Reading 7—When the highest price is right

by Ken Roberts

You are faced with the decision between two products performing the same function. One, however, has a high price. Would you feel the higher-priced product has the higher quality? Do we explicitly trust price to convey information about a product or service? The answer is often, yes. Setting a high price relative to the competition to signal quality to the consumer is known as *price signalling*. It is based on the consumer's trust in a positive price-quality relationship.

Price signalling is used frequently as a price-setting strategy. But it is not for everyone: there are two principal conditions that must be met. Firstly, it is only useful when quality is an important differentiating feature for a sufficiently profitable segment. Secondly, quality must not be determinable simply by inspection. The product or service needs to be more sophisticated than the consumer (fine table wine is a good example).

For consumer durables the second condition (quality must *not* be determinable by mere inspection) is usually met when product innovation is faster than the rate of repurchase. For example, the selling features in microcomputers today are different than five years ago. What we learnt when purchasing our first microcomputer is not helpful in judging today's computer because of the pace of innovation.

One could easily be trapped into thinking it's principally the product, not the buyer, that's important in deciding on the applicability of price signalling. But the key factor is the buyer. For example, it's not the technical nature of the product, but the technical knowledge of the buyer; it's not the rate of innovation, but the frequency of the buyer's purchase; and it is not the firm's gross margin objectives, but rather the needs satisfying attributes of the product that interest the buyer. If you were looking for a single measure for determining the applicability of price signalling, perhaps the most significant would be level of involvement the buyer has in the purchase.

Buyers do not care much about some products. The level of involvement or perceived risk to self-image is relatively low. The product may be purchased entirely on the basis of preference for lowest price, for instance, petrol or dry cleaning. Where the purchase has high impact on self-image, the opportunities for price signalling are greatest. In that instance, the buyer seeks additional information in the form of opinion leader's recommendations, brand names, price or promotions. If a major component of the product bundle is intangible (e.g. perfume), the buyer's involvement is high and their need for seeking additional information becomes even greater. This is very fertile ground for price signalling.

For products such as fine table wine and services such as those of a law firm, price signalling can be used to position the product or service in the prospect's mind. But if the distribution point and promotion do not also suggest quality, the signal may be dramatically moderated. Given the difficulty and cost of repositioning a product or service in the consumer's mind, the decision to use price signalling is usually applicable to new products, products that have been repackaged, remerchandised, or products where noticeable performance improvements result from the upgrading of existing technology. Does the actual product or service need to be of higher quality? Yes. The first rule of marketing is: 'You can sell anything once, but once is not enough!'.

Signalling quality is not the only reason for setting a price above the category average. Buyers are prepared to pay a premium for a number of reasons including, for well-known brand names, the pleasure of being exclusive or for superior reliability. Brand names with which buyers have had past experience can carry substantial power of attraction (goodwill). The price premium in that instance is a return on goodwill. A relatively high price can also provide cues to those consumers who have a desire to be exclusive. Demand is greater because a product bears a higher rather than lower price. Such conspicuous consumption is often associated with very high fashion garments. Purchasers are sometimes prepared to pay a premium for quality because future costs, such as after-sales-service, are believed to be lower. The relatively high price for the IBM computer was acceptable to some buyers because the IBM was perceived to be more reliable. For industrial markets, where the purchaser is usually well informed, any price-setting discretion is likely to be due to goodwill or tangible product differentiation rather than price signalling.

We cannot always assume that the retail price you set will be the price the channels charge. Cadbury Schweppes Australia went on the offensive against Nestlé in the family block sector of the confectionery market by advertising they had added an extra 25% to their family block 'at no extra cost'. Cadbury received a flood of consumer complaints when numerous route trade retailers unilaterally decided to increase the price of the family block in line with the increased size.

The *Trade Practices Act* sets out to ensure marketers do not have price control over the channels (resale price maintainence, s. 48) and so your price-setting strategy may fall down in the implementation. The strategic imperative of price signalling is well documented. In 1989 the Trade Practices Commission (TPC) alleged Penfolds Wines Pty Ltd 'attempted to induce the wholesaler not to advertise or sell Penfolds' wines to retailers at less than Penfolds' prices'. The Court dismissed the TPC's application but the case provided wine makers with a timely reminder of the prohibitions of attempts to enforce minimum prices through the channels.

In the short-term, regaining control over price-setting at retail outlets may be a matter of co-operation with the channels. In the long-term, however, marketers should aim to increase price-setting discretion through marketing techniques which result in creating greater consumer pull. Buyers often trust the price of a product or service to convey information on quality. Marketers who are aware of these instances can set prices above the category average. Opportunities are greatest when the purchase is high involvement, quality is important to a sufficiently large segment, quality is not easily determined by mere inspection, and the product or service is new or noticeably different from past versions.

Reproduced with permission from *Marketing*, June 1992, pp. 46-48.

Questions

1. What branded products do you think lend themselves to premium pricing? Why?
2. Outline the marketing strategy you would recommend for a high quality perfume.
3. Price is the most important element of the marketing mix. Discuss.

Case 8—Oldies under the microscope

by St George TAFE

A new research report on mature consumers has been released, this time the result of a project by a 'new' marketing consultancy.

Like most Westernised nations, the Australian population is getting older. Government projections indicate that by the year 2001 more than one out of every three Australians will be over the age of 45.

The aging of the Australian population presents new challenges and opportunities for marketers. For some time, marketers have concentrated their efforts on reaching the younger age segments in the market-place, neglecting the older age groups. This prompted a group of part-time marketing students to research the mature-age market segment (50 years plus). Researched and compiled by a team of sixteen final-year students at St George TAFE in Sydney, the project took twelve months to complete, with many hours of effort resulting in an extensive research report ' 'Marketing to the Mature Australian'.

The report was designed to:

1. gain general information on a poorly understood market segment;
2. establish how mature consumers obtain information to make purchase decisions, including;
3. the degree of brand loyalty, and how experience impacts on the purchase decision; and
4. develop marketing strategies that enable organisations to better target and promote their products to mature consumers.

A comprehensive literature search revealed few direct sources of marketing information. However, a number of significant trends were observed in the literature, trends supported by primary research. These include:

- People in the 50 and over age group are highly individualistic. This leads to the need for marketers to address the many segments in the mature market.
- Age is not the only segmentation criterion for many markets of goods and services.
- The needs of mature consumers in many areas, particularly finance, are not properly satisfied.
- Most mature-age people are vital, healthy and active and have subsequent needs that are not currently met.
- Many mature-age consumers adapt well to changes in the fabric of society, particularly technological changes.

Primary research consisted of face-to-face interviews, the use of questionnaires and discussion groups. The questionnaire format contained 58 questions divided into five main areas:

1. Demographics.
2. Mobility.

3. Brand loyalty.
4. Advertising.
5. Purchase behaviour.

Further information on specific topics was gained from discussion groups, with each discussion group consisting of eight participants and a mediator from the project team.

The research investigated the effects of a number of different types of advertising on mature Australians. The forms of advertising covered in the report are Radio, Magazines, Newspapers, Television and Direct Mail. Some of the most definitive results came from radio advertising, which indicated the most effective stations for reaching different segments of the Mature Australian market. The report also gives the best times of the day to reach these segments: early morning and late night on talkback shows. Women's magazines totally dominated the types of magazines read by both sexes. Nearly three times as many women read magazines as men. This trend is not evident in the case of newspaper readership. Newspaper readership is evenly distributed amongst males and females, with the Sunday papers' readership being significantly higher than that of the daily papers. Incomes and occupations were the main determinants of the type of newspaper that was read.

By far the most influential form of media in relation to purchase decision is television. The majority of mature Australians watch television, on average, between one and four hours per day. A very small number of respondents do not watch television. This group, however, does listen to the radio. The majority of mature Australians surveyed responded negatively to direct mail, although a significant number of the 50–54 age group indicated that direct mail was informative and helped them make their purchase decision.

The results achieved in relation to finance are quite significant. Mature Australians are not comfortable with many finance products or dealing with financial institutions. One-third of all respondents in all age groups did not understand the financial terms used in advertising. This frustration is one area that financial institutions must address. All the age groups showed a very strong preference for passbook accounts, with the 50–54-year-old age group having more plastic card accounts than the other age groups. The people who use passbook accounts prefer to use cash when shopping, even for major purchases over $500. Mature Australians who have a salary as their main source of income are more likely to have and use credit cards. Nearly two-thirds of those surveyed who were on the pension indicated that they do not use credit cards. Credit card owners showed a higher level of ownership of electrical appliances and are more likely to adapt to technological change.

The majority of Mature Australians are brand loyal. Although many respondents indicated that brands would be switched if a satisfactory price incentive was offered, an almost equal number said that they would not switch brands on price. On purchases over $500 trusted brands rated significantly over any other alternative, including bargain price.

Retirement is no longer viewed as an end to a career, but is viewed as a third stage of life. This change in attitude has led to a whole generation of people looking for new experiences when they retire, which creates many opportunities for marketers of travel, sports and recreation.

For general marketing of goods and services the report indicates there are only a few golden rules that apply to the mature market: brand loyalty is strong and should be initiated and developed. A lifetime of experience is brought to each purchase decision and this presents many market segments to marketers.

Reproduced with permission from *Marketing*, June 1992, pp. 54–55.

Question
Devise and outline a strategy for selling to the fifty-plus market.

Case 9—The Queensland grocery industry
by Alan Dowsett, Peter Graham and Robert Young

Introduction
Changes in food retailing and consumer shopping behaviour are forcing the participants in the Queensland grocery industry to rethink how they can best compete for the consumers food dollar in the 1990s. In 1990, the Queensland grocery industry employed in excess of 75 000 people and its total sales exceeded $4 billion per year. The grocery industry is one of the few Queensland retailing segments which is showing growth (approximately 3–4% p.a.). In terms of an industry life cycle the Queensland grocery industry is fast approaching saturation stage, typified by the intensity of competition amongst the competitors, and the distinct chance that many participants may face profitless prosperity over the next two to three years. The major participants in this industry include the chain operations of Woolworths, Coles New World and Franklins, who account for nearly 75% of the grocery volume. Queensland Independent Wholesalers, Davids Holdings and Pick-N-Pay Hyper-market make up the independent sector of the market, and represent the remaining 25% of grocery volume. Important driving forces within the industry include regulatory influences and government policy changes, marketing innovation and the change in the long-term industry growth rate. The industry is essentially price driven and can be affected by economic factors such as rising interest rates and inflation.

Five key success factors have been identified in the industry of which two relate directly to the independent sector of the market. These factors include the ability of the independent operator to focus upon a niche strategy and the importance of the independent operator achieving high levels of operating efficiencies. The key success factors relative to the chain operations include the availability of qualified professionals who can focus their attention on specific areas of the business, the rise of regional shopping centres in prime locations which offer speciality stores assisting in generating customer traffic, and the economies of scale enjoyed by the large chain store operations. To remain competitive in such an environment the independent operators must increase their focus upon developing a market niche and improve upon their levels of management expertise. This in turn will assist in improving the existing levels of operating efficiency.

Industry structure

(a) *Chain Stores*
   In 1990, six major players constituted the Queensland grocery industry, three of which can be viewed as being chain store operations:
   (i) *Woolworths*
       Woolworths account for 29.5% of the Queensland market with 127 stores, of which 51 actually trade under different banners than that of Woolworths.
   (ii) *Coles New World*
       Coles have a 28% market share in Queensland with 88 stores, of which 12 are Bi-Lo stores.
   (iii) *Franklins*
       Franklins have achieved a 17% market share in Queensland with 46 stores all trading under the Franklins name.

In total, chain operations in Queensland represent some 74.5% of total Queensland grocery volume turnover which, in dollar terms, equals $2.98 billion (1990).

(b) *Independents*
   The independent sector of the 1990 Queensland grocery industry represents some 25.5% of grocery volume. There are three major independents in the Queensland market:
   (i) *Queensland Independent Wholesalers (QIW)*
       QIW account for 15.5% of the market.
   (ii) *Davids Holdings*
       Davids Holdings have a 9% market share in Queensland.
   (iii) *Pick-n-Pay Hypermarket*
       Pick-n-Pay has one store, which represents 1% of the total grocery volume in Queensland.

The independent sector of the Queensland grocery industry is extremely fragmented. QIW, for example, has some 1074 independent operators utilising their wholesaling operations, under eight different banners. Davids Holdings in Queensland have 287 independents utilising their wholesaling operations under nine different banners.

In 1990, Queensland represented 17% of Australia's population but had 18% of the total grocery outlets in Australia. Significantly, Queensland had 21% of the total independent outlets in Australia and 19% of the total chain outlets, which indicates that Queensland is slightly over-represented in both independent and chain store outlets.

A national survey of the grocery industry in 1990 revealed some interesting findings in relation to independent and chain stores:

- 10% of independents turn over one-third of the total business done by independents;
- the top 20% of independents turn over 50% of all business done by independents;
- 33% of independents compete for 10% of the turnover generated by independents which represents only 3% of all grocery business;
- the top 33% of chain stores have 50% of all the chain business and 33% of the total grocery business.

Historical context

The early 1970s were generally typified by the local grocery store which was the community focal point. It was an enjoyable place to visit where people intermingled with their neighbours and were served by someone who knew them personally as well as their grocery needs and desires. It represented a time when this type of establishment was the most common outlet and where the chain stores were the minor players in the market. Overall, the grocery industry during this period can be considered to be in its early development. There was no dominant leader amongst the chain stores and the small operators held a significant market-share level.

By 1980 a trend had emerged towards the establishment of major suburban shopping centres which led to the one stop shopping concept. A gradual transition in customer allegiance took place from the independents to the new-style chain store operations, slowed by a degree of customer loyalty towards the local shop owner. The change in the independent operator-customer relationship saw this area of the grocery market change from being a main source of supply to being a 'top-up' operation. These transitions reflect the start of the decline for the independents and the early development of the chain stores.

At the beginning of the 1980s, there was ample evidence that the chain store concept was experiencing rapid growth. With the emergence of Jack the Slasher operations, there commenced a period of major influence in retail trading techniques. Evidence of this phenomena was the introduction of minimal servicing and the use of loss leader targeting of high profile national brand products.

The emergence of Jack the Slasher operations may have been assisted considerably by the complacency of Woolworths and Coles in the Queensland industry during the early part of the 1980s. Similarly, the purchase of the Jack the Slasher operations by Safeway several years later (who almost immediately began to move away from the previously successful low cost and low service strategy) was seen to be the beginning of the end for Jack the Slasher operations.

It was about this time that the industry witnessed the emergence of the Franklins Chain whose strategy was similar to that of a low status, low margin, low price operation, to fill the void left by Jack the Slasher. Similarly the rise of Bi-Lo operations in Queensland came shortly after Franklins. This was Coles New World's attempt to gain a share at the low cost, low price end of the market. It remains to be seen whether one or both of these operations begin to upgrade facilities, offer additional services and ultimately leave themselves vulnerable to still newer types of low cost operations entering the Queensland market. Furthermore, Pick-N-Pay Hypermarkets, whose strategy was also consistent with this approach, commenced operations during the early 1980s.

Despite the growth of the low cost, low price operations, within a few years both Woolworths and Coles emerged as leaders within the Queensland grocery industry and began an intense battle for market share. Coupled with low inflation and an increase in retailer concentration, the specialisation of food discounters marked the start of the early maturity stage of the grocery industry.

By 1988, there were signs that the industry was reaching saturation point with a slow-down in sales growth to 3-4% per annum which was only slightly higher than the Queensland population increase of 2.5% at the time. This trend has continued through to 1990, caused mainly by a slow-down in the economy and expendable income. Industry sources suggest that current trends are the beginning of a consolidation phase. For the chain stores, the most likely scenario is a slow-down in new building supplemented with refurbishment of existing stores. The independents, in turn, will experience a rationalisation within this segment of the industry as evidenced by the emergence of the Foodstore supermarket concept. This change of direction by some of the independents places them in direct competition with the chain operations.

Dynamics of the grocery industry in Queensland

Industries evolve because forces are in motion that create incentives or pressures for change. A number of such forces are at work in the grocery industry.

Political and legal

Perhaps the most significant political break small business experienced in Australia was the 1990 appointment of Queensland M.P. David Beddall as the first Federal Minister for Small Business and Customs. Beddall chaired a Parliamentary Committee which produced a 300-page report on small business problems. The importance of this report in terms of government policy changes was seen as a driving force, evidenced in that there are some 66 specific policy recommendations covering tax reform, finance, regulation, trade practices, retail and commercial tenancy, franchising and management education and training. All these issues have an impact on the small business sector.

In particular, tax reporting for the independent operator has, in discussions with many independents, been the most complex and burdensome of government policies faced by the independent grocery retailer in Queensland. As such, any form of relief in terms of tax reporting on PAYE, prescribed payments, sales tax, provisional tax or capital gains tax would offer assistance to the small business operator.

Equally important is the revamped State legislation which will enable some service stations to sell groceries. In 1990, the Local Government (Planning and

Environment) Bill lifted a ban prohibiting service stations from selling groceries. The danger in terms of the grocery industry is that it may enable service station owners to transform service bays into grocery stores thus impacting significantly on the structure of the grocery industry and its environment.

Marketing innovation

An example of marketing innovation was the attempt by QIW Retailers in 1990 to launch the Foodstore supermarket concept with one stop shopping, including fresh meat, fruit and vegetables, and serviced delicatessen. This can be viewed as an attempt by QIW to market the independent operator in a new manner which will spark a burst of shopper interest, lower unit costs, provide the consumer with a supermarket range of product with the service level of the traditional independent and thus set in motion new forces to alter the industry and the competitive position of other supermarket outlets.

Long-term industry growth rate

The final industry dynamic identified in the Queensland grocery sector is the change in the long-term industry growth rate. It has been suggested by many Queensland grocery operators that the rate of growth of the grocery industry has greatly slowed over the last two years, thus impacting the extent of structural and strategic changes. Quite clearly the rate of growth has impacted investment decisions with the two major industry players (Woolworths and Coles) opting to refurbish existing stores rather than to open new stores.

Industry price-cost economics

A number of salient economic factors impinge on the performance of the Queensland grocery industry. Although the demand for grocery items in most instances suffers no significant seasonal variations, economic factors such as inflation and rising interest rates can have serious implications for the industry. Industry sources believed that by late 1989 sales within the industry would increase as a direct consequence of improvements in disposable income resulting from tax cuts and increases in employment. This did not eventuate and has been blamed on consumers becoming more cautious. This is supported by Australian Bureau of Statistics data showing the average Australian household saved 6.3% of its after tax income in 1987 as opposed to 8% in 1989.

In addition to the increased levels of saving by the public, grocery sales in Queensland have similarly been impacted by high interest rates and the burden of mortgage repayments faced by the majority of consumers. This necessarily imposes greater problems for the independent grocery retailer as they struggle to be price competitive with the larger chain stores who can absorb lower prices for sustainable periods in an attempt to attract many of these reluctant spenders.

Due to the high degree of power possessed by grocery customers and the intense rivalry of retail grocery competitors, the grocery market, to a large extent, is price driven. The three major competitors, Coles, Woolworths and Franklins, are advanced along the experience curve. As long as all three continue to follow pricing and growth strategies to maximise their market shares, it will be a difficult struggle for the minor industry players, namely the independent operators. Any gains made through experience further encourage price competition amongst the chain operators. Unless the independent operators can position themselves in an exclusive market niche, an inability to match the prices of the largest competitors will contribute to their problems.

Queensland grocery industry strategies

Rather than attempting to identify every possible factor which may contribute to success, it is more useful to select the major factors which will impact on strategy development and implementation in the Queensland grocery industry. Hence the strategies, specific skills and competences of the independent operator will be discussed, followed by those of the chain store operations.

Independents

The key success factors of the independent operators can be grouped under two broad headings—firstly, their ability to niche market and, secondly, their degree of operating efficiency.

(a) *Niche marketing*
The ability of the independent operator to adopt a niche strategy may be the primary success factor of independent grocery retailers. This basically involves the independent operator filling or creating gaps in the market that grocery chains find unsuitable with their large capacities. It involves specialising in customers or products and emphasises the non-price elements of the marketing mix, such as service quality and satisfying a small, clearly defined target market or segment which have these specialised needs. In many instances, the independent grocery retailers are stressing their inherent strengths in flexibility or personalised service.

(b) *Degree of operating efficiency*
The second of the key success factors of the independent operators is their degree of operating efficiency. Given that the average independent operates with only a 28-30% gross margin, it is imperative that sloppy management practices and inefficiencies in all methods of store operations are avoided as these quickly erode the typically slim 3.0–3.5% pre-tax profit margin.

Chain stores

The key success factors of the chain store operations can be seen to involve three specific kinds of skills and competences.

(a) *Qualified professional personnel*
The first success factor of the chain stores is the availability of suitably qualified professional personnel who can focus their attention on the areas of business for which they have special expertise. For example, the three major chain operators

have specialised departments to deal with promotional, personnel and marketing activities, each of which is normally supervised by persons who are professionally qualified in their field and who have many years of experience. This is in direct contrast to the independent operator who attempts to be an expert in all areas of the business but, unfortunately for many, ends up as master of none.

(b) *Prime Locations*

The second of the chain operations key success factors involves their ability to draw consumers via their prime locations offering first-class facilities and amenities, such as the large suburban shopping centres with large customer car parking. Most chain operations stress the importance of having easily accessible sites on well travelled routes in rapidly growing areas of population.

(c) *Economies of scale*

The final key success factor involves the chain operations economies of scale, particularly in terms of advertising, financing and the ability to sell at lower prices than the independents, allowing volume turnover to be much greater.

Problems facing the industry

The Queensland grocery industry in 1990 was facing a number of issues, or problems, that needed handling effectively to ensure continued prosperity.

The economy

Recent research suggests that the 1990s will see consumers in Australia shift from being debtor-orientated to savers of disposable income (up to 14.0% by the end of the decade). This would result in a slow-down in consumption growth which will, in turn, affect the income levels of the grocery trade. The grocery trade will need to carefully evaluate customer needs as market share will be keenly contested and the mortality rate, particularly among small businesses, will remain high.

Technological change

One area that is likely to have a major impact on the market is the change taking place in technology. Two significant developments in computer management are Scan Data and Apollo. Through the use of standardised numbering (APN) on all products, organisations can now scan goods at checkouts which provide information on stock levels, product movement, generated dollar sales and seasonal fluctuations. This data can then be evaluated and used in financial, logistical and marketing management. All chain stores have taken advantage of this technology, but there remains some independent operators who are not using it. In doing so, they deprive themselves of up-to-date information that can be used in assessing the store's efficiency.

With the exception of Tasmania, Queensland has the highest chain store throughput of groceries which are utilising scanning technology. This technological advantage provides the chain stores with information which enhances their management systems.

Table B3.1 *Grocery scanning*

Australia—November 1989 estimates	
States	Cents in the dollar scanned
Tasmania	82.3
Queensland	48.7
South Australia	47.9
New South Wales	47.3
Western Australia	39.1
Victoria	38.5

Source: A.C. Nielsen Reports, April, 1989

Apollo is a computerised shelf management system that provides data on areas such as packet dimensions, layout area, turnover and dollar advantages. The use of this technology minimises stock refilling and provides more information for allocating additional space to better sellers. To date, only Woolworths and Coles have installed this technology which will give these companies an advantage in floor layout technique over both Franklins and the independent operators.

Finally, only Woolworths and Coles have commenced using a computerised documentation system known as Electronic Data Interchange (EDI) which can reduce paperwork and duplication costs. EDI is a paperless system whereby data, in all forms, is transported through networks and modems to be accessed by others.

Management

This issue could well become the most important influence on the grocery trade in Queensland. Because the industry has now begun the saturation stage of its life cycle, both the chain stores and the independent operators will move into a period of consolidation. The chain stores will place more emphasis in consolidating from an internal perspective. This phase will be highlighted by:

- the introduction of new technology;
- reviews in pricing policies (and possible redevelopment in pricing strategies);
- more emphasis on refurbishment and renovation of current stores;
- more usage in management expertise; and
- increased personnel administration of staff (as a result of award restructuring).

The independent operators, on the other hand, will enter the consolidation period differently, with a more balanced focus between the internal and external perspective, namely:

- a re-emphasis towards niche marketing;
- a re-evaluation by the owner-manager as to whether he should undertake an expansive or a defensive strategy (e.g. operators have opted to compete directly

with chain operations via the introduction of new food store supermarket banners);
- a need to maintain and improve cash flow; and
- a self-assessment by the owner-manager as to business efficiency.

Each of the management functions mentioned involves a skill level that is based on more than just experience. It requires a level of education in the management of both chain stores and independent operations. Although it is hard to correlate the exact effect of management skill (as opposed to experience and luck), it is nevertheless a resource threat influencing significantly the future of a business. The advantage of good management can be taken on by both groups; it is not the domain of larger organisations such as the chain stores. It can be the difference between running an ordinary enterprise compared to a prosperous one.

Questions

1. Discuss the concept of the 'wheel of retailing' in relation to the Queensland grocery market.
2. Conduct a SWOT analysis for both independents and chain stores.
3. A competitive position assessment focuses upon the success of strategies employed in an industry. Apply this to chain stores and independents.
4. Two areas of advantage for the independents were highlighted in the case study:
    (i) the ability of the independent grocery retailer to focus upon niche marketing; and
    (ii) the extent to which management expertise levels can be raised, particularly in relation to operating efficiencies and basic skills of small business management.

    Critically analyse both areas, devising strategies for independents to adopt, with particular reference to Williams' (1982) research on patterns of small business failure and Burgoyne and Stuart's (1976) research.

References

A. C. Nielsen Reports, April, 1989

Burgoyne, J. and Stuart, R. (1976), 'The Nature, Use and Acquisition of Managerial Skills and Other Attributes', *Personnel Review*, 5 (4), pp. 19–29.

Kotler, P., Shaw, R., Fitzroy, P. and Chandler, P. (1983), *Marketing in Australia*, Prentice Hall, Sydney.

Williams, A. J. (1982), *Patterns of Small Business Failure*, Small Business Research: Proceedings of a Conference held at the University of Newcastle.

# Case 10—Garden centre retailing in Australia

by Peter Graham

'Garden centre retailing in Australia' is the follow-up case study to 'the Australian nursery industry' and should only be attempted by students who have at least read the first case. Both cases are based on the research project commissioned by The Horticultural Research and Development Corporation. The study produced a comprehensive picture of the national nursery industry, and covered both nursery retailers and the broader Australian population.

'Garden centre retailing in Australia' covers a number of issues facing retailers in particular. The case study gives a detailed description of the retail garden centre industry structure, market dynamics and strategies involved.

The retail garden centre industry structure

Employment and staff

Generally speaking, the owner of the retail nursery is the main 'employee' at the establishment. Overall, across all of the retail nurseries included in the study 84% of retail nurseries employed the nursery owner. Variations did occur ranging from 90% of owners being present at smaller nurseries (those establishments with under $400 000 turnover per annum) falling to 75% at the largest category of nurseries (turnovers of $700 000 per annum). Not surprisingly, smaller nurseries employ fewer staff in all occupations, whilst for larger nurseries employment is common across all occupations. Table B3.2 in the appendix shows in detail the employment structure of retail nurseries in Australia.

The structure of full-time, part-time and casual employment at retail nurseries was also examined. The findings show that an average retail nursery employs 3.5 people and most are employed on a full-time basis. Part-time and casual staff are predominantly shop or sales assistants.

Qualifications of staff

Staff qualifications were also examined and it was clearly found that relevant certificate or diploma qualifications were only required from staff in the occupations of nurseryman, horticulturist or nursery manager. Very little in the way of formal qualifications was required for shop or sales assistants, labourers or garden attendant staff.

The need for less formal skills, however, was a different matter with sales and people skills and plant identification skills being necessary for all categories of staff. Additionally, landscaping and garden planning skills were felt to be necessary for labourers, cash register skills were required for shop or sales assistants, and trade buying and management skills were rated as necessary for managers.

There is almost a consensus among management and nursery owners that full-time staff should have either a Certificate or Diploma of Horticulture as a minimum standard. There is also a strong view about the importance of good people skills and sales skills. Most owners/managers agree it is very important for all employees to be able to get on with all types of people.

Minimum standards/qualifications for part-time staff and casuals were not specified, though the comment was made that they must again understand people of all ages and backgrounds, and be able to meet their needs. People skills are highly regarded at all levels.

Demand dynamics

Nursery retailers were asked for their views on demand dynamics in 1990. Most retailers were found to stock a wide range of plants and product categories. There were no major differences between large, medium and smaller retailers. Larger retailers tend to stock most of everything. For the product category of nursery hardware (such as garden tools) smaller retailers were less likely to stock such items. Products and plant categories sold also varied depending on the city in which the nursery retailer was located.

Demand changes

Nursery retailers' perceptions of trade dynamics were also assessed. It was clearly found retailers perceive strong growth occurring throughout 1990 for most plant and product categories. Notwithstanding this strong overall demand, some negative growth was also found.

Table B3.3 in the appendix illustrates the full picture of consumer trade dynamics as perceived by retailers, and it can be seen that, although demand is generally perceived to be very strong it is not without problem spots.

Retailers' perception of the reasons for demand changes was documented in the research and many felt that several reasons were responsible for demand increasing. These were:

- changing trends and fashions largely due to customer awareness of environment issues;
- because of a weakening economy gardening is becoming more popular since consumers perceive it as a cheap leisure activity; and
- greater success of retailer advertising and promotion efforts and the influence of radio and TV gardening programmes.

These reasons were relatively consistent across each of the seven cities.

For those retailers who mentioned that in some plant or product categories, consumer demand was falling, the main reasons given were:

- the weakening economy is depressing the level of household purchases, particularly in plant or product categories where hardware stores, variety stores and supermarkets can offer the same item at a cheaper price; and
- heightened consumer concern about the environment has depressed sales of chemical fertilisers and sprays.

New products sold

Nursery retailers were also asked to indicate any plant or product categories that they sell now but did not sell 12 months ago. Generally speaking organic fertilisers and sprays, potted colour, and ornaments and giftware are the categories where nursery retailers are introducing new products.

However, despite perceptions of increasing consumer demand over the last 12 months, most retailers (66%) have not added new plants or product categories. This was because half (51%) felt their existing product range is sufficiently comprehensive to meet customer needs.

However, some (17%) have extended the range of products within existing plant and product categories. The remainder state:

- they had insufficient space to extend their product range (16%);
- they just specialise in a particular product category such as natives (7%); or
- they have decided not to extend their product range due to economic conditions (4%).

Nine per cent felt no major new categories were available.

Strategies to cope with seasonal demand changes

To help develop strategies to assist the nursery industry overcome variations in seasonal demand, the research attempted to understand the ways individual nurseries try to overcome seasonal influences. Generally, buying stock more often, advertising more in local newspapers, and letterbox drops were the main sales strategies adopted, a detailed synopsis can be seen in Table B3.4 in the appendix.

These strategies however, vary significantly in different seasons. For instance, retailers who adopt gift/discount vouchers predominantly do so in summer and winter. For the small number of retailers who offer coupon prize response, nearly half (44%) offer such items in summer. Thirty-nine per cent offer coupon prizes in autumn. Advertising more in local newspapers is also common in summer.

Retailers who adopt catalogues or use letterbox drops do so more in autumn and during winter and spring, the emphasis shifts to different approaches. For instance, in winter many retailers advertise more in local newspapers. Also nursery retailers who employ sales and specials as a strategic approach, employ such methods strongly in winter (as well as in spring).

Value of the average nursery sale

Retail nursery owners and managers were asked about the average value of a sale. They claimed $11.00–$20.00 is the most common sale. There is little variation between small, medium and large retailers except that smaller retailers are more likely to have sales of $10.00 or less, whilst larger retailers are more likely to have sales (per customer) in the $21.00–$50.00 range. Table B3.5 in the appendix details the value of nursery sales.

Customer services

Retailers were asked to outline the most common requests made by customers and these can be seen in detail in Table B3.6 in the appendix. Nearly two thirds of requests (65%) were found to be for retailers to recommend a plant for a specific location. Retailers were then asked to describe the services they offered to their customers; likewise this list can be seen in the appendix in Table B3.7.

The research found a large range of services were offered to customers with (free) general advice being offered by all nurseries. Most nursery operators see customer service as an essential part of operating at a retail level. The services shown in Table B3.7 are perceived to effectively promote goodwill among customers. Goodwill is thought to encourage a return visit, leading to an ongoing relationship with the particular retail outlet. Nursery operators perceive free advice as the most important of all services offered as it is felt to be very effective in developing a good rapport.

Although general advice was offered universally, other customer services provided were less universal, with major differences depending on the size and location of the nursery. Although smaller nurseries are strong in offering most customer services, larger retailers offer more in the areas of:

- garden planning;
- guaranteed return policy;
- gift baskets;
- alternatives to using chemicals; and
- gift vouchers.

Only in one area do smaller retailers offer a greater service to customers—free delivery.

Strategy promotion

Major promotion techniques employed by nursery retailers are:

- front entrance displays (78% of responses);
- gift vouchers (62% of responses); and
- special occasion promotions (such as Mother's Day) (51% of responses).

Variation in promotion techniques existed and the research found differences between activities of larger retailers as compared to those of smaller retailers. Larger retailers place stronger emphasis on:

- participation in garden shows and festivals;
- product catalogues;
- gift vouchers;
- promoting special occasions;
- hiring out plants for major functions;
- garden personalities in store;
- in-store displays; and
- displays in other businesses or shops.

Nevertheless, smaller retailers are active in the promotion of their business, albeit if only in certain areas. Smaller retailers are just as active as larger retailers in:

- front entrance displays;
- newspaper garden columns;
- school promotions;
- newsletters;
- discount vouchers; and
- free breakfasts, barbecues on location.

Nursery retailers were asked which promotion techniques they felt were the most successful:

- front entrance displays;
- letterbox drops;
- participation in garden shows (and festivals); and
- a newspaper garden column in local newspaper.

Smaller retailers particularly felt that front entrance displays are a successful way to promote their nursery. Sydney and Melbourne retailers had very strong views that front entrance displays were effective.

Less successful approaches were felt to be:

- gift vouchers;
- hiring plants out for major functions; and
- school promotions.

Advertising techniques used

Closely related to promotional activities are the advertising approaches adopted by nurseries. Respondents were asked to outline the range of advertising forms that they have adopted over the last two years.

Leading by far is Yellow Pages and newspaper (typically suburban newspaper) advertising, followed by letterbox drops. Radio advertising was important (over one in three nurseries claim to have used radio) while television advertising was the least used. Table B3.8 in the appendix illustrates these findings.

Again, however, the range of advertising methods used was found to vary significantly between large and smaller retailers (which probably reflects the different resources available for advertising in each sector). Larger retailers are more likely to use the following media for advertising:

- television;
- radio;
- magazines;
- garden club newsletters; and
- leaflets.

Smaller retailers, nevertheless are active, and just as active as larger retailers in advertising in:

- newspapers;
- billboards;
- Yellow Pages;
- newsletters; and
- letterbox drops.

Appendix

Table B3.2 *Employment structure of retail nurseries*

(N = 202)	%
Owner	84
Manager/assistant manager	53
Shop or sales assistant	50
Horticulturalist	37
Labourer	29
Nurseryman	27
Garden centre attendant	20
Florist	5
Other	9

Source: HRDC Study 1990

Table B3.3 *Perception of demand—increase or decrease*

Base: Total sample (N = 202)	Increasing sales %	Decreasing sales %	Static sales %
Organic fertilisers and sprays	78	5	17
Bedding plants	70	9	21
Potted colour	67	7	25
Herbs	61	8	31
Perennials	58	10	32
Trees/shrubs	52	9	39
Citrus trees	50	6	44
Seeds	49	7	44
Roses	45	20	34
Pottery	41	16	43
Ornaments/giftware	38	20	42
Indoor plants	37	18	45
Stone fruit	36	29	35
Climbing plants	34	11	55
Chemical fertilisers and sprays	33	38	29
Hardware (garden tools, etc.)	27	16	58

Source: HRDC Study 1990

Table B3.4 *Sales strategies used to cope with seasonal demand changes*

(N = 202)	%
Buy stock more often	59
Advertise more in local newspapers	43
Letterbox drops	32
Hold sales in slow periods	29
Gift/discount vouchers	23
Catalogues	18
Hold more sales	12
Coupon price response	9
Other ways	15
Nothing	9

Source: HRDC Study 1990

Table B3.5 *Value of average sales*

(N = 202)	
$	%
1.00–10.00	14
11.00–20.00	47
21.00–50.00	31
51.00 and over	5

Source: HRDC Study 1990

Table B3.6 *Most common requests from customers (n=202)*

(N = 202)	%
Recommendation of plant for specific position	65
How tall plant will grow	47
Reason for plant failure	31
Fertilisers (what to buy, when to use)	27
Pest control methods	23
Whether plant needs shade or sun	19
Length of, and when, flowering	17

Source: HRDC Study 1990

Table B3.7 *Customer services offered by retailers*

	%
General advice	100
Garden planning	76
Gift vouchers	71
Alternatives to using chemicals	70
Free delivery	52
Guaranteed return policy	49
Gift baskets	26

Source: HRDC Study 1990

Table B3.8 *Advertising media used*

(N = 202)

	%
Yellow pages	82
Newspapers	81
Letterbox drops	46
Radio	35
Magazines	28
Leaflets	26
Newsletters	18
Billboards	18
Garden club news	17
TV	16

Source: HRDC Study 1990

Questions

You are the owner/manager of a medium sized garden centre, based in Brisbane and employing two other people full time. The centre offers a wide range of plants and garden equipment. Whilst business has been steady for a few years, you recognise the fact that you must try and 'grow' the business for continued future development.

1. Using the brainstorming technique, devise a list of promotional ideas that could be developed into a promotional strategy for your nursery. Outline the strategy.
2. What growth strategy would you, as the owner/manager, implement? Would you recommend market development or product development? Why?

References

Kotler, P., Chandler, P., Gibbs, R. and McColl, R. (1989), *Marketing in Australia*, Prentice Hall, Australia.

National Consumer and Retailer Study of Nursery Industry Opportunities, 1991, Horticultural Research and Development Corporation, The Research Arm of the Australian Horticultural Industries.

4. APPLICATIONS OF MARKETING

Introduction 120

Readings
8. Deeds, not words, says Japanese guru, by Robert Gottliebsen 121
9. US airline makes itself at home away from home, by Neil Shoebridge 124

Cases
11. Non-profit organisations take on new discipline, by David James 128
12. The globalisation of Fosters, by Alan Kilgore and Terry Alchin 132
13. Marketing Drug Arm Brisbane, by Terry Gatfield 146

Introduction

Section four in this part of the book examines the different applications of marketing. Industrial marketing, service marketing and the marketing of organisations, places and ideas are also covered here. Non-profit marketing and international marketing are also examined.

Two readings and three case studies have been selected for this section of the book. Robert Gottliebsen, editorial director of BRW, provides us with a detailed look at the impact of Asia, as a market, on Australian companies. His reading is entitled, 'Deeds, not words, says Japanese guru'. In 'US airline makes itself at home away from home', Neil Shoebridge documents the success of Northwest airline's segmentation strategy. The US company targeted business travellers with a clever promotional campaign.

David James' case study 'Non-profit organisations take on new discipline' examines what business can learn from successful non-profit organisations. Similarly, Terry Gatfield's 'Marketing Drug Arm Brisbane' takes an in-depth look at a non-profit organisation and encourages the student to analyse financial data and also perceptions. 'The Globalisation of Fosters' by Alan Kilgore and Terry Alchin is a thorough account of Fosters' international strategy. The case tracks the rise of Fosters from A. L. Elder's days of 1839 to Fosters Brewing becoming the world's fourth largest brewer in 1991.

Reading 8—Deeds, not words, says Japanese guru

by Robert Gottliebsen

Australia is accused of failing to take up opportunities because its attitudes to Asia are 'schizophrenic'.

Kenichi Ohmae, the chairman of McKinsey & Company in Japan and the best-known management expert in Asia, is not frightened to express views about Australia that most Japanese keep to themselves. He sees the fall in the Japanese sharemarket and problems being encountered in the Uruguay Round of Gatt as opportunities for Australian enterprises to forge a much wider range of links with Japan, Taiwan and South Korea, but he questions whether Australians have the necessary resolve.

Ohmae, author of the book *Borderless Trading*, says: 'The Australian mentality is a very strange mentality. In a way it is ambivalent at best; if you use a not-so-good word, it is schizophrenic.' Australia has made net progress over the past couple of years turning away from a 'nostalgic Oxford-Cambridge mentality' to saying its future is with these Asian countries, he says. But, on the other hand, Australia has not performed the tangible actions that should flow from such a conclusion.

Australia has an 'FOB (free-on-board) mentality', he says. After the commodities go on to the boat, Australians expect to receive the money in 100 or 120 days. So, although Australian executives now have a commitment to Japan, Korea and Taiwan, when it comes to really 'having a go and living in the countries, there seems to be a big gap'. Very few Australian executives have lived in Japan for longer than two years and many Australian mining houses that have 60% of their sales in Japan do not have Japanese as senior executives.

Ohmae says executives of large Australian companies are very experienced 'in investment, in capacity expansion, cost reduction and logistic systems but when you talk about a $5 million investment to establish a research operation in Japan, they would be very reluctant. But that's where the market is.'

The fall of the Tokyo stockmarket means that Japanese property prices will come down and Japanese companies will be much more affordable and accessible. Australian companies will be able to take a 5% or 10% equity position and forge much closer links with the Japanese market. 'But Australians are sometimes afraid of Japan; they have a realisation that the Japanese market is huge but say those guys could eat us alive,' Ohmae says. An encouraging sign is the recent zinc-smelting joint venture in Japan by MIM which is, Ohmae says, 'a very, very proactive activity. It is the first major step I have seen in this direction'.

Ohmae says the Taiwanese market is about the same size as the Australian domestic market. 'So I ask Australians: Are you willing to put the same kind of resources, quality thinking and attention to Taiwan (as you would to your local market), because it is the same size?' And it is virtually left open because there are not many well-managed companies in Taiwan,' he says.

Australians are reluctant to go to Taiwan partly because there is no diplomatic recognition. Often they choose China instead. 'But then I query Australians: "Do you think you can really establish a good, trust-based 100% relationship with China because it, too, is resource-based and may be competing with you? Isn't Taiwan more complementary?" And they they will say "Yes", but they are so ambivalent about going out and establishing fully fledged relationships with Taiwan'.

Ohmae believes that if the Uruguay Round fails, Japan will have to develop either multilateral or bilateral relationships to safeguard its security of supply. 'We cannot ignore the United States because that is a very important political and trading partner. On the other hand, if you really believe in complementary relationships I would think that Korea, Japan, Taiwan and Australia should sit down and really form a trust-based relationship, similar to the Japan-US security treaty and to what you've got with New Zealand,' he says.

'The problem of APEC (Asia-Pacific Economic Cooperation group) or ASEAN (Association of South-East Asian Nations) is that they've got countries with conflicting interests, countries at very different economic development stages and some countries with whom you compete on resources. But if you pick up those three (Korea, Taiwan and Japan), they have so many things that are complementary.

'Korea, Taiwan and Japan all have something in common: they are small countries in terms of land mass, do not have very much in resort facilities; they are basically industrial and mountainous. Amenities are secondary to industrial development and professional services are not well developed.'

Koreans have begun to come to Australia, and love it, but they prefer a different style of accommodation from the Japanese, and Qantas has no direct flights from Sydney to Seoul. 'You say these countries are important but . . . it is just amazing that you haven't shown these things by physical actions; you know that is the problem,' Ohmae says.

'Australia has the best medical system in Asia but has never offered it to these people. We need to beg so that Brisbane hospital can be used by some guy (who is critically ill) in Japan. But Australian patients and taxpayers then complain. You have tremendous professional services, ranging from architects and engineers to medical. In addition, I think you could become an education centre, as was the case with the United States.'

Although Ohmae acknowledges there are many Asian students already in Australia, he says: 'I don't know of many Koreans who are doing this. I don't see why you couldn't establish yourselves as the academic and medical centre for Asia. Australia is the only Asia-Pacific country where the amenities preceded the development. 'You can teach us in many ways: in furniture, interior design ideas, bold architectural design. We have been working with an Australian computer software company. Over time they just dominate. They are much smarter, faster . . . they are much better than the Japanese.

'Australians have had this tremendous luck with resources and higher standard of living. Now they have to find the means to sustain this. The only way is to globalise and become much more market-oriented and to start offering professional services, because they are very high value-added'.

However, Ohmae warns that Japan is very wary of Australia. 'Australians negotiate like cowboys. So while Australia is a natural partner, it is dangerous to depend too much on Australia,' he says. The Japanese perspective on resource negotiations is very different from Australia's. Ohmae says Australia had a 60–70% share of the Japanese market in many commodities but when it found Japan did not have any other source of supply, it was tough in negotiations on prices'.

'Years ago, when Whitlam was in power, he went to China; that threatened Japan because a communist government was tying up with a socialist government. The Japanese said: 'In the long term this is dangerous, so we have to diversify into Brazil and a few other places.' The rest is history: we have diversified. It's the same with sugar and woodchips. In woodchips, Australia had a 60–70% share of the Japanese import market but negotiated on price for short-term gain. Japan immediately diversified into Chile and then increased the American portion,' he says.

'I think what happens is that Australians feel exploited so when the first moment arrives to negotiate from power, they just dump everything.' Ohmae says that this forcing up of the prices scares the buyer. 'In steel, I think they have learned this lesson. Now Australians have invited Japanese capital, and the supplier-producer-buyer mentality is much more stable. I think there is a trust base between companies like CRA and BHP with the Japanese producers and, amazingly, it is profitable for Australians, too. So after 20 years, they have a full trust-based relationship.'

But Ohmae says this good experience is not shared with the community, so other industries are going through the same learning process and journalists and politicians want to talk about the problems. From the Japanese side, one of the problems is property. Ohmae says Australia has never attracted Japan's top property developers nor has it really wooed Japanese investment in manufacturing.

'If foreigners buy a piece of land, they have to start construction within a year. Then, during this construction they have to sell 50% (of condominium units) to foreigners. But the remaining 50% must be sold to Australians. Given the different requirements of layout and all kinds of amenities, it will take a schizophrenic architect to give 50% to Australian and 50% to Japanese. It is much better to say you can't do it, or to say, in this zone or in this area it's OK to do so. The country is big enough.'

Against this background Ohmae brings a Japanese view of the multi-function polis. 'I will tell you what is wrong with the multi-function polis. It was a mirage to begin with, it was just a painting in the sky. And then you took it seriously and debated every which direction. It was in Queensland, now (it is) in Adelaide and I wish them good luck, because there is no substance behind it. If you have the energy to debate such trifling issues, I think one thing you should do is to think about establishing your own research facility in Japan. It is much cheaper and much more helpful because there are very strong trends in the main.

Reproduced with permission from *BRW*, Australia's leading business magazine, 17 April, 1992, pp. 32–33.

Questions

1. Is international marketing as simple as Kenichi Ohmae says? Why or why not?
2. How does international marketing differ from national marketing? What factors must the marketer consider?

Reading 9—US airline makes itself at home away from home

by Neil Shoebridge

After only nine months on the trans-Pacific route, Northwest says it is having success with a clever campaign aimed primarily at business travellers.

Timing is not Northwest Airlines' strong suit. When the US carrier made its first Australian landing in Sydney last July, the international air transport industry was reeling from the effects of the Gulf War and a worldwide slump in travel. The trans-Pacific market had shrunk an estimated 20% during 1990–91, with no sign of a recovery. Northwest could not have picked a tougher time to enter a new market.

Nine months later, Northwest maintains that the move has been a success. The number of passengers it has carried between Australia and the US is not available, but it claims that the count is ahead of budget. It has snared an 8% share of the trans-Pacific market, a respectable achievement given that it operates only seven flights a week on its Australian route, compared with 34 weekly trans-Pacific flights by Qantas, 19 by United Airlines and 28 by Continental Airlines.

Northwest executives are also crowing about the success of the marketing programme that launched their airline to Australian fliers. From last July to December, Northwest pumped $1.5 million into television, newspaper and magazine advertising, plus $600 000 into sponsorships. According to research conducted in January and February, awareness of Northwest's advertising among business travellers trailed slightly behind that of Qantas, but was well ahead of the other trans-Pacific airlines.

Northwest gained access to Australia via a $26 million deal with Hawaiian Airlines in December 1990. Northwest bought 25% of Hawaiian and took five of its routes, including Honolulu-Sydney. In May 1991, it started putting together its Australian company, poaching several senior executives from Continental's local operation, including general manager Col Hughes and marketing manager Philip Mills. Hughes was installed as general manager (South Pacific). Six weeks later, the first Northwest plane landed in Sydney.

Initially, it operated four flights to the US via Honolulu. In October, it launched three non-stop flights to Los Angeles (the Sydney-Honolulu service was subsequently chopped to once a week). At the same time, Northwest provoked an angry response from Qantas and the Japanese Government when it secured the right to fly from Sydney to New York three times a week via Osaka—thus becoming the first non-Australian and non-Japanese airline to gain access to the lucrative Japan-Australia route. Japan Airlines had been the only carrier servicing Australia from Osaka.

When Northwest came along, the trans-Pacific market was home to five airlines: Qantas, United, Continental, American and Air New Zealand (American quit the market last month). Earlier, Northwest had operated a small sales office in Sydney. A study conducted by Woolcott Research found that just 8% of Australian business travellers were aware of Northwest.

Hughes last May hired the Sydney advertising agency Creative Connection, owned by Michael Corbett, who had worked on Continental's account at other agencies and as a consultant. Creative Connection was officially established after Corbett won the Northwest account. It has since attracted other clients, including Pirelli Tyres and Matchbox Toys.

The Woolcott study was commissioned to help Northwest position itself in Australia. The airline set business travellers as its key target market. Andrew Denman, its marketing programmes manager (South Pacific), says the head office in Minneapolis instructed the Australian company to 'fill the plane from front to back'—in other words, to concentrate on high-yield first-class and business-class travellers, rather than less-profitable holiday-makers.

'Filling the back of the plane is dependent on pricing and destination—that is, the holidays and prices offered by the airline,' Corbett says. 'To some degree, holiday-makers are influenced by the image and awareness of an airline, but price is their main concern. In the business market, the criteria for selecting an airline are very different.'

The Woolcott study found Australians would not welcome Northwest if it was positioned as a US airline, and that business travellers see Qantas as the yardstick against which others are measured. Northwest decided to position itself as an international airline that happens to be American, rather than as a US airline that operates internationally. At the same time, Creative Connection was asked to promote Northwest as 'the Qantas of North America'.

'The brief to the agency was clear,' Denman says. 'Position Northwest as the sophisticated Qantas of North America, an airline with experience, history, technology and so on. Announce Northwest's arrival in Australia. Promote its modern fleet and the fact it is an airline that wants to get to know Australia and Australians.'

Last June, Creative Connection launched a TV commercial that simply listed facts about Northwest. The ad ran for three weeks before it was replaced by a second commercial that featured an eagle and the slogan, 'Northwest: tipped to be number one'. The second ad ran for two weeks.

In mid-June, Denman and Corbett attended a two-day training seminar in the US for Northwest staff. The seminar was designed to teach US staff about Australia and was attended by flight and cabin crews, checking agents, caterers and cargo handlers. Corbett returned to Australia and created a 60-second TV ad called 'training course', which featured Northwest's US staff wrestling with the pronunciation of Melbourne and Brisbane, expressing amazement that Australians eat Vegemite and puzzling over a cricket bat. The ad was launched in late July.

Northwest and Creative Connection were worried about how some Australians might respond to the ad. A Woolcott study conducted in January and February assuaged their fears: only 10% of respondents described the commercial as patronising.

'Most airline advertising is wallpaper,' Denman says. 'The 'training course' ad stood out because it was different. It was not full of shots of pretty flight attendants or Disneyland.' The TV commercials have appeared only in Sydney, although some newspaper and magazine ads have been run nationally.

The campaign ran from July to December last year, with a media budget of $1.5 million (Qantas spent $5 million on advertising in Australia during 1991, and United's ad budget was $1.7 million). Northwest also ran a direct-marketing programme for its World Perks frequent flier programme. Its sponsorship deals include a three-year, $900 000 contract with the South Sydney rugby league club, the NSW Open tennis tournament, the Australian Jockey Club's Epsom Handicap and the Royal Sydney Wine Show.

The Woolcott study discovered that 60% of business travellers were aware of Northwest's advertising campaign, compared to Qantas' 62% awareness score, United's 47% and Continental's 37%. Northwest also scored high marks on image factors such as 'new, modern aircraft' and 'staff are interested in learning about Australia'.

Northwest had limited success in the business market until last October, when its non-stop services to Los Angeles started. Traffic on its Sydney-Osaka-New York run was also sluggish at first. 'New York is a difficult destination to market, but we are starting to see an increase in traffic,' Denman says.

Access to Osaka was conditional on Northwest devoting no more than half of its capacity on the final leg route to passengers joining flights in Japan. It exceeded that limit in late 1991, with Japanese accounting for as much as 90% of the passengers flying between Osaka and Sydney. Denman claims this was because the carrier did not have sufficient time to market its link to New York, and says the 50% condition has been met over the past month.

Northwest entered the Australian market with several discount fares. Last June, it halved fares for US travellers, selling economy return tickets from the US west coast to Sydney for $724. In Australia, it offered return fares to Honolulu for $747. When its New York service started, it sold return tickets for $1,299.

Denman describes the price-cutting as 'promotions rather than discounts.' He says: 'Price-cutting does not give an airline any real marketing edge. Rivals invariably match a discount the next day, so all you do is destroy your yields.'

Qantas, United and Continental have cut some of their trans-Pacific fares since Northwest arrived, while Qantas has resurrected the Honolulu-San Francisco service it ditched in 1990 and extended its daily Sydney-Los Angeles service to Melbourne.

Northwest started a new marketing programme early this month with the return of TV advertising. Corbett says the campaign will become 'harder-edged and more product-related' over the next few months, covering corporate, destination and price advertising.

Northwest hopes to extend its services to Brisbane and Melbourne this year, although its expansion in Australia hinges on the outcome of a number of corporate moves. It is discussing a financial link with Continental and has also expressed interest in acquiring a stake in Qantas (April 30 is the deadline for lodging indicative bids for Qantas with the Federal Government). Meanwhile, Northwest will continue trying to build its trans-Pacific operation. 'We did not expect to make money during our launch phase, given the costs associated with starting a service from scratch,' Denman says. 'But the losses are not as large as we expected.'

Reproduced with permission from *BRW* Australia's leading business magazine, 17 April, 1992, pp. 64–66.

Questions

1. How would you describe Northwest Airlines' international marketing strategy?
2. Bearing in mind the volatile nature of the airline market, do you think their strategy is sound?
3. Have Northwest segmented their market? How? Why?

Case 11—Non-profit organisations take on new discipline

by David James

What was once a labour of love requiring few specific skills has become an important branch of management that can teach business a few things.

Non-profit organisations do not always figure in the economic statistics, but their total annual income in Australia of between $7 billion and $10 billion makes them a significant element of the economy and an important area in fostering managment skills. The non-profit organisations work for cultural and special-interest causes or carry out philanthropic and charity work. Australia cannot match the stature of the philanthropy industry in the US, where the non-profit organisations are the biggest employment sector—they provide about 80 million full-time and part-time jobs—but nonetheless there are about 100 000 non-profit organisations in Australia. About 45% of them are charities.

Management in these organisations has traditionally been regarded as a labour of love, and has not usually attracted the same scrutiny as management in industry and commerce. Many of the non-profit groups will continue to use many volunteer workers, but the attitude to management skills and accountability is changing. The US management theorist Peter Drucker says that in the past non-profit organisations believed they did not have to pay much attention to management because they did not have a bottom line. But increasingly, he says, they are finding they have to manage well—precisely because they lack the discipline of the bottom line. 'They are learning that good intentions, of themselves, only *spawn bureaucracy*,' he says.

It has also become evident that the non-profits have some lessons for business. Drucker says non-profit groups are more money conscious than businesses, because money is always difficult to raise and they always have less than they need. Drucker says they overcome this by focusing on a mission. 'Non-profits start with the environment, the community, the customers-to-be,' he says. 'They do not, as American businesses tend to do, start with the inside, that is, with the organisation or the financial returns.'

Ian Hook, the executive director of the Arthritis Foundation of Western Australia, says non-profit organisations are becoming more important because of a trend by governments to devolve an increasing degree of authority to them. This has changed their nature, he says. 'More than ever, accountability, performance monitoring and effective management become strategic issues facing non-profits and, consequently, the pressure is on all aspects of the executive leadership,' he says.

What, then, are the usual stages in the growth of a non-profit organisation? Peter Lonsdale, general manager of the Asthma Foundation of Queensland, says that although a non-profit organisation should in principle be managed along the same lines as a business, in practice the two tend to have differing growth patterns. 'The growth of the organisation is often not accompanied by the growth of perception in the people who are involved in it,' he says. 'People are sometimes committed to such an extent that they don't want to let go; that can happen at executive level as well.' Hook says non-profit organisations often go through a predictable five-stage cycle: creative, conflict, crisis, negotiated conciliation and trust.

He says the creative phase typically involves group participation, in which energy is focused on forming the vision, aims and forms of the organisation. Then comes the conflict phase, during which the organisation is perceived to have lost direction. 'The attempt to delegate the vision of where the organisation should go results in a competition between the process thinkers and the visionaries, who feel the organisation is losing impetus,' he says. 'This usually leads to a crisis. The competing perspectives become sectional, and factional debates usually result in friendships being destroyed.'

Hook says the organisation can then go in one of three directions. It can split, it can return to the creative stage, or it can begin to work towards a resolution. He says returning to the creative stage simply means an organisation repeats the previous stages. In the short term, the visionaries bring back the impetus, but they do not have the staying power, and the same problems return.

There can only be a resolution if the organisation moves to negotiation and conciliation. Hook says the corporate plan usually needs to be reworked or created, and a new vision needs to be established. 'It is possible at this stage that the membership could rise and fire the whole board because of a dissatisfaction with the process,' he says. 'Grieved visionaries in particular may choose this process.' If the organisation survives this process, Hooks says the final stage is trust. He says this usually involves a strategic plan for the organisation. Management authority is delegated and there are criteria for the evaluation of employee performance.

None of these changes is made without considerable resistance within the organisation. Hook says the difficulty with any voluntary organisation is that the people involved have a personal commitment to the cause. Hook says this means that debates are often defended on a personal level rather than on the issues. There is also potential for burn-out on a massive scale. He says the job of the chief executive is to remain detached from the debate and to concentrate on implementing the decisions of the organisation. 'People commit themselves and their ideology to the issues, then fight a campaign of such personal value that it burns them out completely,' Hook says. 'It is not unusual to have significant players within a non-profit organisation withdraw completely after they have lost a debate, leaving the organisation with great hurt and hatred.'

Who are the typical players in the non-profit organisation? Hook says the behaviour is fundamentally tribal. For example, each organisation will usually have a 'tribal chief'. This is an informal leader, who is acknowledged as an authority. The 'authority figures' in organisations are recognised by the fact that everyone heeds them when they speak. 'My experience is that tribal chiefs often do not fully understand their role within the organisation, and consequently corrupt the leadership by not taking true and proper counsel from the executive leadership,' he says. 'Any executive leadership that does not brief the tribal chieftain before going public, or does not take time to keep the tribal chief happy, is going against the power base of the organisation.'

Hook says the organisation will also typically have a 'tribal witchdoctor'. This person is the ceremonial leader and the custodian of traditions. Hook says the chief executive can use this person to defuse conflict, depoliticise debates and gain commitment in times of difficulty. 'Within a board debate, the tribal witchdoctor offers a human view of the issues and, if well briefed by the chief executive, can be used to take the venom out of many issues.' Hook also defines what he calls the 'opinion leaders' in an organisation. These are resident specialists who are considered by the tribe to be qualified and competent, assessing the issues and describing them to the tribe. Hook says the chief executive must know who influences opinions in the organisation, and should learn to stage-manage some issues so that the issues come to the board as suggestions by the opinion leaders.

Finally, Hook says, non-profit organisations will usually have an 'elder statesperson', someone respected by the tribe for what he or she has contributed, and who can become the closest confidant of the chief executive. If the opportunity provides, the elder statesperson will explain the traditions, background, personality conflicts, restructuring and other events in the history of the organisation. 'These are necessary lessons for the chief executive to learn in order to interpret the power games in the organisation,' Hook says.

Much of the success or failure of a non-profit organisation rests on the ability and skills of the chief executive, according to Hook. He says the chief executive's role is to stand between the organisation and the staff, ensuring that there is no interference in day-to-day management, and implementing regular reporting mechanisms. The selection of the chief executive, Hook says, must be based on the 'tribal chief's' understanding of the role, or conflict will develop quickly. 'I am aware of non-profit organisations in Australia where the tribal chieftain, often the board chairman, believes he is the day-to-day chief executive of the organisation and the appointed chief executive is simply a secretary. In these situations, an outside counsellor is needed.'

More crucial is the balance between the board and the chief executive. Drucker says the relationship between the board and chief executive is more dynamic in non-profit organisations than it is in business. 'Precisely because the non-profit board is so committed and active, its relationship with the chief executive tends to be highly contentious and full of potential for friction,' he says. 'Non-profit chiefs complain that their board "meddles". The directors, in turn, complain that the chief executive "usurps" the board's function. It is the main cause of guerilla warfare in the non-profit institution.'

Drucker and Hook have firm opinions about the ideal structure of the board of a non-profit organisation. Drucker says: 'I have rarely seen strong boards in co-ops, where the boards are elected by the membership. The chairperson has no say about who sits on the board, nor has the CEO. Problems are likely to arise on these boards, sometimes from troublemakers who abuse the board to create a political platform for themselves or just to hear themselves talk.'

Hook says the board of a charity organisation should not draw any of its members from the group of people who benefit from the organisation. 'A board filled with parents of children who are the benefactors of the organisation, or who are themselves afflicted by the problem being addressed, can skew the debate of the organisation towards their particular interests,' he says. 'They fight harder, they die harder, they hang on tenaciously to their position and they can corrupt the workings of the board because they lack objectivity. The same should apply to the senior management. Over the door of every non-profit board should be placed a sign clearly stating that board membership is not power, it is responsibility. There is no reward, there is little recognition, there is just service to those whom the organisation is assisting. It is not a place for grandstanding or power mongering.'

Lonsdale says the chief executive's role is to make suggestions about board membership, but says the recruitment of the board should be the board's responsibility. He also believes there should be board members who have direct personal involvement in the issue. 'Saying that people with arthritis shouldn't be on the board of an arthritis foundation is wrong: they are precisely the sort of people you want. They are the creative people you need.'

Why, then, can non-profit organisations prove so productive? Certainly, traditional methods of analysing incentive and the relationship between payment and output do not suffice. Few businesses, for example, would be able to attract voluntary labour in the manner of a non-profit organisation. Drucker says a crucial advantage possessed by non-profit organisations is the ability to provide clear goals. He argues that this makes the establishment of accountability measures and career structures crucial. He says there is a warning for business in the popularity of non-profit organisations.

'The students in the programme for senior and middle-level executives in which I teach work in a variety of businesses, but most of them also serve voluntarily in non-profits,' he says. 'When I ask them why they do it, far too many give the answer: "Because in my job there isn't much challenge, not enough achievement, not enough responsibility; and there is no mission, there is only expediency".'

Hook says non-profit organisations maintain many of the essential strands of community in an increasingly depersonalised urban environment. 'All too often, the environment in which we work is emotional, sectarian and sensitive, yet, at the same time, we still get a great deal done,' he says.

Lonsdale says the success of non-profit organisations demonstrates that there is greater scope in industry for motivating people through an improved demonstration of leadership skills. 'Non-profits have shown what can be done with a vision: a world without asthma or arthritis or hunger,' he says. I believe industry could achieve something similar, although I accept that it is a lot harder. But I think motivation is something we have to relearn. We need to go back to looking at people. Thinking of them as "human resources", for example, is absurd. Who says we are human resources? We are people who make things happen, not resources like land or capital. That kind of view is a totally wrong concept.'

Reproduced with permission from *BRW*, Australia's leading business magazine, 24 April, 1992, pp. 85-87.

Questions

1. Identify the key constituent groups of non-profit organisations. (In some texts these may be referred to as 'publics' or 'stakeholders'.)
2. In what ways do these constituent groups differ from profit-oriented organisations?
3. What are the implications of these differences for effective marketing by non-profit organisations.

Note: Students may find it helpful to review the article 'What Business Can Learn from Non-profits', by Peter Drucker in *Harvard Business Review*, July–August 1989, pp. 88–93.

Case 12—The globalisation of Fosters

by Alan Kilgore and Terry Alchin

Elders IXL had planned to put Fosters beer into Europe from a British base such as Watney, Mann & Truman, or Courage, or Scottish & Newcastle, or Grand Metropolitan. Elders used various techniques to establish itself in Britain and this case reviews these techniques. They include licensing, direct investment and takeovers. In addition Elders is penetrating the North American market through its merger with the giant Canadian brewer Molson. Elders IXL (or Fosters Brewing as it is now named) is fast becoming one of the main players in the international brewing game and has moved to being the world's fourth largest brewer in 1991.

Introduction

In the summer of 1839, Alexander Lang Elder set sail from the Scottish port of Kirkcaldy for a new colony of South Australia. His ship, the 89-ton schooner *Minerva*, carried a mixed cargo of the materials required by hardy pioneers developing a farming-based economy. On arrival in what was to become Port Adelaide, Alexander hung up a single shingle: 'A. L. Elder, General and Commission Agent'. From this simple basis was built Australia's largest farm service organisation, and now one of the world's foremost brewers. Elders IXL was also a major processor and trader of agricultural commodities worldwide, a successful merchant bank, and through Elders Resources NZFP, a significant participant in resource industries. More than 150 years later, the company is still successfully satisfying customer needs.

The origins of the Elders IXL company in its present form can be traced back to 1972. John Elliott and his management team merged with Henry Jones IXL and in 1981 eventually assumed overall control. John Elliott as managing director, turned the then ailing and lacklustre Tasmanian jam maker Henry Jones IXL, with falling market share and poor financial performance, into a highly successful company. Sales increased five-fold and pre-tax profits increased dramatically from $1.5 million in 1972 to $56.6 million in 1981. Elliott transformed the company into Elders IXL: a brewing, agribusiness, resources and finance empire with annual sales of $14.1 billion in only 18 years. In 1983, the acquisition of Carlton and United Breweries (CUB) was Elders IXL's first major venture into the alcoholic beverage industry. This takeover included the acquisition of the already successful beer brand Fosters.

The principal activities of the Elders group for 1989–1990 were the brewing and marketing of beer; the provision of agency and other services to wool, meat and other primary producers; the processing and trading of agricultural commodities; and the provision of financial services and investment in forestry and paper operations, metals recycling, coal and gold mining, oil and gas ventures and trading of mineral commodities. Of these activities the brewing, pastoral, and finance were considered to be core activities. These function were undertaken under the various divisions such as Elders Resources Limited, Elders Brewing, Elders Pastoral, Elders International and Elders Finance.

The structure was decentralised and semi-autonomous with the central management exercising control over finance and accounting matters. This was a strong feature of Elders IXL making it the market leader in its fields. The management philosophy in Elders IXL was such that economies of scale through market leadership create further business success. This was illustrated by Elders' building up to a 48% share of the Australian beer market, 48% of Australia's wool production, 68% of domestic sheep sales and a 29% share of Australian cattle sales in 1989.

Management objectives

Some of Elders IXL's management objectives were:

(i) to maintain market leadership in Australia in each of the core businesses through internal growth and acquisition;
(ii) progressively to internationalise the company to provide real growth opportunities in markets which provide attractive returns;
(iii) to remain entrepreneurial and opportunistic in building investment stakes and capturing opportunities that arise, particularly those related to the core businesses.

The decision to internationalise

These management objectives generated the globalisation of Fosters. In addition the following factors contributed to Elders IXL's decision to expand overseas from a home base in Australia where Elders IXL holds a majority of beer sales.

Firstly, since the mid-1970s the Australian beer market has shown a steady decline in per capita beer consumption which has been parallelled by a growing interest in locally produced wine and increased spirit consumption especially by younger drinkers. Table B4.1 shows the most recent picture of decline in Australian beer consumption.

Table B4.1 *Apparent per capita beer consumption (litres) in Australia*

	Low-alcohol beer	Other	Total beer
1985–86	12.7	102.8	115.5
1986–87	11.5	99.8	111.3
1987–88	12.1	98.7	110.8
1988–89	16.4	96.7	113.1
1989–90p	18.8	92.8	111.6
1990–91p	19.6	88.5	108.2

p = preliminary figures

Source: Australian Bureau of Statistics, Apparent consumption of selected foodstuffs, Australia, 1991–92 Preliminary, Table 2, p. 3, 4315.0

Secondly, as might be expected the Australian beer market, being a very mature and fairly saturated one, exhibits a seasonal swing. On past experience the variation between peak and trough does not normally exceed 15 to 20% of average annual production. Expansion overseas, especially to the Northern Hemisphere, could help to level out overall consumption.

Thirdly, there is increased competition and a slow rate of growth in the Australian market. Thus for Elders IXL who held about 40% of the saturated Australian market to achieve its minimum projected requirement of 18 to 20% return after tax and maintain its market share, expansion was required overseas.

Elders Brewing had another successful year in 1989 with domestic sales up just under 2% while the overall beer market was static. This sales growth increased Carlton's market share to approximately 50%. The continued success of Foster's Light, Australia's leading light beer, and Victoria Bitter have been the major contributors to this sales growth.

The acquisition of Matilda Bay Brewing Company in May 1990 provided Elders with a base to compete effectively in the important Western Australian market. The company's major brand is Redback, which is growing rapidly in the expanding boutique beer market. As well, Fosters Brewing continued its high profile marketing activities in Australia with the Fosters Australian Grand Prix and the Fosters Melbourne Cup.

The restructuring of Elders IXL

1990 was a year of substantial change in direction for Elders IXL. In March 1990 Elders IXL announced a reconstruction of the company into a single purpose international brewing company called Fosters Brewing and the divestment of non-brewing interests. This was partially due to peculiar internal tensions. John Elliott became non-executive chairman.

The 1989–90 Elders IXL Annual Report gave four reasons for this restructuring decision. Firstly, equity markets were downgrading conglomerates and this process was expected to continue. Secondly, single purpose companies with lower gearing were increasingly favoured by equity markets. Thirdly, the company had significant low yielding investments which were adversely affecting earnings of Elders Finance as a non-bank financial institution. Fourthly, the economic and financial environment was not conducive to the continued operation of Elders Finance as a non-bank financial institution.

Considerable progress has been made on this restructuring. The sale of non-brewing assets to 30 June 1990 exceeded $1.6 billion and, in addition, the gross assets of Elders Finance Group were reduced from $5.9 billion to $2.7 billion. In addition to the reduction of Elders Finance Group assets, the company has disposed of its shareholdings in Elders Resources NZFP Limited, Scottish & Newcastle Breweries PLC, AFP Group PLC and the company's grain businesses in North America. Elders IXL sold its interest in SA Brewing which it had acquired in 1981 when Elders IXL bought a 19.9% stake to fortify the fellow brewer's register after widespread concern about a raider. Since the date of the reconstruction announcement the directors of Elders IXL have responded to changing circumstances and have made a number of alterations to the original plan, particularly as a consequence of deteriorating economic conditions in Australia and the resultant uncertainty of financial markets.

Elders IXL was unable to arrange the float of Agribusiness, but maintained its plans for the sale of the wool, meat, and brewing materials divisions. In 1991 Elders IXL sold 55% of Australian Meat Holdings to Nebraska-based Canogra for $300 million. Interestingly in April 1992 the remaining 45% is estimated at around only $58 million. Part of this decline has resulted from being attached to the 'badly muddied' Elders brand name and the consequential reduction in intangibles associated with the name. The pastoral business will be retained and the possible return of prosperity to the agricultural sector and the implementation of rationalisation programmes should restore the profitability of this business. When conditions in the agricultural sector, and improvements in the profitability of the pastoral operations become evident, the directors will seek an appropriate long-term shareholding structure for the pastoral business. In 1991 the pastoral business reported losses of $37.6 million and for the first half of 1992 losses totalled $9.4 million. There were also doubts about the rural land portfolio assets valuations in the cyclical rural slump in Australia.

As well, it has been difficult to sell a number of Elders Finance businesses as going concerns, resulting in increased costs where businesses have instead been closed or wound down. An example is Elders IXL's inability to sell the property business (Lensworth) of Elders Finance. This business will be retained until an improvement in the Australian property market facilitates its sale at an acceptable value.

Elders IXL and the UK

Watney, Mann & Truman Ltd

In 1984 Watney Mann & Truman (Watney) signed an exclusive 15-year manufacturing licence with Elders IXL to produce Fosters. At that time Watney owned around 6500 pubs and Elders IXL saw this as an initial means of penetrating the UK lager market.

Elders IXL decided to licence the manufacture of Fosters because it seemed advantageous to produce in the host country, as opposed to the disadvantages of shipping. In Britain in 1983 the average price of imported Australian beer was 43p per litre, as compared with 25p for West German imports and 14p for Irish imported beer.

Many companies licence their products in overseas markets because they are reluctant to make direct investments abroad and are unable to service foreign markets via exports, thus finding an attractive alternative in the use of licensing. This can be seen to be consistent with Elders IXL's actions at the time of the Watney's licensing contract. The 15-year contract showed that Elders IXL was committed further than just an initial market penetration trial.

As an alternative to licensing Elders IXL would have preferred to have full control over its operations but in this case Elders IXL had to pass over trade information that normally would be kept secret. This data had to be disclosed in order that the product would be produced in the same manner that the customers and prospective customers would expect.

Allied-Lyons PLC

In 1985 Elders IXL decided to further pursue their interests in the UK beer market through direct investment. They decided on this approach because Elders IXL wanted 'to get much more control from the market end on a lot of the products we handle ... to build a much greater control over the operations right through from production to sales'.

This process of acquiring a brewery in the UK presented an arduous and time-consuming task, which ultimately resulted in a highly successful venture for Elders IXL. The initial move in February 1985, by Elders IXL to establish their own brewing facilities in the UK was by way of share purchases in the UK giant brewer, Allied-Lyons (Allied). Allied-Lyons in February 1988 had 13% of the ale market and 16% of the lager market which provided it with 14% of the total market, just behind Bass at 21%. As well, Allied-Lyons had 2010 managed (about 16% of all managed) pubs and 4861 tenanted (about 15% of all tenanted) pubs giving a total of 6871 pubs (about 15% of all pubs).

By August 1985, Elders IXL had already obtained 5% of Allied capital costing about $55 million. In September 1985 Elders IXL made a bid for Allied of $4 billion which at that time was the biggest takeover bid in UK history. Allied at the time were not interested in being taken over by the Australian brewer. Allied attempted to place obstacles in the path of Elders IXL. The first was by taking a controlling interest of 51% in the Canadian liquor company, Harim Walker Spirits, to help head off any new bid from Elders IXL.

The takeover battle was taken to the press through advertisements from both corporation, Allied and Elders IXL. The second phase in Allied's attempt to present obstacles for Elders IXL's takeover included statements proclaiming Allied's long established history with household name brands and steeply increasing profits. They claimed that Elders IXL were 'aussie upstarts'. Elders IXL retorted these claims with advertisements stating the success of the Fosters launch in Britain and Elders IXL's association with internationally known companies, and how these were examples of their 'energetic youth'. Elders IXL also claimed that the Allied management were unsuccessful and uninspired.

A further obstacle for Elders IXL in their Allied takeover bid was the referral of the proposed takeover to the Monopolies and Mergers Commission (MMC). This investigation began in December 1985 and continued for several months. During this time Elders IXL were blocked officially from completing their bid for Allied.

While Elders IXL waited for the MMC decision, expectations on the British stockmarket grew and grew. As a result and views that the Elders IXL takeover was imminent, the Allied shares rose sharply, and for Elders IXL to obtain Allied they would have had to have found $7.54 billion compared to the original bid of $4 billion. The Allied chairman was quoted as saying, with reference to the Elders IXL bid, 'Let them come, we are not out of reach. But it is going to be pretty expensive for Elders IXL, or anyone else to bid for Allied now. That is the only true defence we have ever had'. As a result of the increased share price, Elders IXL sold their entire 5% stake in Allied. This resulted in a profit of $90 million.

In September 1986 the Monopolies and Mergers Commission cleared the Elders IXL purchase of Allied and gave a glowing testimonial for its management. However Elders IXL declined to buy due to the high price of Allied's shares.

Courage

Due to the referral of the Allied bid to the Monopolies Commission Elders IXL investigated another way of penetrating the UK beer market. Courage emerged as a possibility because the Courage breweries were already modern and efficient and could quickly adapt production to changes in demand. Of the three breweries, the Bristol and the Tadcaster ones had just been renovated at a cost of £21 million and the third, the one at Reading, is considered to be Britain's most efficient. Courage then had about 9% of the market.

Elders IXL decided to bid for Courage and met with competition from the Bond Corporation, Phillip Morris, and Scottish & Newcastle (S&N) Brewers. The bidding battle was fierce. Elders IXL thought it had sewn up the deal at least two weeks before the final announcement, but competition had risen from strong interest being shown by the US giant brewer Anheuser-Busch which produces Budweiser beer.

In September 1986 Elders IXL made a successful bid for Courage of £1.3 billion from the property group the Hanson Trust making Elders the eighth largest brewer in the world. Mr Elliott said: "Elders IXL had decided to go for Courage because of the price and the relative ease with which the company could be acquired . . . Courage would be used as a spring-board for Elders IXL's expansion in the UK and Europe". Courage had extensive beer, wine and spirits interests and was Britain's sixth largest brewer, accounting for about 9% of the British beer market at the time. It had three breweries and 5000 tied estate pubs located in London and the south of England. In 1985 Courage had made £86.7 million in pre-tax profit.

To finance the purchase of Courage, Elders IXL raised £1 billion in a syndicated facility with 22 banks for three years. The facility was to be repaid through a special first mortgage backed security. The second part of the funding was accomplished through a convertible bond issue which was the second largest bond issue made in the world. It totalled over $700 million and was made in four different currencies. The convertible bond issue allowed Elders IXL to fund $700 million worth of debt at a price of less than 5%. Bond holders had the right to convert into Elders IXL' shares at a price of $6 per share at any time in the next 12 years.

To reduce the debt incurred in the Courage takeover, Elders IXL proposed to float a company called Courage Pub Company (PubCo). The arrangement being for PubCo to purchase the real estate from the publicans and list as a public company. This would enable Elders IXL to keep the tie on their pubs whilst giving publicans the opportunity to take an ownership position. Elders IXL would retain one-third of PubCo and offer the remaining shares to the publicans, and then to the public. In this way Elders IXL could reduce its debt by £900 million and the publicans could have the benefit of dividend payments and profits through sale of shares which would increase in value with the proposed real estate revaluation every three years.

However, the stock market crash in 1987, along with the British Government's privatisation programme, forced Elders IXL to review its strategy to float PubCo. The crash would have made the listing price too low, thus not covering the £900 million required. Also the share-paper glut on the London stock market, a consequence of the British privatisation programme, made floating of PubCo no longer a viable solution.

So Elders IXL decided on a joint venture with Hudson Conway to set up PubCo which was an incarnation of the original proposal to sell the pubs to the tenants. Hudson Conway, a Melbourne-based property developer of whom Elders Investments own 32%, gets 50% of one of the biggest pub estates in Britain for an actual outlay of only $50 million. Elders IXL put in $345 million in preference shares and the rest of the cash came from banks such as Citibank and First Boston. This joint venture released over £900 million to Elders IXL and allowed control of the tied pub estate to be retained. Elders IXL have given Hudson Conway what amounts to a money-back guarantee in the form of a 'put' option. If Hudson Conway is dissatisfied with the deal in five years time, it can oblige Elders IXL to buy it out at cost plus a satisfactory return.

The manufacturing licence Elders IXL signed with Watney still had 13 years to run when Elders IXL purchased Courage. Watney wanted £150 million to end the contract early, Elders IXL was however able to establish a deal with Watney to share the brewing of Fosters. The arrangement would double the number of pubs that Fosters is sold through, as Courage operates 5000 pubs and Watney operate 6500 pubs. Watney will still however have the sole rights to sell Fosters in packaged form to the entire UK off-licence trade until 1996.

Courage continues to put up a good trading performance with volumes up 7.2% in 1989 over the previous year and the company improving market share to 10%. The financial performance of Courage has been depressed by continuing high interest rates in the United Kingdom and subsidies paid to the PubCo joint venture.

Courage became principal sponsor of the British Grand Prix under the Fosters brand name and a new and high profile advertising campaign was aired for Fosters Lager in 1989.

Greene King

In October 1987 Elders IXL purchased a 5% stake in the UK brewing company Greene King. Greene King was chosen due to their 770 pubs situated in the East Anglia region which is one of the fastest growing economic regions in Britain, and represented no overlap on Elders IXL's existing distribution of Fosters. A 5% stake was not enough to coerce Greene King into distributing Fosters throughout its tied estate. However, by December Elders IXL had acquired a 13% stake in Greene King which was more than enough to secure the further distribution of Fosters.

Scottish & Newcastle

During 1986 Elders IXL planned the takeover of S&N in an $3.4 billion deal to give Elders IXL more than one-fifth of the British beer market and to become at the time the second largest in Britain behind Bass which controlled about 22% of the British market.

One of the major strategic reasons for the takeover was that S&N had a stronghold in the north of England and Scotland where S&N has 1820 pubs and has around 10% of the total ale and lager market in the whole United Kingdom through its major beers, including McEwans Export and Newcastle Brown. These areas are where Elders IXL had few pubs and where the flagship Fosters sold poorly. This is mainly due to the fact that 90% of Courage pubs are located in London and the south of England.

In reaction to the latest Elders IXL bid, the attempted takeover of S&N was referred to the MMC and in early April 1989 the MMC presented its findings to the British Department of Trade and Industry (DTI) secretary Lord Young, who announced that the bid was not acceptable to the 'public interest' of the British people.

The MMC considered that the merger would reduce consumer choice and competition between brands and reduce competition for the supply of beer to the free trade and off-licenses. As a result, the report announced a number of planned measures to loosen breweries' control over Britain's retail beer trade, after finding that a 'complex monopoly situation' exists in the supply of beer. Paramount among these measures would be limiting to 2000 the number of public houses any single brewer could own.

This measure alone could force the sale of 3000 of the 5000 pubs owned by Elders IXL and by Hudson Conway through PubCo. If the latter pubs are deemed to belong to Elders IXL, this could also attract MMC attention, with the possibility that these pubs may be put on the market, thus limiting the potential for capital growth.

The DTI announced that it planned to bar breweries from issuing new low-interest loans to independent public houses in exchange for an exclusive contract to supply them. Tied pubs, representing about 55% of a total of about 82 000 public houses, are to sell only those beers that are supplied by the breweries which own the pubs. The remaining 45% of pubs, the so-called 'free houses', may buy beer wholesale from any supplier.

The DTI has also demanded that Elders IXL reduce its current 23.6% shareholding to 9.9%. Elders IXL had built up its holding since early 1988 when it had initially purchased 3% at the time that Anheuser-Busch had purchased 2%. The American purchase was a signal to S&N that relations with a long-time ally would continue.

Elders IXL was also required to sell to buyers vetted by the S&N board. The UK Office of Fair Trading has made it clear it will supervise Elder's disposal of its shareholding and intervene if it does not like the buyers the company finds. The most obvious candidates would be off-shore brewers, someone like Anheuser-Busch or a European brewer. There could also be interest from companies interested in cash flow such as industrial conglomerates like the Hanson Trust.

These edicts, and the removal of the theoretical 'floor price' the proposed Elders IXL bid had placed under S&N, sent the Edinburgh brewer's price into a tail-spin thus placing Elders IXL in an invidious position if and when it sought to comply with the DTI edict.

Based on share purchase disclosures in the original Elder's offer document and supplementary share buying, Elders IXL had about $750 million invested in its 23.6% shareholding in S&N. After the slump in S&N's share price that stake is worth considerably less, leaving Elders IXL staring at a paper loss of nearly $100 million and the unenviable task of having to scale down its holding in a retreating market. S&N has since announced that it had spent $12.69 million in fighting the takeover bid but more interesting to the executives of Elders IXL is the continued insistence by S&N executives that they had not ruled out the possibility of buying the Elders IXL's share of S&N.

The share price of S&N jumped late in April 1989 on rumours that Elders IXL had found a buyer for its 23.6% stake of S&N. According to signals from the UK stockmarket, Elders IXL was on the brink of selling the stake to United Breweries (UB) of Denmark as a result of the MMC's decision on S&N earlier that year. UB, which brews Carlsberg and Tuborg lager, felt that its contract with Grandmet to brew under licence in the United Kingdom deserved at least some support. A deal with S&N would help strengthen Carlsberg in its UK-brewing role but even if UB declines the Elders IXL offer there would be no shortage of buyers including Japan's Kirin Brewery Co Ltd, the Dutch brewer, Heineken NV, and the huge US brewer, Anheuser-Busch.

It was not until March 1990 that Elders IXL finally placed its 23.7% stake in S&N for $530 million. The sale of almost 88 million shares was broken up among institutions who stand to make tidy profits as they purchased their shares at 290p a share and this price bounced to 307p after the sale. The S&N shares were the last vestiges of the aborted takeover bid for S&N. The sale represented a loss for Elders IXL of more than £90 million.

The sale of the S&N shares finally cleared the way for Elders IXL to proceed with its elaborate expansion plans in British brewing with Grandmet.

Grand Metropolitan

Elders IXL then turned its attention to closer alliances with the British brewer Grand Metropolitan (Grandmet) which brews its own brands such as Ruddles and as well produces other brands under licence. It also owns about 5000 hotels. Grandmet has continually argued that both British and international brewing were set for a period of rationalisation. This is in complete agreement with comments from Elders IXL who believe that beer companies of the future will either be large international corporations or smaller niche players and that there would be no room for operators with the size of Grandmet's brewing interests.

Early in 1989 there had been informal talks between the then Elders IXL chief, John Elliott, and Grandmet chairman Sheppard. Both leaders are known to believe in the merits of further concentration in the British brewing industry. These early discussions occurred about a 'wide range' of possible deals involving Elders IXL's Courage brewing interests and the Watney & Truman brewing operations of Grandmet. Grandmet already brews Fosters Lager under licence in Britain and imports Fosters into the United States through its Allbrands subsidiary. But neither company would enter into any formal agreement until they knew the final outcome of the MMC's investigation of Elders IXL's bid for S&N.

Elders IXL formally announced its deal with Grandmet in which Elders IXL has swapped some of its 5000 hotels for ownership of all of Grandmet's four British breweries. Elders IXL was very keen to acquire the Mortlake Brewery which currently makes Fosters under licence. United Breweries of Denmark had been eager to acquire the Halifax facility where its Carlsberg beer is brewed by Grandmet under a similar agreement. By offloading its breweries, Grandmet could keep full control of its 5000 hotels and gain the outlets from Courage. Elders IXL wanted the four breweries to step up its production of Fosters in Britain.

The joint-venture company, Intrepreneur (IEL), with assets valued at £2.8 billion, would be formed by the two companies to operate nearly 5000 Courage pubs and 3500 Grandmet pubs. The proposal would enable Courage to expand its brewing activities in the UK as part of the planned launch of Foster's Brewing in the UK and Europe and enable Grandmet to quit brewing and concentrate on retailing.

The Elders IXL-Grandmet transaction involving two of the big six British brewers was the first deal since Lord Young in the 1989 MMC decision on S&N gave them a 'new world' for brewers to become used to. This superdeal consists of spinning off one giant brewer and an amalgamation of a huge property venture. This industry restructuring appears to be agreeable to both parties. There was a prototype deal in late 1989 with Lord Young in mind when the regional brewer Boddington auctioned its real ale to Whitbread to concentrate on retailing but that involved only $109 million compared with the billions of this deal.

An obvious side effect of cutting a superdeal is that the attention of the UK Office of Fair Trading is attracted. The Grandmet-Elders IXL plans, as the first substantial response to the 1989 Monopolies and Mergers Commission industry recommendations, look especially ripe for referral to that body. The OFT focused on forbidding 'the creation of a second major beer group which, together with Bass, would control over 40% of the supply of beer' when it scotched Elders IXL's bid for Scottish & Newcastle in May 1989.

There may be even greater problems in the Intrepreneur Estates joint venture and its 8500 public houses. Even though 3500 of those pubs have to be freed, Intrepreneur's initial regional concentration in some areas will make the OFT uncomfortable. The venture will own three in every ten pubs in London.

Reflecting their diverging objectives, Grandmet and Elders IXL have been running their estates quite differently since 1986. Grandmet, with its flair for property management, has been building its managed estate and paring its tenancies down to a core of 3500 premium sites. Almost 2000 of its 3500 pubs have been 'incentivised' under its Intrepreneur's scheme, which offers tenants a 20-year lease and 'freed' trade in wine and spirits if they agree to sell a minimum barrelage and do their own repairs.

In contrast, Elders IXL, the brewer, 'parked' its pubs off-balance sheet and set about unloading its managed houses on to tenants. There has, in fact, been relatively little 'weeding'. PubCo was notorious in the industry for spending very little on capital improvements.

These different approaches have two consequences. Grandmet's tenancies will more than likely go into the new venture at a higher value. At the same time Elders IXL pubs will be of a less uniform quality because many of them were once superior managed houses turned over to tenants. If surplus pubs have to be shed, Intrepreneur Estate's manager, Grandmet Estates has had practice in that it had sold some 1000 of its parent's expendable outlets in the past year.

The partners, in fact, do seem to have significant rationalisation on their minds. Considering the recent decline in pub prices they have been placing a relatively high £320 000 unit value on the properties, which suggests more than a few of the smaller pubs will be turned into cash pretty quickly. As these were always likely to struggle with the rise in rents that is facing the industry under the new 'commercialisation' of leases under the *Landlord and Tenant Act*, they will be no great sacrifice. Apart from their need to address OFT problems, both Grandmet and Elders IXL have a vested interest in shaking up the estate further. Operationally it means better pubs for higher rents. Under the Intrepreneur scheme so far, improved volumes and better trading from those outlets have been shown over the last two years.

Grandmet, like Elders IXL, already ran its Mortlake, Trowbridge and Halifax facilities at close to their rated capacity of 3.2 million barrels. So it is unlikely that Elders will tamper with the production mix of these facilities even though Elders has paid a high price of £375 million for them.

Its main initial impact there would seem to be that it just makes life a lot simpler. Elders IXL will, for the first time, control Fosters in the UK where ever since the Courage purchase it shared the honour. That had resulted in all sorts of anomalies, like the fact that Elders IXL has never been able to put Fosters Lager into its own can. Grandmet, although it shared Fosters Draught production with Courage in the UK, retained the exclusive right to make the canned lager for the take-home trade.

The proposal was referred to the MMC on 27 April 1990 by the former trade and industry secretary, Mr Nicholas Ridley, and its report was forwarded in August 1990. The director-general of the Office of Fair Trading, Sir Gordon Borrie, was asked to negotiate a new proposal with Courage and Grandmet by 18 November 1990.

The MMC report recommended that Courage and Grandmet should:

1. *Amend* the transaction by disposing of beer brands or brewing capacity to limit market share to no more than 15% from an estimated 40%.
2. *Release* an extra 1000 pubs from the tied supply agreements operated by Intrepreneur Estates Ltd (IEL) before November 1992 in addition to the 2000 required by law.
3. *Reduce* the period of the exclusive supply agreement from ten to five years.
4. *Cut* the proportion of pubs tied to Courage by 25% before November 1992.

Also, Courage made arrangements to ensure it does not control the voting rights from their 50% stake in IEL.

The initial rejection by British regulatory authorities of Elders IXL's deal with the drink group Grandmet was a 'significant blow' in terms of market sentiment. It was considered likely there had already been negotiations between the parties and the regulators, with a compromise unable to be found. This would explain the long delay in the release of the government's findings by the Secretary for Trade and Industry,

Mr Peter Lilley. With the Office of Fair Trading 'notoriously unfriendly to this deal', common ground was considered to be hard to find.

Trade and Industry Secretary, Mr Peter Lilley, said he would approve the then deal if the exclusive beer supply deal was cut to five years and other terms, including the release of an extra 1067 pubs from the tied beer supply deal and the foreshadowed restriction on its market share to 15%, were met. Elders IXL had already said it could do three of the five conditions specified ahead of the announcement of the findings in the UK. The major sticking point was the cutting of the exclusive supply arrangements from ten years to five. Elders IXL considers that the deal is obviously not ideal but it was at least part of the freeing up of the brewing and pubs market in the UK.

Besides meeting the British Government's terms, Elders IXL and Grandmet will have to renegotiate their original cash-neutral deal to reflect the modifications. The shortening of the exclusive beer supply contract will cut the value of Grandmet's offerings.

Grandmet chairman Sheppard considered that the final restructuring will be both financially attractive and strategically beneficial to both Courage (Elders IXL) and themselves and, of course, ultimately in the UK 'public interest'. This results from the build-up by Elders IXL of a portfolio of brands in the UK which would be crucial once the market became untied as it has recently.

The deal would mean that profits would, however, increase significantly because Elders IXL could unwind PubCo, ending expensive subsidies to the joint venture controlling Courage's pubs. That deal had disadvantaged Elders IXL because Elders IXL had to subsidise the interest by 100% (at a cost of £45 million in 1990). If there is sharing of the subsidy then Elders IXL is immediately better off. Mr Lilley said that suggested alterations to the original proposal by Courage and Grandmet had gone some way to meeting the Government's concerns but did not go far enough.

The pubs-for-breweries swap between Courage Ltd, the Elders IXL brewing arm in the UK, and Grandmet was finally approved on 19 November 1990 by the UK Secretary for Trade and Industry. This was after substantial modifications to the original proposal were taken and certain undertakings were negotiated with the UK Government.

The revisions to the original deal, which were negotiated with the UK Office of Fair Trading focus on a shorter (ten down to seven years) secured beer supply agreement between Courage and Grandmet and their joint operating company, Intrepreneur Estates Ltd (IEL) and terminate after four years the secured beer supply agreement between Courage and retail estates managed by Grandmet. As well, there is an undertaking that from 1 November 1992 the parties will have no more than 25% of pubs tied to Courage in any Petty Sessional Division and no more than 20% after four years.

The financial arrangements between Courage and Grandmet were renegotiated with some 'give' by Grandmet and some 'take' by Courage to compensate for the revised terms and conditions. The new deal means that Elders IXL will be able to proceed with the restructuring of its worldwide brewing operations under the new name, Fosters Brewing, which aims to expand its operations in Europe. As well, Grandmet will be able to finalise arrangements for restructuring of their interests.

During 1991 Courage effectively doubled its size by the acquisition of the Grandmet brewing operations. The pubs of the two companies were placed in a jointly owned property company called Intrepreneur Estates. Some 1100 Courage pubs are being sold, as is the former Grandmet Brewery at Trowbridge. These sales are part of the policy of Fosters to concentrate on the core business of brewing and marketing beer.

This mechanism would circumvent the 1989 MMC report that put a limit of 2000 tied pubs on all big brewers and allowed tied pubs to carry at least one independent brand. This was designed at reducing concentration among the so-called 'big six' brewers and providing greater competitive scope for the small regional and independent brewing companies.

The Canadian market

Elders IXL first entered the Canadian market through its purchase in April 1987 of Carling O'Keefe from Rothmans and public shareholders. At the time Carling was Canada's third largest brewer with a 23% share of the market and produced leading brands such as O'Keefe Ale and Carling Black Label. From this base Elders conducted a major deal with Molson Companies run by the Molson family, which had run the company since its founding almost 200 years ago and still retains control.

The relationship between Elders IXL and the diversified Molson companies was forged in July 1989, when, after six months of negotiations between chairman Cohen of Molson Companies and chief executive Bartels of Elders Brewing the merger of their Canadian brewing operations was announced. Elders' Carling O'Keefe was sold into Molson and in return, Elders IXL acquired half of the new joint venture company, Molson Breweries, which virtually overnight became the Canadian market leader in a difficult market.

As part of the strategic brewing alliance between the Canadian brewer, Molson and Elders IXL, Molson had taken a 6% ($C148 million) investment in Harlin Holdings Pty Ltd. This was in the form of direct equity and a guarantee for a note.

The advantages of such a deal to Molson are a little more difficult to pin down. But there is no doubt that Molson, or at least Cohen and his advisers, believe that taking the equity position in Elders offers more opportunities. But there are complications. One of these is the growing concern that Elders' preference shareholders in Canada could initiate legal action to ensure that they take part in any cash return to the ordinary shareholders. This is a vital part of the Harlin funding package, which requires that returns from the sale of Elders assets be distributed to shareholders. It is believed that legal precedent in Canada would support such an action. Elders Finance issued the preference shares in a $C400 million raising to finance the acquisition of the Carling O'Keefe brewing operation in 1987.

In forgoing these links Molson wanted to expand overseas and was interested in acquiring some of the Elders IXL concerns when they came up for purchase to so expand. But being able to afford to take advantage of it is another thing. Molson's 'war chest' is said to hold about $C1.4 billion, built from $C400 million in cash drawn from its brewing business in accordance with the merger agreement. This recognised the greater value of the Molson assets and provided for a future cash payment; $C300 million from an equity and unsecured floating note issue and the rest in potential borrowings. The company would need to boost its spending power greatly before it could take a big stake in Elders' brewing business.

Molson was interested in a deal that would give Molson a direct minority stake in Elders assets including Carlton in Australia and Courage in Britain. But, in the light of Elders' present strategy of selling all but its brewing operations, an investment in Elders IXL would do as well. It remains to be seen whether Elders' independent directors would be more inclined to accept a deal that left them with a reduced majority position in the brewing business.

Molson Breweries performed well in 1991 with production and sales volumes up and market share at over 52%. The merger process which created Molson Breweries has made significant progress and rationalisation benefits place the partnership in a sound position for future growth and profitability. This is a result of Molson Breweries holding 53% of the market at the formation date of 1 August 1989 and a planned three-year rationalisation and capital expenditure programme which is expected to result in considerable cost savings. These cost savings could occur because both individual brewers had excess capacity so that the 16 breweries of the joint venture will be reduced to nine with a reduction of the workforce by 20%.

One of the group, Molson USA, is strengthening its position and in 1991 is the second largest beer importer into the United States. The Fosters profile was further lifted in Canada and the US with sponsorship of the Foster's/Porsche Indy Car Team. It is interesting to note that in 1987 Elliott had had talks with the Busch family in the US who control around 15% of Anheuser-Busch with a plan for a joint venture to market Fosters in the US. The negative reaction that John Elliott received was predictable given that their company produced a lager that alone sold more than four times the total product of Elders.

During 1991 Molson completed the consolidation of its production activities. Breweries were closed in Montreal, Vancouver and Toronto achieving a more efficient infrastructure of nine breweries from the original 16 when the merger was completed in August 1989. Molson's strong performance was led by a marketing and sales emphasis on key major brands and introducing, in 1991, the first 0.5% alcohol beer in Canada. This new brand continues Molson's goal of offering consumers a range of high quality beers with different alcohol content.

Conclusions

Fosters has attained a 6% share of the lager market since arriving in the UK market seven years ago. When comparing this to the world's best-selling beer, Budweiser, the full impact of Fosters success can be recognised. In the four years since Anheuser-Busch of the US took Budweiser into the UK it has barely been able to attain a 1% share of the UK market.

The purchase of Courage has been one of Elders IXL's most successful acquisitions. Elders IXL purchased Courage for £1.35 billion. At the time of the Pub-Co deal the pubs were valued at just over this amount, meaning that Elders IXL acquired the brewing business of Courage for considerably less than its market value. This 100% ownership of Courage along with the 100% ownership of Carlton forms the basis of the corporate structure.

The Elders IXL move into the UK market appears systematic and well planned. This move was initiated by supporting their Fosters beer brand awareness through TV commercials featuring Paul Hogan. Fosters had been exported to the UK for some 30 years, and held a small percentage of the imported beer market. Elders IXL followed the internationalisation process, which in Elders IXL's case included exporting, licensing and eventually foreign direct investment.

Elders IXL's bid for Grandmet has been cleared by the British Department of Trade and Industry, opening up Elders IXL's entire European strategy after the decision on S&N had thrown the strategy into doubt. The S&N MMC ruling had ended Elders IXL's aspirations for control of the Edinburgh brewer and for achieving a 21% share of the British beer market, and was thought to jeopardise its long-term vision for expanding into Europe and floating its brewing operations as an independent company. The revised Grandmet deal allows this to go ahead.

Elders IXL had planned initially to play the European game post-1992, with S&N and Courage as its main stepping stones from potentially number one or two in the UK. Now Elders IXL has changed course towards becoming a major force in the European market by the acquisition of Grandmet and the possibility of becoming more involved with Holsten Breweries in the European Community.

In Europe the Courage export business grew in 1991 with Fosters enjoying growth in Southern Europe in Spain, Italy and Greece. Fosters has also obtained a strong selling position in Sweden after just two years. These grounds follow on from the historic agreement with Holsten Breweries in Germany where Holsten brewed Fosters to the standards of the Rheinheitsgebot from 1 September 1991. This is the first real agreement for a foreign international premium brand in one of the major beer markets in the world and certainly the largest beer market in Europe.

Questions

1. Summarise the cultural factors involved in the globalisation of Elders IXL.
2. As a marketing manager for Elders IXL, what would you have done differently?
3. Summarise the strategies that Elders IXL have used in their globalisation programme.

References
Australian Bureau of Statistics

Case 13—Marketing Drug Arm Brisbane

by Terry Gatfield

This case study builds on the material presented in 'Marketing the non-profit way' (section B6). The student should read that case to gain an understanding of the concepts and terminology used for examining the non-profit sector before attempting this case.

Drug Arm Brisbane

Drug Arm is a non-profit, Christian-based, drug and alcohol agency with 17 full-time and 4 part-time staff and about 750 volunteers who collectively contribute over 1400 hours to the work. It has bases in eight cities operating out of two states. The organisation has served Queensland for over 150 years with five name changes. Its mission statement is:

> To provide a vital ministry of compassion and caring through education, awareness, prevention and welfare services in the areas of alcohol and other drug use and misuse, solidly based on a Christian foundation.

Unlike most non-profit organisations Drug Arm provides an unusual cluster of services to the community, a very active lobbying process and a complex network of funding arrangements. Drug Arm is critically aware of the three separate sectors of donor publics, moderating publics and client publics. The network is illustrated in figure B4.1.

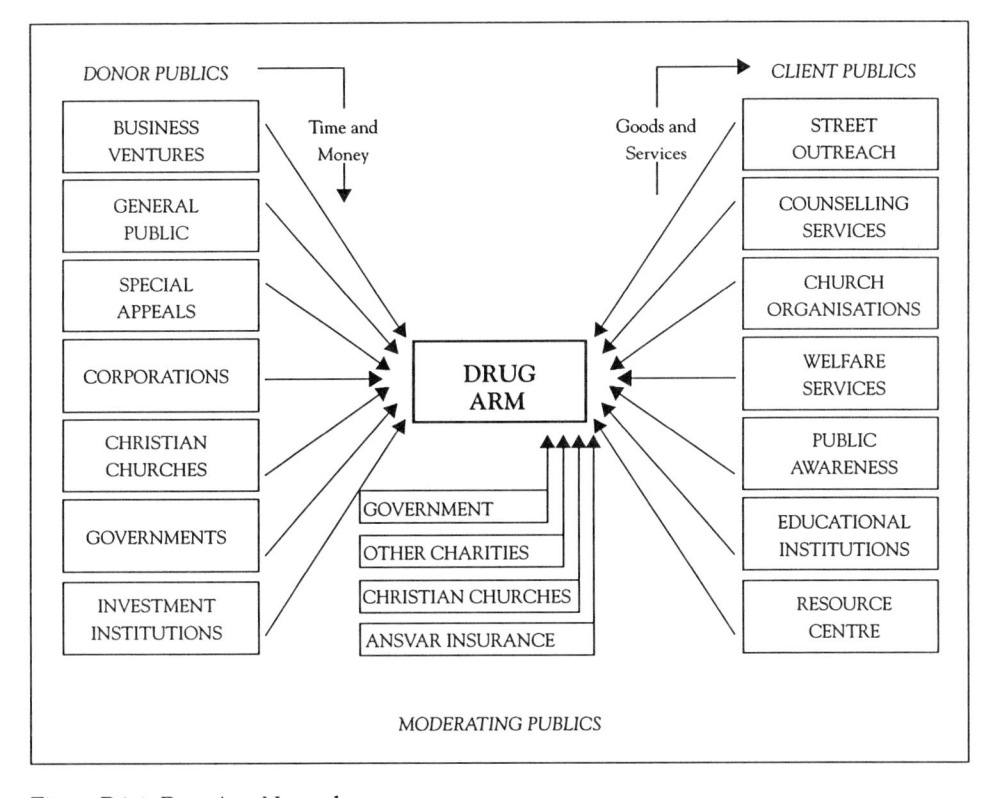

Figure B4.1 Drug Arm Network

Supply side marketing

On the supply side, the income mix is from seven different streams:

- General public gifts and bequests.
- Commercial business ventures which include 'helping hands', a general cleaning and maintenance activity and the sale of non-alcoholic wines.
- Four special annual public databased mail appeals, special fund-raising events such as a No-Booze River Cruise, and a concert with the Queensland Pops Orchestra.
- Corporations such as the Ansvar Insurance Company.
- Christian church and community support agencies such as Rotary, Apex and Lions groups.
- Investment institutions and property investments held by the parent organisation, the Queensland Temperance League (QTL).
- Government bodies.

Table B4.2 *Drug Arm operating expenditure and income 1990–91*

Income	1990–91	%
QTL subsidy	600 952	70
Government grants	38 050	4
Community and other funding	221 284	26
Total	$860 286	100
Expenditure		
Administration	243 516	27
Welfare	169 105	19
Marketing	155 660	17
Education	141 422	16
Fund-raising	67 472	7
Awareness	120 267	13
Miscellaneous	8783	1
Total	$906 225	100

The two noticeable factors in Table B4.2 are the deficit between income and expenditure of approximately $46 000 and government support of only 4%. A factor disguised by the data is the changing dynamics of the need to generate additional funds through commercial and fund-raising activities and to rely even less on government funding. The following changes that have emerged are illustrated in Table B4.3:

Table B4.3 *Changes in funding*

Year	1987–88	1988–89	1989–90	1990–91
Total income $	428 499	699 350	1 021 814	860 286
Amount raised by community and other funding $	47 169	116 056	187 206	221 284
% of total income	11	17	18	26

For this reason the organisation has established an Enterprise Division which has the objective of creating revenue to assist in funding. Currently the Helping Hands operation is functional and operates through an extensive promotional campaign. A commercial management training programme is being investigated as a potential venture. In general, the separate parties of the supply publics act as independent groups and Drug Arm designs a specific marketing mix for each group.

Demand side marketing

For the majority of non-profit organisations the client publics are generally a single well defined group. For example, Teen Challenge is centred primarily on teenage drug users and abusers. By contrast Drug Arm has a legion of client publics as illustrated in the Figure B4.1 depicting the three public groups and their memberships. The reason for the multiplicity is that it is a frontier organisation working on the streets with the destitute, in telephone and face-to-face counselling to the needy, in schools and institutions, in educational programmes, in-house as a resource base for the general community and to governments as a lobbying force. Many of the factors are market and demand driven such as educational requests from schools. Other factors are satisfied only as long as funds and resources are available to meet the needs.

An example of this is the recent employment of mobile rescue street vans for alcohol abusers. The cost of the fully equipped vans is about $25 000 each and these are staffed with fully trained volunteers who now number 450. Thus it is a matter of not just monetary and material resources but voluntary staff recruitment, training and support.

A new method of marketing has recently been introduced which has meant that several of the vans are now completely maintained by the local communities within the areas they service. This represents not only considerable cost savings but facilitates community ownership and involvement. This aspect, although only one component in the overall operations, has been mentioned because in some aspects it represents a prototype of what is proving to represent a departure from the traditional tripartite model which separates the donor public from the client public by the agency. In this application Drug Arm becomes the facilitator in the linkage between the donor and the client and the 'ownership' of the resource is linked more firmly to the community.

Drug Arm and the future

Drug Arm is one of the rare non-profit organisations not only to employ a marketing manager but to be actively engaged in an extremely proactive marketing strategy. To give three of the most significant factors for the organisation's future Denis Young, the executive director of Drug Arm, provides these indicators:

1. The public is now extremely aware of the damage caused to individuals, families and society by alcohol and tobacco companies. But the multinational conglomerates exercise very powerful lobbying pressure on State and Federal Governments in order to increase, or at least maintain, their markets. Whereas we cannot match the funding mechanism of those organisations we must match their energies. This aspect will become extremely important in this current decade and it will be necessary to increasingly mobilise and centralise the concerned community groups to increase our lobbying power on governments. Currently there is not a peak organisation to facilitate that process but Drug Arm will be actively engaged in pressing for the formation for that group.
2. There is an endless set of needs for our organisation to address. It is impossible for us to even suggest that we can meet every need that we confront. There are many charities and welfare agencies that perform excellent services but the overlapping and duplication of services creates unnecessary cost to the organisations and confusion to the public. Drug Arm will be increasingly active in the coming years in monitoring the activities of other ministries to ensure that there is minimal overlap in our activities. Thus we will be endeavouring to make optimal investment of donors time, money and staff resources.
3. Lastly, funding is going to be a critical aspect for the next decade. The demand for the donor dollar is increasing and the dollar availability is reducing in the current climate, and will be for many years to come. The traditional backstop of reliance on government support has been for a number of years a misnomer. The current economic political climate is user-pay, independence and self-support for government sectors as well as non-profit organisations. Thus increased creative marketing efforts are being made to expand donor support to be generated to ensure that existing programs can be maintained and future development work kept on schedule. A key factor of the marketing arrangements will be to make stronger linkages with donors to community projects. This will not only create stronger social linkages with the donors and client groups but it represents substantial cost benefits to Drug Arm. In general one factor is clear—Drug Arm will be placing increasing emphasis on the marketing concept as an integral component of its structures and planning to achieve its mission in this decade.

Questions

1. It is thought that Drug Arm is ranked very low in public perception of their name and knowledge of the organisation's operations. What would you do to increase this awareness? Consider your approach in line with a five-year strategic awareness plan.
2. The financial data in the case study depicts that for the past four years there has been an increased reliance on community support and the organisation's commercial business ventures and less on Government support. Is there, in your opinion, any reason to doubt this trend will change and, if not, what additional commercial ventures could be entered into?

5. DESIGNING COMPETITIVE MARKETING STRATEGY

Introduction 153

Readings

10. How do you know they're satisfied? by Robert Orth 154
11. Statistics reveal major move in supermarkets, by Bernard Holt 158
12. How a steady job turned into a frantic scramble, by David James 160
13. CUB gets the Tooheys blues, by Neil Shoebridge 165

Cases

14. The Australian financial services industry, by Michael Harker 171
15. St George Bank, by Michael Harker 176

Introduction

Section five in this part of the book deals with competitive marketing strategies and competitive advantage. Four readings and two case studies have been included and students are encouraged to critically analyse the wealth of information provided.

In 'How do you know they're satisfied?' Robert Orth looks at IBM's multi-layered measurement system for gauging customer satisfaction, whilst Neil Shoebridge's 'CUB gets the Tooheys blues' discusses the issue of marketing strategy and competitive advantage. In 'Statistics reveal major move in supermarkets' by Bernard Holt, students are encouraged to analyse and interpret statistics provided on the grocery industry. Students will find this reading helpful when analysing the case in section three, 'The Queensland grocery industry'. Similarly, David James' 'How a steady job turned into a frantic scramble' looks at the effects of deregulation on the banking sector and ways of defining efficiency. This reading will greatly assist students when analysing case 14, 'The Australian financial services industry'.

The two cases in this part of the book both deal with financial services. Although the topics are similar, both cases address different issues. Michael Harker is the author of both case studies and in 'The Australian financial services industry' he provides the student with a detailed review of the industry and asks how profitable it is. In 'St George Bank' the focus is turned on the St George Building Society and its attempts to enter the Queensland market.

Reading 10—How do you know they're satisfied?

by Robert Orth

How does IBM know when customers are satisfied? Robert Orth reveals IBM's multi-layered measurement system.

Businesses today are embracing quality as a way of gaining competitive advantage by improving efficiency, increasing business effectiveness, growing market share, and creating satisfied customers. Ultimately, the only quality which counts is that which satisfies and delights customers.

Focusing on satisfying the needs and wants of customers requires the use of new measurements of performance. When asked how they would measure customer satisfaction, managers will give a variety of answers:

- the quality of our products and services;
- ask the customer;
- repeat business;
- increased market share.

These are all appropriate. Gaining a clear understanding of customer satisfaction requires a balanced set of measurements which directly or indirectly indicate the level of customer satisfaction.

What are the types of measures that are used to evaluate customer satisfaction? Aside from surveys, there are numerous measures which can be used to gauge customer satisfaction effectively. An appropriate mix of measures can be used to ensure a comprehensive view of performance and to validate analysis.

Trend measures, such as customer satisfaction surveys or product performance surveys, provide a method of measuring performance over a long period of time, the term *trend* indicating measurements which show a general direction, up or down. These surveys use diagnostic questions to ascertain customers' perceptions and allow you to analyse general trends in one's own performance and that of your competitors. For example, IBM participates in a yearly survey across the market-place to gauge customer satisfaction levels. The analysis of this data enables us to:

1. identify areas which are declining year by year;
2. identify areas which are diverging from competitor performance (positive and negative);
3. develop a set of improvement plans with annual goals; and
4. review the impact of previous improvement plans.

Complementary to this activity is the use of *specific measures* of customer satisfaction. Specific measures relate to the satisfaction of individual customers. There are two categories of specific measure: proactive and reactive. *Proactive measures* involve actively seeking out customer needs or issues and responding to them. Examples are the conduct of user group meetings and regular client reviews. *Reactive measures* are systems or procedures for reacting to customer feedback such as complaints and return mailers.

The value of specific measures areas derives from your ability to correct the customer issue immediately. In addition, the aggregation of data from specific measurements over a period of time allows you to confirm problem areas and understand these problems. A combined evaluation of trend and specific measure provides an opportunity to assess better the reasons for positive or negative moves in satisfaction, validate observed trends, and confirm the effectiveness of action taken to improve customer satisfaction. Benchmarking allows for comparative measurement.

The *Macquarie Dictionary* defines *benchmark* as 'a standard from which quality or excellence is measured'. One example of IBM's benchmarking is the customer satisfaction survey which reviews all participants in the market-place and allows us to compare our performance against many competitors across a range of products and services. We look at the average of competitors' results, and then the highest result, defined as *best of breed*. If we are not best of breed in a specific product or service, related answers are further analysed to establish the areas in which we fall short. We then use other market information to develop improvement plans, or enhancement plans if we have already achieved best of breed. Further benchmarking is performed with these survey results by comparing results in Australia with those achieved in the US and Japan.

Most measurements of customer satisfaction are obtained through feedback channels. We attempt to answer questions: 'How well am I performing today' and 'What can I improve?'. We may also obtain information on changes required to our products or services for the future based on customer comment or explicit questions. We use a concept we term *feed forward*, that is, the opposite of feedback. A feed forward system is designed to answer the questions. 'What else should I be doing for my customers or market?' This is a logical extension to the measurement of customer satisfaction as it assists in identifying improvements and changes that will make the customer more satisfied.

The concept is important because the onus is on the provider of a product or service to decide what will be provided while the customer has the role of assessing and taking a decision to buy that offering. It is essential when instituting new or changed measurement systems that consideration is given to capturing the customers' view of the future. You should ask the customer. However, our customers do not spend a great deal of time contemplating what each of their many suppliers should provide to them, nor are they burdened with knowledge of their suppliers' business logistics when suggesting a change. When seeking future requirements from customers you need to ask for some of their time and effort, in order to gain an understanding of their real needs. The processes employed to do this could include market research and product trials.

IBM has developed and implemented a new programme called *quality service planning*. The process involves a one-day workshop with customers, consisting of five key steps:

1. Defining the product or service to be reviewed and the appropriate customer set.
2. Taking the customers through a guided session designed to elicit from them their vision of the service they require.
3. Listing all the requirements they identify and defining for each, that which constitutes good service.
4. Assigning priorities by means of a voting system.
5. Assessing current performance.

The end result is a clear understanding from the customer of what they require and what they value in the specific offering. This must then be compared with current plans to reset any misconception of customer needs. This planning methodology has proved very effective in focusing on service to the customer.

A balanced set of measurements is required to supply a total view of how well customer requirements are met. A valid system for the measurement of customer satisfaction requires measures which closely reflect the customer's own view. The next section will examine direct and indirect measures.

Direct Measures

The most direct source of information is the customers themselves. If the customers say they are satisfied with the product or service, and demonstrate this by purchasing the product or service, they are indeed satisfied.

There are two categories of direct measurement: *business* and *relationship* measures. These two measures must be in balance. If a customer places business elsewhere while saying they are satisfied with their existing supplier, then the supplier must review their satisfaction measures. If customers place business with a supplier (perhaps due to lack of alternative), while stating dissatisfaction with the supplier, then that supplier should know they are in a precarious position.

Key business measures are:

- market share;
- participation—being considered in more customer buying decisions indicates approval for your offering;
- business mix—increased penetration of the market-place with all products and services offered.

Key relationship measures are:

- quality;
- value—perceived value for money by the customers;
- loyalty—customers' preference for continued business.

Measurements in the relationship area are best obtained by asking customers for their views and performance ratings in surveys. The quality of a relationship with a customer is measured by their perception of actual performance against performance.

Indirect Measures

The measurement of customers' satisfaction can be developed further by establishing which aspects of business performance influence the direct business and relationship measures. These 'indirect' measures observe internal processes based on our understanding of the level of achievement required. We categorise these measures in terms of people, products or processes. Many items can be identified under these headings as contributing to customer satisfaction and, ultimately, to business success.

People measures have to do with the quality of service provided by staff to customers. One measure may be staff skills, as these are directly related to the quality of service delivered. The skill levels needed for support of a particular customer set are assessed, achievement levels set, and progress against these objectives measured *Product measures*, for example production line defect rates, involve measurement of the quality of product to be provided to customers. *Process measures* encompass all those areas of processes which act together to deliver offerings to customers. For example, we could record the number of incorrect invoices issued and the reasons for error.

Establishing a structure of direct and indirect measurements of customer satisfaction provides a very powerful tool for measuring and improving the satisfaction of customers. Measurements form the basis for successful management of customer satisfaction. People are the key to achieving the results. How then do we link the measurements we have in place to rewarding our people?

Customer satisfaction measures provide a mechanism for the assessment of performance and progress of staff and a basis upon which to reward their efforts. People whose responsibility is 'front-line' contact with customers can be paid incentives based on appropriate balance of direct customer satisfaction measures. Staff who support the business operations in areas such as administration and finance can be rewarded for quality improvements. In a pay-for-performance system all employees can be remunerated on the basis of quality and customer satisfaction measures.

Business focus is shifting. The demands of customers are changing and so is their expectation of a supplier. Customer satisfaction is now being recognised as an important asset. Strategically, where the business focus might have been product, it has now become the customer. The key measures are shifting from volume and revenue to satisfaction and market position. The strategy is moving from one driven by only price and function to one broadly described as quality service differentiation. The basis for a competitive, profitable business in the long-term has changed.

Successful management of today's business cannot be achieved without a comprehensive customer satisfaction strategy. An essential part of this strategy is the effective measurement of customers' satisfaction.

Reproduced with permission from *Marketing*, June 1992, pp. 69–70.

Questions

1. Why is customer satisfaction so important to IBM?
2. Is customer satisfaction the same as TQM?
3. Not all companies can afford to worry about customer satisfaction. Discuss.

Reading 11—Statistics reveal major move in supermarkets

by Bernard Holt

What is the proper mix of advertising for both above and below the line to give maximum impact at retail? Most retail turnover is in the doldrums. Why is the grocery industry the exception? What has been the retail experience over the last five years?

Looking back on a very tough 1991 there are some significant surprises. For the five years ending December 1991, total retail turnover in Australia went up each year, although at a reduced rate. The figures, expressed in millions of dollars and calculated on a calendar-year basis, excluding motor vehicles, are:

1987	1988	1989	1990	1991
$58 976.6	$73 626.4	$80 552.7	$88 178.9	$91 118.1

If you accept that advertising is one of the main engineers of retail turnover, it is worth noting that all forms of retail advertising (including print, television, radio, etc.) represented only a tiny fraction of the retail turnover which it helped to bring about. From our annual survey, *Advertising Expenditure in Main Media*, retail advertising in a calendar-year basis for the five years under review, in millions of dollars was:

1987	1988	1989	1990	1991
$1148.8	$1236.3	$1386.3	$1307.8	$1350.0

Advertising as a percentage of the above:

1987	1988	1989	1990	1991
1.94%	1.68%	1.72%	1.47%	1.40%

The percentages of retail advertising to retail turnover are comparable with nationally advertised product categories such as foodstuffs (1.57% of total turnover), liquor (1.24%), confectionery (2.91%), and travel and tours (0.80%). But at a time of high inflation, they have been dropping instead of increasing.

Only one of the retail categories measured by the ABS managed to make any significant and consistent increase—food and groceries. This is quite remarkable for several reasons. Two of which are: there has been no increase in the population and unemployment is over 10% of the workforce.

The record shows that the bulk of grocery buyers have traded down to house brands and generics to the extent that both Coles and Woolworths are reputed to be selling 10% to 12% in generics and Franklins 30%. This raises some fascinating questions for grocery marketers. Is it a growing component of married women in the workforce using larger quantities of ready-prepared foods which are more expensive than raw materials? Is it that the average family is eating more at home and less outside? Is it that grocery manufacturers' consistent use of below-the-line support for their products is the main reason?

Below-the-line support in the grocery industry includes all forms of promotions, new entry fees, case deals, co-operative advertising and all other support charges arranged between food and grocery retailers and their suppliers. This support is substantial. Here are the figures from *Advertising Expenditure in Main Media*, Australia-wide, in millions of dollars:

1987	1988	1989	1990	1991
$1100.0	$1400.0	$1500.0	$1665.0	$1814.8

The next-largest category after food and grocery was hotels, liquor stores and licensed clubs, with estimated turnover around Australia in millions of dollars of:

1987	1988	1989	1990	1991
$7098.0	$7695.0	$8234.0	$8275.0	$8272.9

Our estimates of support are:

1987	1988	1989	1990	1991
$259.0	$307.8	$332.4	$413.7	$413.6

Although we do not measure below-the-line support in other industries, we are aware that it is quite significant.

One of the other ingredients in the mix, however, is the national advertising support given to the various retail categories. In 1990, the latest figures which we have produced at the time of writing, food and grocery was around $500 million, liquor $50 million, furnishings $25 million, clothing $32 million, electrical $33 million.

To give a full perspective of the 12 retail categories measured by the Australian Bureau of Statistics, we have included the Table B5.1 of five years performance in terms of annual turnover. At the time of writing March quarter figures were not available; however, anecdotal evidence suggests that, in spite of some success for department stores and some others through heavy discounting during January sales, the first part of 1992 was even tougher than 1991, with the full force of the domino effect within the recessed economy biting hard, particularly in the retail sector.

Table B5.1 *Retail turnover—Australia (calendar-years in $ million)*

Description	1987	1988	1989	1990	1991
Grocers, confectioners, tobacconists & other food stores	22 590.6	24 768.9	27 343.4	30 415.9	32 593.9
Butchers	1855.3	1788.5	2043.1	2295.1	2189.3
Hotels, liquor stores & licensed clubs	6757.3	9968.1	10 738.2	11 953.8	11 663.3
Cafes & restaurants	—	4933.5	3722.5	4369.2	4472.6
Clothing & fabric stores	5235.3	6179.7	6233.7	6415.2	6675.6
Department stores	6710.9	9102.6	9435.9	9775.5	9954.7
Footwear stores	1000.7	1004.9	1068.0	1166.6	1231.0
Domestic hardware stores & jewellers	1595.3	2479.2	2703.1	2598.0	2687.8
Electrical goods stores	3057.2	4244.4	4869.6	5319.1	5135.4
Furniture & floor covering stores	2095.2	2370.1	2411.1	2593.3	2743.9
Pharmacies	2440.0	2681.2	3081.0	3526.2	3927.4
Newsagents	2160.2	2567.7	2951.8	3148.1	3143.7

General stores and other stores not included

Source: Australian Bureau of Statistics

Reproduced with permission from *Marketing*, May 1992, pp. 56–58.

Questions

1. Do you agree with Bernard Holt's interpretation of the figures?
2. To make a more detailed analysis, what other sources would you consult?
3. Apart from statistics, what other factors affect the retail market?

Reading 12—How a steady job turned into a frantic scramble

by David James

Deregulation plunged bank managers and policymakers into areas they were not equipped to handle. The scars are taking a long time to heal.

Perhaps the most dramatic changes in Australian management during the 1980s were those that occurred in the banking sector. The big banks have moved from heavy regulation and almost completely predictable behaviour to intense competition and instability. When the effect of increased computerisation is also considered, it is clear that bank management now bears little resemblance to what it was.

How are we to evaluate Australian bank management? One way is in terms of efficiency. Ian Payne, deputy managing director of the Commonwealth Bank, says that after banking was deregulated, efficiency became the focus of attention. He says: 'Previously, the banks were underwritten, but once the regulations were opened up, and the banks realised they were no longer underwritten, we all had to focus on efficiency. I think all the banks understood the consequences. If you were operating in a competitive environment and overheads were running above those of the competitors, the business would be bid away.'

The spate of bad and doubtful debts encountered by the banks since deregulation suggests their efficiency drive was not altogether successful. But efficiency itself is open to definition, as indicated in research undertaken for the Australian Bankers Association by Robert Ackland and Professor Ian Harper of the Melbourne University economics faculty. Their research gives three ways of defining efficiency: operational or cost efficiency, allocative efficiency and dynamic efficiency.

The first, *cost efficiency*, is simply the minimising of operating costs. The Ackland and Harper report says the banks have improved their cost efficiency, partly because they were inefficient before deregulation. The operating costs of the main banks, as a proportion of total assets, fell from 4.2% in 1982–83 to 3.6% in 1988–89 and are continuing to fall. Unit labour costs were reduced significantly and the ratio between employee numbers and funds deposited was improved.

But while these gains were being achieved, there was a sharp fall in net interest margins, the main source of income. The net result is that profitability is no higher in spite of greater cost efficiency. The net return on assets dropped by 30% for the six years to June last year. A banking study by Merrill Lynch shows that in 1989–90 the return on equity (minus the ten year bond rate) of Australian banks was well behind the returns in the US, Britain, Spain, Canada and France, although ahead of the returns in Japan and West Germany.

The picture is even gloomier for the State banks and the new foreign banks in Australia. For the four years to June 1989, the State banks had a 72% fall in net returns to assets. The foreign banks in Australia lost 23% on assets in the 1988–89 year. Indeed, Alan Cullen, executive director of the Australian Bankers Association, says that if the banks had not increased their efficiency they would not even have remained profitable. He also says that the rate of improvement in cost efficiency will tend to slow in the future, suggesting that the profit performance is not likely to improve dramatically.

The second type of efficiency, *allocative efficiency*, is the degree to which services can be priced in relation to the cost of providing them. The banks have not been highly successful in this regard, mainly because of consumer resistance to some charges. The Ackland and Harper report says the income of the banks from sources other than interest has not changed significantly in relation to total income. This means that net interest margins are continuing to subsidise other bank services. The report says: 'The Commonwealth Bank was forced to withdraw a proposed flat fee on low-balance accounts in the face of public outcry.'

The third type of efficiency, *dynamic efficiency*, is the extent to which the range of services reflects the needs and preferences of the market. The banks have done well here. Westpac had eight retail products before 1980, and has since introduced 54 others, including automatic teller machines, electronic banking, approved deposit funds, stockbroking services and personal investment funds. Cullen says: 'You don't have to go back very far to see that the bank manager's job was to say no all the time. The customers had a cheque account, an overdraft, a term deposit and a savings bank deposit, and they adapted to the product. Now the banks adapt the product to the customer. There has been a profound switch in attitude.'

But improvements in service have not been without management difficulty. Don Argus, managing director of the National Australia Bank says moving away from paper to electronic delivery has involved a huge education programme for management. He says the process will continue and is one of the biggest challenges for the banks.

In her book *The Bankers*, Supriya Singh says the push to improve levels of education has fragmented the management structure. She says: 'There is a sharper line differentiating the counter staff from the management. Graduate enrolment and recruitment from outside are already changing the kind of social mobility that is possible in banks today. Will Bailey, Stuart Fowler, Nobby Clark and Don Sanders made it from tellers to chief executives. For the tellers of today, this will not be possible without tertiary and technological education.'

Robert Harper, co-author of the Ackland-Harper report, agrees that the increase in the number of products has created a management headache. He says: 'The banks are responding, but it is not without pain. It is an endless headache for people in the retail branches.' A customer walking into a bank could want anything from a new cheque book to a sophisticated international transfer, and Harper says the wide range of products is a source of confusion for bank staff. 'Now that the banks have a hunger for well-trained university people, they are facing the sociological problem of mixing the university graduates with the old guard,' he says.

Harper has found that the long-established practice of sending employees into the field for training no longer works. Graduates who are given this introduction tend to leave the job because it does not use their skills and they find it dull. Sometimes they are discouraged because the local branch manager and staff do not like the new system of staff intake. The banks have no problem placing the newcomers in treasury work, but the growing need is to place them in retail banking.

One way of assessing the quality of bank management is in intangible qualities, including judgment and discretion. Australian bank management—on average, anyway—appears to have been less than impressive in these fields. The total of non-performing loans is estimated to be $15 billion, suggesting problems in managing the higher levels of risk that accompanied the deregulated market. Harper says: 'With hindsight you can explain very easily what happened. You had these big institutions with the freedom to expand lending. They were worried about loss of market share to non-bank financial institutions, and were anxious to protect their existing market share from the competitive pressure of 16 foreign banks.

'They suddenly had much greater discretion and a barrage of new products. But they didn't have the appropriate training, so they made mistakes. In the country branches, you would get farmers coming and saying they wanted to borrow in Swiss francs. The bank manager was not going to admit he didn't know how the foreign currency market operated. So he gave the loan. The centre of the wheel was rotating faster than the edge.'

The problems were perhaps even worse in the wholesale lending market. Cullen says: 'In lending to the larger corporates, the banks were competing in the international market, and they were not fully informed. Many of the loans were syndicated, and in that background the banks had less than full knowledge. So in the trickle down, the borrowers could demand favourable security positions.'

Argus says problems started in the late 1970s when traditional trust deeds began to lose their position of influence in company accounts. He says: 'These deeds had all the usual covenants in there in the balance sheet. They gave an investor the comfort that the balance sheet would be kept in shape. But companies recognised that they had to use their capital better, and realised that it was possible to use their balance sheets differently. That started the first breakdown of the covenants that shareholders, and I suppose lenders also, look for.

'Then we saw the lenders get away from their traditional role. When the environment was regulated, the lenders tended to rely on the collateral support to a loan. In the deregulated market, I think it would be fair to say that many banks in Australia did not really know how to handle balance sheet and cash flow lending. That was the education period, post deregulation. You also had asset accumulation in the country running in excess of 20%, and if your economy is creating that sort of growth factor, then what do the banks do? Do they retreat so that the credit unions, or the non-bank financial institutions, handle the lending? The big banks were not going to move over and give their markets to the newcomers. They have a lot of money invested in their branches around Australia—there are 1400 branches—and they simply have to generate a fair profit in order to generate a fair return.'

At the Commonwealth, Ian Payne agrees that the banks could not have been expected to stay out of the market. In retrospect, he says, it would have been better to let much of the business walk out the door, but it is idealistic to believe that such a course of action could have been taken time and time again. He says: 'I think we are all chastened by what happened, and we have all spent valuable time asking why, and looking to understand the process that brought this about, but no single participant could have influenced the outcome'.

'In the Australian context, the greatest weakness is the focus on blue-chip property as the focus to lend. That has been bred into Australian banking for a long, long time. So when property was inflated to unsupportable levels, it was not well identified. We must also question the extent of the attitude that allows funds to be diverted into property as an inflation hedge rather than into the tradeable goods sector.'

Harper, though, suggests the banks might have chosen the right strategy without being aware of it. Certainly, their efforts to protect market share have succeeded. He says: 'I think you can also argue that they knew they exercised the advantage of incumbency. They may have picked the eyes out of most deals, knowing that what the new banks got would be of a poor quality. They knew that they would be caught in some of their lending, but they also knew that the proposals they couldn't even look at would go to the competition.'

Nevertheless, there is no dodging the fact that the banks are going to have to wrestle with some very bad loans. Argus rules out any move by the National Australia Bank into taking substantial equity positions, but Chris Stewart, managing director of the Bank of Melbourne, says such a move will become inevitable for some banks. He says: 'The banks are effectively proprietors in many cases. It is inevitable that they will take some shareholding positions rather than try to dispose of an asset in a market in which there are no buyers.'

There is a third element of banking management in a deregulated environment that is almost entirely new: the management of public opinion. Whether banks like it or not—and it is clear often they do not—management success is not judged merely in terms of the ability to make money; it is inevitably assessed in terms of its social effect. According to Singh, bankers see themselves as responding purely to economic imperatives. She says: 'No major trading bank details how it conducts its banking activities with a view to future economic growth, or how it helps the credit needs of the communities that deposit with it.'

Cullen says managers have tended to concentrate on efficiency and have been slow to react to changes in public perception. He says: 'Bankers now have to be like politicians, with media skills being part of their abilities. The public insists on being well informed and will no longer accept what the banks tell them without an explanation.'

For many managers it is a shock to be exposed to such scrutiny. Payne says: 'I find it most uncomfortable to be on the pages of the newspapers and the television screens of the nation. The trouble is that it is not a balanced presentation, because it tends to be an incident-based picture. It is difficult for a banker to argue a specific incident because we are bound by all sorts of requirements of secrecy.' Payne says the best answer to adverse publicity is to work harder at the relationship with the customer.

Stewart agrees that the need to cope with a high level of public exposure is a new requirement for the bank manager's art. He says: 'Politicians get this sort of thing all the time, and they have developed thick skins, but until the last few years, banks have been pretty insulated from the media. Now they have been hit with such a lot at once, and it is very taxing. When the media is doing a story the best thing to do is to lay out the problem as you see it in the hope that you will get your point across. Sometimes, the media has a fixed idea of what it is trying to achieve and you can't always affect that even if you give them the facts. But I suppose the older you get, the less upset you get by it.'

Deregulation has indeed brought radical change to banking management in Australia and has given a new edge to competition, but volatile lending conditions in themselves—for one reason or another—are as old as Shylock. And Payne has an overview that sums up the background neatly. He says: 'I think one of the conclusions you can draw is just how strong the competitive process can be when it is unleashed.'

Reproduced with permission from *BRW*, Australia's leading business magazine, 22 March, 1991, pp. 68–70.

Questions

1. Ackland and Harper identified three ways of defining efficiency in the banking sector. Critically analyse all three.
2. What other measures of efficiency are you aware of? Can they be applied to the banking sector?
3. How has deregulation affected the banking sector:
   (a) from the bank's point of view?
   (b) from the customer's point of view?

Reading 13—CUB gets the Tooheys blues

by Neil Shoebridge

Australia's biggest beer maker has been caught napping in Victoria by the success of two upstart NSW brands. It is counter-attacking with new products but, as Neil Shoebridge reports, its hold on its home market has been shaken.

For the past ten months, executives from the New South Wales brewing company Tooheys Limited have steadfastly claimed that their latest products, Tooheys Red and Tooheys Blue, were launched in Victoria in response to demand from local beer drinkers and retailers. The claim is not entirely true. The Victorian launch of the two brands in the middle of last year was part of a long-term plan devised by Lion Nathan, the New Zealand brewer that acquired 50% and management control of Tooheys' former owner, Bond Brewing, in October 1990. Lion Nathan's plan was simple: break Carlton and United Breweries' (CUB) near-monopoly on Victorian beer sales.

Lion Nathan's chief executive, Douglas Myers, and chief operating officer, Kevin Roberts, saw Victoria as CUB's strongest and weakest market. CUB dominated it, capturing 97% of beer sales, the highest share of any brewer in any Australian state. But that dominance bred an environment of marketing myopia. The beer business has changed dramatically since the late 1980s, with Australians drifting to new types and brands. CUB had failed to respond to those changes. Victorian drinkers were looking for something new. Myers and Roberts believed there was an opening for their brands.

The quiet launch of Tooheys Red and Tooheys Blue in Victoria caught CUB napping. Australia's largest brewer was distracted by the boardroom battles of its parent company, the Foster's Brewing Group. Foster's was pumping money into its British and Canadian operations and had pruned its investment in Australia. CUB had failed to develop any big new products since its low-alcohol Foster's Light was launched in 1988. Its range included some increasingly tired brands.

Still, the success of the two Tooheys brands in Victoria has taken both Lion Nathan and CUB by surprise. Industry sources estimate that the newcomers have snatched 9% of sales since mid-1991, trimming CUB's market share to 89%. The combination of Lion Nathan's attack, a sharp decline in the State's beer market and a cool summer has chopped CUB's Victorian sales by an estimated 15% during the past six months.

CUB will not discuss precise figures, but Peter Williamson, its group executive director (Australian operations) confirms that its Victorian market share has fallen since the middle of last year. Williamson says a public comment by CUB's managing director, Pat Stone, that Lion Nathan is 'a mere irritant' in Victoria was an understatement, but he maintains that the company's biggest problem is the recession. 'Our greatest competitor is not within the beer industry,' Williamson says. 'Our greatest competitor is the economy, and the impact it is having on beer sales. The economy is our number-one rival; Toohey's is number two'.

Victoria's beer market is the most depressed in Australia. Sales there fell 4% in 1990–91, compared with a 2% decline nationally. Victorian sales have slipped a further 7% over the past six months, versus 3–4% nationwide. CUB's national market share is believed to have fallen from 49.5% early last year to 47%, while that of Lion Nathan's National Brewing Holdings has risen from 37% to 40%.

Victoria represents 22% of the national $5-billion-a-year beer market, but it generates 40% of CUB's sales and is its most profitable outlet. The company traditionally has treated its home state as a cash cow, using the revenue generated there to fund marketing and promotional activities elsewhere, particularly in NSW and Western Australia. Since the late 1980s, it has done little to promote its brands in Victoria. Now it is paying the price.

CUB recorded a 14.9% profit decline in the six months to December 31; its profits had already fallen to $111.5 million from $131 million in the same period the year before. Last month the company sacked 120 people from its Victorian operation, blaming the recession and the loss of market share. At the same time, it started discounting its brands in Victoria for the first time, shaving 3–6% from the wholesale price of Foster's Lager and Foster's Light. This week, a new CUB beer, Foster's Special Bitter, is appearing around Australia.

The launch of the new product, which is a low-alcohol bitter like Tooheys Blue, has surprised liquor retailers. 'CUB should have launched a low-alcohol Victoria Bitter,' says one Melbourne retailer (Victoria Bitter is the top-selling beer in Victoria and nationally). 'The Foster's brand name is sinking like a stone.' Asked whether CUB considered introducing a light version of Victoria Bitter, Williamson says the company considered 'various brand combinations'. He adds: 'Foster's is the best property we can use. Foster's is seen (by consumers) as an innovative brand.'

Critics of CUB say the launch of Foster's Special Bitter represents the company's first acknowledgement of the changes that have taken place in its industry during the past five years. The rise of boutique beers during the 1980s changed consumer attitudes, particularly among 18 to 25-year-olds, the so-called 'swinging' beer drinkers who have not yet formed firm brand allegiances. The specialised brews introduced Australians to new styles and tastes, and created a wide gap between 'traditionalists' and younger drinkers. Boutique beers began losing favour in 1990–91, but Wayne

Honeywill, marketing manager of SA Brewing, says they have created a new generation of drinkers with no brand loyalties, no parochial ties to State-based brands, and an increased willingness to experiment.

Tooheys has targeted these people with products such as Tooheys Red, Tooheys Dry and Tooheys Blue. Lion Nathan's Queensland division, Castlemaine Perkins, has rolled out Fourex Light Bitter and Malt 75 (a 'naturally brewed' bitter similar to Tooheys Red that was launched in February). SA Brewing has introduced West End Super bitter and West End Eagle Blue low-alcohol brews. Until Foster's Special Bitter appeared, CUB had failed to respond. 'CUB had tried to cater for a changing, evolving market with its existing products,' says Mike Wesslink, managing director of Tooheys Limited. 'It has been the wrong strategy.'

New products have been a key part of Lion Nathan's strategy for reviving the old Bond Brewing operation. With Australian Consolidated Investments, it acquired Bond Brewing in late 1990 and quickly relaunched the company as National Brewing Holdings. The three Bond breweries—Tooheys, Castlemaine Perkins and Swan Brewery—now operate as autonomous companies, reporting to Myers and Roberts. The national brand marketing and distribution strategy developed by Bond had started to disintegrate in early 1990 and was killed when Lion Nathan took control.

In November 1990, Lion Nathan embarked on a cost-cutting programme to boost National Brewing's earnings, which had dropped from $201 million in 1987–88 to an estimated $168 million in 1989–90. Contracts with can, bottle, hops and malt suppliers were renegotiated and staff numbers cut in all three breweries. Tooheys has trimmed its workforce by 10% during the past year and reduced its raw materials and packaging costs. It has also shifted marketing dollars away from the expensive television ad campaigns favoured by Bond into radio advertising, point-of-sale material, sponsorships and consumer competitions. Analysts estimate that National Brewing's pre-tax margin has climbed from 22% in 1989–90 to 25%.

Tooheys has received the most attention from Lion Nathan. NSW is the biggest beer market in Australia, generating 30% of national sales. Tooheys is the biggest division of National Brewing, accounting for an estimated 40% of sales. In late 1990, it was also the division with the most problems. Tooheys' NSW market share had sunk from 52% in 1987 to 43%, thanks to Bond's prickly relationship with local publicans and expensive marketing flops such as the launch of Swan Premium and the relaunch of Tooheys Draught. When Wesslink moved from Swan to Tooheys, he announced plans to push its market share to 55%.

Wesslink claims Toohey's share of NSW beer sales has increased since late 1990, but declines to provide figures. Industry sources say its share is now 47%, to CUB's 49% (down from 52% late in 1990). Its growth has been driven by new products such as Tooheys Red and Tooheys Blue, the relaunch of Tooheys Old and an expanded customer service department. Wesslink claims the decline of Tooheys Draught—which generates half of the NSW brewer's sales—has been arrested. Industry watchers say Tooheys is planning to relaunch the brand.

Tooheys Red bitter beer was launched by Bond Brewing in May 1990 and now accounts for 10% of NSW packaged beer sales. Tooheys Blue appeared in the packaged and bulk markets in March last year. It has grabbed 9.6% of NSW beer sales during the past year and a claimed 80% of the low-alcohol segment, which represents

12% of the total market. Before Tooheys Blue appeared, CUB's Foster's Light held about 80% of the state's low-alcohol beer sales. Toohey's executives claim its share is now 20%.

Tooheys started selling Tooheys Blue outside NSW in the middle of last year, starting with Victoria and the Northern Territory. It moved into South Australia and Western Australia in January. Tooheys Blue is not yet available in Queensland, where Castlemaine is posting strong sales with Fourex Light Bitter, launched in April last year. Fourex Light Bitter accounts for 47% of low-alcohol beer sales in Queensland, versus 30% for Power's Light and 17% for Foster's Light.

'Tooheys Blue has changed the face of the low-alcohol beer market', says SA Brewing's Wayne Honeywill. 'It is a light beer that doesn't look or taste like a light beer. Its blue packaging has drawn people who did not like to be seen holding a can or bottle of light beer, most of which are sold in white packaging. Its taste has won people who didn't like the light taste of low-alcohol beers.'

Bond Brewing has tried hard to crack the Victorian market with Swan Premium, Fourex and Tooheys 2.2 Lite. It ran costly advertising and price-cutting campaigns, set up Swan Premium bars in hotels around Melbourne and staged expensive publicity stunts such as the $56 million purchase of Melbourne's famous Young and Jackson's hotel. It enjoyed little success. Its share of Victorian beer sales rose from 2.9% in late 1985 to 6% in late 1986, before slipping back to 4.1% in 1988, 3.7% in 1989, 3% in 1990 and 2% in the middle of last year.

In November 1990, Lion Nathan pruned Bond's Victorian sales and marketing staff from 50 people to 13 and slashed the number of brands it sold in the state. A new company, National Brewing Victoria, was set up under regional director, Michael Molloy, who reports to Wesslink. It now has a staff of 17. 'CUB had no competition in Victoria,' Wesslink says. 'It was spending nothing on promotion in Victoria and using Victoria to fund its marketing programmes in other states. We wanted to force CUB to compete with us in its home market.'

The marketing of the two Tooheys brands in Victoria has been low key, with bus-side and outdoor ads and limited TV campaigns (a similarly low-key programme has been used in NSW). CUB is adopting the same sort of low-key approach for Foster's Special Bitter, employing public relations, in-store and outdoor advertising programs. 'I don't think people see a TV commercial for a new product and rush out to buy it,' Williamson says.

Tooheys Blue holds an estimated 7% share of Victorian beer sales; Tooheys Red has 2%. Wesslink says Tooheys Blue is selling strongly in the bulk beer market, despite the fact that hotels owned by Australian Pub Company—a joint venture between CUB and the Cascade Group—are not carrying it on tap. Some Melbourne retailers report that Tooheys Blue is the second best-selling beer in their stores, after Victoria Bitter. Meanwhile, Victorian sales of Foster's Lager and Foster's Light have tumbled an estimated 20% during the past six months. 'Foster's lager is not performing as well as I'd like it to perform', Williamson says. 'The Tooheys products represent a true challenge to us.'

Wesslink admits that the success of Tooheys Blue and Tooheys Red has surprised him. 'I didn't expect them to be successful because Victoria is a very hard, competitive market,' he says. 'But we have the right brands at the right time. Our beers are good—good enough to convince Victorians to switch from CUB products.'

CUB regularly uses price-cutting in NSW and Queensland to boost sales of its brands, but its present discounting of Foster's Lager and Foster's Light to retailers represents the first time CUB has offered price cuts in Victoria (in the past, it has offered free product as incentives). Wesslink claims CUB is about to start discounting Victoria Bitter in Melbourne.

Williamson plays down the price-cutting. 'We are simply trying to stimulate consumer spending,' he says. 'Because of the nature of the economy, pricing must be very keen'. But Melbourne retailers have been stunned by the discounting. 'How desperate is CUB?' asks one retailer. 'Desperate enough to cut its Victorian wholesale prices for the first time in living memory.'

CUB is also funding special deals with retailers to blunt the growth of the Tooheys brands. Woolworths' Safeway supermarkets have banished all National Brewing brands to their coolrooms and refrigerators, and are only displaying CUB products on shop floors. Safeway store managers have also been told to replace National Brewing's in-store display material with signs for Foster's Light and Victoria Bitter. Williamson declines to comment on this. Wesslink is circumspect. 'Safeway is a very good and valued customer,' he says. 'We are working very hard to treat all our Victorian customers equitably.'

CUB declines to reveal its targets for Foster's Special Bitter, but Williamson says it is confident the new brand will be a success. CUB spent 12 months developing the product, which is sold in green cans, and bottles with green labels. It has an alcohol content of 2.8% (versus Foster's Light's 2.5% and Tooheys Blue's 2.7%). CUB is expected to launch another new brand by the end of this year.

Lion Nathan's success has encouraged other brewers to attack CUB in its home market. Early this month SA Brewing launched West End Super and West End Eagle Blue in Victoria. SA Brewing already offered West End Draught, West End Export and Southwark Premium there, but Honeywill says sales were negligible. 'The time is right to launch West End Super and Eagle Blue in Victoria,' he says. 'Victorians are ready for the products.'

West End Super was launched in South Australia last October and by December it had seized 16% of packaged beer sales there (it is not sold on tap). West End Eagle Blue appeared in November. In a month, it captured 22.2% of low-alcohol beer sales in SA, or 5.3% of the total market. The two newcomers have pushed SA Brewing's market share in its home state from 73% last June to 75.7% in December.

Honeywill admits that West End Super and West End Eagle Blue are similar to Tooheys Red and Tooheys Blue respectively, but denies they are copies. Other brewers are developing similar products, a fact that worries Tooheys executives. 'We are concerned about Tooheys Blue knock-offs,' Wesslink says. 'If there is any evidence of passing off, we will take legal action. We must protect our brands. We don't want "blue" to become generic for low-alcohol beers.'

Reproduced with permssion from BRW, Australia's leading business magazine, 13 March, 1992, pp. 22–25.

Questions

1. The case study, 'The globalisation of Fosters' gives a rigorous account of the rise of Fosters. Include this reading, and any other information you can uncover, to provide a critical analysis of the Australian brewing industry.
2. Do brands compete on price alone or is there some other form of differentiation involved?

# Case 14—The Australian financial services industry

by Michael Harker

Students are directed to read the complementary case, 'St George Bank'.

Introduction

The marketing of financial services is big business in Australia, but it is a complex business which has witnessed significant change. Once, neatly compartmentalised by government regulation, each industry sector was able to operate without reference to organisations in other industry sectors. Market change was gradual and competition 'gentlemanly'.

The industry went through a metamorphosis in the 1980s during the deregulation era. The changes were profound in nature and scale. Mark Baker of Barclays International, a major organisation specialising in banking and financial services, sat in his office overlooking St Paul's Cathedral in London, England, contemplating these changes as he prepared a report for his boss on the structure of the industry in Australia.

The Australian financial services industry

The industry comprises: banks, building societies, finance companies, insurance companies and credit unions.

Deregulation

Prior to 1983 the industry was closely controlled by government whereby markets and the businesses which operated in those markets were regulated by government legislation. This legislation effectively ensured that banks, finance companies and insurance companies would only compete in specific markets with defined product ranges. Deregulation changed all that. The controls came off, markets were opened up and the scene was set for real competition.

Proactive players

Once it became clear that government control of financial markets would be reduced, the financial institutions became more proactive in the market-place. Financial institutions were merged in order to offer a broader range of services and to gain market share. Marketing improved and technology was exploited. Automatic

Teller Machines (ATMs) were introduced in 1980 by Westpac and by 1986 88% of people between the ages of 26 and 45 years were using them regularly. Service quality improved and products were developed to satisfy niche markets.

The customer in the deregulated market

Customers changed in the deregulation period. The deregulation issue heightened consumer awareness of financial institutions and their activities. Strong competition between institutions gave customers greater knowledge of products and services and enabled them to evaluate the competing offers being made by the institutions. Banks, in particular, were seen as institutions offering products for sale just like any other retail outlet, and the awe in which banks had previously been held started to dissipate. Consumer loyalty diminished as people and businesses started to shop around for a better deal and multiple account holding became more common. Customers started to demand better service and convenience from their banks.

Competition in the deregulated market

Finance companies

The relative monopoly finance companies had in certain sectors of the market, particularly higher risk loans and domination of commercial lending was eroded by deregulated competition. The removal of restrictions on banks allowed them to attack the now traditional markets of finance companies. Banks such as ANZ drew closer together with its finance arm, Esanda, and the distinction between the pre-existing markets was lost. Furthermore, banks with their ownership of finance companies were now able to offer prospective clients a far wider range of products (including more competitive lending rates) than 'stand alone' finance companies.

The banks had begun the first stage of their expansion into other markets and since then finance companies have experienced a continual decline in market share.

Insurance companies

The era of deregulation has also affected insurance companies, mainly in their sales of life, superannuation and investment products. There has been an increase in the number of companies competing in the insurance market. Major banks, particularly Westpac and ANZ, have established significant sales operations for these products, and then attached them to their branch network. The clients for the bank life products are drawn from the existing bank client base. The implications for insurance companies are that a previously accessible customer base is now being contested.

The major life offices of AMP, NML and Capita have attempted to combat the deregulated market-place by using or extending their network of finance intermediaries. This era has also seen the development and sale of investment and unit trust products by the insurance and insurance/banking industry.

Building societies

Building societies are registered and controlled under State Legislation and are mutual institutions designed to channel people's savings into providing finance for home ownership. The impact of deregulation on banks had an adverse effect on the roles of building societies in the market-place. The benefits enjoyed by building societies pre-deregulation, such as lending flexibility and interest rates advantages were neutralised. In broad terms this meant that banks were no longer disadvantaged. In fact they were in an advantaged position compared to building societies. Building societies have been losing market share to banks ever since about 1984.

The building society share of total financial assets in Australia has decreased from 11.3% in 1980 to 5.2% in 1990. A similar decline has been experienced by Queensland building societies which currently hold 9% of the assets of deposit-taking institutions in Queensland, compared with almost 15% in 1980.

Since 1985 non-Queensland building societies have grown at an annual rate of nearly 20%, while Queensland societies have grown at only 11% per annum. This period coincides with major reforms to building society legislation in other States.

Generally the maturity of funds placed with permanent building societies is very short. Less than 2% of the deposits of permanent building societies have maturities greater than 12 months. On the other hand, virtually all lending by building societies is to finance housing, which normally is long-term. This results in a major maturity mismatch, which requires building societies to manage carefully their liquidity exposure.

1985 saw the NSW Building Society convert to bank status with the formation of the Advance Bank—the first building society to do so. Advance Bank has more than 200 branches. The Advance Bank maintains 65% of its loan portfolio in residential housing. In 1988 the Metropolitan Permanent Building Society in Queensland converted to the Metway Bank. This was the first institution in Australia to offer seven-day trading when banks in Brisbane and Surfers Paradise opened on Saturdays and Sundays. In 1992 St George Building Society converted to bank status and declared that its loan portfolio will emphasise relatively safe home loans.

Legislation introduced in 1992 has brought new controls over building societies regarding capital adequacy, liquidity and management control systems.

The banks

The banks were the major beneficiaries of the deregulation legislation. They were able to extend their range of products and services and enter new markets such as insurance. The banks used their extensive client bases and large branch networks to 'sell on' new products to existing clients, for example personal loans, insurance, home loans, mortgage protection, home/property insurance, life cover, superannuation and travel. The cross-selling of services to clients creates what is known as 'switching barriers', that is, it becomes increasingly inconvenient for a client to take his business elsewhere, to switch to another institution.

Although the banks benefited from funds transfers in the 1987 stock market crash, the intense competition between the 'big four' (Westpac, ANZ, NAB and the

Commonwealth Bank) started to affect profitability as the decade progressed. The cross-subsidisation of services was becoming a problem, as new banks attracted the profitable business and the banks started to explore user-pay strategies and introduce transaction charges in order to make unprofitable services pay. Branch managers were given more autonomy and became more profit responsible—a move which was quickly detected by the public who became increasingly cynical about banking activities and motives. To this was added a feeling of mistrust as failures and bad management in the financial sector emerged.

State banks

The State banks which were owned and founded by the States under state legislation have had to adapt to the new environment if they wished to compete and this has lead to crises and problems at some of the major institutions, for example, the collapse of the State banks of Victoria and South Australia; and privatisation has become a necessity at others. Meanwhile the Bank of Queensland continues to make steady, sound, but unspectacular progress under shrewd and prudent management. Table B5.2 below summarises the situation with regard to the six State banks:

Table B5.2 *The State banks, 1990*

Bank	Share of State mket	Total assets ($m)	Total loan book ($m)	Bad debt provs. ($m)	Non-accrual debts ($m)	Pre-tax profit/(loss) ($m)
South Aust	50	21 620	15 360	42	1895	(0.4)
NSW	11	18 400	10 800	441	555	34.8
Victoria	21	23 806	15 896	243	2132	310.6
Tasmania	22	888	529	20	n/a	(6.6)
WA	24	8271	5304	60	232	(127.5)
QLD	3	845	699	5	—	15.3

Source: *Financial Review*, 18 February, 1991, p. 12

Overseas banks

Another consequence of deregulation has been the market attack by overseas banks, namely:

- HongkongBank.
- Chase/AMP.
- Barclays.
- NatWest.
- Standard Chartered.
- Citibank.

However, all incurred significant losses in 1990.

Competition has bred innovation and subsequently won business for new entrants. For example, a computer system at Citibank was introduced to carry out credit approvals for personal loans which enabled the bank to process lengthy procedures in hours and, for routine personal loan applications, in a few minutes. Citibank's niche marketing strategy seems to be working. Citibank's average new deposit is worth $30 000, compared to an industry average of just $2000 (BRW 8 May, 1992).

Credit unions

The 'cheap, cheerful, local' image of the credit unions has also had to undergo some change. The unions were seriously threatened by deregulation and affected by the uncertainty of the financial sector. Although the number of credit unions has declined, deposits have increased since deregulation. More professional management are developing successful and progressive images and an enhanced range of products and services are being welcomed by their loyal clientele.

The future?

The dramatic changes which have been experienced in the last decade in the Australian financial sector are not yet at an end. In this age of discontinuity further significant developments are inevitable. Technology and market demands will drive the main changes and an industry shake-out is a distinct possibility in this crowded market-place.

And back to the present

Australia, like most advanced economies, suffered from the effects of the worldwide recession in the late 1980s and early 1990s. Unemployment, at levels which had not been experienced since the Great Depression, has affected consumption and savings patterns with adverse effects on investment and borrowers' confidence.

Question

Mark Baker glanced up from his papers and peered through the London gloom to see the numbers 17:48 shine brightly on a clock on an adjacent building. He wondered if he would be able to devise a strategy which would help Barclays to perform better in its Australian venture? The first question he decided to tackle was just how profitable is the Australian financial services industry?

References

Brown, L. (1991), *Competitive Marketing Strategy*, Nelson, Melbourne.
Lewis, G., Morkel, A. and Hubbard, G. (1991), *Cases in Australian Strategic Management*, Prentice Hall International, Sydney.
Neale, S. (1991), 'State Bank's Fate in Question', *Financial Review*, 18 February, p 12.

Porter, M. E. (1985), *Competitive Advantage—Creating and Sustaining Superior Performanc*, Free Press, New York.

Shoebridge, N. (1992), 'A Big But Careful Spender, Citibank', *Business Review Weekly*, 8 May, p. 70.

Case 15—St George Bank

by Michael Harker

Students should not attempt this case without first addressing the complementary study 'The Australian financial services industry'.

Introduction

The St George Building Society developed a large and loyal client base in New South Wales and the ACT and operated very successfully in these markets. Dramatic changes in the financial services industry during the last decade, however, are influencing the way in which St George conducts its business and competitive pressures are eroding the Society's traditional client base. The Society took the decision to become a bank on 1 July, 1992, to arrest this process and to be able to offer a wider range of services to its customers. With limited expansion prospects in its traditional NSW market, the top management team of St George is casting envious glances at the growing market in Queensland, in its endeavour to sustain the growth of its business. In these difficult times St George seeks to establish itself with a new status in a new market—conservative Queensland, the Sunshine State.

The Queensland scene

Queensland has not suffered to the same extent as the southern states of Australia. Unemployment is lower and the State continues to attract a diverse range of migrants. Including natural increases and both interstate and international migration, the population has been growing steadily.

Table B5.3 *Population growth in Queensland*

Total population growth	1985	1986	1987	1988	1989	1990
Number	50 022	52 594	56 949	79 064	85 363	67 399
% increase	2.0	2.0	2.1	2.9	3.1	2.3

Source: Australian Bureau of Statistics, 1990 Demography Queensland, Table 3, p. 10, 3311.3

Compared to other Australian States, the Sunshine State appears to be the most popular destination for migrants, after the ACT. Although, the population of the ACT is only 10% that of Queensland.

Table B5.4 *Growth rate summary, by State, 1990*

	Total increase	% increase
Australia	253 996	1.5
ACT	6971	2.5
Queensland	67 399	2.3
WA	35 148	2.2
Victoria	56 904	1.3
NT	1851	1.2
NSW	64 658	1.1
South Australia	16 117	1.1
Tasmania	4948	1.1

Source: Australian Bureau of Statistics, 1990 Demography Queensland, Table 1, p. 1, 3311.3

Where do these people go to live in Queensland? Housing 'starts' (commencement of dwelling construction) in Queensland in 1990/91 numbered 30 996 with more than one third being in the State capital, Brisbane and two-thirds in S.E. Queensland.

Table B5.5 *Number of dwelling units commenced by type of new residential buildings in statistical divisions and statistical districts, Queensland*

	1989–90 Houses	1989–90 Other res. buildings	1989–90 Total	1990–91 Houses	1990–91 Other res. buildings	1990–91 Total
Brisbane	7781	3166	10 947	8329	3118	11 447
Moreton	6726	2407	9133	7025	2804	9829
Wide Bay-Burnett	2213	440	2653	2333	417	2750
Darling Downs	1046	220	1266	1199	492	1691
South-West	54	31	85	80	20	100
Fitzroy	941	161	1102	1088	239	1327
Central-West	21	—	21	15	10	25
Mackay	680	180	860	732	118	850
Northern	935	356	1291	886	372	1258
Far North	1483	534	2017	1304	355	1659
North-West	24	11	35	26	34	60
Queensland	21 904	7506	29 410	23 017	7979	30 996

Source: Australian Bureau of Statistics, Dwelling Unit Commencements Reported by Approving Authorities, Queensland, Table 4, p. 5, 8743.3

But what about the natives? They prefer to settle in the south-east corner of the State also and two-thirds of the three million Queenslanders live there.

The Queensland market for financial services

Queenslanders have a reputation for being laid back but they mirror the behaviour of their southern cousins when it comes to money!

The market for financial services comprises two main segments—the private (personal) market and the business market. The market has changed dramatically over the past ten years as deregulation and increased competition have influenced consumer knowledge, attitudes, behaviour and expectations. Banks are no longer regarded with awe and wonderment and there is less loyalty to financial institutions in general. Account switching and multiple account holding is more common.

People now demand high service levels and innovative products from institutions on which they can rely. Public confidence in the financial sector has been badly dented by failures, bad management and high-handed, uncaring behaviour from some financial institutions. In Queensland there is still considerable trust and respect for the State bank (Bank of Queensland), the building societies and the credit unions. The security offered by the financial institution is still important in the buying decision process, particularly with older people, but so is service, convenience and flexibility.

The business market segment is more concerned about the cost of finance and range of services provided. Businesses also look for flexibility, business acumen, and local decision making from their bankers.

'Switching costs' for both sectors are a problem but multiple account holding is a more common practice, particularly with new institutions which 'do things differently', and offer new services (AGB Research, Brisbane, 1991). Queenslanders tend to support established institutions, for example the Commonwealth Bank has a significant and loyal following, and the Bank of Queensland has a sound business in house loans. The relatively new Metway Bank with its friendly efficient service and free cheque accounts is establishing itself successfully in this market. Suncorp is also well regarded in Queensland. It is a unique institution offering a 'one stop' shop service for home loans and deposit and cheque accounts through its building society arm, insurance for home, car, boat and person through its insurance division, and business finance through its financial operation. Suncorp's acquisition of the L.J. Hooker business gives it direct access to the estate agency market, for home loan accounts.

Technology plays an important part in the marketing of financial services. The financial sector has benefited considerably from advances in technology and indeed most financial institutions rely heavily on their technology. Services such as Automated Teller Machines (ATM), Electronic Funds Transfer at Point-of-Sale (EFTPOS) and Electronic Data Interchange (EDI) offer consumers new service levels and increased convenience; but customers have come to expect this level of service in this highly competitive market, and much of the investment in technology by the institutions which is cost-driven is not apparent to the customer.

Another convenience product on which the market has come to depend is the credit card. The number of credit card accounts is approximately 7 million and the number of transactions in 1991 was 168 million, valued at $15 billion. Big business indeed—and big costs for the financial institutions. One major bank has recently disclosed that it employs 1100 staff directly on credit card operations with an annual wage bill exceeding $40 million. The annual capital spent on technology to support this operation is $24 million and postage costs another $14.5 million since the law demands written notification of changes in credit card conditions. Another cost attached to credit cards is write-offs, currently running at 1.3% of outstanding balances, or $4 billion across the nation (*Financial Review*, 20 May 1992, p. 12).

The banking business

The Australian banking market was worth $374 billion in 1990, whilst the Queensland share of this business was $45.7 billion or 12%, (*Financial Review*, 1991). Seventy per cent of Queenslanders state that a bank is the best financial institution for their financial needs and the Commonwealth and Westpac are the most used institutions. Some disquiet in the market-place, however, concerning the attitudes and behaviour of some banks has enabled Metway to get a profitable foothold in this market (AGB Research, 1991). The National Bank is the most favoured bank of the business community (AGB Research, 1991).

The building society business

The number of permanent building societies in Queensland has declined from 18 in 1980 (with assets of $1.4 billion) to nine in 1990 ($2.8 billion assets) as a result of mergers and the conversion of the Metropolitan Building Society to Metway Bank. The industry has become more concentrated as the three largest societies held 78% of the market in 1991 compared to 70% in 1980 (Queensland Permanent Building Societies Association, 1991).

The building societies also hold almost 10% of the assets of deposit-taking financial institutions in Queensland. Table B5.6 below shows the Queensland building society organisations as at 30 June 1990:

Table B5.6 *The Queensland Building Society organisations 1990*

Society	No. of branches	Market share (%)
Suncorp	61	51.9
Heritage	27	16.5
Northern	23	9.7
Wide Bay Capricorn	19	5.8
Ipswich and West Moreton	9	4.7
The Rock	4	3.9
First Provincial	6	3.3
Mackay	9	2.8
Pioneer	4	1.3

Source: Queensland Permanent Building Societies Association

The credit union business—Alive and kicking in Queensland

In 1990, Queensland boasted 34 Credit Unions with 439 232 members. They had deposits of $1072 million and loans of $917 million, with assets of $1179 million. Nationally, the credit unions held reserves of $662 million and, in attempting to compete with other financial institutions, offered a mixed bag of services, just like their competitors. Amongst other services, the credit unions offered their 'Redicard' (a debit card) and 250 000 members had obtained one in 1990. They also offered Visa cards and a number of ATMs.

A breakdown of loan purpose, nationally, in 1990 showed that used cars accounted for 24% of loans, debt consolidation 15% and new cars 9%.

Table B5.7 below shows the 'top' 5 credit unions in Queensland in 1990, by number of members.

Table B5.7 *Queensland Credit Unions, 1990*

Name	Operating revenue after tax ($M)	No. of branches	No. of members	Total members deposits ($M)	Total assets ($M)	Total loans ($M)
Credit Union Australia	0.26	53	122 324	—	214.5	158.2
Qld Teachers Credit Union	1.35	12	72 000	179.5	195.3	164.2
CPS Credit Union	0.4	6	33 745	95.0	107.65	41.9
Sunstate Credit Union	0.3	5	25 560	—	49.61	16.4
Qld Police Credit Union	0.49	1	22 310	96.0	104.06	68.6

Source: Business Queensland, 1 April 1991

Competitive activity

Competition between financial institutions is extremely fierce. The banks and building societies spend considerable sums of money in marketing their services and establishing a position in the market-place.

Competitive positioning

Each of the major banks and second-tier banks and building societies endeavour to differentiate their offerings by adopting a particular position or business orientation. In the immediate post deregulation period, Westpac, Australia's largest bank positioned itself as Australia's 'World Bank'—a position of little perceived value to the domestic Australian market. Westpac's slogan has been changed to 'You can bank on us.' The Commonwealth Bank proudly claims to be 'Australia's leading bank'. The positions of other institutions are shown below in Table B5.8.

Table B5.8 *Company positions as shown by slogans*

Slogan	Institution
'Australia's leading bank'	Commonwealth
'You can bank on us'	Westpac
'Banking your way'	Metway
'ANZ will help you get there'	ANZ
'National Australia Bank—together'	NAB
'You can count on a Queenslander'	Bank of Queensland
'We'll always be there'	AMP
'We pay more interest to you—that's a promise'	Heritage
'The helpful Queenslander'	Suncorp
'Living money'	Ipswich & West Moreton
'State what you want from your bank'	State Bank of NSW

Source: TV and press campaigns

Marketing activities

Marketing research

The financial institutions have started to invest heavily in research activities as they try to understand the scale and structure of markets, consumer needs, attitudes and behaviours, and the impact of marketing decision variables on consumer knowledge, attitudes and behaviour.

Promotional activity

The 'advertising spend' by key financial institutions in Sydney and Queensland is shown in Table B5.9 below:

Table B5.9 *Total advertising spend, key financial institutions, Sydney and Queensland, 12 months to December 1990*

Institution	Expenditure ($m)
Westpac	6.8
NAB	3.7
Metway	2.3 (mainly Qld)
Bank of Queensland	0.5 (Qld only)
Commonwealth	6.0
Suncorp	2.4 (Qld only)

Source: TART Research

'Total advertising spend' covers all elements of the promotional mix, that is, TV, radio, posters, print but excluding sales-force activity. Promotional activity has concentrated on:

(a) Positioning the organisation.
(b) Promoting particular products/services.

Product and service development

The institutions have responded to market demands to improve service quality and to develop new products which are closer to the needs of the customer. Core products have been expanded to satisfy the various sub-markets and the number and complexity of packages has proliferated. Products and services for the personal and business markets are shown below. In terms of personal products, all ten institutions offer:

- Savings accounts.
- Cheque accounts.
- Credit cards.
- Bank cheques.
- Telegraphic transfers (except Suncorp).
- Home loans.
- Home equity loans.
- Home improvement loans (except Chase AMP).
- Personal loans (except Chase AMP).
- Line of credit.
- Loan insurance (except Chase AMP).
- Home insurance (except Chase AMP).
- Home contents insurance (except Chase AMP).
- Life/super.
- Financial planning.

Table B5.10 summarises the commercial products on offer by the top institutions.

The provision of these services, however, does not totally reflect a consumer-orientated approach on behalf of the institutions—there is some enlightened self-interest. The institutions offer products and services based on the life-cycle concept whereby the client has a need for different products at different life-cycle stages, for example, leaving school, university entrance, car purchase, marriage and house purchase. The more product the client 'takes on', the higher is the 'switching' barrier and the more 'loyal' the client will remain to the providing institution.

Pricing of services

Complex products are often priced in complex and, for the consumer, confusing ways. There is mistrust in the market-place over charges imposed by financial institutions. Cross-subsidisation of services is undertaken in order to offer attractive packages. In the Queensland market free cheque accounts are provided subject to a minimum account balance being maintained.

Table B5.10 *Products offered by the top financial institutions*

	Suncorp	NAB	Westpac	ANZ	Common-wealth	Metway	Advance Bank	Nat. Mut. Royal Bank	Chase AMP	State Bank of NSW
Commercial loan	✓	✓	✓	✓	✓	✓	✓	✓	✓	✓
Leasing		✓	✓	✓	✓	✓	✓	✓	✓	✓
Commercial insurance	✓	✓	✓	✓				✓		✓
Car fleet insurance	✓	✓	✓	✓						✓
Cash pay packets		✓	✓	✓	✓	✓				
Night safe		✓	✓	✓	✓					
Counting daily takings & deposits		✓	✓	✓	✓	✓	✓			
Corp. S'annuation	✓	✓	✓	✓						
Keyman Insurance	✓	✓	✓	✓						

Source: Organisations' promotional material

Branch networks

Australia has almost 6000 bank branches and has one of the highest proportions of branches per head of population in the world. It is 'considered a costly and clumsy way of delivery of services' (*Financial Review*, March 1992). However, convenience is another attribute demanded by the consumer—and the number and location of branches and the opening hours are criteria which are used to assess the convenience factor. Increasingly important also are the number and location of ATMs. Seven-day personal banking is offered in Queensland by Metway at branches in Brisbane and Surfers Paradise, and seven-day 'hot lines' are operated by some institutions for home loans. The number of branches in Queensland of key competitors in this market are shown in Table B5.11, together with performance indicators.

Table B5.11 *Major financial institutions (Qld) size and performance, 1990*

Institution	Total assets ($bn)	Profits ($m)	Branches (No. Qld)
Westpac	107	920	230
NAB	76	3210	226
Metway	2	15	113
Bank of Qld	8	15	69
Commonwealth	67	783	156
Suncorp	5	297	92
St George	8	72	272 (NSW)
Ipswich & West Moreton	0.1	0.6	10
Heritage	0.5	0.2	28
Advance Bank	6	53	3
State Bank (NSW)	16	41	5

Source: Annual Reports

There is a view however that the technological advances in the industry, for example, ATMs, EFTPOS, EDI, are such that it is possible to have an almost branchless banking system (*Today's Computers*, March 1992).

The Queensland market represented a new challenge for St George and the senior managers grappled with a marketing strategy which would assist them to meet their objectives (Appendix 2).

Question

Devise a marketing strategy for St George Bank to be used in the Queensland market.

References

AGB Research Brisbane 1991—Unpublished.
Annual Reports.
Australian Bureau of Statistics.
Brown, L. (1991), *Competitive Marketing Strategy*, Nelson, Melbourne.
Fox, C. (1992), 'It's a Brave New World', *Financial Review*, 18 February, p. 12.
Neale, S. (1991), 'State Banks Fate in Question', *Financial Review*, 18 February, p. 12.
Queensland Permanent Building Society Association, 1991 Report.
'Queensland Credit Unions', *Business Queensland*, 1 April 1991.
'Changing Role for Branch Business', *Today's Computers*, 20 March 92, pp. 20–22.
Listing Memorandum 1992, St George Bank and Annual Report 1990 (St George Building Society).

Appendix I
St George

St George have 289 branches established in Victoria, Queensland and ACT. In 1992, they had 26 580 loans worth $2.152 billion approved for housing. Retail deposits totalled $6.885 billion and the average balance per account holder was $2740.

In 1990, St George successfully launched their Happy Dragon Club for the under-13 years segment. They were inundated with 20 000 accounts in the first month.

St George have an established TQM (total quality management) programme running and all staff must have knowledge of the full product line. St George also had an advertising drive recently to take the mystique out of superannuation (St George 1992).

Table B5.12 *St George Group: Group performance five-year summary*

Profit and loss year ended 31 May	1988 ($'000)	1989 (1) ($'000)	1990 ($'000)	1991 (2) ($'000)	1992 (3) ($'000) (11 months)
Interest revenue	568 971	835 600	1 179 812	1 132 347	982 115
Interest expense	420 938	621 346	928 586	839 693	694 728
Interest margin	148 033	214 254	251 226	292 654	287 387
Other revenue	10 120	30 365	36 335	47 595	54 501
Operating expenses —bad & doubtful debts	1577	2056	6616	27 870	28 897
Operating expenses —other	107 452	172 462	209 215	243 307	242 496
Operating profit before income tax	49 124	70 101	71 730	69 072	70 495
Tax expense	23 717	24 665	26 170	23 454	26 001
Operating profit after income tax	25 407	45 436	45 560	45 618	44 494
Extraordinary items (net of tax)	7130	2129	−830	0	−3040
Operating profit after income tax and extraordinary items	32 537	47 565	44 730	45 618	41 454
Balance sheet at 31 May	($'000)	($'000)	($'000)	($'000)	($'000)
Total assets	4 600 749	6 896 464	7 701 669	8 520 989	9 308 127
Receivables	3 100 622	5 232 589	5 566 674	6 168 792	6 975 545
Liquid assets and cash	1 350 017	1 403 743	1 668 803	1 842 578	1 815 819
Other assets	150 110	260 132	466 192	509 619	516 764
Shareholders' equity	232 089	340 848	378 251	431 331	481 225
Retail deposits	3 873 597	5 431 004	5 874 338	6 052 714	6 885 259
Borrowings and creditors	459 343	1 077 276	1 367 827	1 957 805	1 854 060
Other liabilities	35 720	47 336	81 253	79 139	87 583

Figures for 1989 include the merger with State Building Society Limited, effective 1 October 1988. Figures for 1991 include the acquisition of the VS & L Society, effective 1 November 1990. Figures for 1992 represent 11 months of operations ended 30 April 1992.

Source: Listing Memorandum 1992, St George Bank and Annual Report 1990 (St George Building Society)

Appendix II

The mission of St George Bank is:

> To provide affordable home finance and quality financial services in a friendly, efficient and convenient manner.

Objectives for 1992

Objective: To continue quality asset growth and maintain profitability.
Objective: To maintain strong and consistent home lending and further develop St George core business.
Objective: To provide shareholders with an appropriate return on their investment.
Objective: To reduce the Group's exposure to commercial lending.
Objective: To provide the maximum level of protection for depositors' funds.
Objective: To expand St George operations along the eastern seaboard of Australia.
Objective: To continue diversification of funding sources.
Objective: To participate in community activities and contribute to those in need.

6. IMPLEMENTING MARKETING

Introduction 188

Readings
14. The Gold Coast's mid-life crisis, by Andrew Stewart 189
15. Where Brian Quinn went wrong, by Robert Gottliebsen 194
16. Fosters faces a familar foe, by Matthew Stevens 199
17. Fast food frenzy, by Neil Shoebridge 203

Cases
16. Marketing of the Queensland Art Gallery, by Peter Graham, Neal Hogg, Nicole Licastro and Danielle McEwan 211
17. Marketing the non-profit way, by Terry Gatfield 217

Introduction

Section six looks at the implementation of the marketing effort. The planning, implementing, organising and controlling of marketing programmes is examined. Four readings and two case studies have been selected for this section.

Andrew Stewart's 'The Gold Coast's mid-life crisis' considers the marketing of a place and encourages students to consider the concept of the product life cycle when analysing the reading. Robert Gottliebsen's 'Where Brian Quinn went wrong' analyses the mistakes made by the Coles Myer board. Students will find this reading helpful when reviewing 'The Queensland grocery industry' case in section B3. In 'Fast food frenzy', Neil Shoebridge contemplates the fate of the fast food chains in Australia and, like Reading 14, asks the student to consider what stage of its life cycle the industry is in. The final reading by Matthew Stevens, 'Fosters faces a familiar foe', looks at the corporate battles being fought in the brewing industry. Students will gain greater insight by reading 'The Globalisation of Fosters' case study in section B4.

Case 16, 'Marketing of the Queensland Art Gallery' examines the marketing plan of the Art Gallery and encourages students to research methods of measuring performance and controls. Terry Gatfield's case, 'Marketing the non-profit way', takes a detailed look at the role of marketing in not-for-profit organisations and encourages students to apply the theory to analyse organisations they might be familiar with.

Reading 14—The Gold Coast's mid-life crisis

by Andrew Stewart

As urbanisation catches up with Australia's premier resort, it is becoming more anxious about its future. It must not only attract clean industries to provide jobs for a growing population, but increase tourist numbers as well.

The Gold Coast is somewhat like an aging surfie who has become a bit self-conscious about younger competitors and some of his own past excesses. But out of this mid-life crisis might come the model for the high-tech services and resort city that is destined to be repeated around the Australian coast and in Asia during the next few decades.

Despite the Gold Coast's economy continuing to grow at three times the national average and tourism numbers being at their highest, it is worried that it is being seen as an anachronism of the 1960s and 1970s. As Australia's fastest-growing region becomes increasingly a south-east Queensland growth conurbation, the importance of tourism, which attracted the property buyers, could be diminished. That is why the usual signs of the Gold Coast leading the national recovery—cashed-up locals and Brisbane investors snapping up property bargains to on-sell to southerners and foreigners in a boom—are matched by a new caution. The brash commercial confidence is tempered by an acknowledgment of some mistakes during the 1980s, mainly blamed on the white-shoe brigade, whose Gold Coast headquarters is now said to be firmly closed.

Nevertheless, some of the cyclical turns are the same. Gordon Douglas of PRD Realty resurrected a style of advertisement not seen for eight years, using a frog to promote waterfront land. The advertisement still worked: 127 blocks of Gold Coast waterfront land were sold for between $80 000 and $140 000 in three days. Eddie Kornhauser, who sold his Paradise Centre in 1988 at the peak of the boom, plunged back into the market last month, buying the Pines shopping centre property in the Gold Coast hinterland rather than the Surfers Paradise beachfront, which he previously favoured. Douglas says these are signs that the Gold Coast property market is recovering, but he admits that property and tourism have changed forever, because of the size of the market and new influences, ranging from what competitors are doing to sources of finance. Douglas says some people are confusing the maturing of the Gold Coast with a loss of vigour or growth.

The Gold Coast's promoters are more defensive and less brash than they were. They worry about the success of Cairns, the flood of Japanese, the demolition sites that mar the Surfers Paradise landscape, the shadows on the beach, the $50 price of a round of golf and, most troublesome of all, familiarity.

In May 1992, the Gold Coast launched its biggest promotion campaign, with $3 million worth of give-away holidays, against a background of fear that it may be too well known for the wrong reasons. David Hall, chief marketer of the Gold Coast for the past three months in his job as executive director of the Gold Coast Visitors and Convention Bureau, says: 'People think they will give the Gold Coast a miss as a holiday destination because they've been here before—it may have been ten or 20 years ago—or because it seems so familiar. They have seen the documentaries, the TV series and ads based here. In some ways the Gold Coast has been oversold, in the old image. We have to change people's perceptions for the better.'

The main job for Hall, who moved to the Gold Coast after 12 years promoting Adelaide, is to persuade Australians—and, to an extent, jaded overseas tour wholesalers—that Australia's biggest tourist resort still has the qualities that made it so popular, including the size and variety of attractions and accommodation.

Research based on interviews last year by the Queensland Tourist and Travel Corporation with 3600 potential holiday-makers in the eastern states highlights the Gold Coast's perception problems. Of those interviewed, 68% had spent at least one night on the Gold Coast at some time, but for most it was more than five years ago. Positives for the Gold Coast were its beaches, nightlife, high quality accommodation, restaurants, shopping and a wide variety of activities. Among the negatives were that it was seen as overcrowded with tourists, overdeveloped and too expensive. Only 14% of budget-conscious holiday-makers, which included a large proportion of families, showed any definite interest in a Gold Coast holiday. This was despite the Gold Coast having Australia's biggest bank of value accommodation (58% of Gold Coast beds are in units where a family of four can stay for $60 a night).

The domination of advertising for five-star hotels and the overwhelming image of high-rise hotels and units along the beach was blamed for the perception of the Gold Coast as expensive. However much the locals like to promote the 1960s image of the family at a cheap motel on the beach, the statistics point to fewer long family holidays and more shorter trips, often related to business.

A study by Alan Midwood, of the quantity surveying firm Rider Hunt, shows a 35% reduction in the past four years in the number of motel beds as traditional motels are demolished for high-rise hotels and units. The motels suffered a 40% reduction in bed nights while hotels increased 45%. The number of units (largely high-rise) available for letting has not risen, largely because more owners want to occupy them full time rather than for just a few weeks between holiday lettings. Average ownership time for units has increased from 3.7 years a decade ago to ten years. Sales of 1200 units last year showed the market was not dead, but it does not have the speculative fervour that left 54 cranes on unit towers and 7000 units on the market after the 1982–83 recession.

Gold Coast hotels enjoyed 21.5% increase in room nights in the December 1991 quarter compared with the December 1990 quarter, despite a mere 7% increase in rooms. Occupancy is above 70% and the average rate per room is $115 a night and rising. Hotel and airline packages have encouraged stays of two or three days, particularly when tied to conventions. And international tourism and special events, such as the Daikyo Indy car race, have left May the only dead month. Last year the traditional dead month, November, had higher hotel occupancy than December (74% compared with 72%).

The latest wave of visitors, from Taiwan, South Korea and Singapore, holiday at different times from the Japanese, who prefer the early and late months of the year, away from the Australian peak periods of winter and Christmas.

The news that Cairns has passed the Gold Coast in accommodation takings has cast a shadow over the industry's long-term goal of stable growth and high utilisation. In the September 1991 quarter, Cairns earned $59.2 million (up $18.6 million) while the Gold Coast earned $53.9 million (up $7.1 million). This was due in part to the fact that Cairns charged more per room ($96 a night compared with the Gold Coast's $63) which only highlights the misconception that the Gold Coast is expensive. In that quarter Cairns gained maximum benefit from the airfares war and its increasing share of overseas visitors.

The Gold Coast likes to emphasise that it is primarily a domestic tourism resort and that the perception of hordes of Asians is wrong. Of the 1.75 million visitors to the Gold Coast in 1990–91, 34% were from Queensland, 54% from interstate and only 12% from overseas. Australians patronised the newer attractions, such as Movie World, and stayed in budget units and new hotels offering special deals for Australians in advance of overseas bookings; overseas visitors were more dominant in some older properties, especially Seaworld (where half the visitors on a weekday are often overseas tour groups) and the central Surfers Paradise hotels.

Even while the Gold Coast is trying to emphasise its appeal to Australians, it is complaining loudly about Qantas making Cairns its Queensland hub, thus reducing the number of Asians and Europeans flying directly to Brisbane and the coast. The Gold Coast tourism industry sees the cash flow from 1.3 million international visitors predicted for the year 2000, worries that Asians should not be seen as overwhelming Australian holiday-makers, then worries again that it will miss out on its fair share of both markets.

Despite its size, the Gold Coast tourism industry is relatively unsophisticated. For example, while Cairns has 28 tour options, from snorkelling to whitewater rafting to bus tours of rainforests, the Gold Coast has few that take visitors beyond the nightclubs and golf courses. The tours are not only an important financial spin-off for Cairns because of their high labour and local ownership content, but also extend the range of activities beyond the Gold Coast's perceived limits of swimming, lying on the beach, eating, golfing and visiting theme parks.

One of the new thrusts of the Gold Coast's marketing is to emphasise that it too has rainforest, with better accessibility, and other green tourism exotica that are rated highly by Australian and international visitors. Hall says: 'The Gold Coast needs a strategic plan to cope with these issues of how to be Australia's top domestic tourist destination and attract our maximum share of international business. The issue is whether we can take control of our tourism future, or have it dictated by the development industry. Cairns has been very smart. They got off their butts and marketed. But they are at the stage the Gold Coast was at a decade ago when it just filled up the place and let it boom. It works for a while, but then you get to a size and sophistication where you've got to deal with a number of tourist segments and non-tourist interests.'

Ironically, one possible brake on the Gold Coast's tourism development is the 200 000 people who, having holidayed on the coast in the 1960s to 1980s, thought it was so good that they settled there. They hanker for the quieter coast they know and protest increasingly about crowding, traffic, new developments, and tourist levies to pay for infrastructure. The tourism industry is so concerned that it has commissioned research designed to demonstrate how tourism benefits local residents, not just in more restaurants and nightlife, but by provision of better water, roads and community facilities, such as parks.

The research project is the first real acknowledgment by the tourism industry that the Gold Coast's population growth is not necessarily the positive it was reckoned to be. Last month, the region's population passed 300 000 and it is expected to reach 500 000 by the end of the century.

'Most of the increase is in the hinterland (largely the Albert Shire), so that should not affect the coastal strip where most of the tourism activities are confined,' says Rider Hunt's Alan Midwood. 'We are fortunate that the geography gives us the backdrop of green mountains, so we won't become like Miami, where the hotels back on to a flat plain of suburbs.'

However, planner and developer Geoff Burchill says the Gold Coast should emphasise to governments and communities the planning difficulties involved in new-style cities based on recreation and service industries with little traditional manufacturing. 'The more substantial the Gold Coast becomes, the less spectacular the growth appears. We can build more accommodation than all but one of our competing Australian tourism destinations, but it hardly seems much in the stock we already have,' Burchill says.

'The Gold Coast doesn't have a God-given right to be the major tourism destination, just because it's got great beaches and, increasingly, other facilities (hotels, theme parks, casino). We have to look for new directions because of competition, not just from Cairns, but also from Malaysia and later Indonesia and Vietnam, where they also have spectacular beaches and will develop the infrastructure.

'We've got to understand that the nature of show business is changing. Building shadows on one of our beaches used to be a negative. Now, with the concern about skin cancer, it can be a positive. Similarly, if more people want to live in resort areas, we have to plan the tourism functions so tourists can have a lively atmosphere and party through the night, while the residents can enjoy a quiet life, using facilities when they want to, but not being overly disturbed by tourists.

'If you look ahead 20 or 30 years, the Gold Coast has the chance to lead a number of locations on the Queensland and NSW coasts and in Asia in showing how to meld tourism with modern service cities. Everyone looks at tourism as promotion and airlines and hotels. But as resort areas get bigger, the important part of tourism will be the infrastructure: how to handle lots of people in a fairly confined area without it losing its attractions.'

Burchill strongly backs what is referred to locally as 'not the MFP' as the additive that will round out the Gold Coast both as a place to live and as an attraction. Since the multi-function polis went to Adelaide, the Queensland Government and industry leaders and developers have been pondering how to capture the essence of the MFP: clean industry with intellectually based workers living in resort style.

The Japanese companies that picked the Gold Coast as the most suitable location in the world for its mixture of resort, geography, industrial and education facilities, are quietly supporting the new scheme to set up the Centre for International Business. The new strategy, rather than being seen as a real estate development, leans towards attracting clean industries to various locations in the Brisbane-Gold Coast corridor. The prime example is the Hong Kong Jockey Club, which located its computer research and development arm on the Gold Coast after its workers decided, following a worldwide survey, that was where they wanted to live and work.

One of the main reasons for the interest in clean industries is jobs. The perception that the Gold Coast is filling with retired people is wrong: only one in five people migrating to the Gold Coast are at retirement age. The biggest group of migrants is young families attracted by relatively cheap real estate and the chance to get out of the big southern cities. However, not even tourism can provide enough jobs, particularly permanent, well-paid jobs. The Gold Coast is a big national producer of household detergents, metal products, furniture, technology and tourism support services (everything from software for running conventions to resort design), but it needs industries that harmonise with tourism.

'The Gold Coast will always be tourism-led, which is why we need to lift its tourism image, but in the next 10–20 years there will also be another 400 000–500 000 people living here who need feeding and entertaining,' Burchill says. 'Our challenge is to manage it so we have a vigorous tourism side, which does not suffer from big boom-bust swings caused by the larger population and other industry. We want to have all the peaks, but not the extreme swings. It is not easily achieved, but worth aiming for.'

Midwood is concerned that people have become so depressed by three years of tourism disasters (arising from the pilots dispute) that they do not fully recognise that present facilities will be inadequate within two or three years, depending on the speed of economic recovery. 'Whatever direction the coast goes in, it still needs rooms. Unfortunately, we are suffering from the international capital shortage, just like everywhere from Czechoslovakia to South Africa,' he says. 'It is very frustrating for people on the Gold Coast, where we are not used to sitting on our hands, debating which way we will go, simply because we can't raise the money to do what has to be done: build more rooms. The debate is not whether the Gold Coast will grow, but whether it will reach anywhere near its potential. When people speak as if the Gold Coast is dead or dying, I just point out that it has grown, and continues to grow, at better than 6% a year for the past 25 years.'

Reproduced with permission from BRW, Australia's
leading business magazine 15 May, 1992, pp. 58–62.

Questions

1. In what way(s) has the marketing of the Gold Coast differed to the marketing of any other product or service?
2. What stage of the product life cycle would you say the Gold Coast is at? Why?

Reading 15—Where Brian Quinn went wrong

by Robert Gottliebsen

Although the Coles Myer chief laid the foundations for enormous profits in the future, he and his managers made mistakes that allowed rivals to steal a march on the retailing monolith.

A year ago Brian Quinn was at the zenith of his power at Australia's biggest retailer, Coles Myer. He was chairman, chief executive and chief operating officer of the group. No other business executive in Australia had so much power. Yet as last year proceeded, it became apparent to Quinn and his co-chairman, Solomon Lew, that the best solution for the company was for Quinn to go. Accordingly, last week, Quinn and the man he chose to promote in the 1980s, Russell Stucki, announced their retirements. On the following day, about 400 Coles Myer executives gave Quinn a standing ovation as he stood alongside Lew, the new chairman. Those executives also knew they were witnessing the start of a new era in Australian retailing as the Lew family took over the mantle once carried by the Coles and Myer families who gave the company its name. Lew made it clear to the executives that he was looking for growth.

The saga at Coles Myer has few parallels in Australian corporate history. The company is now in a remarkable position to take advantage of the strong foundation that has been laid by Quinn. At the same time, the mistakes that were made following the merger of the Coles and Myer giants are still affecting the company and are a lesson for all those who might attempt a similar exercise. However, those mistakes are not fatal and can be corrected by the new management team. There is enormous potential in the company for future profits.

The Coles company, which engineered the merger, had a very different heritage to Myer. It was run with a 'five and ten cents' mentality, first by the Coles family and, second, by a remarkable group of expansionist executives headed by Tom North, Bevan Bradbury and Brian Quinn who all started with the company early in their working lives and rose to the top. By contrast, the Myer family and their business operated in an upmarket environment. For the downmarket men at Coles to take over the prestigious Myer business had seemed impossible. But in 1985, the businesses came together as Coles Myer with Coles men taking the key positions.

Bradbury became chairman, Quinn chief executive and two more Coles executives who had started at the bottom, Graeme Seabrook and Russell Stucki, headed almost all the operational departments. The Coles executives wanted to run the company and be seen to be running it. But achieving the 'impossible' had a strange effect on many Coles executives. The task of managing a business three times the size of Coles required different skills and, although no one realised it at the time, the Coles management team was thin. For about 18 months after the merger, the four-person operating team at the top of Coles Myer looked strong. Then, in August 1987, Bradbury retired as chairman. He could have been replaced by deputy chairman Bails Myer, but that would have resulted in the Coles team reporting to the head of the Myer family. The Coles people were still savouring their win and that was not an option. As a result, Quinn took over as chairman and chief executive. At the time, many other chief executives also acted as chairmen of their companies, and the dangers of the dual role did not become apparent for several years.

The job of chairman at Coles Myer was particularly demanding as the holders of half the company's equity stock sat at the board table, putting up plans for capital reorganisation and other ideas that required attention. Quinn believed that if he took on the dual role he would have to appoint either Stucki or Seabrook to take charge of the group's retail operations. In such situations, whoever is passed over for the job normally leaves. It was a decision that Quinn had to get right. He chose the popular Stucki over the more prickly Seabrook who later left the company to move to Britain where he became chief executive of Kwik Save, a discount supermarket chain, owned by Dairy Farms International (part of the Jardine Matheson group). The 770-store Kwik Save chain was recently named British retailer of the year.

In little more than a year, the Coles management team of four had been halved and there were no obvious successors to Quinn in the ranks. But that fact was obscured in 1987–88 by the sheer power of Quinn, the boom in the Australian economy and soaring Coles Myer profits. Quinn seemed to have done everthing right until then, but the boom concealed his first fundamental mistake. Stucki had a good record in the food sector, but was not the person to be managing director of the retail operations of a group as diverse as Coles Myer.

After the merger, Quinn, Stucki and other former Coles executives spent a lot of time studying the new Myer business and, in particular, its department stores. Morale in the Myer stores was low but some beneficial fundamental changes had already been made. However, there was still a lot to be done to unify the cultures of the two companies and give the group a corporate identity. Soon after Bradbury retired as chairman, the company moved into its plush new Melbourne headquarters—a sharp contrast to the previous environment where executives walked through a store to get to their desks. Buoyed by the early success of the merged company, it started to prepare to extend into New Zealand and elsewhere.

The 'five and ten cents' era ended in the 1980s. By then, Coles Myer dominated every segment of Australian retailing and in particular had its foot firmly on the neck of Woolworths, which was reeling from a succession of mistakes in the previous decade. Quinn made his second great mistake by allowing Woolworths to recover. Every Coles Myer executive who walked into his or her new office believed the company was invincible. The new complex, including the lavish quarters for the board and Quinn, seemed to confirm that invincibility. At the same time, enormous corporate energy—particularly from Quinn—was spent on creating a new company. As a result, no one really worried when the aging Paul Simons was recalled by Woolworths. Many years earlier, Simons had been regarded as an up and coming Woolworths executive. Unhappy with the way the company was progressing, he left to co-ordinate the successful establishment of Franklins in Australia. When Simons returned to Woolworths, he set up office at the company's warehouse at Yennora with a black phone and a wall air conditioner—the antithesis of Coles Myer's style. Simons started revamping the Woolworths merchandising policy, including placing greater emphasis on fresh foods and spending money updating the company's stores to give a new approach to supermarket retailing. He also lowered Woolworths prices to within 1% of those at Franklins stores.

In earlier times, North, Bradbury and Quinn, as chief executives of Coles, lived and breathed the supermarket business. But as Simons went about introducing his changes, Quinn was looking the other way and Stucki didn't recognise the trap his wily opponent was setting for Coles Myer. Simons must have been stunned by the lack of response. Not only did Coles Myer not update its stores to match Woolworths, but in some cases, even increased prices in a bid to go upmarket. Stucki imported an executive from the recently acquired New Zealand operation to head the Coles Myer food business and oppose Simons. It was not a fair match. Inevitably, market share fell.

The K mart operation had been a jewel in the Coles crown throughout the 1970s and early 1980s. It was the result of work by a brilliant Coles team that opened up a new era of discount retailing. Coles outflanked Myer and its Target operation. There was great joy at K mart after the merger of Coles and Myer . . . perhaps K mart's rival, Target, could be acquired and made part of a new and wider network of K mart stores.

But Quinn's pride in the Coles victory was aimed at reviving, not killing, Myer businesses. Target was given a new lease of life under the team headed by Peter Wilkinson and Brian Beattie. Like Coles supermarkets, K mart, freed from the day-to-day supervision of Quinn, began to develop an upmarket strategy at odds with its traditional base. K mart outlets were carpeted, signs were changed and different merchandise introduced. Corporate historians will reflect that although the Coles executives won, those in the two great Coles businesses, K mart and goods stores, forgot their heritage and reasons for success and started trying to emulate the company they acquired. The reasons for this go beyond being influenced by the atmosphere of the group's plush new headquarters. Like food, K mart had been heading in the wrong direction for several years before Quinn and his board realised. Technology and buying systems had become vital to modern discount stores.

Perhaps the sense of being part of Coles prevented K mart from adopting the simple but brilliantly effective Target technology developed by former Myer managers. K mart believed that Target's technology would be unsuitable by the year 2000 and aimed at establishing a better system. But K mart fell behind during the long programme to develop new systems. It was only a matter of time before these fundamental mistakes at K mart had an effect on the firm's bottom line. For some time, K mart profits were merely sluggish, but on 12 March the company announced that they had been halved during the past year—a period when well-financed discount stores should have boomed.

At Target, which boasts good technology and a clear sense of direction, Beattie has been taking full advantage of a situation made for discount stores. Not only have customers been looking for bargains, but manufacturers, desperate to stay in business, have been prepared to sell cheaply. Moreover, local manufacturers have been able to supply quickly those items that are subject to fickle fashions. Beattie has been clever in mixing local buying with imports and keeping stock turnover high.

K mart buyers have made many mistakes. They haven't understood that the essence of retailing is to keep stock turning over quickly. In a recession, that means being able to adapt to changes in consumer demand. But K mart buyers had been returning from overseas buying missions with huge volumes of stock that have been wrong for discount stores trading in a recession. K mart established a new distribution centre at Hoppers Crossing, Melbourne, which was, in theory, a sound move. But as the mountain of stock began to leave the wharves (often delayed), the new distribution system became clogged. The centre became a warehouse and extra space had to be rented. Getting rid of the stock caused big losses. Although it was clear last year that something was wrong with K mart, the full extent of the problem did not become apparent until after last August when Quinn gave former Grace Bros executive Bob Dalziel the job of ending Coles Myer's woes.

Although Coles' operations suffered from the merger, the former Myer operations blossomed under the touch of Quinn. Not only did Target emerge brilliantly from the merger, but Quinn picked the right people to head the Myer and Grace Bros department stores. They improved and, at a time when they should have been under pressure from the recession, profits continued to rise. David Jones launched a major assault on Myer in the 1980s and seemed to be a much greater threat to the merged group than Woolworths. But not only have Myer and Grace Bros department stores turned the tables, they are now close to dominating the department store sector, much as Coles food stores did to Woolworths in the mid-1980s.

In 1989 Quinn started to realise that his chosen successor, Stucki, was not the person to be operations manager of the group. Often people in positions of great power do not admit their mistakes, but Quinn faced up to the problem. He abolished the position of managing director of the retail operation and had line managers report to him, giving him almost complete control of the company. About the same time, Lew became vice-chairman, while Bails Myer continued as deputy chairman.

The executive changes in 1989 had important repercussions. Overseas expansion plans had to be set aside, partly because the company did not have the management depth. The New Zealand exercise had been successful, but Quinn had already realised the drain an overseas venture—even one as near as NZ—could have on management time. Had Myer made a major purchase in the US at the top of the market in 1986–88, the Coles Myer story might not have had a happy ending.

Stucki, who spent 25 years in food retailing before his elevation, was sent back to the food division to confront Woolworths and Franklins. But by this time, Woolworths was firing. Quinn had high hopes of Stucki repeating his previous success in the food store sector, but the Coles Myer food operation Stucki returned to had its back to the wall. He devised some excellent promotional schemes, including the computers-for-schools giveaway. New shoppers attracted by the scheme discovered Coles trailed its rivals, not only on price, but on store quality too. Stucki followed the promotions by launching a price war.

It is now clear that Quinn did not deal with the fundamental issues facing Coles Myer. Coles supermarkets require a new approach to give them the sparkle Simons introduced to Woolworths. But the 1989 reshuffle involved more than transferring Stucki. It signalled the end of the dominance by the 'Coles boys' of the senior positions immediately below Quinn. As a result, Peter Wilkinson, who had helped set the foundations for the spectacular rise of Target, was put in charge of Coles Myer department stores, which, like Target, were already on an upward path. It was an excellent appointment. Beattie, who worked under Wilkinson at Target, grabbed the opportunity provided to an aggressive discounter by the recession to vigorously attack his competitors, some of whom went to the wall.

Although it was important for Quinn to place Coles executives in control of the retail arms after the merger, he and Bradbury realised that the Coles team lacked someone with the finance talents of Myer's finance director, John Barner. Not only did Barner win the respect of both sides in the merger, but during its success and failures, Coles Myer has been financially well managed. Most of the present financial strength of the group stems from Barner's appointment.

Barner provided a valuable link between the management and the board. Coles Myer was not a company that was passively owned by institutions and the public, but one where the manager, Quinn, sat at a board table faced by directors who controlled half the equity. Among the shareholders represented at the table, were the Myer family, Westfield, K mart of the US and Solomon Lew.

Bails Myer represented the increasingly diverse interests of the Myer family, which had reaped big gains from the merger at the expense of a loss of power. Frank Lowy and his Westfield group had a long association with Myer and were potentially long-term investors until losses in the media industry forced them to take their profits and leave. K mart has never been active in the management of the company and, a little like the Myer family, has stayed in because of the rewards and the fact that their name is an important brand for the company.

Lew had a long-held dream to head the company, but in the 1980s Quinn's reign seemed likely to extend well into the 1990s. Coles and Myer had a history of executive-dominated boards and the early Coles Myer boards were similarly structured. Gradually, the composition of the board changed with the appointment of people well known to Lew, such as the ANZ Bank's Will Bailey and transport magnate Lindsay Fox.

Lew's appointment as vice-chairman in 1989 was a signal he was heading for the chairmanship. As vice-chairman, he had a much greater mandate to visit the group's various operations and talk to executives. Quinn must have been in an unusual position. A chairman and chief executive can normally relinquish the chief executive officer's job and remain chairman. But Quinn had not trained a successor. The man he selected had been returned to divisional head. Indeed, much of his attention was occupied by his retirement package, and at last year's annual meeting, Quinn's superannuation package was underwritten against any tax changes. When Quinn finally steps down on 24 July, he will take with him a very substanital sum. There was no penalty in leaving early.

Quinn and Lew came to similar conclusions last year: that the company had to overhaul K mart and Coles food stores and that Quinn, in his last year as CEO was not the right person to do it. Lew became co-chairman and started running board meetings. It was proposed to institutionalise the co-chairman's role, but Quinn stepped down and became chief executive only in the months leading up to his retirement. Quinn's retirement was announced along with a virtually steady profit—a good achievement given the recession and the K mart disaster.

Although K mart's earnings were slashed, the chain maintained its sales base. Similarly, the damage to the Coles food stores' sales had been arrested, while the group's department stores and Target were going well. The company was in good shape with much greater potential than either Coles or Myer boasted as separate operations.

During the opening of the new Coles Myer headquarters at Tooronga, Melbourne in 1987, Quinn said 'What we have done is simply lay the foundations for the future. It's a future with no bounds'. He didn't realise that laying those foundations would take until 1992, and that by then the company's 'future' would be in different hands.

Reproduced with permission from BRW, Australia's leading business magazine, 20 March, 1992, pp. 44–48.

Questions

1. Brian Quinn and his board were obviously working to a well formulated marketing plan. How do you think marketing planning would differ for a non-profit organisation?
2. How would you describe the culture of Coles Myer?
3. What do you think was Brian Quinn's biggest mistake?

Reading 16—Fosters faces a familiar foe

by Matthew Stevens

The doubts, personality clashes and struggles for power that have plagued Foster's Brewing Group for years refuse to disappear. Indeed, according to sharemarket analysts, they ensure that the battle for control of the brewing giant is far from over.

International Brewing Holdings is seeking funding for a bid for the minority shareholdings in Foster's Brewing Group. The management of SA Brewing Holdings has requested board approval to build a stake of 3–5% in Foster's, whose chief executive, Peter Bartels, is considering the top job at Coles Myer, having grown weary of the disruption and interference by his major shareholder, IBH. Meanwhile, Foster's former chief executive and chairman, John Elliott, who runs IBH, is talking to SA Brewing's chief, Ross Wilson, about replacing Bartels. Wilson is expected to be appointed chief executive of Foster's by the end of the year. To top that, Foster's Canadian partner, The Molson Companies, has the cash ready to take a 10% stake in Foster's.

These are some of the likely scenarios, predictions and rumors that swept through sharemarkets in Australia, Britain and Canada last week. Of course, none of these may happen. But most observers expect further action. 'The rumours about a potential outcome of Foster's are really hotting up; they are flying around everywhere. It seems to be moving fast,' Potter Warburg analyst Justin Hilford says. Despite the efforts by Bartels to concentrate on the company's continuing climb back from the brink of corporate oblivion, the focus is once again on the fate of its major shareholder, IBH.

Foster's has become the most enduring source of market debate, speculation and occasionally pure fantasy since Robert Holmes à Court's decade-long dalliance with BHP. The battle for Foster's now involves so many local and international groups, so many alliances are being formed and broken, and so many friendships are being made, broken or renewed, that even those who closely follow the emotion-charged battle between Bartels and his former boss and close friend, Elliott, cannot claim to be certain of the likely fate of either man or their companies.

Although the likely victor is unclear, the timing of the victory dash is not so difficult to pick. Certainly, it appears that the battle is reaching its final stages. Elliott must present to his banks and other creditors—most importantly BHP—a solution to his debt problems by May. If Elliott's proposal is accepted, IBH will then have until April next year to repay $750 million it borrowed from BHP and $212 million it owes on preference interest.

Few people in the market or executives at Foster's have any doubt that the latest outbreak of speculation is linked to an attempt by Elliott to flush out one of the potential major shareholders for Foster's. But equally, few blame IBH for emphasising the fluidity of Foster's ownership position and the number of options open to it in seeking an answer to Elliott's huge problem—the shortfall of more than $1 billion between what it paid for and what it would receive in a liquidation of its only asset, 37.8% of Foster's.

The current Foster's share price of about $2 means that Elliott is very close to being able to pay off his big creditors. But Elliott is just as keen to repay his friends, both corporate and personal, who backed his management buy-out of Foster's (then Elders IXL) in 1988. The brewers Molson and Grand Metropolitan, broking firms Prudential Bache and McIntosh, long-time personal backers the Myer family and AFP (now the Lang Corporation), and a host of senior and second-tier managers of the now-dismembered Elders IXL put their faith and money in the hands of Elliott and his management buy-out. Elliott can no longer wait for Foster's share price to boom or for the dividend and capital-return policy to change. To repay his friends, Elliott must engineer a solution.

One option he is believed to have considered is a bid for the minorities, either directly or, more interestingly, through a new entity that would raise equity of $400-500 million from a range of parties interested in acquiring the assets of, or securing supply contracts with, Foster's. But such a king hit is expensive and, in the end, unnecessary, according to ANZ McCaughan senior analyst Terry Povey. He says the hidden value of IBH is that it controls the minorities without owning the shares. Foster's ownership structure is so delicate that a new shareholder prepared to take a 5% stake could swing the balance towards Elliott at an annual meeting.

At last year's meeting, Elliott unsuccessfully tried to seize control of Foster's though a proxy battle, but only 85% of votes were cast. Accordingly, he would need slightly more than 43% of the votes at an annual meeting or extraordinary general meeting for victory. At present, IBH owns 37.8% of Foster's. NML owns about 2% and is largely supportive of Elliott's strategy. One additional big supporter would give Elliott the 5-6% he needs to regain control of Foster's.

The lack of liquidity in the market for Foster's shares must also be of concern to Bartels. There is no question that the shortage of scrip, combined with Elliott's ability to regularly stir the market's interest in the brewing company, has played a significant role in the recent strong performance of Foster's shares. The company has easily outperformed its Australian and international counterparts during the past year and, more particularly, since last November when Elliott's campaign for control began in earnest.

SA Brewing is regularly mentioned in the Foster's battle. Ross Wilson would be a buyer if the price were right and if there were a chance that the IBH ownership issue could be resolved. Wilson also was a bidder for Castlemaine Tooheys assets but walked away from a joint-venture agreement that he decided was too complex. Wilson is taking the same pragmatic view of Foster's. He was angered by the pre-Christmas blow of losing SA Brewing's canning and toll-brewing contracts with Foster's, which resulted in a sustained fall in SA Brewing's share price. According to brokers in London and Australia, Wilson sought permission to start buying Foster's shares with a limit of less than 5%. But Wilson is not buying Foster's shares and the market is reading the company's situation incorrectly. SA Brewing wants no involvement in Foster's until there is a solution to the IBH situation.

Clearly, the market believes that Wilson will buy Foster's shares in a bid to gain leverage in the IBH settlement, and perhaps regain the canning and toll-brewing contracts. Such a short-term response would be quite possible. It is understood that Amcor's five-year contract for the canning business can be reviewed annually, both in terms of price and volume. Potter Warburg's Hilford also believes that the savings on the deal with Amcor will fall short of the $16 million a year suggested by Foster's. Hilford suggests that $11 million a year is a more likely saving.

Molson, which shares ownership of Canada's biggest brewer, the Molson Brewing Group, with Foster's is another company with a keen interest in who owns Foster's. Chief executive Marshall 'Mickey' Cohen admits that he picked a loser when he spent $150 million to gain a share of Elliott's management buy-out effort. It was a decision that nearly cost him his job last year in a management restructuring, prompted by the company's decision to return to more conservative, traditional business.

Although Cohen remains interested in the Foster's battle and is on record as supporting Bartels and his team, he must decide whether IBH or Foster's offers him the best chance of gaining access to the underlying assets of the company, the international brewing business. He will also have to persuade Molson's board that staying in the Foster's battle is worth risking another $2 billion. Cohen has expressed an interest in building a stake as high as 40% in Foster's. But according to a spokesman for Molson, reports that the company is poised to start that process by buying a 10% stake and that it has a $450 billion line of credit ready to fund the acquisition are not accurate. But privately, Molson executives say the company is more than happy to maintain its wait-and-see approach. But it would be ready to start buying if Elliott altered the existing balance.

BHP is also monitoring the battle closely. Indeed, those involved in the corporate struggle emphasise the importance of watching BHP. This week, BHP chief executive John Prescott visited Tokyo, where he met executives of Asahi, the Japanese brewer that owns 19.9% of Foster's. Asahi's support for the existing management was crucial to Bartels fighting off Elliott's attempt to wrest control at last year's annual meeting. Prescott's visit to Asahi is typical of the quiet way BHP has gone about staying in touch with Foster's major shareholders. A working knowledge of the international businesses that have become Foster's major shareholders and allies could prove vital if BHP decides to become more involved in the Foster's battle. Formally, at least, IBH has until April next year to repay more than $900 million it owes BHP. But BHP, along with the bankers, can move in on IBH if Elliott fails to provide an acceptable proposal to its creditors by May.

BHP faces a difficult choice. Many believe IBH is still keen to unlock value from Foster's by forcing the sale of a major brewing asset (the most likely choice being the British brewer, Courage). 'But BHP is the senior corporate citizen in Australia,' Potter Warburg's Hilford says. 'It would be hard to see how they could let Elliott proceed with any plan that required a break-up—not if they had the power to put a stop to it. But what are their alternatives? Elliott still controls IBH, he pulls the strings. But after May the creditors have the power to send in the receivers. BHP then has a far more direct input into the decisions of IBH, presuming I think as you must, that IBH will struggle to meet the requirements of its May deadline.'

When Foster's share price passes $2.05, IBH will cover the principal BHP debt of $750 million. When the price reaches $2.20, IBH can then cover the $212 million BHP is owed on unpaid preference dividends. As a result, BHP's attitude will be influenced by the conditions of its agreement with IBH and how close to covering the debt is close enough, given that there is no requirement to repay the principal until April 1993. At present, BHP is trying to find an arrangement that would allow it to give Elliott more time to repay the debt. As well, it is working to persuade Elliott's bankers to extend the time for repayment.

Arranging breathing space for Elliott could prove easier than many believe. Elliott's major banking syndicate, Vextin, would be comfortably covered by any settlement. Vextin's only concern would be that its leading financier, the Hong Kong & Shanghai Bank, has a guarantee over $180 million that expires in November, but which the other banks in the syndicate would be keen to see extended. Meanwhile, BHP and IBH's other major creditor, Citibank, are not completely comfortable with the state of the ownership struggle but are believed to be reasonably confident that extra time would be more beneficial than closing down IBH.

The key to understanding BHP's role in Foster's is a company called Beswick. It was formed in 1988 to hold 322 million BHP shares, originally bought by Elders IXL from Robert Holmes à Court as part of the settlement of his long-running bid for control of BHP. Those shares were transferred to Beswick when BHP sold its 18.5% interest in Elders IXL to Harlin Holdings, now IBH. At present, BHP is showing a comfortable paper profit in Beswick of more than $1 billion, which explains why the company has so much patience with Elliott and is able to carry the IBH exposure. BHP, with the support of its auditors, is able to link the IBH and Beswick investments, which has saved the company from being forced to make provision for, or write off, any of its investment in IBH, even though other companies, many with far less conservative reputations, have done so.

The pressure on Bartels builds daily. According to Hilford, he should be defending his position as if a full take-over campaign were being mounted. However, Bartels remains convinced that he should concentrate on Foster's daily business, while being forced to privately dismiss rumors that he is leaving to join Coles Myer, or that he is desperately frustrated by the chairman and shareholders meeting that was established after last year's annual meeting.

Bartels and his team are believed to be looking for ways to exercise the share options held by IBH. At current levels, these are 'out of the money', or more expensive than existing shares. If Bartels could get those shares exercised and placed in friendly hands, he would immediately dilute the shareholding of IBH and its allies and create a new liquidity in the Foster's market—a liquidity that could threaten the longer-term performance of Foster's shares.

Meanwhile, Bartels is trying to run a business that is coming under increasing pressure from the arrival of Lion Nathan in Australia. The New Zealand brewer has already made a big impact by bringing new capital and ideas to the Tooheys and Castlemaine Perkins ranges. While Lion Nathan has been grabbing market share in NSW, Queensland and even in Foster's home market, Victoria, the overall market has been squeezed by the effects of the recession. Foster's sales in Victoria last year fell by 7%, resulting in Carlton and United's national net profit falling from $131 million to $111 million. It was only the strong performance of the British and Canadian businesses that enabled Bartels to record a 33% increase in net profit to $333 million.

Bartels says he and his team have some novel ideas for regaining market share. Few would blame him for spending a lot of time working just as hard to develop some similarly dramatic plans to ensure Foster's survival. Certainly, the market believes that Elliott and IBH are now in control of events. For Bartels, that means great danger.

Reproduced with permission from BRW, Australia's leading business magazine, 21 February, 1992, pp. 20–23.

Questions

1. Foster's is an international corporation: how important is the chief executive officer?
2. 'The globalisation of Fosters' case study traces the company's fortunes over 150 years. How would you describe their current marketing strategy?

Reading 17—Fast food frenzy

by Neil Shoebridge

The ubiquitous burger and pizza chains are set to further infiltrate our lives with new outlets, new products and hard-sell marketing drives. But has the industry already reached saturation point?

If Kevin Jurd has his way, Australia will soon be dotted with hundreds of little Pizza Huts. This month, a nine-square-metre kiosk opens in the Sydney Football Stadium. During the next few years Jurd, who is Pizza Hut's director of marketing and business development, will open similar outlets in petrol stations, factories, airport terminals and sports grounds. Bob Bothwell, the South Pacific and Asia vice-president of Kentucky Fried Chicken, is also plotting an ambitious expansion programme. After opening seven or eight new stores a year during the 1980s, Kentucky Fried—which, like Pizza Hut, is owned by the giant US food and soft-drink manufacturer PepsiCo—has been bitten by the growth bug. It opened 35 last year and will build 130 by 1997.

This is only the beginning. Australia's fast food industry is set to explode, with companies pumping more than $1.5 billion into at least 800 new outlets during the next five years. The golden arches of McDonald's and the red roofs of Pizza Hut will soon be everywhere, joined by dozens of other chains. No large country town will be overlooked. Outlets will appear in hospitals, office buildings and convenience stores. New products will be introduced at a head-spinning rate. Franchising programmes will be expanded to lure new recruits into the business.

The fast food chains have taken a page out of the soft drink industry's marketing manual. 'Our aim is to get our products to people where they eat,' Bothwell says. 'We can no longer expect the consumer to always come to us.'

Last year Australians spent $3 billion in fast food chains, up 15% over 1990, plus an estimated $5 billion on take-away food from local Chinese restaurants, fish-and-chip shops and hamburger joints. Meanwhile, the number of fast food outlets has climbed from 2200 in 1990 to an estimated 2500. The industry employs more than 120 000 full-time and part-time workers.

All this points to the beginning of a golden era for the industry. But how much fast food can Australians stand? Indeed, the taste has already begun to sour for some. The recession brought a halt to the rapid growth the chains had enjoyed in their existing stores during the 1980s. Several studies point to a sharp decline in spending on fast food this year. Nagging questions about nutritional value also continue to pose problems.

McDonald's launched 36 new stores last year, the most it has opened in one year since it entered the Australian market in 1971. Chairman Peter Ritchie believes the fast food industry will eventually reach saturation point. 'There is a limit, but I don't know where that limit is,' he says. However, that threat is not crimping McDonald's plans. Ritchie says it will open 195 new outlets in the next five years, lifting its total to 500.

Most of the sales growth achieved by the industry last year came from the addition of new stores. Hungry Jack's, a 110-store hamburger chain owned by Competitive Foods, will finish 1991–92 with sales of $157.5 million, up more than 15% on the previous year. More than two-thirds of that growth was generated by opening 10 new stores; sales in existing outlets grew a modest 4.1%. 'Our growth rate in existing stores during 1991 was down on previous years,' says Jack Cowin, the managing director of Competitive Foods. 'But 4.1% was a good result compared to the rest of the industry.'

Danny Rubenstein, owner of the six-store Rueben's Hot Dogs chain in Melbourne and Sydney, estimates that the fast food industry's real sales—that is, excluding those generated by new stores and price rises—have sunk 25–30% this year. Wilder Ruiz, the managing director of Pancakes Australia, tells a similar story. His company's turnover climbed 8% to $13 million during 1991, thanks to the addition of two new stores. But sales in its nine existing stores fell 7%, while customer traffic slipped 5%. 'The recession has clearly hurt the fast food industry,' Ruiz says. 'People don't want to spend money.' The average amount each customer spends fell to $11 in a Pancakes store last year, from $12 in 1990. McDonald's turned over $670.5 million in 1991, up 12.2% over 1990. But the company's real sales rose just 3%, the worst result in 20 years. Kentucky Fried's sales climbed 12% to $450 million during 1991, but existing stores had zero growth. 'It was our worst year for a decade,' Bothwell says. 'Our average sale is $8, which is not a lot of money. Buying a Kentucky Fried meal is not a big decision. Below our price point, people may as well stay at home.'

That is just what many are doing, thanks to the recession. To lure them out, fast food operators are pushing a bewildering array of special deals, discounts and giveaways. Pizza Hut has a string of special offers, including a $19.90 'family meal deal' (two medium pizzas, two garlic bread rolls and a bottle of Pepsi-Cola) and $5 all-the-pizza-you-can-eat meals on Tuesday and Wednesday nights. These deals are not used as loss leaders to generate customer traffic. Kevin Jurd says the discounts trim the company's profit margin on individual products but boost sales. 'Customer traffic increases and our docket average rises,' he says. 'Fixed costs remain the same, so our total profitability rises.' Pizza Hut has been running various discount offers for 18 months, and Jurd says the programme will continue. 'Consumers are very value-conscious,' he says. 'We must give them real value for money.'

Most fast food companies claim that the sales slow-down is an aberration; when the economy improves, growth will return. But some industry executives are not so confident. Colin Stacey, chief executive of Whitbread Restaurants, which owns the 121-outlet Keg chain, believes Australians' spending on eating out has declined 20–30% annually since 1989. 'I expect to see growth when we emerge from the recession, but I don't believe we will see the high propensity to eating out witnessed during the 1980s,' he says.

A survey conducted by the research firm Yann Campbell Hoare Wheeler late last year found that Australians were planning to trim their fast food and take-away budgets. Convenience stores, the hybrid petrol-and-food stores that are springing up around Australia, have targeted fast food as a growth area. A 1990 report by the marketing consultancy Meyers Strategy Group claimed that fast food accounted for just 5.5% of convenience stores' sales here, compared with 16.3% in the US. Circle K, a convenience store chain owned by Shell, expects fast food to represent 15-20% of its sales in 1995, up from 10% today.

Concerns about fast food's nutritional value also cloud the industry's future. Research by the advertising agency George Patterson last year found that 51% of Australians did not think the chains offered good quality or healthy food, up from 45% in 1990. At the same time, 38% of women said they felt guilty about serving fast food to their families, up from 26% in 1989. But operators say nutrition is not an issue when people decide to visit their stores. 'The image of fast food as junk food is fading,' Jurd says. Last year McDonald's added a low-fat muffin and low-fat hamburger sauces to its menu, but the company has not promoted these products. Ritchie says: 'People don't come to McDonald's for health food. They come to McDonald's for the food we already sell. We added the low-fat items because we could do it without hurting the taste of our products. But it's not a big deal.'

According to many operators, the recession is a short-term irritation. They point to studies such as a report released by BIS Shrapnel in March as proof of their industry's good growth prospects. The report claimed that in 1988–89 Australians spent 24.5% of their weekly food budgets on eating out, up from 18.1% in 1975–76, and predicted that the figure will hit 30% by 1995. (BIS did not isolate spending in fast food chains). The forecast is based on trends in the US, where spending on eating out has climbed from 20% of the average food budget in 1970 to 32% in 1980 and 48% today.

Kentucky Fried's Bothwell argues that demographic and lifestyle changes will fuel growth in Australia. 'The horizon keeps expanding, not because of population growth but because of lifestyle changes such as the rise of working women and two-income families,' he says. 'Fourteen years ago we thought the maximum number of Kentucky Fried outlets in Australia would be 300. Now we are talking about 500.'

Americans spend an average of $317 a year at quick-service restaurants such as McDonald's, Hungry Jack's and Kentucky Fried. In Australia the figure is $102. Annual per-capita spending on pizza in Australia is now $35, up from $24 in 1987. In the US it is $83. 'Australia doesn't mirror everything that happens in the US,' Jurd says, 'but the fast food industries in both countries have developed along similar lines.'

The growth potential of the Australian fast food business attracts a steady stream of new entrants, many of which fail. Sizzler, the industry's present darling, arrived in Australia from the US in August 1985 and did not break even until early 1988. 'Fast food is a tough industry, plagued by high start-up costs, high labour costs, high marketing costs and fierce competition,' says Kevin Perkins, the managing director of Collins Foods, which holds the chain's Asia-Pacific franchise and operates 35 outlets (it is also Kentucky Fried's Queensland franchisee). 'To succeed, you need an excellent concept and a keen understanding of the economics of the local fast food industry.'

Recent flops include Arby's, a US roast beef sandwich chain that opened just one store in Sydney before it collapsed last year; Toucano Char, a Brisbane-based chain of charcoal-grilled food stores that folded in late 1990; and El Pollo Loco, a Mexican-style grilled chicken chain that was lauched by biscuit manufacturer Arnotts Limited in December 1988 and closed eight months later. Existing companies routinely announce big expansion plans that never come to fruition. In 1989 the property and food group Kaasen Limited announced plans to expand its Mr Chow Chinese fast food chain from 10 outlets to 100 by 1994. A year later it had shrunk to four stores. Melbourne businessman Victor Hew bought two Mr Chow stores in December 1990 and is negotiating for the others. Kaasen went into liquidation last year.

Fast food is an advertising-driven business. Newcomers must quickly build a network of stores to be able to finance publicity drives. El Pollo Loco, for example, would have needed to open 15 outlets before it could afford television advertising in

Sydney. Rather than spend the $7.5 million that would have cost, Arnotts pulled the plug after just two stores. 'Fast food is a product that must be advertised on TV,' Bothwell says. The truth of that statement was highlighted in February, when Kentucky Fried launched is new 'I like it like that' campaign. The first phase of the drive, which was created by John Singleton Advertising, produced an immediate sales spike. 'Corporate ads are not designed to send people rushing into a Kentucky Fried store, so it normally takes a while to see any sales growth after you launch a new corporate campaign,' Bothwell says. 'With the "I like it like that" ads, we are seeing sales climb every time the ads go to air.'

Despite the high cost of keeping up with the competition, new entrants continue to appear. The Brisbane company Magic Menu Systems launched A Kebab, a chain of take-away kebab stores, in 1989. It now has 10 outlets in Queensland, NSW and South Australia with annual sales of $3.5 million. It is aiming for 50 stores by the end of 1993. Magic Menu's owner, Doug Miller, says sales in existing outlets are up 25% so far this year. 'We offer value for money and sample our product from every outlet,' he says. 'People are encouraged to try it before they buy it. Eighty per cent of people who try it then buy it.'

The Keg chain arrived in Australia from Canada via Whitbread's $4.3 million purchase of Denny's from Ansett Transport Industries in 1989. Whitbread sold three of the 13 Denny's restaurants and soon started putting the rest under their new banner. Colin Stacey describes Keg outlets as 'middle-market restaurants, not fast food outlets', with average customer spending of $25–30. Flat sales in existing outlets during the past 12 months have forced Stacey to modify his plans; his target of 50 Kegs by 1995 has been extended to 1997 'at the earliest'.

Eighteen months ago, Brisbane businessman Hans van der Drift sank some of the $25 million he had received from the 1989 sale of his Hans Continental Smallgoods company to Japan's Asahi Chemical into Vanders, a chain of upmarket hot dog restaurants. At the time, he told a retail trade magazine: 'I love hot dogs. All my life I've dreamed of owning hot dog outlets.' Van der Drift planned to establish a national chain of 40 Vanders stores. By May 1991 he had two in Queensland. The stores, which featured life-sized statues of van der Drift, sold 'gourmet' hot dogs topped with bacon, cheese and onion, as well as sauerkraut and chilli dogs. After less than a year, van der Drift's dream started to sour. His two stores closed last spring. 'I don't want to talk about it, he says. 'I lost a lot of money on Vanders. For some reason the concept didn't work.' A rival fast food operator offers this assessment of the flop: 'The products and the stores' atmosphere were not up to scratch.'

Although Vanders failed, van der Drift at least tried to establish his chain. In the past few years, several companies have announced big plans, only to suddenly vanish. 'This industry sees a lot of fly-by-nighters,' says one operator, 'people with big mouths, big promises and no money.'

In March 1989, the financial services company MBFI Australia declared it would launch the US chain Grandy's here. There was talk of 210 stores, with 10 to be opened by mid-1990. It never happened here, although Grandy's has been launched in Asia by MBFI's Malaysian parent company. In July 1990, a US company called Cantinas International announced that it would open 12 Mexican restaurants under the Compadres banner. Nothing came of that either. There is one Compadres store in Brisbane, but it has no links to Cantinas.

Mexican food is the industry's hottest item in the US, with sales up 15% during 1990, but it has not really taken off in Australia. Pizza Hut tried with the Taco Amigo chain, but gave up in 1987. Collins Foods persevered with Taco Den for seven years but also quit two months ago, switching its three outlets to a new all-you-can-eat format called Gulliver's. 'It's tough to turn Mexican food into a fast food concept in Australia,' says Kevin Perkins. 'Taco Den's customer traffic fell sharply in 1991, so we stopped trying.'

The newest kid on the block is Western Sizzlin, a Texas-based chain that is launching steak houses under the Western Steakout banner here (the name had to be changed here because of its similarity to Sizzler). The company spent 18 months studying the Australian market and in late 1990 hired George Lopa, a former Pizza Hut executive, to launch its Australian operation. Lopa has signed two franchisees, neither of which he will identify. One will open 10 stores in Sydney during the next six years, while the other will develop eight stores in Brisbane. Each store will cost $1.45 million to build, and Lopa says Western Sizzlin will open 112 outlets in Australia in the next 15–20 years. The first Western Steakout will open in Sydney in August or September. 'Australia is a good market for fast food operators,' Lopa says. 'It holds a lot of growth potential and is underdeveloped compared to the US. The key to success in this market is understanding the local culture and tastes. You can't simply launch a US fast food concept in Australia and assume it will work.'

Sizzler has become one of Australia's fastest-growing food chains. Its sales jumped 60% to $197 million in the year that ended in April, driven by the launch of 20 new stores (lifting the total to 63) and growth in existing outlets of 14%. Collins Foods and its local franchisees, Jardine Matheson and Bob Lapointe, are aiming to have between 110 and 150 Sizzlers around Australia by late this decade. Kevin Perkins says Sizzler's growth is easily explained. 'It fills a gap between limited-menu fast food chains and fine-dining restaurants,' he says. 'It is also clearly positioned as a family-oriented chain that offers quality, value and personalised service. That's what people are looking for in the 1990s.'

The growth of Sizzler is hurting chains such as McDonald's, Hungry Jack's and Pizza Hut. As part of their fight-back strategy, the big chains are pushing into new retail outlets and adding new products. McDonald's and Hungry Jack's are opening small stores in places such as shopping centres and airport terminals. McDonald's is test-marketing a salad roll and is expected to launch McPizza in the next 18 months. Hungry Jack's launched a flame-grilled chicken burger last year. 'The word "new" is very important in the fast food business,' Jack Cowin says. 'Without new products, customers soon lose interest.' During the 1980s Kentucky Fried boosted its sales with new products, including chicken nuggets and chicken burgers. Now the company is searching for products to take it into the non-fried chicken market, which accounts for 70% of chicken sold in Australia. 'There is not a lot of upside in the word "fried" these days,' Bothwell says. Three Kentucky Fried stores in New Zealand are testing a range of new products, included baked chicken. 'The products in test in New Zealand represent the next phase of our development in this region,' Bothwell says.

Home-delivered pizza is the fastest-growing sector of the fast food industry, with sales jumping from $150 million in 1989 to an estimated $300 million last year. Chains that do not offer home delivery have been hurt. Bothwell says 30% of Kentucky Fried's 'heavy users' have bought home-delivered pizza in the past 90 days. 'Clearly we are losing business to the dial-a-pizza chains,' he says.

Home delivery accounted for 50% of Pizza Hut's $350 million turnover last year. The company, which compensated for a late start by acquiring the 110-outlet Dial-A-Dion's chain in 1989, now operates 167 home-delivery outlets, 186 restaurants and nine takeaway stores. Home delivery has stolen sales from Pizza Hut's restaurants, but Jurd says the company will correct this with new products such as all-you-can-eat salad, pasta and desert bars.

Pizza Hut's home-delivery sales jumped an estimated 25% last year, and other dial-a-pizza chains also report strong growth. Silvio's, which is 70% owned by Competitive Foods, acquired 15 new outlets last year and lifted sales 92% to $16 million. The US-owned Domino's now operates 62 home-delivery and take-away outlets in Australia, up from 45 in 1990. Its turnover jumped 20% to $18 million in 1991, and managing director John Walker says it will open 40 new stores by 1993-94.

Pizza Haven is one of the stars of the home-delivery market. Launched in Adelaide eight years ago by the Christou family, the company operates 50 franchised and company-owned outlets in South Australia, NSW and Victoria. It opened 23 new outlets last year and boosted sales 78% to an estimated $25 million. Two Pizza Havens opened in Sydney in March, and the company plans to launch another 40 there by 1993. Alan Tulloch, a former managing director of Budget Rent A Car's chauffeur division, bought the Victorian Pizza Haven franchise in January last year. He has expanded his network from 12 outlets to 29, and plans to open another 31 by 1995. Tulloch says Victorian sales of his company's pizzas, which are priced 'a tick below' Pizza Hut's, doubled last year, driven by the new stores and 40% growth in existing stores.

As fast food companies push to expand, growth will become harder to achieve. Tulloch believes Pizza Haven has the key to sustained growth in an increasingly crowded and, some operators argue, saturated industry. 'We are focused on giving our customers value for money and better service than our rivals,' he says. 'That's why we will continue to grow.'

Reproduced with permission from *BRW*,
Australia's leading business magazine, 15 May, 1992, pp. 44–49.

Questions

1. What barriers to entry exist in the Australian fast food market? (students may find the table 'Top 200 advertisers' in Part C helpful).
2. What part does culture play in the Australian fast food market? How does Australian culture differ from American and British cultures?
3. What do you think prompted Kentucky Fried Chicken to change their name to KFC recently?

Table B6.1 *Top 10 fast food chains*

Chain	Sales ($m) 1991	Sales ($m) 1990	No. of stores 1991	No. of stores 1990	% real sales growth 1991#	No. of staff	Owner(s)
McDonald's	670	597	305	269	+3.0	30 000	McDonald's US
Kentucky Fried	450	402	370	335	0	10 000	PepsiCo, Collins Foods, Competitive Foods
Pizza Hut	350	304	362	337	+10.0*	10 000	PepsiCo, Jardine Matheson, Novell
Sizzler[1]	197	123	63	43	+14.0	NA	Collins Foods, Jardine Matheson, Bob Lapointe
Hungry Jack's[2]	157	136	110	100	+4.1	NA	Competitive Foods
Red Rooster[3]	100*	106	134	NA	-6.0	2600	Coles Myer
Big Rooster/ Chicken Treat	100*	NA	152*	NA	NA	NA	Australian Fast Foods
The Keg	36*	12*	12	4	0	900	Whitbread Restaurants
Black Stump	30*	30*	14	14	0	NA	Parsonage Meats
Pizza Haven	25*	14*	50	27	+30.0	NA	Christou family

NA = not available.
* = estimate.
\# = figures exclude growth generated by new store openings.

[1] 1991 figures for Sizzler covers the 12 months ended April 1992. 1990 figures cover 12 months to April 1991.
[2] 1991 figures for Hungry Jack's cover the 1991–92 financial year. 1990 figures cover 1990–91.
[3] 1991 figures for Red Rooster cover the 1990–91 financial year. 1990 figures cover 1989–90.

Reproduced with permission from *BRW*, Australia's leading business magazine, 15 May, 1992, pp. 44–49

Case 16—Marketing of the Queensland Art Gallery

*by Peter Graham, Neal Hogg,
Nicole Licastro and Danielle McEwan*

The Queensland Art Gallery is a statutory authority within the ministerial control of the Premier's Department. In 1987 the gallery began an approach to its operations which throughout the organisation is now commonly referred to as marketing. The driving force for this change was funding. The growth of the gallery was being constrained by a shortage of finances. Traditionally, organisations such as the Art Gallery have relied substantially on Government funding to supplement their operations. In 1987 reductions in Commonwealth financial grants to Queensland had a major budgetary impact on the gallery. Its funding would not be increased for a number of years.

The gallery's vision was being threatened. This was not measured in terms of money. The vision was measured, and was seen to be lacking, in terms of art and people. In terms of people there was a feeling within the broader gallery community that it was not fulfilling its access potential. The concern was that the gallery was not being utilised by the general public and had an elitist image. Whilst, physically, the gallery was accessible to the public, it was not perceived as being a welcoming place. Basically, access to the collection, temporary exhibitions, professional and educational resources was not being maximised.

Whilst there seemed to be a common vision for the development of the collection, it was unclear how this vision could be fulfilled. The burden involved in acquiring, maintaining, building, administering and securing such a large collection was becoming unmanageable. The gallery saw two options. The vision for the gallery required growth and adjustment through a total restructuring of the organisation, which was bound to be met by resistance. Conversely, a refusal to change precursed the likely inability to maintain the quality of the collection.

The gallery chose the path of change and growth. The vehicle for this change and growth was marketing and in 1987 the first tentative changes were witnessed with the development of the Queensland Art Gallery Corporate Plan, 'designing the future of the gallery'.

Prior to 1987 the art gallery had no clearly defined or commonly agreed organisational direction. Kotler and Andreasen argue that in analysing a non-profit organisation, it is crucial to firstly, develop an effective organisational mission statement and secondly, identify objectives and goals, all whilst considering the culture to which the marketing strategy must contribute (1991, p. 71). In addition, Kotler and Andreasen (1991, p. 71) suggest that decision makers must also consider long-term objectives, the organisation's likely future external environment and its potential strengths and weaknesses.

Mission statement

The mission statement is intended to reflect the purpose of the organisation. The art gallery's mission statement is as follows:

> *To develop and maintain the State Art Collection and programmes in the visual arts for the enjoyment and cultural enrichment of the people of Queensland.*

Kotler and Andreasen (1991, p. 71) define a *mission statement* as 'The basic purpose of an organisation'. Does the statement of the art gallery conform to this definition? Moreover, does the statement conform to the basic purpose of the organisation? This can be assessed by evaluating the organisation's objectives and goals.

Organisational objectives

In order to achieve the mission of the art gallery two organisational objectives need to be specified. The two objectives of the art gallery are *people* and *art*. Firstly, with regards to people, the mission statement refers to the people of Queensland. This seems to consider not just people who are already a part of the art gallery community, but also those who do not traditionally visit the gallery. Secondly, the mission statement specifically addresses the development and maintenance of the state art collection and programmes in the visual arts. This conforms to the common desire for the improvement and development of the collection.

Considering Kotler and Andreasen's (1991, p. 71) definition of a mission statement and the gallery's purpose, manifested in these two aims, it seems fair to say that the art gallery's mission statement effectively serves it purpose.

Organisational goals

In order to address the organisation's objectives it is necessary to define the goals instrumental in achieving these objectives. Kotler and Andreasen (1991, p. 71) define a goal as 'An objective of the organisation that is made specific with respect to magnitude, time and responsibility'. The art gallery's approach in meeting its objectives, as stated in its strategic plan, is the application of marketing techniques.

Culture

In the early stages of a non-profit organisation's life, it is dominated by an internal social culture (Kotler & Andreasen 1991, p. 77). As is the case with the art gallery, when help is sought from marketing specialists advice cannot be effective if it is dominated by the old culture. Therefore, a new corporate culture develops and severe culture clash within the organisation inevitably results.

With the inevitable culture conflict comes a vital reassessment of the organisation 'The organisation is seen as a means to achieving an end, not an end in itself' (Kotler & Andreasen 1991, p. 77).

The external environment

Public environment

A key part of the external environment of a non-profit organisation is its publics. Terry Gatfield's paper, 'Marketing the non-profit way', explains more about publics in a non-profit environment. Kotler and Andreasen (1991, p. 89) describe four main publics:

(a) *The input publics*—donors, suppliers and regulatory publics—mainly supply original resource and constraints to the organisation. In relation to the art gallery the donors consist of the Art Gallery Foundation, the corporate sector, the Government Arts Department and Art gallery Society bequests. The major regulatory body is the Queensland Government through the Premier's department.
(b) *Internal publics* define, refine and carry out original strategy. Within the art gallery these internal publics include staff, volunteers and management.
(c) *Intermediary publics* assist in promoting and distributing goods and services to final consumers. At the art gallery such publics include gift shop merchants, agents, manufacturers, facilitators, mass media and transport companies.
(d) *Consuming publics* have various interests in the output of an organisation: for example, customers, local residents, activists and the general public.

The gallery relies on the input publics for financial support. The art gallery's foundation is instrumental in raising capital to acquire new art and organise exhibitions. The State Government Indemnification Scheme allocates a proportion of funding to the gallery each year, and provides in the statute that it will match the Gallery Foundation's revenue dollar for dollar. Because the art gallery is a statutory authority, it works autonomously from the government yet, it must report to the Queensland Government Arts Committee yearly as a means of justifying its funding.

The art gallery's strategic plan is directly influenced by the Goss Government's Arts Policy. The Queensland Government is commencing an overhaul of all its statutory authorities and, in 1990, (Report of the Arts Committee 1991, p. 7) saw an opportunity within the art gallery. The Goss Government saw the 'arts' and, in particular, the art gallery as being of great economic significance in that it would generate employment and tourism. The government policy states that it is:

> The right of the entire community to cultural enrichment through the arts based on the democratic principles of access, equity and participation.
> (Review of Arts Committee 1991, p. 7).

This policy of access stems directly from the Goss Government's policy that the arts should be used for the benefit of all Queenslanders irrespective of their socio-economic background (Report of the Arts Committee 1991, p. 7). The State Government is involved in all aspects of the operation of the art gallery.

Competitive environment

It is a common perception that service-orientated non-profit organisations such as the art gallery do not operate in a competitive environment. This is not strictly true. Kotler and Andreasen (1991, p. 100) talk of four major types of competitor that could concern the non-profit service organisation. Two of these could be applied to art galleries. Firstly, talk of *service form competitors* which are defined as 'Other service forms that can satisfy the consumer's particular desire'. For example, organisations such as movie theatres and concerts do attempt to satisfy and therefore compete for the art galleries' prospective audience.

Kotler and Andreasen (1991, p. 100) also discuss *enterprise competitors*. They are defined as 'Other enterprises offering the same service form that can satisfy the consumers particular desire'. Sources of enterprise competition would be from private galleries and regional galleries.

Setting the marketing mission, objectives and goals

Having decided upon an organisational mission statement, objectives and goals, Kotler and Andreasen say that the marketing objectives of an organisation must be defined. They define an objective as 'A major variable that the organisation will emphasise, such as market share, profitability or reputation'. The art gallery's ten marketing objectives as outlined in the corporate plan are as follows:

1. *Collection*: To develop, manage, research, preserve and display the collection according to the *Gallery's Act*, By-laws and policies and established art museum standards.
2. *Access*: To maximise access to the collection, temporary exhibitions, professional and educational resources.
3. *Human resource management*: To foster and provide for the development and training of all staff and volunteers to maximise their full potential.
4. *Exhibitions*: To stage exhibitions of Queensland-based, national and international art, with emphasis given to gallery initiated exhibitions.
5. *Interpretation*: To extend enjoyment, knowledge and documentation of the collection and temporary exhibitions.
6. *Regional services*: To provide art services for regional Queensland through touring exhibitions, education programmes and related professional activities.
7. *Art practice*: To provide a greater understanding of art practice through gallery programmes and to provide a venue for innovative visual arts projects.
8. *Institutional profile*: Maintain and enhance the public profile of the gallery, its collection and programme activities within the wider community, corporate and public sectors.
9. *Technology*: To maximise effective use of technology.
10. *Strategic planning*: To continue to develop strategic planning objectives in accordance with the gallery's corporate plan.

Once objectives have been specified, Kotler and Andreasen (1991, p. 71) recommend establishing a detailed set of goals as a means of achieving these objectives. The art gallery's marketing plan contains fifteen objectives and each objective is supported by approximately ten goals. As access is such a pervasive theme throughout the art gallery's organisational culture and marketing plan, it is used as an example to analyse the design and constructiveness of the art gallery's marketing goals.

With regard to the objective of access the gallery's marketing plan describes nine supporting goals. They are as follows:

1. Evaluate and respond to audience needs, including culturally diverse audience.
2. Increase the quality of audience experience.
3. Widen audience base.
4. Continue interpretation of the collection.
5. Extend information services.
6. Articulate the basis of art museum professional practice.
7. Communicate policies.
8. Provide education opportunities in the gallery.
9. Improve physical access to the gallery.

(Strategy Document 1991)

Specific markets

The process of segmenting a market as outlined by Kotler and Andreasen (1991, p. 16) can be broken up into four strategies:

- Mass marketing.
- Differentiated marketing.
- Target marketing.
- Niche marketing.

Kotler and Andreasen (1991, p. 167) argue that organisations should be moving away from mass marketing and differentiated marketing towards target or niche marketing. This is because target marketing allows for better positioning to spot marketing opportunities. The non-profit organisation is also able to interview members of the target market and obtain a clear picture of their specific needs and desires and track how these change over time. Finally, instead of trying to draw all potential buyers with a shotgun approach, the non-profit service organisation can create separate marketing projects aimed at specific markets.

For the art gallery to move towards a more target orientated form of marketing, it needs to identify its segments. After segmentation, three specific types of target marketing can be considered and the most appropriate applied. The three options are; undifferentiated, differentiated and concentrated.

Competitive position

The art gallery appears to be adopting what Kotler and Andreasen (1991, p. 207) would call a market leader strategy. The state government says that the:

> Objective is to see Queensland renowned not only for its sun, surf and spectacular scenery, but also as a major centre for the arts.
> (Report of the Arts Committee 1991, p. 7)

The gallery regularly co-operates with the Australian National Gallery in the exchange of art and national exhibitions. Its marketing leadership is gauged in terms of the quality, the recognition of the quality and the maintenance of the quality of the collection (Strategy Document: 1991). There is little concern with the monitoring or maintenance of market share.

The art gallery has, in attempting to fulfil the organisational objectives and goals, produced a marketing strategy that is customer-centred, visionary, motivating, easily communicated, flexible and sustainable for the long run. However, in attempting to develop strategies that apply to the mass of the general public, they are not reaching a number of important consumer groups.

Questions

1. In the case study *access* was identified as an important marketing objective in the gallery's corporate plan. A supporting goal of 'widening the audience base' was also identified. Using market segmentation, draw up a number of strategies for the gallery to implement in order to maximise access to the collection, temporary exhibitions, professional and educational resources.
2. Kotler and Andreasen (1991, p. 629) have stressed the importance of performance indicators. Briefly outline the performance indicators that you think would be most suitable for the Queensland Art Gallery.

References

Art Gallery Strategy Document, 1991.
Kotler, P. and Andreasen, A. (1991), *Strategic Marketing for Non-Profit Organisations*, Prentice Hall, Englewood Cliffs, New Jersey.
Report of Arts Committee, 1991.

Case 17—Marketing the non-profit way

by Terry Gatfield

'Man shall not live by GDP alone' (Paul Samuelson).

The emergence of the middle way

Our 20th century social and economic system has evolved with two principal players, the private business sector and the government sector. Yet in latter decades we have seen the formal emergence of a new sector, *the non-profit sector*. This sector consists of thousands of groups and individuals covering a large spectrum of industries and interests. Kotler names it as the 'middle way'. The middle way meets social needs without resorting to the profit motive or government bureaucracy. These third sector organisations tend to be socially responsive and service orientated, specialising in delivery of social services which are not adequately provided by businesses or governments. The sector is dependent on private citizens and on grants from the other two sectors.

The non-profit sector in the US is surprisingly large. A recent 1987 study found that there were nearly 1.4 million private non-profit organisations and government entities in the United States (Kotler & Andreasen 1991, p. 11). Tax-exempt organisations accounted for 69% of total non-profits, whilst churches represented 25% and Government entities 6%.

Millions are directly involved with one or more non-profit institutions as donors, volunteers or members (McLaughlin 1986). Yet despite the sector size and value to society very little attention has been given to it by marketeers. It gained little formal recognition in marketing literature until 1969 when Kotler and Levy wrote the controversial paper, *Broadening the Concept of Marketing*. It was not until 1975 that the first classic book on marketing the sector was written which was titled *Marketing for Non-profit Organisations*. In this work the traditional definition of marketing was customised to:

> . . . the analysis, planning, implementation and control of carefully formulated programmes designed to bring about voluntary exchanges of values with target markets for the purpose of achieving organisational objectives. It relies heavily on designing the organisation's offering in terms of the target markets' needs and desires and upon using effective pricing, communication and distribution to inform, motivate and service the market.
>
> (Kotler 1975, p. 5)

The non-profit sector taxonomy lacks definitional clarity and may include any organisation that does not have a profit motive and where there is no distribution of generated surpluses to the public by way of shares or bonuses. This may include organisations such as Telecom, Australia Post, public hospitals and the Australian Army. But this article centres around those organisations that have no formal links with government. These organisations include charities and welfare agencies such as Lifeline, the Salvation Army and Drug Arm.

Generally it is considered that marketing in the non-profit sector, due to the lack of commercial incentives, is considerably easier than marketing in the business sector. Unfortunately the reverse is true. Marketing in the non-profit sector is complex and demanding as demonstrated by the following models.

Profit sector marketing

Profit sector marketing rests on the core concept of exchange between two parties.

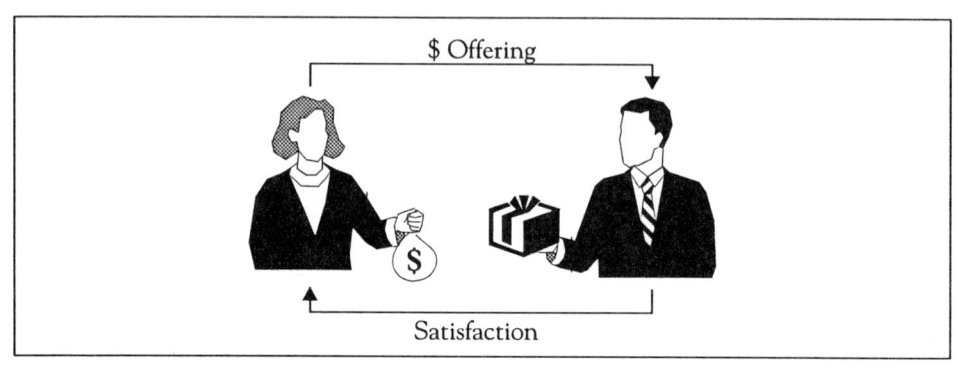

Figure B6.2 *Core concept of exchange*

The basic balanced equation of the operation in the free market is determined by the perceived equality of satisfaction received by the purchaser as measured by the dollar value of market exchange. Price is essentially determined by perceived levels of satisfaction. Although the concept of exchange may be highly complex as each actor is involved in at least one direct exchange and the entire system may be a web of interconnected relationships (Bagozzi 1975), yet the basic underlying equation remains of satisfaction between two parties.

Non-profit sector marketing

By contrast the non-profit organisation consists of three main agent groups and a modifying subset of interested moderating publics. Figure B6.3 illustrates the interaction:

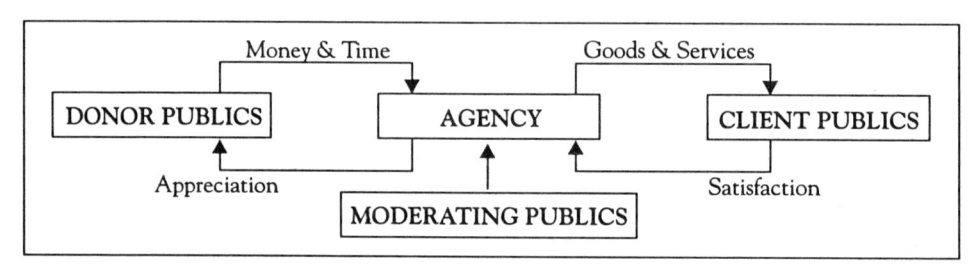

Figure B6.3 *Interaction model*

The non-profit organisation acts as an intermediary player between the donor public and the client public. The organisation may be considered as a resource conversion machine instituted by the donor groups. The organisation's internal publics take the raw resources of time, goods and money from the input publics and convert them into products and services that are carried to client publics. The term *publics* is used in the plural form because it contains individuals and groups which are generally not related to each other or to use the statistical jargon the groups are, 'mutually exclusive and collectively exhaustive'. Thus the model can be expanded as is illustrated in Figure B6.4:

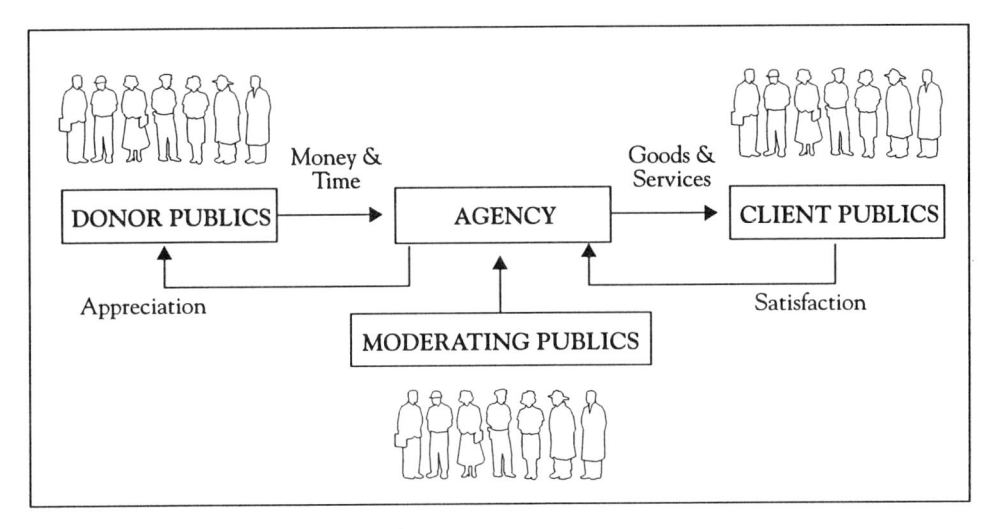

Figure B6.4 *Expanded interaction model*

The donor publics are seen to represent the supply side of the organisation and the client publics represent the demand side. This is a clear deviation to profit sector marketing (Shapiro 1973). For this reason, it is necessary to develop an integrated marketing strategy that will formulate a programme to satisfy both sets of publics. The client publics, or receivers of goods and services on the demand side, are generally marketed through traditional marketing arrangements. By contrast, the donor publics on the supply side are marketed through less understood marketing concepts.

Both supply and demand marketing functions will be substantially different as the two individual groups' publics will not only have radically different needs and wants but the demographic, behaviouristic and psychographic profiles will be substantially different. Yet, given the substantive difference, there must exist a financial aggregate of equality between them, supply must equal or exceed demand—the alternative in the long-run spells disaster. For this reason of short-term financial imbalances it is preferred to use the term *not-for-profit* for describing the sector rather than *non-profit*. The former term suggests that a profit or surplus is allowable in the short-run. This surplus is frequently needed for purchasing future capital items, projects or held as a reserve for possible future trading imbalances.

Supply marketing

Supply marketing arrangements are faced with a number of unusual difficulties compared with conventional demand-style marketing. There is most likely to be a series of different income streams such as business investments, donor publics' subscriptions, wills and bequeaths. Each of these factors will have their own unique 4P marketing mix, that is, product, price, place and promotion; the total marketing mix of each supply element being a unique adjustment to the profile of the donor group.

The first difficulty is that the unit of exchange for donors, money and time inputs, is intangible. Donors are concerned about efficiency, success rates, service availability and, most importantly, recognition for their contributions (Evans 1992). The marketing of intangible benefits is paramount. A typical scenario could be sighted in a large private corporation providing financial aid for a charity project. The project is likely to be marketed to the corporation with specific tangible benefits, such as social advantages, which are linked to gains for them in terms of organisational or product endorsement. The project must be costed in terms of quantitative and qualitative social values and these must be related in 'partnership terms'. If funding is received as a result of such a submission, then a continuous stream of reinforcement benefits must flow back to the corporation. This may be in the form of special appreciation functions to directors and administrators, regular progress reports and substantial linking with particular media items. This continual follow-through is critical.

A second difficulty is the changing comparative advantage of different income streams over time from differing competitive institutional mechanisms. Thus it becomes essential for long-term survival viability to study the life cycle of income streams. This is illustrated in Figure B6.5:

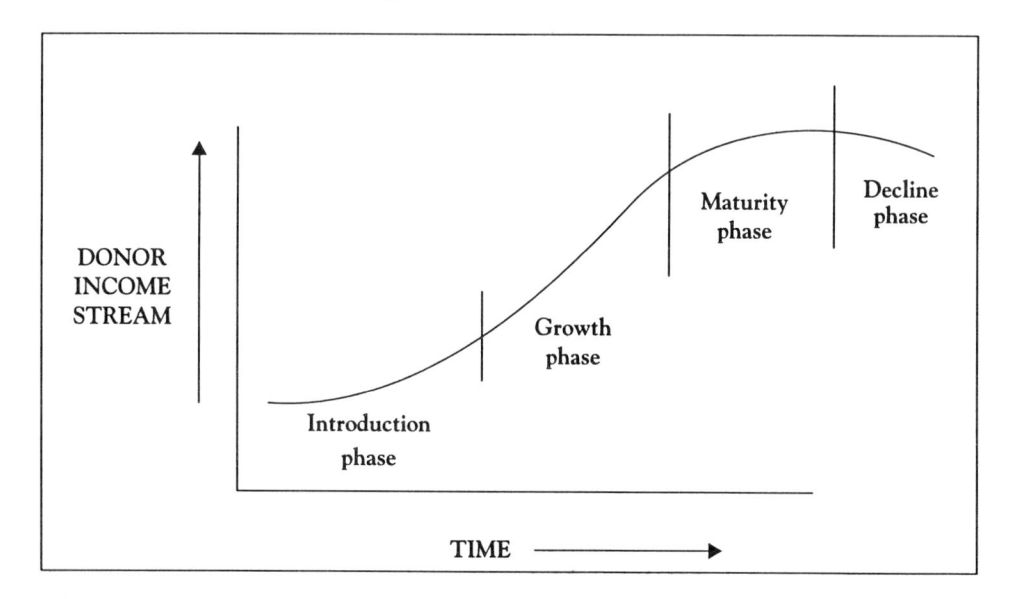

Figure B6.5 *Income stream life cycle*

Each income stream can be broken up into four phases. The objective for the non-profit organisation should be to study the life cycle to try and ensure the individual income stream is in the high marginal gain area of the growth stage. An income stream in the maturity stage or decline phase is not to have such a high commitment of time and money given to it due to the lower marginal gains. An example of this may be the traditional door knock appeals which may not only be out of the maturity stage but may be substantially in the decline phase. This may be due to changes in donor attitudes towards giving for this type of funding. The phenomena is likely to mirror the United States where such donor giving is now virtually superseded by other methods which appear to be in the high marginal gain area, such as direct mail based marketing, corporate sponsorship and product endorsements.

Demand marketing

Demand marketing arrangements in a similar way also use the 4P marketing mix, yet a number of special variations and difficulties are encountered in comparison to traditional marketing.

Price, in dollar terms, for most non-profit organisations, seldom has an exchange property as services are usually offered free of charge to the public. Also price involves the full economic and psychic costs to the consumers receiving the service. This may include travel time, waiting time, travel costs, provision for child care, social stigma and impact on self-worth. There may also be a psychic price to others who are poor yet self-supporting who resent the dependency on others (McLaughlin 1976).

Place must also be considered in the mix. Many non-profit organisations are highly centralised which means that most clients have to travel to receive a benefit. With the advent of increasing urban sprawl this aspect needs to be monitored to ensure place is tailored to clients needs rather than modifying clients needs to the place.

Promotion costs may represent a substantial cost for an organisation. The expenditure may be seen by some to be an unnecessary cost and perhaps, on ideological grounds, be curtailed. However there is a substantial cost involved in changing clients' and donors' beliefs, values and attitudes. The amount spent should be viewed as an investment in awareness arousal and a tool which should yield better services and a more satisfied clientele in the long-run.

A further difficulty is encountered in output measurement. For commercial business ventures success is measured in terms such as profit, market share and repeat business. But in the case of a non-profit organisation the outcomes are sometimes very difficult to measure, for example a successful client/counsellor contact may yield substantial healing and wholeness of a person which results in no repeat business and a substantial financial loss on the transaction. In general, success of the non-profit organisation can only be measured in terms of attaining goals related to client satisfaction and not in financial gain, repeat business or customer referrals.

General problems facing non-profit organisations

In the profit sector of the economy, when moving into a recessionary period, product demand decreases, prices adjust, and signals are given to decrease supply. This mechanism fails to work for the non-profit sector. In a recessionary period the non-profit welfare sector services demand increases and funding usually decreases. This is compounded by the shrinking government purse in assisting welfare and non-profit agencies. This is further frustrated by the increase in society's social problems such as rising divorce, family disintegration, and sexual, drug and alcohol abuse. Thus it is unfortunate for the non-profit sector that an increase in demand cannot equate with an increase in supply.

A factor which has been given little attention is the management composition in charitable institutions. They are usually governed by voluntary boards who are ultimately placed as custodians of donor resources. As a consequence the boards and management compositions tend towards conservatism and this may result in inhibition towards marketing ventures that may have any elements of risk. Very few charitable institutions are actively engaged in marketing on a broad scale, and if marketing is undertaken at all it is usually on an ad-hoc basis which is usually done in reaction to crisis rather then in proactive response to changing market supply and demand frontiers.

Questions

1. For a non-profit organisation that you are familiar with, design a graphical model that incorporates the donor groups, client groups and moderating groups. Out of the donor groups, rank them according to the value they represent to the organisation and how much they cost the organisation in maintenance. With the findings, what are the implications?
2. The RSPCA is a very well established non-profit organisation yet they still have difficulty in raising community financial support. Suggest a number of creative ventures that would substantially increase their support base and increase public awareness without undue cost and time burdens on their staff.

References

Bagozzi, P. R. (1975) 'Marketing as Exchange', *Journal of Marketing*, 39.
Evans, J. R. and Berman, B. (1992) *Marketing*, Macmillan Publishing, New York.
Kotler, P. and Andreasen, A. (1991) *Strategic Marketing for Non-Profit Organisations*, (4th edn), Prentice Hall, New Jersey.
Kotler, P. and Levy, S. J. (1969) 'Broadening the Concept of Marketing', *Journal of Marketing*, 33.
McLaughlin, C. P. (1986), *The Management of Non-profit Organisations*, John Wiley, New York.
Shapiro, B. P. (1973), 'Marketing for Non-profit Organisations', *Harvard Business Review*, New York.

7. MARKETING AND SOCIETY

Introduction 224

Readings

18. Is there more to ethical marketing than marketing ethics? by Mike Brennan 225
19. Fear and loathing can sell anything, by Graham Haines 234
20. How to protect trade secrets, by Margaret Lyons 237
21. Consumers ain't what they used to be, by Tony Wheeler 240

Cases

18. The Quit Club, by Peter Graham and Debra Harker 246
19. Ethics and international business, by Daniel W. Skubik 251

Introduction

Section seven of this book examines marketing's role in society. Four readings and two case studies assist the student in understanding the impact of marketing on society. The ethical side of marketing is explored by Michael Brennan in his paper 'Is there more to ethical marketing than marketing ethics?'. 'How to protect trade secrets' by Margaret Lyons examines the dilemma facing companies when employees leave with sensitive knowledge, whilst Graham Haines discusses the ethics of using emotion to sell. His article 'Fear and loathing can sell anything' questions where the line should be drawn. The final reading, by Tony Wheeler, 'Consumers ain't what they used to be discusses the issue of corporate image and its impact on society.

Case 18 is by Peter Graham and Debra Harker and is called 'The Quit Club', documenting the 1990 Quit Club campaign, run by the Queensland Health Department. The 1990 campaign differentiated itself from previous years by specifically targeting smokers who had already formed a desire to give up, rather than all smokers. The final case study in this section of the book is by Daniel Skubik and is called 'Ethics and International Business'. The case gives students a number of ethical frameworks to apply, together with some practical examples.

Reading 18—Is there more to ethical marketing than marketing ethics?

by Mike Brennan

Recent events in New Zealand have focused public attention on business ethics, and led to calls for stricter controls over business practices. This paper outlines a variety of ways in which people deal with ethical issues, and suggests that most simply add to the problem. It is suggested that the objectives of business and even the language of business also put business people 'at risk' of unethical conduct, and that the commonly cited moral imperatives and 'rules of thumb' do not adequately equip people to deal with the types of moral dilemmas commonly encountered. Instead, it is suggested that, if we want people in business to *be* ethical rather than merely *appear* ethical, a completely different paradigm and method of enquiry may be required.

Introduction

While it may have been acceptable in the past for businesses to pursue profits single-mindedly with little or no consideration for the wider social and environmental impact of their activities, this is not the case today. The consumer movement and the environmental lobby are now firmly established as vigilant and powerful watchdogs, and have successfully brought about changes in business practice and in the laws which govern how businesses must operate.

This is not to say that businesses have not responded to the criticisms levelled against them. Many have voluntarily changed their ways of operating to take these wider concerns into account. For example, in marketing, the *marketing concept* has become synonymous with having a consumer orientation (Houston, 1986), and the more recent *societal marketing concept* extols the need for marketers to consider the wants and long-run needs of both society and consumers (Kotler 1986). At first glance it would appear that marketers at least are facing up to their responsibilities to the world at large.

Unfortunately, as recent events in New Zealand have demonstrated, the problem of unethical conduct is ever present; it is usually just not so visible. The sharemarket crash in particular exposed numerous examples, including blatant fraud, and not only within the business sector. Government departments, and members of the legal, accounting and medical professions, and even the police, have been found guilty of unethical conduct in recent times.

This state of affairs has, understandably, prompted commentators, practitioners and the public at large to demand an end to this type of conduct. The purpose of this paper is to consider what can and should be done about ethics in business, using marketing as the focus for the discussion. The paper will begin by examining the ways in which people deal with ethical issues, then examine aspects of business practice that may affect the way in which people deal with, or fail to deal with, moral and ethical issues in business. Possible courses of action will be considered, along with their limitations. The paper will conclude by suggesting a radical approach to the problem.

Methods of dealing with ethical issues

Denial of responsibility

One option for people faced with a moral dilemma is to deny responsibility, and one way of doing this is to claim 'moral sanctuary' (Burt 1986; Konrad 1982; Roberts 1986). That is, the person essentially argues that the normal rules and constraints of ethics and morality do not apply in that situation. Adopting this approach, some have argued that there is no such thing as business ethics (Beversluis 1987).

Supporters of this argument either claim that business is like a game, and therefore the normal rules of society do not apply, or that 'one cannot survive in business if one is too ethical'. Neither of these arguments is convincing. In response to the first, it can be pointed out that, since games are governed by rules that specify not only how, but where and under what conditions a game is played, even games require ethical conduct. Futhermore, unlike games, where players can choose to participate and therefore voluntarily suspend normal ethical considerations, no one has this option in business. Insofar as a person must make a living or purchase goods, he is of necessity a participant in the game.

The second argument also falls down on two counts. First, by claiming a right to survive, claimants are in fact accepting that there is such a thing as business ethics. Second, the assertion is simply not true; it is possible to be ethical and survive in business.

Neutralisation

A second option available to people faced with a moral dilemma is to transgress, then justify the transgression. Vitell and Grove (1987) refer to this process as *neutralisation*, and write:

> Those who employ techniques of neutralisation do not feel that the norms they may be violating should be replaced, only that they do not or should not apply in these particular instances . . . (these techniques of neutralisation) . . . are essentially a learned vocabulary of motives for misconduct used to protect one from self-blame. By employing verbal symbols and rationalisations shared by society at large, the techniques allow one to make use of widely pursued and accepted, but publically un-verbalised values, such as revenge, as a means of diminishing one's culpability for a socially approved act. (p. 434)

Examples of neutralisation techniques, identified over 30 years ago (Sykes & Matza 1957), include:

(i) *Denial of responsibility*
   Individuals argue that they are not personally accountable for their actions because factors beyond their control are operating, for example, 'I couldn't help myself, I was desperate.'

(ii) *Denial of injury*
Individuals contend that their norm-violating behaviour is not really serious, since no party directly suffers because of it, for example, 'What's the big deal? No one was hurt.'
(iii) *Denial of victim*
Individuals counter any blame for their actions by arguing that the violated party deserved whatever happened, for example, 'If they're foolish enough to believe that, it's their own fault they were taken advantage of'.
(iv) *Condemning the condemners*
Individuals deflect moral condemnation to those ridiculing them by pointing out that they engage in similar disapproved behaviour, for example, 'I was only doing what others do all the time'.
(v) *Appeal to higher loyalties*
Individuals argue that their norm violating behaviour is the by-product of their attempt to actualise a higher order deal or value, for example 'I did it because it was better for all concerned'.

Hosmer (1987) suggests that if people within an organisation use these techniques, the unethical behaviour may have become institutionalised. In such cases, changes to the current strategic planning systems, or the CEO, may be required.

Good business is good ethics

A third approach, adopted by some people, accepts a need for ethical conduct, but never actually considers the question of ethics because proponents believe they behave ethically; that 'good business is good ethics'. The rationale for this approach is that the very requirements of profitable business constitute a morality, and leave managers with little choice but to 'do good and avoid evil' (Newton, 1986).

Various groups have promoted this approach in New Zealand. However, organisations who adopt this philosophy put themselves seriously *at risk* of unethical conduct, simply because they do not acknowledge the ethical consequences of their actions.

Good ethics is good business

The view that 'good business is good ethics' should not be confused with an alternative view that 'good ethics is good business', expressed in books such as *In Search of Excellence* (Peters & Waterman 1982). Proponents of this argument suggest a corporation must have integrity in order to achieve long-term profitability, therefore good ethics is good business.

While this appears an admirable sentiment which would ensure ethical conduct, some writers take a far more cynical view, and argue that some corporations may be more concerned with public relations than action; 'they want to *appear* good, not *be* good' (Newton 1986, p. 250). On the other hand, this option does seem the most likely to lead to ethical behaviour, even if the hypothesied links between profitability and ethical behaviour are suspect.

Factors contributing to unethical behaviour in business

Business objectives

Clearly, a variety of views about the role of ethics in business exist, and it would seem that most of these views actually put business people *at risk* of unethical conduct. However, the problem extends even further than the arguments used to justify particular business and practices. To use marketing as an example, the objectives of marketing, the marketing concept and even the language of marketing may also contribute to the problem.

Houston (1986) points out that the ultimate goal in a commercial venture is some sort of profit achievement. As a consequence, the needs and wants of consumers and the wider concerns for the impact on society are only of concern to the marketer to the extent that they affect the objectives (e.g. profitability) of the operation (see also, Cressey & Moore 1983).

He argues that:

> Few if any . . . organisations come into being through altruism; that is, organisations do not come into being to achieve the goals of a non-member constituency. Instead, it is the set of objectives defined by the membership that guide the organisation . . . The initiators of a commercial venture do so to satisfy their own needs. (Houston 1986, p. 82)

Put another way, the question these organisations ask is: 'How might these factors affect what I am doing (i.e. profitability)?' not, 'What effect might what I am doing have on others?'

Marketers adopting this orientation may well remain oblivious to the likely consequences of their actions, unless there is a perceived threat to their operation. Furthermore, even if aware of possible consequences, business people faced with a moral dilemma will be predisposed to act in a way that has the least detrimental impact on profitability, even if this means adopting an unethical course of action.

The language of business

The language of business also presents problems. Two pervasive metaphors in marketing are those of *war* and *competition* (strategy, tactics, competitors, heroes, targets). This language emphasises the notions of power, control and dominance—the antithesis of concern, caring and co-operation, and scarcely consistent with the notion of moral or ethical behaviour.

Paradoxically, even the marketing concept and particularly the societal marketing concept may add to the risk of unethical behaviour. Because these concepts appear to put the needs of consumers and society first, they may lead the public to believe marketers are behaving in an ethical manner, regardless of whether they are. Since the concepts embrace an ethical dimension, they may also lead marketers to believe their actions are ethical by definition. This may result in a situation where ethics are given little thought.

This is not to suggest business and marketing practice is totally unethical. The point being made is that the language of business, the objectives of business, and the ways in which business people perceive their roles, put them at risk of unethical conduct. The onus is therefore on business people to ensure that they are not unwittingly contributing to the problem.

Possible courses of action

A number of different approaches to the problem of unethical conduct have been suggested:

Examination of values

Business people could, and arguably should, examine their own attitudes, values and behaviour. A recurrent theme in the recent literature is the importance of an organisation's value system to the conduct of its members, and the importance of the CEO in establishing this system (Chonko & Hunt 1985). For example, William Wiess, CEO of Ameritech, claims that a corporation can, and must, create a moral environment in which there is a distinct set of values and standards to which it holds people accountable. He further argues that it is a key responsibility of corporate leadership to set the pattern and tone of this 'corporate conscience' (Wiess 1986). A method designed for developing or reformulating a corporate culture is presented by Robin and Reidenbach (1987).

Apply normative principles

Business people could be introduced to different systems of ethical analysis. Hosmer (1988), for example, refers to four normative first principles that he believes should be taught:

(i) *The utilitarian principle:* Act in a way that results in the greatest good for the greatest number.
(ii) *Kant's categorical imperative:* Act in such a way that the action taken under the circumstances could be a universal law or rule of behaviour.
(iii) *Personal justice:* Act so the least advantaged members of society will be benefited to some extent.
(iv) *Personal liberty:* Act so the ability of other members of society to lead lives of self-fulfilment and self-development will be maximised.

Apply rules-of-thumb

There are also less formal rules-of-thumb that can help one get in touch with one's own feelings and conscience about the decisions that have been made. Peter and Olson (1987) provide the following summary:

230 PART B

(i) *The golden rule:* Act in the way that you would expect others to act toward you.
(ii) *The professional ethic:* Take actions that would be viewed as proper by a disinterested panel of professional colleagues.
(iii) *The TV test:* A manager should always ask: 'Would I feel comfortable explaining to a national TV audience why I took this action?'

Employ a checklist

A number of people advocate the use of a checklist. For example, Nash (1981) suggests that the following 12 questions should be used for examining the ethics of a business decision:

1. Have you defined the problem accurately?
2. How would you define the problem if you stood on the other side of the fence?
3. How did this situation occur in the first place?
4. To whom and to what do you give your loyalty as a person and as a member of the corporation?
5. What is your intention in making this decision?
6. How does this intention compare with the probable results?
7. Whom could your decision or action injure?
8. Can you discuss the problem with the injured parties before you make your decision?
9. Are you confident that your position will be as valid over a long period of time as it seems now?
10. Could you disclose without qualm your decision or action to your boss, your CEO, the board of directors, your family, society as a whole?
11. What is the symbolic potential of your action if understood? If misunderstood?
12. Under what conditions would you allow exceptions to your stand?

Limitations

While these methods of analysis may offer some assistance, they are of only limited help to people faced with a moral dilemma. A common difficulty with a moral dilemma is that of identifying clearly what the issues are. It is relatively easy to identify violations of widely held norms or moral principles, thus the responsibilities of managers in such situations are well defined. Sometimes, however, the norms or moral principles themselves substantially conflict, and it is not clear which option should be chosen. King (1986) observes that western moral philosophy offers no guidelines for dealing with what he calls 'moral dilemmas of the second kind'. His suggestion is that we must therefore begin to examine the types of social relationship that must exist for there to be agreement on what is right, good and just.

Re-examine the moral paradigm

King argues that mainstream philosophy accepts the ideal of the theorist as a detached observer, and operates according to what he calls the 'ethics of justice', which emphasises objectivity and detachment. He suggests that this moral paradigm is also prevalent in business. The consequences of managers remaining detached, however, are that they can avoid accepting responsibility for the effects of their actions. A detached manager is therefore at risk of acting in an unethical manner. A similar point has been made by other authors, particularly with regard to accounting (e.g. Tinker 1985; Tinker, Merino & Neimark 1982).

The problem, according to King, is that mainstream philosophy, and business, ignores what he calls the 'ethics of caring', with its connotations of compassion, empathy and relatedness. Drawing on the work of MacIntyre (1981), King suggests that the ethics of caring is a necessary condition of any ethics of justice—that the ethics of caring is *the* moral paradigm and that the ethics of justice is subsumed under it.

King suggests that human endeavour consists of empirical, interpretive and evaluative dimensions, but that while we have well developed empirical methodologies, we do not understand the methodologies of interpretation and evaluation. He argues that everything we know is necessarily interpretive in nature—that we do and must construct our social realities. Since narrow interpretation leads to limited or stupid behaviour, it is possible to construct realities in which evaluation becomes unintelligible. He concludes that caring is an essential part of the methodology of evaluation, and that this is the key to understanding the nature of 'ethical encounters of the second kind'.

The implications of what King is saying suggest radical changes to the way managers are educated. If we want managers to behave in an ethical manner, we must take into account the interpretive and evaluative, as well as the empirical dimensions of human endeavour. Since people construct their social reality and this affects evaluation, they must have a *broad based* or *general* education so they do not end up with a narrow interpretation of the world and construct a constricted or blinkered social reality. Furthermore, since caring is an important component of evaluation, education must encourage *involvement in* rather than *detachment from* issues and problems, and managers must be trained to understand others' point of view, to see the world through other people's eyes.

Adopt alternative methods of enquiry

The ideas presented so far suggest a different approach to ethics is required in marketing and in the training of marketing and business graduates. One possibility is presented by Hirschman (1986), who argues that since marketing is a socially constructed enterprise, it requires different methods of enquiry developed specifically to address socially constructed phenomena. In particular, she suggests that marketers should embrace humanistic methods of inquiry. In essence, the humanistic method:

1. requires participation on the part of the researcher (manager); and
2. results in an interpretation of the phenomenon about which one is enquiring.

Hirschman argues that interpretation requires both intuition and empathy. Empathy is required because the investigator must be able to learn the other's reality, to understand how they think, feel and believe. The comprehension attained through investigator empathy must then be combined with personal intuition to arrive at an interpretation. The key to developing these skills is practice.

Conclusion

Most examples of unethical conduct that make the headlines probably are those where the perpetrator knowingly and intentionally transgressed, and such behaviour will always be a possibility in business as in other spheres. The concern of this paper was not with this group of people, but with those who seek ethical solutions to complex moral dilemmas, and those who are oblivious to the ethical implications of their actions.

This paper has argued that conventional wisdom is of limited use for resolving complex moral dilemmas, and that there exist many situations that put business people 'at risk' of unethical behaviour. It is further suggested that many people are ill-equipped to deal with moral and ethical issues, because of a way of thinking that contributes to blinkered vision and a narrow concept of reality.

The suggested solution is to expose people to alternative ways of looking at the world, and to encourage them to become *involved with* rather than *detached from* everyday problems. To put this into practice in business, perhaps business students should take courses in languages or anthropology, or other papers in the humanities or social sciences, in addition to their business courses.

Quite clearly, the suggested adoption of a humanistic method of enquiry would be a radical departure from conventional approaches to ethical problems. However, such a paradigm shift may be a necessary prerequiste for the development of an 'ethics of caring' that is perhaps necessary to resolve ethical dilemmas 'of the second kind'.

Reproduced with permission from *Marketing Bulletin*, 1991, 2, pp. 8–17.

Questions

1. 'If it is legal, it is ethical.' Comment.
2. Why are ethics important to marketers?
3. Should ethics be a compulsory part of university courses in marketing? If so how should it be implemented? Do you think Mike Brennan's suggestion is viable?
4. Would Mike Brennan agree with Daniel Skubik (see case on Ethics and International Business)? Why or why not?

References

Beversluis, E. H. (1987), 'Is There "No Such Thing as Business Ethics"?' *Journal of Ethics*, **6**, pp. 81–88.

Burt, D. X. (1986), 'Moral Sanctuary in Business: A Comment on the Possibility', *Journal of Business Ethics*, **5**, pp. 209–11.

Chonko, L. B. and Hunt, S. D. (1985), 'Ethics and Marketing Management: An Empirical Examination', *Journal of Business Research*, **13** (August), pp. 339–59.

Cressey, D. R. and Moore, C. A. (1983), 'Managerial Values and Corporate Codes of Ethics', *California Management Review*, Summer, pp. 53–77.

Hirschman, E. C. (1986), 'Humanistic Enquiry in Marketing Research: Philosophy, Method, and Criteria', *Journal of Marketing Research*, 23, pp. 237–49.

Hosmer, L. T. (1987), 'The Institutionalisation of Unethical Behaviour', *Journal of Business Ethics*, 6, pp. 439–47.

Hosmer, L. T. (1988), 'Adding Ethics to the Business Curriculum', *Business Horizons*, July/August, pp. 9–15.

Houston, F. S. (1986), 'The Marketing Concept: What It Is and What It Is Not', *Journal of Marketing*, 50 (April), pp. 81–87.

King, J. B. (1986), 'Ethical Encounters of the Second Kind', *Journal of Business Ethics*, 5, pp. 1–11.

Konrad, R. (1982), 'Business Managers and Moral Sanctuaries', *Journal of Business Ethics*, 1 (August), pp. 195–200.

Kotler, P. (1986), *Principles of Marketing*, (3rd edn), Prentice Hall, Englewood Cliffs, New Jersey.

MacIntyre, A. (1981), *After Virtue: A Study in Moral Theory*, University of Notre Dame Press, Notre Dame.

Nash, L. L. (1981), 'Ethics Without the Sermon', *Harvard Business Review*, November–December, pp. 79–90.

Newton, L. H. (1986), 'The Internal Morality of the Corporation', *Journal of Business Ethics*, 5, pp. 249–58.

Peter, J. P. and Olson, J. C. (1987), *Consumer Behaviour: Marketing Strategy Perspectives*, Irwin, Homewood, Illinois.

Peters, T. J. and Waterman, R. H. (1982), *In Search of Excellence: Lessons from America's Best-run Companies*, Harper & Row, New York.

Roberts, IV. D. (1986), 'Moral Managers and Business Sanctuaries', *Journal of Business Ethics*, 5, pp. 203–8.

Robin, D. P. and Reidenbach R. E. (1987), 'Social Responsibility, Ethics and Marketing: Closing the Gap Between Concept and Application', *Journal of Marketing*, 51 (January), pp. 44–58.

Sykes, G. M. and Matza, D. (1957), 'Techniques of Neutralisation: A Theory of Delinquency', *American Sociological Review*, 22 (December), pp. 664–70.

Tinker, A. M. (1985) *Paper Prophets: A Social Critique of Accounting*, Paeger, New York.

Tinker, A. M., Merino, B. D. and Neimark, M. D. (1982), 'The Normative Origins of Positive Theories: Ideology and Accounting Thought', *Accounting Organisation and Society*, 7 (2), pp. 167–200.

Vitell, S. J. and Grove, S. J. (1987), 'Marketing Ethics and the Techniques of Neutralisation', *Journal of Business Ethics*, 6, pp. 433–38.

Weiss, W. L. (1986), 'Minerva's Owl: Building a Corporate Value System', *Journal of Business Ethics*, 5, pp. 243–47.

Reading 19—Fear and loathing can sell anything

by Graham Haines

While humour is but one human emotion to which advertisers appeal, fear and anxiety is another. How effective advertising is when this technique is used is open to debate, but unlike humour, we have a better understanding of what causes anxiety and fear than what makes people laugh.

Fear is an extreme form of anxiety. Therefore you can view both emotions as a spectrum. The level of anxiety induced by the advertising and the point at which anxiety becomes fear will vary from person to person and from group to group. Similarly the point at which a level of anxiety is raised which causes someone to do something—whether to buy a particular brand of toothpaste or to avoid drinking and driving—will also vary.

The fundamentals of good marketing practice remain unchanged—aim your advertising at a specific target audience of homogeneous consumers and encode and transmit the message in a form that will give the desired response.

Anxiety appeals by advertisers must be as old as those based on humour. From the 'ring around the collar' to Close-up toothpaste, to deodorants, the message is that the user will be more readily accepted by his or her peers, if these particular products are used. These ads create anxiety about one's social acceptability and the fear of social ostracism is a most powerful motive governing our actions. Another common technique is to create anxiety about one's personal and family security. All forms of insurance, from life to travel insurance, are frequently advertised via fear appeals and Lockwood deadlocks, Michelin tyres and Munroe shock absorbers further illustrate this technique.

These campaigns all have one thing in common. They are all positive appeals in that they encourage one to purchase or use the products concerned. However, in recent years, there has been an upsurge in social marketing and frequently the appeal here is to persuade people not to do something—not to speed, not to drink-drive, not to smoke, not to practise unsafe sex.

Despite the negative positioning, the technique of creating fear and anxiety is commonly used and the reason for their effectiveness is because the agencies concerned struck the right balance between creating the degree of anxiety necessary to achieve a behavioural change in the target audience without over stepping the mark that would cause that audience to switch off and say to themselves—this won't happen to me.

The classic campaign and the one chosen to illustrate the theory behind its success, is that produced by Grey Advertising for the Transport Accident Commission of Victoria (TAC). The vanguard of the campaign consisted of five TV commercials which were designed to meet the Commission's objective to 'outrage, appal and upset' Victorians. They were all based on extensive consumer research by Brian Sweeney & Associates and there appears to be a remarkable correlation between the findings of Brian Sweeney and the theory of consumer behaviour.

'Perception is reality' is a catch-phrase, but theory tells us that people's perceptions and therefore realities differ markedly from one another. The theorists tell us that our perceptions are based on a four stage process. Firstly, we *selectively* expose ourselves to a message, then we *selectively* pay attention to it. Thirdly, we *selectively* comprehend it and, finally, we *selectively* retain it.

This process of *selective perception* is used by everyone to limit the number of messages that we pay attention to and then having been through this filtering process, we embark on a further process of selectively comprehending and retaining the messages concerned. It is well recognised that people are more likely to retain information that is consistent with their own beliefs and predispositions and that they will tend to ignore or discount information that is in conflict with that they believe or what they do. This is called *perceptual defence* and what the TAC's campaign did was to overcome the barrier of perceptual defence among the targeted audiences at which the ads were aimed.

Mr Sweeney's research revealed that those in the 18 to 25-year-old age group were generally not receptive to statistics quoting the chances of being killed or crippled for life or images of twisted metal and broken bodies. Their perceptual defence mechanism told them that it wouldn't happen to them but that if it were to, it was simply the luck of the draw—the lottery of life. Statistically, there is a very strong foundation for this argument. Few 18 to 25-year-olds who drive while drunk do not live through this period; not everyone who smokes dies of lung cancer. A more subtle approach to overcome perceptual defence was required and this in turn reflects the behavioural theory of balance or equilibrium.

There is an interrelationship between beliefs and behaviour, and the vast majority only feel comfortable—or in equilibrium with themselves—if their actions reflect their beliefs. Suppose you find a wallet on the floor of a Coles supermarket. There is no indication as to whom it belongs and it contains $200 cash. If you decide you could do with the $200, you might pick up the wallet. I bet you would glance around you to see if anyone was watching and you might well experience remorse at your action at a later date. Your disequilibrium—the conflict between your beliefs and behaviour—might become so unbearable that you finally decide to hand the wallet in at your local police station. Would you tell the police where you found it?

So the key to changing behaviour is firstly to change people's beliefs and in the context of the Grey 'If you drink, then drive, you're a bloody idiot' ad, you have to convince the target audience that it can happen to them and that there is a very good chance that it will. The way that this was achieved was to place much greater emphasis on the indirect victims of drink-driving—in this case, the driver, the parents of the girl, and by implications the driver's family and friends and the friends and other members of the girl's family.

There would be very few people in this demographic age group who can then convincingly say to themselves—this won't happen to me either directly or indirectly. The barrier of perceptual defence has been overcome. Who hasn't had too many drinks at a quiet dinner party with friends? Who hasn't been speeding to make an appointment? Who hasn't lost concentration in an attempt to bring the noisy kids to heel in the back seat of the car? Who hasn't felt themselves nodding off and failed to stop and take a rest? In all cases, one might begin to raise the barrier of perceptual defence but as one of the ads says—'don't fool yourself', it can happen to you and so to maintain equilibrium, you modify your behaviour.

A further technique used to overcome perceptual defence is to ensure that the ad is highly credible. Any aspect of an ad that makes an anxiety or fear appeal will fail if it is not totally credible to the target audience. That target audience is looking for the slightest excuse to distance themselves from the message.

How hard some people will try to disassociate themselves from a fear appeal can be illustrated by a student of mine who claimed that the impact of the 'concentrate, or kill' ad in the TAC series was negated because one of the occupants of the car was found after the accident lying on the road apparently some distance from the wreck of the vehicle in which he had been travelling. Any member of the traffic police or ambulance service will tell you that bodies being thrown from a vehicle in an accident is common, but to this person at least the position of the body allowed her to rationalise that advertisement's message. The importance of the tiniest detail is further illustrated by one of the latest series of ads where the word 'morgue' was subsequently deleted from the dialogue, when research showed that its use was too fearful for some of the audience and caused them to switch off.

The fear of social ostracism is the most powerful motivator for changing people's behaviour and the TAC ads, particularly the drink-driving one, play upon this factor when the charge nurse from the Royal Melbourne Hospital says: 'If you drink, then drive, you're a bloody idiot'. Now no one likes someone else to come up to them in private and say: 'you're a bloody idiot' but that person likes it a whole lot less if their peer group perceives them as a bloody idiot.

Again the theory supports the practice. In consumer behaviour, marketers recognise that attitudes are comprised of three components—beliefs, attitudes, and intentions which result in some form of action or behaviour. If one wishes to change a group's behaviour, then the best place to start is by changing that group's beliefs. Change beliefs and you will change attitude; change attitude and you will change intent; change intent and you will change behaviour.

It's not fear or anxiety appeal, but reference to Clemenger's highly effective campaign for rice illustrates this sequence well. The reason for the 20% rise in rice consumption was because the ad changed consumer's beliefs about rice. Rice was no longer that boring substitute for potato and a complement to curries and other eastern cuisine. It was a miracle food, possessed of all the benefits of meat, fish, fruit and poultry with none of the less than welcome side effects. The previous ads, based on the theme of 'rice power', were merely attempting to change attitudes rather than firstly changing beliefs. They were less than successful.

The TAC ads are playing a leading role in a bid to change people's beliefs about speeding and in particular drink-driving. In the most vulnerable age group for drink-driving accidents, the TAC's ultimate goal is to make drink-driving socially unacceptable. If behaviour is to be permanently changed, then this process must start with changing beliefs.

In one respect, the TAC and other authorities responsible for promoting road safety are in a race of their own. Many believe that the ads themselves are already pushing the frontiers of the barriers of perceptual defence. Yet conditioning theory would suggest that even these graphic ads have a 'wear-out' effect and the temptation must be to produce ads which go even further in their attempt to 'outrage, appal and upset' their targeted audience. Some observers would claim that they have gone too far already and that the ads are so graphic that the audience switches off. So the challenge is to change the community's beliefs before such 'wear-out' occurs.

So far I have concentrated on the dangers of creating too much anxiety or fear. But ads that create too little are equally ineffectual in eliciting the hoped-for response from the audience. In contrast to the 1950s and 1960s current ads for household cleaning agents are rarely, if ever, promoted using anxiety appeals.

The suggestion that your neighbour will look down upon you if your kitchen floor is not spotless is hardly likely to raise the consumer's anxiety to the level where he or she fells compelled to purchase a particular brand of floor cleaner. What the neighbour thinks about your kitchen floor is not that important to you. Close-up's positioning on fresh breath is effective with its target market, but such a positioning would not influence an elderly married couple for whom garlic was a staple of their diet.

Fear appeals in advertising work if these rules are followed. Firstly, it must be established what it is that the targeted audience might be fearful of; secondly, the degree of anxiety raised must not exceed the level which leads to perceptual defence; and thirdly if the objective is to change social attitudes on an issue, then the message must be aimed at changing beliefs, if the resultant attitude and behaviour changes are to be permanent.

Reproduced with permission from *Marketing*, April 1992, pp. 28–29.

Questions

1. Explain the theories of:
   (i) selective perception; and
   (ii) cognitive dissonance.
2. Nominate some social marketing campaigns you are familiar with and discuss why some appear to be effective and others have little impact?
3. How do you personally deal with disequilibrium?

Reading 20—How to protect trade secrets

by Margaret Lyons

What can you do if an employee walks away with confidential information? The issue is tricky, but remedies are available.

When engineers Robert Leonard and Thomas Schalk took copies of their computer files before leaving their jobs at Texas Instruments, they sparked a six-year legal battle with their former employer. Late last year the Texas Court of Criminal Appeals finally upheld convictions against the two men for stealing trade secrets.

The question of whether they had actually used the information was never raised; the company had only to show that they had 'neither requested nor received permission to copy the files'. Encouraging as this verdict may sound for employers in the United States worried about protecting sensitive information, the situation in Australia is proving somewhat different.

'If you give an undertaking when you enter a job that you will not divulge trade secrets (upon leaving), that becomes an enforceable intellectual property agreement,' says Michael Brereton, a partner with law firm Barker Gosling. But the reality is more complicated. To get the protection of the courts, the employer must show that what was taken was a trade secret that could be used to his detriment. Unless the former employee has taken written material without authorisation—which amounts to theft because work produced by staff is the employer's property—it has so far proved difficult for Australian employers to meet this condition.

This is illustrated by a recent Victorian Supreme Court case, *Secton Pty Ltd and BWN Pty Ltd versus Delawood Pty Ltd*. The court ruled that knowledge of a process for separating oil and water developed by Secton and BWN and later used by three former employees who formed their own business, Delawood, was not a trade secret. This is despite the fact that two of the defendants learned of the process while working for the company, and all of them had signed confidentiality agreements that included a seven-year worldwide restrictive covenant.

The court concluded that stopping the defendants from using the process would unfairly limit their freedom to employ their personal skills and knowledge—a clear signal of reluctance to reduce anyone's employment options. The reasoning is that in the course of their duties employees acquire not only confidential information, but also a stock of general knowledge and expertise that they are entitled to use in competition with their former employers.

Employers in the information industry accept this as a fact of life. Brian Wilson, national managing partner of Andersen Consulting, says he 'cannot stop ex-employees from making use of things they have learned at Andersen Consulting'. Wilson believes forcing staff to sign agreements that they will not set up in direct competition with his firm, presumably making use of procedures learned while working there, is 'not very viable'. He prefers to rely on employees' discretion and professionalism, he says, and to date has not been given any reason to do otherwise. The only people required to sign non-competition agreements on departure are partners in the firm's Asia-Pacific consulting group, who must not approach Andersen clients for a designated period after they leave.

Nevertheless, Andersen Consulting keeps very thorough records of all material issued to staff in the course of their employment. 'When a person is leaving, we routinely have a final meeting with that person to cover a number of things,' Wilson says. 'One of the things we do cover is a discussion about whether all training materials issued to that person in the course of their employment have been returned.' Because the firm asks staff to return everything, taking anything would be a 'very clear-cut' breach of copyright laws, if not theft, Wilson says.

Dr Tony Smithyman, managing director of Cellabs, says that in the scientific community 'the industry standard is that when you employ people you get them to sign an agreement that they will not disclose information for a certain period of time after they leave your employment'. But he adds: 'Unfortunately, this is not worth the paper it is written on. (However) scientists generally have a lot of integrity. Also, it is an international industry, so if you do something silly everyone around the world knows about it'.

Smithyman says there have been cases of research scientists leaving jobs and taking with them samples of the actual cell line they had been working on. This has been treated as straight theft. But the scientific community is generally agreed that it is impossible to stop people from transporting the knowledge acquired in one job to their next position, even if the former employers' competitors may inadvertently benefit.

In the *Texas Instruments* case, the engineers, Leonard and Schalk, claimed they took information that they believed they were entitled to, with the intention or sorting through the files later. But Barker Gosling's Brereton says that when employees take written material their employers would have refused to let them have, it is clearly theft. 'The classical situation is where somebody who works for a company has access to clients, helps develop a product and before leaving takes copies of the client list or other data. This is a clear breach of their duties as an employee,' Brereton says. 'These disputes are not about innocent things.'

Employers have three ways of protecting themselves, says Louise Herron, technology partner at Minter Ellison. The first is to develop an intellectual property agreement stipulating that anything an employee creates in the course of employment is the property of the company. The second is a confidentiality agreement that remains in force after the employee has left for as long as the information is confidential. This is really only useful as a deterrent and, as in the *Secton versus Delawood* case, can be easily overturned if the courts decide that the information in question is not a trade secret. The third method is a non-competition pact that remains in force for a reasonable period, although it should be noted that no court will enforce an agreement that prevents someone from earning a living.

Herron notes that it is important to distinguish between intellectual property that belongs to the employer, and material that is created by someone working on a consulting basis. Employees are entitled to take the 'general stock of skills and knowledge' acquired in the course of their employment and apply it to their next job, Herron says, but cannot take specific information such as client lists.

So what remedies are available? In the short-term, employers can get an injunction to stop staff from using information or, in less urgent cases, sue for damages. A more dramatic option is to go to court for an Anton Pillar order, on the basis that it is believed someone has taken material that might be destroyed if they were sued. The lawyer, plaintiff and police then do a 'search and seizure' of the employee's premises. But Brereton cautions that the police generally regard such matters as civil issues even when they are clearly theft, and are rarely interested in, or able to pursue, a criminal conviction.

Reproduced with permission from *BRW*, Australia's leading business magazine, 15 May, 1992, pp. 70–71.

Questions

1. What do you think? Where should the line be drawn? When does knowledge become theft?
2. What insights does Mike Brennan's article in this section provide for such situations?
3. Read Daniel Skubik's case. Does it provide guidelines? How would they work?

Reading 21—Consumers ain't what they used to be

by Tony Wheeler

Consumers in the Age of the Apocalypse are horses of a different colour, according to Tony Wheeler—so managing your image is a delicate balancing act.

Futurist Faith Popcorn is warning that companies who made money out of the fiscal hedonism of the 1980s have cause to worry—because the consumer world has changed.

In Australia, from a survey we have conducted we know that only one adult in three believed that life will be 'back to normal' once the recession is over. Many people are over their heads in debt; we're consumed-out, and there's a feeling that if we go on living as before then we'll be consuming our future, and our children's future. Consumers are holding on to whatever money they have, balancing their resources. Their first priority is to work-off their burden of debt, and begin saving for tomorrow.

'The undertones of heaviness and gloom that are pervading the consumer world will turn into anger—anger directed at corporations that have been on a century long "search-out-and-destroy mission", and towards governments that have been co-conspirators. We can only stand pessimism for so long,' says Ms Popcorn.

Our survey shows that consumer priorities will change once the recovery occurs and the mood of the market-place rises. People will buy more carefully. There will be a new focus on utility. Impulsive extravagance will be a thing of the past. As Ms Popcorn says, buying will be a political act, having ramifications all the way up the chain of life.

The new theories about the behaviour of things—theories of chaos and catastrophe—are teaching us that the future can be discontinuous with the past; that things can change in leaps and bounds; that so-called orderly systems have invisible thresholds beyond which predictable behaviour fails to materialise.

A researcher in the UK, Peter Coveney, pointed to a dramatic demonstration of this when he drew attention to the environmental force that has gripped the Western world in the last few years. Concern for the environment was certainly not new, but yet in the late 1980s it exploded in prominence with significant implications for businesses. Within two years, CFCs disappeared from aerosols, lead-free petrol became compulsory for new vehicles, McDonalds changed its packaging.

The growth in environmental activity can be plotted by tracing the number of articles published in the consumer press about these topics from 1980 onwards in the UK. There was a slow, steady growth in the number of articles, but nothing that prepared us for the explosion in the last two years of the decade. This almost certainly mirrors the change that occurred in the level of consumer concern which surfaced at the time.

If chaos theory teaches us that dramatic change can be the norm, then we should not be surprised at a dramatic call for change in the corporate role. This consumer-driven shift in behaviour has a crucial message for companies; they will have to realise that 'you don't sell only what you make. You sell who you are'. Is this what is meant by corporate image? Yes. Popcorn talks about the corporate 'soul', underlining the proposition that corporate and consumer interaction is about relationships between human beings.

It used to be enough just to make a decent product and market it. Not anymore. Now the customers will want to know who you are before buying what you sell. They will not merely be asking about your identity; they will want to know:

- a biography of the product;
- the ethics of the maker;
- the maker's stand on environmental issues, human rights, equal employment opportunities, issues like animal welfare in product testing, health care and child care, and so on;
- the company's support of the arts, sport and other activities that make up the fabric of our society.

These things used to be the concern of fringe groups. Now the concern is everybody's. It is no surprise, then, that the fastest-growing sector of marketing research is in the field of measuring consumer satisfaction. Never before have so many companies and institutions laid themselves open to scrutiny, interrogation, and criticism.

There is a parallel to what is taking place in corporate positioning and what is happening in the field of sponsorship. Unlike advertising, in the main media, sponsorship doesn't confront the consumer with a proposition, but rather it comes alongside, like a friend, because the sponsor is supporting something which the consumer wants supported. The sponsor and the consumer have a common purpose. And that common purpose serves to form relationships between the company and the consumer. Corporations need to form relationships with their customers, beyond the commerical transaction that links them together. Corporations—in trying to edge closer to their customers—need to be aware that they are 'not opening the door to strangers'. What will make us buy one product over another in this decade is a feeling of partnership with the seller, and the feeling that together we're both buying for the future. This is implicit in the theory and practice of measuring customer satisfaction.

Faith Popcorn has labelled the 1990s as the decency decade, growing out of the now-universal realisation that society as we know it is under threat. It is dedicated to the three critical Es: environmental, education and ethics.

Consumers are crying out for action, and smart marketers are listening. Success stories make heroes out of consumers and companies alike. It is not the mistake a company makes that the consumer finds unforgivable, but how the company responds to the discovery of the mistake. The relationships people are seeking are based on trust. Decency inspires trust. Companies that do good, are good. As our survey data shows, the more familiar a company is to its consumers, the better they think of it. It is almost a one-to-one correlation. Familiarity does not breed contempt.

Bob Worcester, the chief executive of public opinion research company MORI in the UK, defines *corporate image* as, 'The net result of the interaction of all the experiences, impressions, beliefs, feelings and knowledge that people have about a company'. He describes it as 'the perception of the outward expression of the company's personality'. This definition has been superseded by Faith Popcorn's definition as 'the soul of the company'. This gets behind the imagery, disallowing the notion that corporate image might be nothing more than a public relations camouflage.

Some time ago, a highly respected researcher in Australia said that the pursuit of building a corporate image was a total waste of time, effort, and money. His conclusion is based on a belief that because a consumer can't 'use' the information about the company, in the same way he or she uses brand or product information, then it is redundant. Wrong. And any marketer who thinks otherwise has failed to recognise that the market-place is changing dramtically, spurred by the collapse in consumer confidence. As the chief executive of a major US food producer says, 'the development of consumer relationships is just as important as product development'.

The development of corporate image embraces everything the company is and does. Corporate advertising, sponsorship programmes, involvement in community projects, in education, and so on are the obvious things. This is where you find budgets allocated to image-making. But implicit in the definition outlined earlier, it is the inside of the company that counts just as much. What is the company's stance on affirmative action or the environment or equal employment opportunities? Bob Worcester was able to show conclusively that knowing somebody in a company was 25% more important than the company's advertising in terms of the favourability of its image, even more important than using their products and services.

Corporate image is not simply a means of generating sales. If that sounds ridiculous, think about these 'publics' a company should be concerned about when it is developing its personality, or 'soul': employees, the stock market, the board of directors, potential employees, final-year undergraduates, the financial press, politicians and governments, distributors, retailers, wholesalers, consumer groups, trade unions, and the competition.

The image of a company is a function of things as diverse as sponsoring a Rugby League team, endowing a Chair at a university, or providing a forum among employees for the interchange of ideas. As a senior vice-president of American Airlines said: 'More and more service companies are awakening to the fact that their internal employee constituency is one of their most important target markets. The better employees feel about themselves and their company, the better they feel about the customer'. How many chief executives think of their staff when they sit down to chart a corporate image campaign? Developing a corporate image is about relationships with everyone who might be called a stakeholder in the company, real or otherwise, customer or not. It is about digging a 'well of goodwill' an investment in the future to be drawn on in times of need. But whether the image-building vehicle is in the public domain or not, research shows that the more people can be told about the programme, whether it be sponsorships or philanthropy, the more the company can reap the benefit of an increase in goodwill (see Figure B7.1).

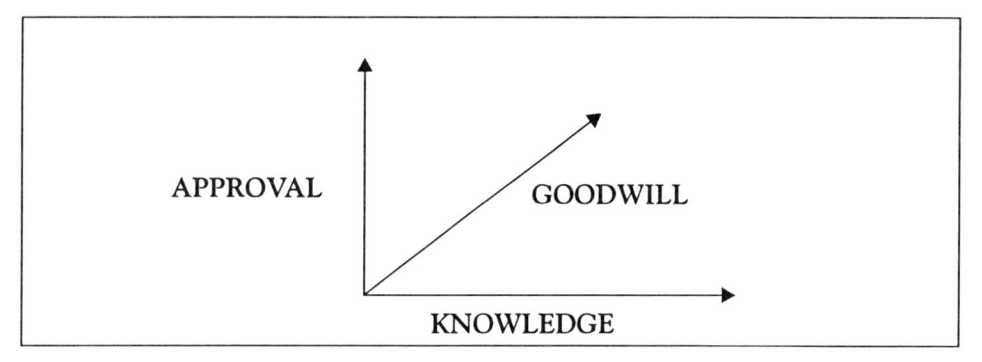

Figure B7.1 *There is, almost without exception, a one-to-one relationship between increases in knowledge about the company, and increases in the favourability score the company can achieve.*

To create a favourable image, programmes need the fuel of publicity. For every dollar spent on an image programme, another dollar needs to be spent on telling people about it. When Esso sponsors the Australian Opera, only 8% of the population are directly reached by that event. But if the population who do not go to the opera are told of it, then significant extra benefits emerge.

How do you measure corporate image? What we set out to measure is consistent with our view of what constitutes corporate image. The first stage in the research process is an undestanding, or discovery stage, to target and help develop an appropriate idea, the image-making vehicle that is best for the company, the synergy of the match, and how best to promote the vehicle to maximise its effectiveness. We're not talking about whether or not it is 'right' for IBM to sponsor the Australian Chamber Orchestra in terms of its target market. That's a tactical issue. We're not talking here about sales promotion. We're talking about building a 'personality' for the company that is above customer relations. Every stakeholder is involved, customer and non-customer alike.

The second phase is the post-launch audit. Typically, it is tracking research to measure the impact of the campaign on the imagery of the brand. As image-making is no more than a vehicle for enhancing the value of a company in the mind of the public, and not a call to action, tracking research focuses on the image characteristics of the company. In particular, we look at:

- its saliency, or awareness (not in relation to the event, but independent of it);
- its familiarity (how well people feel they know the company); and
- its favourability (how well people position the company).

All of this is embedded within industry measures, and among the players in that industry, as well as those from other industries. These are core measures, and by reference to benchmark data we can tell how the company's image shifts over time. It is not possible to separate the effects of a company's image-making from a main media campaign, but image-making comprises a multitude of elements in a company's public activities, even though these activities are designed to create a reservoir of goodwill. It is this reservoir which is the object of our analysis, not any one particular activity. Ultimately, we are looking at the consequences of image-making activities. We measure the soul of the company in the same way all of us assess the quality of our relationships with other people, by how well we know them and whether we like what we learn.

The real value of image research lies in its tracking function, measuring changes in image over time. A good deal of the work in this area is connected with corporate advertising programmes. The objectives of corporate advertising can be condensed into five main factors:

1. *Increase awareness.* Awareness is the base upon which all corporate image is built. To become better known is, nine times out of ten, to increase favourability.
2. *Correct misimpressions.* If research reveals negative perceptions of your company which do not correspond to the facts, advertising and other communications can form the basis of a corrective strategy.
3. *Project positive truths.* Commercial success, research and development of new products, qualities as an employer, export performance, contribution to improving life can all be identified with the company.
4. *Establish corporate links.* Symbols or slogans can be important linking devices between a company and the image characteristics it wants to project. They can provide the nexus between subsidiary companies and their parent company, and between products (brands). The image strengths of a group can be conferred on subsidiaries and their products and vice-versa.
5. *Enhance morale.* People like to be associated with successful, growing, well-regarded organisations. Companies that project this image successfully have employees who 'walk tall'.

There are four generations of corporate advertising: (1) 'here's who we are'; (2) 'here's what we can do for you'; (3) 'here's what we think'; and (4) 'here's what we want you to do'. An attempt to convey the fourth without building the foundation of the first three is likely to be met with suspicion and even hostility. Contrast these with Faith Popcorn's advice about the steps required for a company to find a corporate soul and win the consumer's heart in the 1990s:

1. *Acknowledgment.* Our industry hasn't always done everything in its power to make the world a better place.
2. *Disclosure.* This is who we were. And this is the company we're trying with your help, to become.
3. *Accountability.* Here is how we define our arena of responsibility, and who can be held responsible.

4. *Presentation*. Here is what we pledge to you, the consumer; you'll find our corporate soul in all our products.

There is much in common with these four steps and the four generations of corporate communications. It seems, however, that the focus of Popcorn's is a better prescription for the difficult years ahead, if we are to forge real, lasting links between company and customer. The communication process itself must be founded on mutual understanding, and the responsibility for this lies with the company, not the customer.

Corporate image-making is about building goodwill. That goodwill may ultimately translate into increased demand for a company's products or services. But it also translates into increased productivity through employee commitment, better labour relations, increased saliency in the minds of investors and financial journalists, better relations with politicians and government departments, and with distributors and dealers.

With the future in mind, Faith Popcorn quotes from *Alice in Wonderland*:

> "It takes all the running you can do, to keep in the same place. If you want to get somewhere else, you must run at least twice as fast as that!" said the Queen.

Reproduced with permission from *Marketing*, June 1992, pp. 62–66.

Questions

1. How important is corporate image?
2. What does the importance of corporate image say about changes in society?
3. Corporate image is really just a form of internal selling. Comment.

Case 18—The Quit Club
by Peter Graham and Debra Harker

Introduction

Smoking kills more than 20 000 people each year and costs Australia around $7 billion annually. A recent survey has shown that all smokers will experience some form of related disease or physical deterioration and more than one quarter will die prematurely. After a six-year study of one million smokers, British researchers have found that one in three smokers, and possibly half, will die from tobacco-related diseases. A separate study has found that workers who smoke take more sick days than their non-smoking counterparts but, paradoxically, visit the doctor less often. The study, by the Industrial Programme Service, found smokers over an 18-month period took 66.1 hours off work while non-smoking workers were absent for 52.1 hours.

A recent report by Melbourne's Centre of Behavioural Research in Cancer asked people to comment on three proposals relating to cigarette labelling and packaging. Two of the proposals, detailing tar, nicotine and chemical content, and the inclusion of messages such as 'smoking kills', received unqualified support from 85% of respondents. The third proposal, to include the national QUIT campaign telephone number and an explanation on the pack of the harmful effects of smoking, received support from 87% of those interviewed. When asked to comment on a proposal to introduce generic packaging, 87% said they approved if it would discourage children from taking up smoking. Current estimates suggest that more than 200 000 children in Australia smoke.

Federal and State health ministers have agreed that by 1994 plain brown packaging could replace trademarks and cigarette packs will have almost half their surface taken up with anti-smoking warnings by 1993. The ministers also predicted that within five years smoking would be banned in all public places. Tobacco companies are already banned from sponsoring sports events.

The market

The three tables below indicate the size of the adult smoking market in Australia, the duration of addiction, and consumption patterns.

A current estimate suggests that if there had been no smoking from 1951 onwards there would be at least 350 000 more Australians alive today.

The 1990 Quit Club campaign

On 13 May 1990 the Queensland Health Department (QHD) launched their annual campaign encouraging smokers to stop smoking. Previously, the QHD had run a radio campaign called 'cool turkey'. 1990 was the premier launch of The Quit Club and, for QHD, it was unique in that only those determined to quit were targeted. The Department differentiated this campaign by giving their target market the 'how to' component.

Table B7.1 *The smoking market in Australia, 1989–90 ('000)*

Smoker status	Total
Manufactured cigarettes only	3186.4
Manufactured cigarettes and cigars or pipes	78.9
Roll your own cigarettes only	200.8
Cigars or pipes and roll your own only	14.7
Total smokers	3530.7
Ex-smoker	2891.2
Never smoked	6022.2
Total persons aged 18 years and over	12 444.2

Source: Australian Bureau of Statistics, 1989–90 National Health Survey Risk Factors, Australia, Table 15, 4380.0

Table B7.2 *Duration of addiction to smoking by adults in Australia, 1989–90 ('000)*

Duration of smoking	Total
Less than 1 year	14.0
1 to 4 years	356.8
5 to 9 years	562.1
10 to 19 years	1011.4
20 years or more	1586.4
Total smokers	3530.7

Source: Australian Bureau of Statistics, National Health Survey, 1990

Table B7.3 *Smoking consumption by adults in Australia, 1989–90 ('000)*

No. of cigarettes smoked daily	Total
1 to 10	901.3
11 to 20	1207.6
21 to 30	868.9
31 to 40	186.3
41 or more	100.3
Not stated	*
Total smokers	3265.3

Source: Australian Bureau of Statistics, 1989–90 National Health Survey Risk Factors, Australia, Table 16, 4380.0

At the time, the QHD was the only organisation to actually run a major campaign aimed at changing behaviour, rather than the relatively tame ad hoc attempts made by other bodies. For example, television advertisements shown in 1990 by other bodies included the 'Kathy' commercial which appealed to adult smokers to give up for the sake of their children. Children themselves were targeted with the 'sponge and jar of tar' advertisement demonstrating the harmful effects of smoking. Other advertisements recruited popular television soap stars from 'Neighbours' and 'Home and Away' to try and encourage youngsters not to smoke. The Australian Medical Association distributed educational pamphlets through doctors, emphasising the risks of smoking to pregnant women and children and also highlighted various smoking-related illnesses.

Description and mix of Quit Club campaign

The 1990 Quit Club was a State-wide quit smoking programme developed by the QHD with the support of the Queensland Cancer Fund and the National Heart Foundation. It was aimed at reinforcing the conscious desire of smokers to give up by giving them the 'how to' component to cease smoking. Medical surveys at the time confirmed that 60–80% of smokers had the wish to quit, but lacked the means to do so. The Quit programme endeavoured to give smokers the means by which to achieve a smoke-free lifestyle.

The QHD realised, at the time, that bombarding smokers with scary facts about the consequences of smoking was futile. They identified the clear distinction between those who wanted to give up and those who did not.

Objective

The underlying objective of the Quit Club was to educate smokers who wanted to quit in how to actually do so.

Target market

The target group of the Quit Club was defined as all smokers in the Queensland Community who wanted to cease smoking. The Central Queensland region was used as a control group for future evaluation.

Product

The 1990 Quit Club programme entailed television intervention segments, a support hotline and a kit which contained a booklet, registration form and cigarette wrap and record sheets. All these aspects of the club were new and have been utilised, in some form, in more recent campaigns.

(a) Intervention segments
The intervention segments involved a media personality; David Fordham, a sporting commentator for Channel Ten. He was also the mediator for the programme and offered encouragement and support to those who were giving up. The segments were broadcast each weeknight between 6.30 and 7 pm during the then Anna McMahon current affairs show.

(b) Support hotline
The support phone line was open 24 hours a day for the 19 days that the programme ran. The operator offered counselling, encouragement and support to the quitter who phoned in. However, the 'hotline' was not a success as only 1% of participants utilised it. The QHD have since downgraded the 'hotline' to a 24-hour telephone counselling service.

(c) Kit booklet
The booklet was a day-by-day schedule for the quitter to adopt and follow for 19 days. The booklet was divided into three weeks. Research suggested that three weeks was the optimal time frame for a project of this type, encompassing preparation to quit an addiction, quitting, and a maintenance period.

The first week was a guide to prepare the smoker for the challenge of quitting. The last day of that week coincided with 'World No Smoking Day', which was the first quit day. The second week lent support to becoming used to not smoking. It helped in learning to resist the temptation and for receiving praise for doing so. The final week reinforced the achievement and helped the smoker to look forward to a smoke-free future.

(d) Kit registration slip
The registration slip rendered the adopter a member of the Quit Club, the main benefit of which was group membership and support. Membership also allowed the Health Department to gauge the number of participants and to evaluate the programme.

(e) Kit wrap and record sheets
The cigarette wrap and record sheets, used in the first week, were designed to give the smoker an indication of any patterns in their smoking habits, as it had a time slot, a 'need' rating and asked what the smoker was doing as they smoked. This was wrapped around the cigarette packet in an attempt to discourage the smoker from lapsing too often.

Promotion

The Quit Club was advertised for two weeks leading up to the launch. This informed people about the club and how they could obtain a kit. The advertising took the form of mass communication through 30-second television commercials. These were designed to impact 80% of smokers above the age of 18, 5.3 times per week. The advertisements were shown on the following stations (Table B7.4):

Table B7.4 *The Quit Club campaign, target audience, TV viewers, by area, 1990*

Station	No. of people in area
Vision TV Toowoomba	156 000
ITQ Mt Isa	16 600
NQTV Cairns	104 300
NQTV Townsville	112 300
MVQ Mackay	76 100
SEQ Maryborough	177 800
QSTV Satellite Service	55 250
TQV Channel 10 Brisbane	1 220 000
Total	1 918 350

Other promotional material

Other promotional material included posters and promotional stands designed to be displayed in the channels of distribution.

Distribution

The Quit Club kits were made available from participating general practitioners surgeries and all Medical Benefit Fund (MBF) offices. The Quit Club intervention segments were viewed throughout Queensland through the participating stations with the exception of Central Queensland.

Price

The price of the Quit Club to the adopter was time, effort and dedication. There were no monetary costs for the kit or to register, only a cost of motivation. The price of the Quit Club in terms of implementation costs, such as design and printing of booklets, promotional material, assembly of kits and postage was $196 591. The cost of the Health Department office's time in developing, implementing and evaluating the programme was not recorded as the department did not keep records of those costs. The cost of the television commercials and intervention segments was zero, as each participating station provided their services free of charge, including air time.

The outcome

According to the QHD 65 000 smokers obtained the Quit Club booklet in 1990. By the end of the programme 17% (11 050) had 'succeeded' in giving up smoking. One year later the 'succeeders' were contacted and interviewed by the Department about their progress, 3900 had resumed smoking. This left a net 'success' rate of 11% (7150), a figure with which the QHD are extremely satisfied.

> (Data used in this case study was collected by Tracey Hill, Claude Labreaux and Greg McMillan as part of a marketing assignment at Griffith University.)

Questions

1. Critically analyse the Quit club campaign in terms of social marketing theory. You may find the following texts helpful:
   — Kotler, P. A. and Roberto, E. L. (1989), *Social Marketing*, Free Press, New York.
   — Kotler, P. A. (1985), *Marketing for Non-Profit Organisations*, (2nd edn), Prentice Hall, New Jersey.
   — Peter, J. P. and Olson, J. C. (1987), *Consumer Behaviour*, Irwin, Illinois.
2. Kotler and Andreasen (1991) define seven major steps in planning a campaign within social marketing theory. Do you think the QHD implemented this theory? Why?
3. As an independent social marketing consultant, what broad recommendations would you make to the QHD in order to improve the Quit Club campaign in future years?

References

Kotler, P. A. and Andreasen, A. (1991), *Strategic Marketing for Non-Profit Organisations*, (2nd edn), Prentice Hall, New Jersey.

Case 19—Ethics and international business

by Daniel W. Skubik

Questioner: 'And what do you do?'

Academic: 'I lecture in business ethics.'

Questioner's Rejoinder:

(a) 'Must be a short lecture!'; or
(b) 'Business ethics! Isn't that a contradiction in terms?'; or
(c) 'Business ethics? I didn't know there were any!'; or
(d) 'What sort of joker are you?!'.

Such comically cynical responses were the chronic bane of those pioneers who developed courses, workshops and institutes in professional and business ethics during the late 1970s and early 1980s. More recently the value—indeed the necessity—of these endeavours has been widely recognised, with comic cynicism being steadily displaced by serious welcoming of ethical deliberation in the practical affairs of life.

Of course some suspicions and barbs may be encountered occasionally even today, generally traceable to contemporary revelations of less-than-honourable activities by some notable (notorious) financial figures in North America, Western Europe and

Australasia. Yet, the very fact that such actions by those figures were perforce secretive, and once revealed were soundly deplored by the community, itself provides evidence that ethics in business is seen to be important by traders and members of the general public alike. This does not mean that everyone in Australian society agrees about what specific ethical standards are appropriate to various spheres of business activity such as marketing. Much less is there agreement amongst peoples of different societies when business activities involve crossing nation-state borders.

Transnational Corporations (TNCs) and smaller, export-oriented firms regularly face circumstances where ethical clashes may jeopardise business dealings. An inability to recognise and resolve, or blatant ignorance of such differences are often damaging to the credibility and profitability of these trading firms. Insensitivity to disparities in judgments rarely passes unnoticed by the other party; emphasising the need to carefully analyse the host country's ethical practices and business judgments.

Since we can take as given that business practices and moral judgments about those practices do clash, domestically and internationally, some framework is required to aid business managers in their decision making. Unless we are simply to throw up our hands and declare that 'anything goes' (usually advanced with the caveat 'as long as you don't get caught'), some guidelines—however rough—are needed.

Ethical frameworks

Donaldson's ethical algorithm

Thomas Donaldson has devised a provocative ethical algorithm for corporate decision making in his recent work, *The Ethics of International Business*, as an attempt to address just this sort of practical problem. There, he offers a way of cataloguing clashes, a typology of conflicts, and advances some corresponding formulae for resolving them. His typology specifically addresses conflicts which arise from a practice which is permitted in the host country of a transnational corporation (TNC), but is not permitted in the TNC's home state. Where there exists a clash in permitted business practices, we can discern and divide the moral judgments offered about these practices into two broad types according to the sorts of reasons advanced which support them:

- *Type 1*. The moral reasons underlying the host country's view that the practice is permissible refer to the host country's relative level of economic development.
- *Type 2*. The moral reasons underlying the host country's view that the practice is permissible are independent of the host country's relative level of economic development.

Examples here include clashes between practices concerning the governments' mandated industrial safety measures (strict at home vs. loose in host), permissible pollution levels (low at home vs. high in host), and racial or religious discrimination (not permitted at home vs. permitted or mandated in host). If the conflict is a Type 1 conflict, Donaldson claims that 'the following formula is appropriate':

> The practice is permissible if and only if the members of the home country would, under conditions of economic development relevantly similar to those of the host country, regard the practice as permissible.

If home country moral agents would determine that the practice is not permissible, then regardless of host country permissibility the practice should not be followed by the TNC. Thus, adherence to higher host country worker safety measures (say, steel-tipped boots on heavy construction sites) should on moral grounds (generally speaking or all other factors being equal) be cross-culturally transferable. That is, the standard at home ought to be followed at the host site even though not legally required. On the other hand, morally permissible air or water pollution levels may soundly differ. That means that some trade-offs in the host permitting higher pollution levels for the sake of industrialisation can be morally reasonable ones.

The other category of clashes, Type 2 conflicts, Donaldson suggests, requires a different approach. In this instance, 'the practice would be permissible if and only if the answer to both of the following questions is "no"'.

- Is it possible to conduct business successfully in the host country without undertaking the practice?
- Is the practice a clear violation of a fundamental international right?

If either question can be answered in the affirmative, then the practice should not be adopted. Thus, petty official bribery may be tolerated: it may be necessary but it is not a violation of any fundamental international right. Still, racial or religious discrimination is not to be adopted as good practice: even if necessary, the practice is a clear violation of a fundamental international right and so is impermissible.

These algorithms represent exciting new ground, and we can be grateful for Donaldson's attempt at providing a schema for ethical managerial decision making. It comprises the first comprehensive framework made available to business people who take seriously their ethical obligations. Yet, these algorithms may ultimately fail to deliver.

First, they fail at the pragmatic level of managerial competence. Requiring managers to make the global judgments mandated by these algorithms is too Herculean a burden. Assume for a moment a single, separable, coherent set of moral reasons grounding a host country's permission to turn its rainforest into pulp or for fuel to cure its tobacco cash crop. How are these reasons to be discovered?: from government press releases . . . asking the environment minister for a declaratory letter . . . scanning local newspapers . . . talking to people on the street . . . seeking anthropologists' advice . . . ? In short, how does the manager identify or construct the relevant principles and judgments for a society not one's own and then go on to type them as dependent on or independent of the society's relative level of economic development?

Second, the algorithms fail at another level, not of relevance but of conflict. By this I mean that even assuming there are sufficient devices which can be employed by the TNC manager, a single, separable, coherent set of moral reasons is not likely to be compiled. Rather, a set of somewhat disparate, potentially or actually conflicting judgments will be discovered. And which are to be given priority, thereby specifying the host country's view? In a similar vein, there is no less a problem in the conflict to be found in applying the counterfactual formula for simple Type 1 conflicts: discerning or constructing one's own home country view is surely just as problematic as constructing a view for your host. Perhaps more so, since one is likely to be more sensitive to the variety of judgments in one's home state than in any host country's society.

Third, the algorithms fail at a more complex level. Donaldson writes from the position of one committed to a particular set of values and a particular calculus for formulating and manipulating judgments about those values. I, too, having been born and raised in the US, happen to share many of those values and am sympathetic with many of the judgments about those values he constructs. But if ethical certainty about our own judgments has evaded us, then Donaldson's algorithms may well force us and TNC managers into a position of ethical imperialism, where one takes a host country's ethics only as seriously or to the extent that they can be catalogued and manipulated according to one's home country judgments.

An alternative framework

What is required, then, is a somewhat different approach. Let me suggest the following. Assuming there is a *prima facie* conflict between practices of a host and the typical practices of a TNC; the TNC manager should:

1. take the possibility of cultural relativism seriously enough to empathetically sketch the practices and judgments taken in the host country; and
2. sketch the compatibility of the factual and ethical judgments compiled in (1) with one's own factual and ethical judgments; then
3. if the host country practices and judgments are congruent with one's own, engaging in the practice is at least permissible; but
4. if the host country practices and judgments are not congruent, engaging in the practice is not permissible unless lack of congruence is grounded on differences in factual judgments alone; if so, the practice is only permissible after good faith attempts at attaining congruence fail.

How do these algorithms escape my own criticisms of Donaldson's schema? Don't they require the same sorts of problematic judgments on the part of the TNC manager? The claim is that they escape earlier criticisms, both pragmatic and theoretic on the grounds of their do-ability and their ethical tract-ability. Let me briefly explain.

The sketching required of the manager at Step 1 can be accomplished without assuming or requiring specialist knowledge of the culture in which one is operating. Rather, the sketch can be compiled from a set of reports and surveys, the kind of which any profit-maximising corporation would commission before entering a new market in a new cultural setting: what expectations or demands are there on the part of the government . . . on the part of the labour force . . . on the part of the customers? This sorting out of expectations will then more easily lead to asking relevant questions about judgments which inform these expectations. One need not look to constructing basic moral principles here. Expectations and second-level judgments of moral utility will suffice.

The sketching required of the manager at Step 2 is of the same sort of inquiry; it does not require a theoretically critical evaluation of factual or ethical judgments, just a side-by-side sorting list covering both sets of facts and judgments.

The third step is the crucial one, both in the sense that much of the analytical work required is going on here, and it is here that the manager's competence may come into question. But unlike Donaldson's, this schema does not require of the manager a critical construction of disparate moralities, whether based on perceptions of economic or non-economic requirements, at home or abroad. Instead the manager need only decide whether the practices and judgments are congruent, a much simpler judgment based upon commonality/similarity and universality of relevant factors. In addition, note that the assessments here and at Step 2 are based upon the ethics of the manager, and not upon some theoretically reconstructed home position. Thus, I am quite prepared to take for granted that the manager is in a managerial position in part because the life of that individual reflects some set of mores which in turn reasonably reflects the broader moral framework of the home culture. Now this does require or raise the hopeful expectation that managers have had or will receive some training in moral theory so that notions such as universality are analytic tools available to the decision makers. But this schema does not require of them that they be ethicists proper; critical analysis of another or even one's own culture is not the crucial factor.

Finally, once the congruence judgment is made, the algorithms lead to justifiable outcomes. That is, they are justifiable with reference to the frameworks of the two cultures involved; it is not the task of the manager to be able theoretically to justify adopting a practice to all possible critics from any society.

Practical examples

To put some flesh to these rather abstract frameworks, let's try two real-world examples of clashes between host and home business practices.

Example 1:
> Samsonite, the great American luggage company, moves its manufacturing plant to a maquiladora in Mexico. Instead of paying the US labour wage of $8–$15/hour, the company can bargain to pay the prevailing $8–$15/day. What level of wages ought Samsonite pay its Mexican labor force?

Under Donaldson's schema, we as managers are first to ask ourselves whether the moral reasons underlying the practice of paying bare subsistence wages is related to Mexico's relative level of development. Then we can decide what type of conflict case we may have and so refer to the appropriate algorithm for the conflict's ethical resolution. With all due respect, asking Donaldson's first sort of practices-in-moral-conflict question in this case seems incredulous. Mexican officials, labourers and customers have no moral reasons underlying the practice; what reasons exist are typically simple economic imperatives. If true, Donaldson's schema can tell us nothing here; managers will remain at a loss as to how to decide and may well then say there is no moral issue about which we ought to worry; let's pay as little as we can for an acceptable work force.

Under my schema, the question of congruence of practices can and must be asked to formulate decisions about the ethical nature of wage levels. I shan't take the space and time to go into great detail, so let me straightforwardly assert the following quite plausible managerial findings:

1. Mexican factual judgments covering subsistence wages are grounded in economic realities of overpopulation and underemployment of able bodied workers;
2. ethical judgments about the value of labour (not the wage rate itself) are grounded in international political development theory assumptions which may include more-or-less sophisticated notions from, say, the Prebisch thesis of the 1960s or more modern dependency theories promulgated since the late 1970s, concerning underdevelopment in Third World peripheral economies and that their workers are being exploited by First World core economies in great measure through the cores' TNCs;
3. we would surely expect Samsonite's practices and the manager's judgments not to be congruent with such Mexican practices and judgments, the former being grounded in capitalist market economics; and thus,
4. the algorithm leads us to the conclusion that the Mexican practice of paying subsistence wages is impermissible, or to put the conclusion in more positive terms, the company must be prepared to re-evaluate an ethical wage level before operating across the border.

This re-evaluation is then grounded upon taking seriously the point of view of the host, negotiating a non-exploitative wage package by bringing forward the economic judgments of host costs and benefits related to the maquiladora regime.

Example 2:
IBM Australia wants to locate a new screwdriver factory outside Kuala Lumpur (i.e. a production facility for assembling computer components manufactured elsewhere, the finished product then being exported to countries throughout South-east Asia). IBM seeks to establish negotiations with a Malaysian landowner and representatives of the Government, and is told that while the parties are quite interested in IBM's proposal and so will agree to arrange face-to-face negotiations in KL, the IBM negotiators must be older non-drinking males sympathetic to Muslim traditions. Of course, IBM's principal negotiator in this production area does not fit the description being a 38-year-old fundamentalist Christian female. Whom does IBM send?

Assuming with Donaldson that one might reasonably say this sort of discrimination is not morally grounded on reasons referring to the relative economic development of Malaysia, and so is one of his Type 2 conflicts, we will require a negative answer to both his queries about the necessity of the practice to business success and whether a fundamental right is at stake. While the necessity point is admittedly problematic, let's assume that the practice is necessary, or to rephrase in Donaldson's terms: it is not possible to conduct business successfully without adopting the practice. This response then brings us to the second question about rights violations. And for Donaldson at least, this second query concerning the violation of a fundamental right not to be discriminated against on the basis of race or religion or sex is clearly answered in the affirmative since such discrimination is a violation of a fundamental international right. Thus, changing negotiators for IBM on the basis of the request cannot be morally justified.

Once again, I haven't space or time to go into detail, but let me claim that there is good reason to believe that the judgments of IBM's principal negotiator would be congruent with her Malaysian counterparts: that is, there exists a recognisable commonality and universality to the religious judgments of differentiated roles for men and women with which the IBM negotiator can empathise, though the practices simpliciter may be incongruent due to differences in other (e.g. factual) judgments concerning male/female physiological and psychological constitutions. Thus, we are led to the caveat from my point (4) about good faith attempts at attaining factual congruence, which in this case means making good faith efforts to change the others' minds on the issue. Yet, if these particular agents persist, adopting their practice will be permissible: negotiations can go ahead without IBM's original principal negotiator but with a substitute male who better meets their criteria.

Now, I would not want to suggest that these two schemas which Donaldson and I are proffering must or will always be in opposition as these two sample cases might infer. There will be significant congruence in required outcomes between them in a variety of cases and so significant external broad coherence between our possible ethical judgments and our moral experiences both intra- and inter-culturally. But I would submit that it is only under the alternative schema outlined here that students and managers can come to take their own and others' ethical positions seriously, empathetically and critically, without either 'giving away the store' or 'packing up and going home' because the problems are just too hard to handle. And isn't that a key criterion of practical wisdom after all what we should do, we can do.

Questions

1. Now, try working through a case or two for yourselves. You might begin with the facts of Example 2, above. You are part of the IBM team negotiating the establishment of a screwdriver factory. You have successfully resolved the problem of who should lead the team to everyone's satisfaction (whatever that resolution may have been). Now you are told that while the production facility would be quite welcome in KL, the Government is concerned that the workers be properly selected. In this instance, proper selection means job offers should go first to ethnic Malays, and sourcing of any goods and services needed by the factory is likewise to be Malay in the first instance. Others, such as ethnic Chinese, are to be called upon only after all reasonable attempts at attracting the preferred group have failed. Do IBM agree to these operating conditions? (You might begin discussion by focusing on differences, if any, between legitimate modes of affirmative action and illegitimate types of racial and ethnic discrimination. What facts and what judgments may be clashing here?)
2. One further case for group discussion. You are the marketing director for Dow Corning's silicone breast implant, a product commonly used by cosmetic surgeons in countries such as the United Kingdom, the United States and Australia. A

number of law suits have recently been filed in the US alleging 'leaks' of silicone from the implant into surrounding tissue, causing cancer. The US Food & Drug Administration (the government agency charged with oversight of such products) has responded by directing temporary suspension of use of the implant throughout the US until medical tests can better determine the actual rate of 'leakage' and any linkage to subsequent cancers. The UK and Australian medical authorities express some concern, but neither their medical boards nor governments demand suspension of the use of the implants. Do you continue marketing your silicone implants in these countries?

References

De George, R. T. (1990), 'Ethics and Coherence', *APA Proceedings*, **64** (3), pp. 39-52.

Donaldson, T. (1989), *The Ethics of International Business*, Oxford University Press, New York

Goodin, R. E. (1989), *No Smoking: The Ethical Issues*, University of Chicago Press.

PART C

SELECTED AUSTRALIAN STATISTICS

Introduction and sources of selected statistics

by Peter Graham and Debra Harker

Part C of this book is in two sections. The first, detailed below, includes examples of statistics that the student will find helpful when attempting cases. The second section gives a brief overview of relevant sources of information that students may wish to explore. The overview is not meant to be a definitive 'list' of sources, rather a place to start the research journey.

Selected statistics

Part C also contains two articles. In the first, 'How quickly will advertising expenditure bounce back?' Bernard Holt looks back at the 1982/83 recession to see if anything can be learned. A table showing Australia's top 200 advertisers and their brands is also contained in this section, together with a selection of the top 300 advertising agencies. Three small tables follow, showing the top ten Australian-owned agencies and the top ten agencies with the fastest rising, and fastest falling incomes, in 1990 to 1991.

The second article, 'God is in the details' is by Deane Russell, director of marketing and public relations for the Bureau of Statistics. The article uses a simple example to ably demonstrate the role of statistics in marketing. An example of a typical ABS table, showing Australia's mean resident population is also shown in this section.

Two other ABS tables are contained in this section. 'Users and non-users of cultural venues/activities by region' will assist students when attempting 'The marketing of the Queensland Art Gallery' case study in Part B6 of this book. Similarly, 'Ex-smokers of packet cigarettes: Age last quit smoking by reason for quitting smoking by age' will assist in preparing for 'The Quit Club' in Part B7. Full copies of these tables can be located in your library.

The Australian Stock Exchange provides a number of publications and is a very good source of information for students. The examples shown in this section of the book are taken from the *All Ordinaries Index Companies Handbook*. The companies listed in the handbook account for over 90% of total market capitalisation and turnover and form a significant part of Australian share investment portfolios. Four company profiles have been selected from the handbook to be included here and students will find all four useful when tackling certain case studies.

Sources of Australian statistics

The Commercial Economic Advisory Service of Australia

The CEASA is a research, forecasting and publishing company which was established in 1967. The company specialises in preparing statistical and background information on Australian markets and the economy. Current publications include:

- 'Advertising Expenditure in the Main Media'—annual survey.
- 'The Grocery Industry Review'—a detailed insight into all aspects of the industry.
- 'Australian Profile'—a ready reference to everyday economic statistics.

The principal of CEASA, Bernard Holt, has contributed to this book with the article following this section, 'How quickly will advertising expenditure bounce back?'

The Australian Planning and Systems Company Pty Ltd

APASCO was founded in 1973 and was a pioneer in the provision of computer-based marketing reports and maps. Since that time APASCO has provided marketing services to more than 1000 of Australia's major business organisations. APASCO can be contacted through their head office:

> APASCO Pty Ltd
> 7th Floor,
> 140 Arthur Street
> North Sydney NSW 2060
> Telephone: (02) 922 2088
> Fax: (02) 929 8376

Trades Practices Commission

Periodically the Commission publishes, through the Australian Government Publishing Service in Canberra, detailed research reports. The reports are an excellent example of thorough market research and the index is worth interrogating for relevant reports. The AGPS Sales Operations Department can be contacted on: (06) 295 4411. AGPS publications are available in Commonwealth Government bookshops, in every state and territory capital city in Australia.

Bureau of Industry Economics

Another product of the Australian Government Publishing Service is the work conducted by the BIE. A regular publication from the Bureau is their, 'Australian Industry Trends'. The Bureau of Industry Economics is the research arm of the Department of Industry, Technology and Commerce. It operates with independence in the conduct of its research and the reporting of its results. The Bureau can be contacted in Canberra:

The Director
Bureau of Industry Economics,
Department of Industry, Technology and Commerce
51 Allara Street
Canberra ACT 2601

The Australian Bureau of Statistics

An ABS information sheet is contained in this section of the book and they have an office in every Territory and State in Australia where their information officers are keen to be of assistance. The Bureau provides many excellent publications, too numerous to mention here. Catalogues and indexes to ABS sources are available in your library but a good quick reference is the ABS pocket yearbook, published annually and covering individual states and territories as well as an Australia-wide version.

The Australian Stock Exchange

The Exchange has an office in every state and territory and publishes regular in-depth products which students will find extremely helpful. Apart from the *All Ordinaries Index Companies Handbook* the Exchange also markets *Australia's Top 100 Listed Companies* and the *Gold Producers Handbook*. Head office for the ASE is:

Australian Stock Exchange
Market Information Department
PO Box H224
Australia Square
Sydney NSW 2001
Freephone: 008 029 962

Bureau of Tourism Research

The BTR was established in late 1987, in accordance with the recommendations of the Australian Government Inquiry into Tourism. Its aim is to provide a national focus for the collection, analysis and dissemination of official tourism statistics and thus provide key decision makers in government and private enterprise with the statistical and analytical support necessary for effectively planned and balanced tourism development. It is a co-operative venture, jointly funded by the Commonwealth and State/Territory governments. The Bureau publishes various reports on all aspects of the Tourism industry. They can be contacted in Canberra:

Bureau of Tourism Research
GPO Box 1545
Canberra ACT 2601
Statistical information:(06) 274 1716
Publication officer:(06) 274 1760

University libraries

Most libraries are now computerised which makes life, for the researcher, much easier. Apart from interrogating the library catalogue, students can also use the subjects covered on CD-ROM disks. A printout of your selection is easily obtainable. Access is often provided through your library to on-line databases but these are costly. Your library information desk will be able to provide details of the services they offer.

Journals and magazines

Once again, your library will hold copies of most magazines relevant to marketing and they serve as an excellent source for up to the minute information. Quality newspapers and periodicals are also useful. Marketers will find the following publications particularly helpful:

Business Review Weekly	(03) 603 3888
Marketing	(02) 310 1211
PROFIT	(02) 439 5133
Australian Business Monthly	(02) 282 8300
The Bulletin	(02) 282 8200

How quickly will advertising expenditure bounce back?

by Bernard Holt

Are there any pointers from the 1982–83 recession or are all recessions different? Bernard Holt discusses our history of recession and depression and relates them to advertising expenditure.

For the first time since 1960 when I issued my first report, advertising expenditure in 1990 went down. This calls into question expenditure behaviour in previous recession years. Perhaps the most appropriate recession period might be that of 1982–83. When talking about recession we are really talking about the business cycle, and each one has been different.

Collins' *Dictionary of Economics* describes a recession as: 'A phase of the business cycle characterised by a modest downturn in the level of economic activity. Real output and investment fall, resulting in rising unemployment'. This is distinct from a depression which talks about a severe slump in economic activity and a high rate of unemployment. There have been depressions in the late 1820s, the early 1840s and the first part of both the 1890s and 1930s. Recessions on the other hand have been plotted in 1952, 1957, 1961, 1975, 1977, 1982–83 and, of course, our current agony. Conventional wisdom has it that a recession arrives when there has been two successive quarters of contraction in the economy.

The 1982–83 recession was caused by a combination of world recession, a wages blow-out and a severe drought. The non-farm economy did not contract sharply but just stalled for about two years. When combined with the blow-out in labour costs there was a wave of job retrenchments with unemployment jumping from 6% to 10.3%.

This time around there are new factors to consider. Many of the world economies are in recession, notably the United States and also a question mark over Japan. In addition there are the unknown economic effects of the European upheavals. Our economy's large foreign debt burden, a highly geared corporate sector and a debt exposed banking sector lead to the suspicion that banks are imposing their own lending restrictions or squeeze. The rapid decline of small business and of course unemployment at 11% as at December 1991 according to the ABS statistics. Sustained high interest rates and uncertain commodity demand and prices have severely affected country areas some of which are experiencing drought conditions. So what has this got to do with advertising expenditure? A great deal.

Manufacturing and retailing are the engine room for advertising and buying power is related to real household disposable income, unemployment levels and CPI. Product categories which were advertised most and the total expenditure for them in calendar years 1982, 1983 and 1984 (bearing in mind that the economy was stalled for two years) compared with 1990 are:

Table C1.1 *Advertising expenditure on product categories*

Year	Product category	Expenditure ($)
1982	Foodstuffs	129 725 146
	Cars & trucks	97 276 571
	Household equipment, furnishings and appliances	80 754 097
	Travel and tours	50 137 616
	Building materials & industrial machinery	47 972 896
1983	Foodstuffs	151 238 447
	Cars & trucks	116 289 095
	Household equipment, furnishings & appliances	88 795 579
	Finance loans & debentures	52 966 574
	Travel & tours	52 308 409
1984	Foodstuffs	176 830 322
	Cars & trucks	156 730 867
	Household equipment, furnishings & appliances	103 299 303
	Finance loans & debentures	66 543 522
	Building materials & industrial machinery	64 767 336
	Travel & tours	60 575 736
1990	Cars & trucks	260 537 247
	Foodstuffs	237 818 973
	Travel & tours	135 166 977
	Banks	133 458 860
	Records	79 806 783

As marketers in all the product categories mentioned above will know, there is a story to tell as to why categories have come and gone and why expenditures have fluctuated. Even though the total advertising expenditure went down in 1990, clearly major advertisers kept the pressure up.

Product categories which went down between 1989 and 1990 included: men's and women's toiletries; men's wear and accessories; household equipment; electrical goods; radio, television and sound equipment; pharmaceuticals; building materials and industrial machinery; paints and accessories (marginally); liquor (marginally); fabrics textiles and linens; foodstuffs; gardening; office equipment; watches and jewellery; toys and games (marginally). And those which went up were: children's wear; women's wear and accessories; toilet soaps; dental; household products and cleaners (marginally); car accessories; tyres; soft drinks; confectionery; travel and tours; banks; governments; educational; radio and TV stations; photographic equipment; recorded music.

At the time of writing, talks with major advertisers suggest that the increase is only likely to be of the order of 3% to 4% after a 2% drop in 1990. Interestingly enough AIS Media recently did a comprehensive survey of advertisers concerning 1992 expenditure on advertising. Their prediction for this year is an increase of 7.7%.

It will be fascinating to see which product categories do what in both 1991 and 1992.

Reproduced with permission from *Marketing*, April 1992, pp. 16–17.

The top 200 advertisers

Estimated main media advertising budget ($m)*

* Expenditure in Australia only

Number	Company	1992	1991	Key brands/products
1	Coles Myer	110	120	K mart, Target, Myer-Grace Bros, Coles Supermarkets, Bi-Lo
2	Federal Government	66	70	Various government departments
3	Unilever	62	60	Streets, Omo, Continental, Flora, Bushells, Rexona, Lever 2000
4	AOTC	60	42	Telecom, OTC, Yellow Pages
5	Coca-Cola South Pacific	40	36	Coca-Cola, Sprite, Diet Coke, Fanta, Lift
6	Pacific Dunlop	40	22	Birds Eye, Rio, Holeproof, Four'n Twenty, Bonds, Beaurepaires
7	McDonalds Australia	37	36	McDonald's
8	PepsiCo Inc	37	36	Kentucky Fried Chicken, Pepsi, Pizza Hut, Ruffles, Thins, 7Up
9	Kellogg Australia	36	32	Kellogg
10	Goodman Fielder Wattie	36	19	Uncle Tobys, White Wings, Eta, Meadow Lea, Praise, Buttercup
11	Toyota Motor Corporation	33	35	Toyota, Hino
12	Cadbury Schweppes	30	28	Cadbury, Red Tulip, Cottee's, Schweppes, Sunkist, Solo
13	Reckitt & Colman	30	32	Mortein, Decore, Lemsip, Preen, Down to Earth, Pea Beau
14	Nestlé Australia	30	30	Nescafe, Kit Kat, Feast, Maggi, Violet Crumble, Buffet, Findus
15	Mars Inc	29	27	Pal, Uncle Ben's, Mars Bar, Snickers, Dolmio, Kan-Tong, Whiskas
16	Mitsubishi Motors	27	33	Mitsubishi
17	Eastman Kodak	25	3	Panadol, Kodak, Glen-20, Kodak Express, Pluravit
18	Woolworths	25	NA	Woolworths, Big W, Rockmans
19	GMH's Automotive	23	25	Holden
20	Commonwealth Bank	22	24	Commonwealth Bank, State Bank of Victoria, CBFC
21	NSW Government	21	23	Various government departments
22	Victorian Government	21	25	Various government departments
23	Coca-Cola Amatil	20	16	Smith's Crisps, Deep Spring, Twisties, CC's, Shelleys
24	Ford Motor Company	20	21	Ford
25	Vox Limited	20	18	Chandlers, Venture, Billy Guyatts, Kresta
26	Colgate-Palmolive	19	17	Palmolive, Plax, Cold Power, UV, Sard, Colgate, Fab
27	Nissan Motor Company	18	26	Nissan

The top 200 advertisers (continued)
Estimated main media advertising budget ($m)*
*Expenditure in Australia only

Number	Company	1992	1991	Key brands/products
28	Procter & Gamble	18	17	Vicks, Pert, Pringles, Pampers, Cover Girl, Max Factor, Flash, Whisper
29	Johnson & Johnson	17	16	Stayfree, Meds, Reach, Sure & Natural, Family Shampoo
30	Phillip Morris	17	15	Kraft, Vegemite, Milka, Toblerone, Peter Jackson, Longbeach
31	Lion Nathan	17	16	Tooheys, Swan, Fourex, Castlemaine
32	Guinness	16	17	Johnnie Walker, Guinness, Bundaberg, Rebel Yell
33	ANZ Banking Group	15	14	ANZ Bank, Esanda
34	Arnotts Limited	15	20	Arnott's Sunshine
35	News Corporation	15	25	Telegraph-Mirror, Herald-Sun, Festival, Courier Mail
36	Village Roadshow	15	13	Village Theatres, Movie World, Nightmare, Roadshow Home Video
37	Foster's Brewing Group	14	12	Victoria Bitter, Reschs, Foster's, Melbourne Bitter
38	Hoyts Corporation	14	16	Hoyts, 2MMM, 3MMM, 4MMM
39	Harvey Norman Discounts	13	12	Harvey Norman
40	Mitre 10	13	12	Mitre 10
41	Westpac Banking Corporation	13	12	Westpac, AGC, Ten Network
42	AMP Society	12	13	AMP
43	National Australia Bank	12	12	National Australia Bank, Custom Credit
44	Swift & Moore	12	11.5	Tia Maria, Malibu, Baileys, Jack Daniel's, Grand Marnier
45	Aust. Meat and Livestock Corp.	12	13	Beef, lamb
46	Mazda Australia	12	8	Mazda, Eunos
47	Sanitarium Health Food Co	12	11	Weet-Bix, So Good, Crunchy Bix, Good Start
48	Bowater Industries	12	12	Sorbent, Libra, Fleur, Lady Scott
49	NRMA	12	11	NRMA
50	Sara Lee Corporation	12	8	Sara Lee, Kiwi, Razzamatazz Moccona, Harris, Stubbies
51	Davids Holdings	11	7	Festival-IGA, Clancy's, Campbell's Cash &Carry
52	Honda Australia	11	11	Honda
53	National Mutual	11	11	National Mutual
54	Thorn EMI	11	10	EMI, Radio Rentals, HMV
55	Time Warner	11	NA	Time, Who, Movie World, Time-Life, Warner Music

The top 200 advertisers (continued)
Estimated main media advertising budget ($m)*
* Expenditure in Australia only

Number	Company	1992	1991	Key brands/products
56	ICI Australia	10	12	Dulux, Vetcare, British Paints
57	Pacific Magazines	10	NA	TV Week, New Idea, Home Beautiful
58	David Jones	10	11	David Jones, John Martin, Georges, Clark Rubber
58	Australian Airlines	10	10	Australian Airlines
60	Just Jeans	10	9	Just Jeans
61	National Foods	10	9	Allowrie, Bodalla, Glad, Sunburst, Fruche
62	SA Brewing	10	10	Penfolds, Rheem, West End, Dishlex, Lindemans
63	Ansett Transport Industries	9	8.5	Ansett, Ansett Air Freight
64	Kimberly-Clark	9	8	Huggies, Kleenex, Kotex
65	Aust. Consolidated Press	9	NA	Aust. Women's Weekly, Woman's Day, Cleo, Bulletin
66	John Fairfax Group	9	9	Sydney Morning Herald, Age, Financial Review, Sun-Herald, BRW
67	Retravision	9	8	Retravision
68	Amalgamated Holdings	9	10	Greater Union, Rydges Hotels
69	George Weston Foods	9	8.5	Chocolate Wheaten, Big Ben, Top Taste, Tip Top, Ryvita
70	Aust. Dairy Corporation	9	8	Cheese, butter, milk, cream
71	Queensland Government	8	9	Various government departments
72	Mattel Inc	8	NA	Barbie, Nintendo, Disney
73	Shell Company of Australia	8	7	Shell, Circle K, Autocare
74	Baillieu Knight Frank	8	10	Baillieu Knight Frank
75	Advance Bank	7	7	Advance Bank
76	Burns Philp	7	6.5	BBC Hardware, Chicken Easy, Dilmah, Eastern Feast
77	EAC Plumrose	7	6	Leggo's, Yoplait, Petit Miam, Leggo's Fresh
78	Foodland Associated	7	6.5	Foodland, Four Square, Supa Valu
79	GIO Australia	7	NA	GIO
80	J & B Records	7	7	Concept, Hit Bound, J & B
81	St George Bank	7	6.5	St George
82	Philips Industries	7	7	Philips, PolyGram
83	Sony Corporation	7	6	Sony, Sony Music
84	State Bank of NSW	7	6	State Bank of NSW
85	Astre Limited	6	6.5	Hyundai
86	American Express	6	8	American Express
87	Suncorp	6	5	LJ Hooker, Suncorp Building Society, Hooker Corporate

The top 200 advertisers (continued)
Estimated main media advertising budget ($m)*
*Expenditure in Australia only

Number	Company	1992	1991	Key brands/products
88	SC Johnson	6	7	Raid, Agree, Glade, Charge, Flush Duck, Closet Camel
89	Panasonic Australia	6	7	Panasonic
90	Brash Holdings	6	5	Brashs
91	BP Australia	6	7	BP, Food Plus
92	Gillette Australia	6	7	Sensor, Gillette, Oral-B, Aapri
93	Competitive Foods	6	6	Hungry Jack's, Kentucky Fried Chicken, Silvio's
94	Dino Music	6	NA	Dino
95	Vic. Dairy Industry Authority	6	6	Big M, Rev, Skinny, Revital
96	George Adams Estate	6	4	Tattslotto, Keno
97	HJ Heinz	6	5.5	Heinz, Weight Watchers, Greenseas
98	Hasbro Inc	6	7	Monopoly, Tonka, Cluedo, GI Joe, Cabbage Patch Kids
99	McCain Foods	6	5.9	Healthy Choice, McCain
100	Ingham Enterprises	6	7	Ingham
101	Email Limited	5.5	6.5	Simpson, Westinghouse, Kelvinator
102	Helene Curtis	5.5	4	Salon Selectives, Finesse, Degree, MQ Optimum
103	Amcal Chemists	5	6	Amcal
104	Freedom Furniture	5	2.5	Freedom
105	Boniac Foods/Bega Co-op	5	5	Western Star, Bega, Less
106	Best & Less	5	NA	Best & Less
107	QIW Retailers	5	5.5	Q Superstore, Foodstore, Four Square
108	Seagram Australia	5	6	100 Pipers, Black Douglas, Chatelle Napolean, Seagram
109	Optus Communications	5	0	Optus
110	Levi Strauss	5	5	Levi Strauss
111	West Australia Government	5	5	Various government departments
112	Wrigley Company	5	5	Extra, PK, Hubba Bubba
113	Challenge Bank	5	5	Challenge Bank
114	Copperart	5	5	Copperart
115	Wesfarmers	5	NA	Alco, Masters Dairy, Wesfarmers Insurance
116	Estee Lauder	5	NA	Estee Lauder, Clinique, Aramis
117	Taubmans Industries	5	5.5	Taubmans
118	Toshiba Australia	5	5	Toshiba
119	Volvo Australia	5	3.5	Volvo
120	Voyager-Solo	5	5	Ronson, Kidz Biz, Metro, Witchery

The top 200 advertisers (continued)
Estimated main media advertising budget ($m)*
*Expenditure in Australia only

Number	Company	1992	1991	Key brands/products
121	Tozer Kemsley & Millbourne	5	6	Audi, Subaru, Volkswagen
122	Collins Foods	5	4	Sizzler, Kentucky Fried Chicken, Gullivers
123	Galore Group	5	NA	BBQs Galore, Optic Express
124	Bank of Melbourne	5	5	Bank of Melbourne
125	Jennings Group	5	5	Jennings
126	Associated Retailers	4.5	5.5	Mensland, Toyworld, Zig Zag, Shoex
127	McEwans	4.5	7	McEwans
128	Jetset	4.5	5	Jetset
129	Jenny Craig	4.5	4.5	Jenny Craig Weight Loss Centres
130	Cussons Limited	4.5	4	Imperial Leather, Radiant, Morning Fresh, Tampax
131	QUF Industries	4.5	4	Danone, Dany, Pauls
132	Suntory	4.5	NA	Gravox, Fountain, Salad Magic, Midori, Opal Nera
133	Australia Post	4	6	Australia Post
134	IOOF	4	3.5	IOOF
135	Roche Products	4	4	Aspro Clear, Berocca, Supradyn
136	SSW Supermarkets	4	4	SSW
137	Sega Ozisoft	4	NA	Sega
138	Daihatsu Australia	4	4	Daihatsu
139	SA Government	4	5	Various government departments
140	Gandel Group	4	NA	Priceline, Chadstone, Blockbuster Video
141	Singapore Airlines	4	4	Singapore Airlines
142	Qantas Airways	4	5	Qantas
143	Jones Lang Wootton	4	4	Jones Lang Wootton
144	Betta Stores	4	4	Betta Stores
145	Milk Marketing NSW	4	4.5	Moove, Shape
146	Power Brewing	4	2.5	Power's
147	Bayer Australia	4	5	Baygon, Drontal, Bayson
148	Lend Lease Corporation	4	4	MLC
149	Parke Davis	4	4.5	Schick, Listerine, Parke Davis
150	Canon Australia	4	6	Canon
151	Westfield Holdings	4	5	Westfield shopping centres
152	Medical Benefits Fund	4	4	Medical Benefits Fund
153	Whitman Corporation	4	5	Midas Mufflers, Old El Paso, Pasta to Go
154	Medibank Private	4	3.5	Medibank Private
155	Black & Decker	4	6	Black & Decker

The top 200 advertisers (continued)

Estimated main media advertising budget ($m)*
*Expenditure in Australia only

Number	Company	1992	1991	Key brands/products
156	Citibank	4	4	Citibank
157	Intertan Australia	4	4	Tandy Electronics
158	Mobil Oil	4	4	Mobil
159	Kambrook Distributing	4	5	Kambrook, Goldstar
160	Bristol Myers Squibb	3.5	4	Mum, Mr Muscle, Sustagen, Clairol
161	Sussan Corporation	3.5	4	Sussan, Suzanne Grae
162	Sharp Corporation	3.5	3.5	Sharp
163	Royal Auto Club of Victoria	3.5	3.5	RACV, RACV Insurance
164	K&D Bond International	3.5	3.5	Bond International
165	AAMI	3.5	3.5	AAMI
166	Garuda Airways	3.5	3	Garuda
167	Natural Gas Company	3.5	3.5	Natural Gas Company
168	Bunge Australia	3.5	3.5	Don, Sunnicrust Eastcoast
169	P & O Australia	3.5	3	P&O Holidays, Berkeley Challenge
170	BMW Australia	3.5	3	BMW
171	IMB Building Society	3.5	3.5	IMB Building Society
172	OPSM Industries	3.5	3	OPSM, OPSM Express
173	Eveready Australia	3.5	3.5	Eveready
174	Pfizer Inc	3.5	3.5	Combantrin, Visine, Obiron
175	Jardine Matheson	3.5	3	Sizzler, Pizza Hut
176	Jeanswest Corporation	3.5	3.5	Jeanswest
177	Sanyo Australia	3.5	3	Sanyo
178	Amstrad Computers	3	2.5	Amstrad
179	El Du Pont de Nemours	3	4	Fibremakers, Du Pont, Stainmaster, Lycra
180	Angus & Coote	3	3	Angus & Coote
181	Health Australia	3	3.5	Health Australia
182	Southern Cross Airlines	3	3	Compass Airlines
183	Daimaru Inc	3	4	Daimaru
184	Rothmans Holdings	3	3	Winfield, Holiday, Dunhill, Rothmans
185	Ampol Limited	3	4	Ampol
186	Cathay Pacific	3	3	Cathay Pacific
187	Murray-Goulburn Co-op	3	3	Devondale
188	Nine Network	3	3	Nine Network
189	Milk Products Holdings	3	3	Mainland, Riviana
190	W.D. & H.O. Wills	3	3	Horizon, Wills, Benson & Hedges
191	Visa International	3	2.5	Visa
192	MasterCard International	3	2.5	MasterCard
193	Goodyear Tyre and Brake Service	3	3	Goodyear
194	CSR Limited	3	5.5	CSR, Monier, Bradford Batts
195	NEC Australia	3	5	NEC

The top 200 advertisers (continued)

Estimated main media advertising budget ($m)*
*Expenditure in Australia only

Number	Company	1992	1991	Key brands/products
196	Victorian Gas & Fuel Corp	3	3	Gas and fuel
197	BTR Nylex	3	NA	Nylex, Amatek, Con-Tact, Laminex
198	Orlando Wyndham	3	3.5	Jacob's Creek, Orlando, Wyndham Estate, Carrington
199	Video Ezy	3	3	Video Ezy
200	Rural & Industries Bank	3	3.5	Rural & Industries Bank

Reproduced with permission from BRW, Australia's leading business magazine, 11 September, 1992, pp. 74–77.

The top 10 Australian-owned agencies

Agency (rank in top 300)	1991 income ($000)	1991 billings ($000)
1. Neville Jeffress (16)	13 288	120 800
2. Magnus Nankervis & Curl (20)	8643	54 018
3. Charlton Group (21)	8584	54 296
4. John Singleton Advertising (22)	7659	52 136
5. Samuelson Talbot & Partners (24)	6548	35 348
6. McCarthy Watson & Spencer (25)	6500	40 600
7. John Bevins (27)	5300	30 600
8. Luscombe & Partners (28)	5104	31 575
9. Biddle Ogle Anderson & Co (30)	5041	31 507
10. Advertising Partners (30)	4447	27 519

Reproduced with permission from BRW, Australia's leading business magazine, 14 February, 1992, p. 76

A selection of Australia's top 300 advertising agencies

Rank 1991	Rank 1990	Agency	Income ($000) 1991	Income ($000) 1990	% change	Income ($000) 1991	Income ($000) 1990	% change	Staff/Billings 1991	Staff/Billings 1990
1	1	George Patterson	102 400	108 800	-5.9	640 000	680 000	-5.9	0.7	0.6
2	2	Clemenger BBDO	63 507	64 960	-2.2	396 918	406 022	-2.2	NA	NA
3	4	Mattingly & Partnrs	40 667	40 549	+0.3	261 452	253 432	+3.2	1.1	1.5
4	3	Young & Rubicam	39 711	44 766	-11.2	249 737	279 790	-10.7	1.2	1.2
5	5	DDB Needham	36 000	33 711	+6.8	240 000	224 526	+6.9	1.3	1.2
6	6	Chiat/Day/Mojo	32 137	33 396	-3.8	208 843	208 727	+0.05	0.9	1.0
7	11	Lintas	24 300	18 200	+33.5	151 700	118 300	+28.2	1.0	1.2
8	8	Saatchi & Saatchi	22 640	24 560	-7.8	141 500	153 500	-7.8	0.7	0.8
9	NA	Leo Burnett Connaghan & May	21 616	NA	NA	144 178	NA	NA	1.2	NA
10	7	McCann-Erickson	21 000	27 040	-22.3	140 000	169 000	-17.1	1.0	1.3
11	9	Foote Cone & Belding	20 160	19 840	+1.6	126 000	124 000	+1.6	0.8	0.8
12	10	J Walter Thompson	18 877	19 426	-2.8	133 215	135 607	-1.8	1.1	1.1
13	15	The Campaign Palace	15 040	14 593	+3.1	94 000	87 000	+8.0	0.9	1.0
14	14	D'Arcy Masius Benton & Bowles	14 880	14 594	+1.9	93 000	91 214	+1.9	1.0	1.0
15	12	Ogilvy & Mather	13 370	18 100	-26.1	83 559	121 700	-31.3	1.0	1.2
16	13	Neville Jeffress	13 288	16 098	-17.4	120 800	146 347	-17.4	2.7	2.5
17	17	Marketforce	11 225	11 888	-5.6	70 156	74 300	-5.6	1.4	1.3
18	20	The Ball Partnership	9280	9000	+3.1	58 000	56 000	+3.6	1.1	1.4
19	21	Grey Advertising	9055	8579	+5.5	56 595	54 983	+2.9	1.2	1.2
20	19	Magnus Nankervis & Curl	8643	9544	-9.4	54 018	59 650	-9.4	1.0	1.1
21	23	Charlton Group	8584	8540	+0.5	54 296	53 378	+1.7	1.0	1.0
22	24	John Singleton Advertising	7659	7200	+6.4	52 136	50 300	+3.6	0.8	0.8
23	22	SSB Advertising	6813	8561	-20.4	42 581	53 424	-20.3	1.1	1.3
24	27	Samuelson Talbot & Partners	6548	5440	+20.4	35 348	34 000	+3.9	1.1	1.2
25	26	McCarthy Watson & Spencer	6500	6100	+6.5	40 600	38 200	+6.3	1.0	1.0
NR	NR	Sudler & Hennessey	6020	6137	-1.9	39 170	37 705	+3.9	1.1	1.2
26	29	Clemenger Direct Response	5369	5019	+7.0	33 555	31 368	+7.0	1.3	1.1
27	36	John Bevins	5300	3780	+40.2	30 600	26 300	+16.3	1.2	1.2
28	30	Luscombe & Partners	5104	4990	+2.3	31 575	31 450	+0.4	1.2	1.4
29	38	Biddle Ogle Anderson & Co	5041	3549	+42.0	31 507	22 185	+42.0	0.2	0.2

Rank 1991	Rank 1990	Agency	Income ($000) 1991	Income ($000) 1990	% change	Income ($000) 1991	Income ($000) 1990	% change	Staff/Billings 1991	Staff/Billings 1990
30	35	Advertising Partners	4447	3980	+11.7	27 519	24 615	+11.8	1.0	
31	25	Omon	4260	6150	-30.7	26 140	32 410	-19.3	0.8	1.1
32	31	Pemberton	4192	4548	-7.8	26 202	28 430	-7.8	1.2	0.6
33	32	Hertz Walpole	4050	4122	-1.7	22 800	23 800	-4.2	1.0	1.4
=34	28	Maher & Holmes	4000	5360	-25.4	25 000	33 500	-25.4	1.0	1.1
=34	34	Adcorp	4000	4000	0	25 000	25 000	0	2.1	2.0
36	36	Box Emery & Partners	3876	3912	-0.9	24 226	24 450	-0.9	0.8	0.9
NR	NR	Wunderman Worlside	3810	3197	+19.2	23 817	19 981	+19.2	NA	NA
37	44	Harris Robinson & Associates	3800	3199	+18.8	23 000	22 143	+3.9	1.5	1.3
=38	54	Foster Nunn Loveder	3600	2880	+25.0	22 500	18 000	+25.0	1.1	1.2
=38	40	Moffatt Sharp	3600	3410	+5.6	22 000	21 000	+4.8	1.4	1.4
40	48	Badjar	3596	3072	+17.1	22 478	19 200	+17.1	0.7	0.9
NR	NR	BBDO	3360	5987	-43.9	21 000	37 426	-43.9	1.1	1.1
41	42	Ian Kennon Advertising	3200	3200	0	20 000	20 000	0	0.8	0.8

Reproduced with permission from BRW, Australia's leading business magazine, 14 February, 1992, p. 79

Australian advertising agencies, fastest rising incomes, 1990–91

		Income rise (%)	Billings rise (%)
1.	Mak Advertising	358.0	NA
2.	Smoker & Hellier Partnership	300.0	300.0
3.	Simon Richards Direct	110.0	86.0
4.	Us	108.3	110.2
=5.	Hale & Collins	100.0	120.0
=5.	Dala St Claire	100.0	–16.7
=5.	Smith Ross & Muir	100.0	–0.9
8.	Cahill Wickham Fairweather Stennet	93.9	91.7
9.	B.F.I. Etcetera	89.9	114.5
10.	The Marketing Factory	79.8	26.7

Reproduced with permission from BRW, Australia's leading business magazine, 14 February 1992, p. 76

Australian advertising agencies, fastest falling incomes, 1990–91

		Income rise (%)	Billings rise (%)
1.	Pace Advertising	73.7	73.7
2.	Shapcott Advertising	73.1	3.5
3.	Ad Dimension Davidson	66.4	63.5
=4.	McLean Advertising	62.5	62.5
=4.	The Drawing Room	62.5	62.5
6.	Ad Vantage	61.4	+28.6
7.	Middleton Beverley	59.9	37.3
8.	Beeby Advertising	56.6	+54.1
9.	The Bank Advertising	51.6	51.6
10.	O'Brien & McGrath	50.7	+21.9

Reproduced with permission from BRW, Australia's leading business magazine, 14 February 1992, p. 76

God is in the details

by Deane Russell

Deane Russell, director of marketing and public relations, Australian Bureau of Statistics, explains how to find marketing revelations in statistics.

The Australian Bureau of Statistics (ABS) plays an important role in the marketing process. It provides data on a wide range of topics, but the big trick is to know what data, in what form, and how this translates into a marketing action plan that can be understood and implemented.

Taking one industry as an example—footwear and clothing—we find that the ABS has a huge amount of information. This information could be used by marketing people who have:

- the task of establishing a new outlet;
- to supply a new product or service to this industry;
- determine the competition;
- assess the market share.

The process should begin by looking at the market as a whole and then examining the data at a micro level. Here are some details of the type of reports that the ABS can produce on footwear and clothing.

1. *Trade highlights.* There was a net trade deficit of $360 million for women's footwear for the previous financial year. For the same period total imports came to $383 million and exports $23 million. Our major trade in women's footwear is China for imports and New Zealand for exports.

Table C1.2 *Imports: Footwear trading partners 1990–91*

		December 1991
	$m	$m
1. Taiwan	53 885	3565
2. China	90 581	8336
3. South Korea	79 515	3944
4. Italy	36 932	2618
5. France	4652	232
Others	174 883	7618
Total	383 750	26 313
Previous total	338 954	26 751

Table C1.3 *Exports: Footwear trading partners 1990–91*

		December 1991
	$m	$m
1. New Zealand	12.9	0.654
2. Canada	0.121	0.19
3. UK	0.536	0.184
4. Singapore	0.536	0.29
5. Turkey	0.0009	—
Others	9.2	1.3
Total	23.4	2.6
Previous total	24.9	2.1

2. *Production highlights.* Average monthly production was 1.2 million units for the last financial year compared to 1.6 million units for the previous year.

Table C1.4 *Production: Australia, women's footwear*

1991	Pairs '000s
January	463
February	1960
March	908
April	842
May	805
June	679
July	752
August	772
September	731
October	797
November	758
December	612

3. *Household expenditure highlights.* Average weekly household expenditure for women's footwear is $4.35.

Table C1.5 *Household expenditure: Australia, clothing and footwear*

	$ weekly
Single parent households	25.09
Couple households	24.99
Couples with 3 or more dependent children	37.93
Single	12.55

4. *Retail prices highlights.* The cost of footwear has increased 3.4% between 1989–90 and 1990–91 for the last financial year compared to 3.7% between 1988–89 and 1989–90.

Retail turnover

Average monthly retail turnover for footwear is $102.5 million for the last calendar year compared to $96.5 million per month for the previous calendar year.

With this overall data about footwear and clothing (with footwear isolated in some cases), the marketing manager can start to add some of the company's own data about its turnover, average sale, costs, and prices, and so on.

Table C1.6 *Retail turnover at current prices: Australia, footwear stores*

	$m
September	99.2
October	109.6
November	99.2
December	136.7
January	109.4
February	81.3
March	93.7
April	105.9
May	111.0
June	102.0
July	96.5
August	86.5

Table C1.7 *Consumer Price Index, weighted average of eight capitals*

	Footwear subgroup	Clothing group (includes footwear)
June 90	183.5	188.7
September 90	184.3	190.0
December 90	187.4	193.2
March 91	188.9	194.1
June 91	190.7	196.8
September 91	192.0	196.2
December 91	192.4	197.0

The ABS also has other data that may help the marketing person examine the possibility of opening at a new location. Let's look at opening a new location at either Randwick, Waverley or Woollahra, all in the eastern suburbs of Sydney. This table shows the number of all footwear stores in these three suburbs, including those that sell boots, men's, women's and children's footwear.

Table C1.8 *Footwear stores*

Location	Number of establishments
Randwick	17
Waverley	11
Woollahra	24

Look at the demographics. Say your company's product were aimed at those professional women, over the age of 35, whose incomes were higher than $35 000 at 1986 levels. (1991 Census will be available later this year).

Table C1.9 *Demographics*

	Randwick	Waverley	Woollahra
Number of women aged 25–64	29 790	16 077	14 300
Women with annual income of $32 000–$40 000	526	351	798
Households with income over $32 000–$40 000	4822	2651	2066
Number of women managers administrators & professionals	4376	2933	4028

It is important to realise that this information should be used as a tool towards informed decision making, and not as the sole basis for any marketing decision. (Figures are correct at the time of printing. For further classification please contact the ABS.)

Reproduced with permission from *Marketing*, May 1992, p. 33.

The following tables have been selected to demonstrate the broad cross-section of statistics published by the Australian Bureau of Statistics.

Australian Bureau of Statistics: Information sheet

For more information . . .

The ABS publishes a wide range of information on Australia's economic and social conditions. A catalogue of publications and products is available from any of our offices (see below for contact details).

Information Consultancy Service

Special tables or in-depth data investigations are provided by the ABS Information Consultancy Service in each of our offices (see below for contact details).

Electronic data services

A growing range of our data is available on electronic media. Selections of the most frequently requested data are available, updated daily, on DISCOVERY (Key *656#). Our TELESTATS service delivers major economic indicator publications ready to download into your computer on the day of release. Our PC-AUSSTATS service enables on-line access to a data base of thousands of up-to-date time series. Selected datasets are also available on diskette or CD-ROM. For more details on our electronic data services, contact information services in any of our offices on the numbers below.

Bookshops and subscriptions

There are over 500 titles available from the ABS bookshops in each of our offices. You can also receive any of our publications on a regular basis. Join our subscription mailing service and have your publications mailed to you in Australia at no additional cost. Telephone our publications subscription service toll free on 008 02 06 08 Australia wide.

Sales and inquiries

Telephone:
    Sydney (02) 268 4611   Adelaide (08) 237 7100
    Melbourne (03) 615 7000   Hobart (002) 20 5800
    Brisbane (07) 222 6351   Darwin (089) 43 2111
    Perth (09) 323 5140   Canberra (06) 252 6627

Postal address:
    Information Services, ABS, PO Box 10, Belconnen ACT 2616
    or any ABS State office.

Mean resident population[a] ('000)

Period	NSW	Vic	Qld	SA	WA	Tas.	NT	ACT[b]	Australia
1986	5533.1	4161.2	2623.5	1382.4	1457.8	446.5	154.5	258.9	16 017.9
1987	5614.6	4206.8	2674.9	1392.4	1494.2	449.1	158.5	265.3	16 255.8
1988	5705.2	4259.7	2741.7	1404.5	1534.1	451.4	159.6	271.6	16 527.8
1989	5773.1	4315.2	2826.7	1418.2	1576.2	455.6	161.5	276.3	16 802.9
1990	5828.6	4369.5	2899.6	1431.4	1609.6	462.3	163.8	281.8	17 046.7
1991	5902.9	4417.8	2966.7	1447.1	1637.1	467.4	166.8	289.3	17 295.2
1985–86	5497.3	4140.4	2597.0	1376.8	1437.5	444.6	151.9	255.4	15 901.0
1986–87	5571.8	4183.0	2649.2	1387.3	1476.8	448.1	156.7	262.1	16 135.0
1987–88	5660.5	4232.1	2705.5	1398.2	1513.0	450.1	159.2	268.7	16 387.2
1988–89	5744.5	4288.7	2783.2	1411.6	1556.0	453.1	160.6	274.0	16 671.8
1989–90	5797.6	4341.7	2865.6	1424.5	1594.0	458.8	162.4	278.7	16 923.3
1990–91	5864.4	4395.3	2933.0	1439.1	1623.5	465.5	165.5	285.5	17 171.7

[a] For the method of calculation of mean populations see *Australian Demographic Statistics* (3101.0). Further explanation of this procedure is available on request to the ABS.
[b] Includes Jervis Bay.

Source: Australian Bureau of Statistics, Monthly Summary of Statistics, Australia, October 1992, p. 1, 1304.0

Note: Population statistics shown on this page, at all dates after 30 June 1986, have been revised to incorporate preliminary 1991 Census results. A further revision will be made when final Census results become available.

Users and non-users of cultural venues/activities by region, 12 months ended June 1991, Queensland

Venue/Activity	Captial city Users '000	Captial city Non-users '000	Captial city Participation rate %	Rest of State Users '000	Rest of State Non-users '000	Rest of State Participation rate %	Total Users 000	Total Non-users 000	Total Participation rate %
Library	328.2	624.1	34.5	384.9	728.0	34.6	713.0	1352.1	34.5
Art gallery	249.0	703.3	26.2	233.4	879.4	21.0	482.5	1582.7	23.4
Museum	292.6	659.7	30.7	267.1	845.8	24.0	559.7	1505.4	27.1
Popular music concert	301.5	650.8	31.7	303.0	809.9	27.2	604.5	1460.7	29.3
Dance performance	104.1	848.1	10.9	123.8	989.1	11.1	227.9	1837.3	11.0
Musical theatre	238.5	713.8	25.0	179.4	933.5	16.1	417.9	1647.3	20.2
Other theatre performance	190.0	762.3	20.0	163.0	949.9	14.6	353.0	1712.2	17.1
Classical music concert	88.5	863.8	9.3	53.9	1059.0	4.8	142.4	1922.8	6.9

Users and non-users of cultural venues/activities by region, 12 months ended June 1991, Australia

Venue/Activity	Captial city Users '000	Capital city Non-users '000	Capital city Participation rate %	Rest of State Users '000	Rest of State Non-users '000	Rest of State Participation rate %	Total Users 000	Total Non-users 000	Total Participation rate %
Library	2935.7	4821.5	37.8	1506.8	2831.4	34.7	4442.5	7652.9	36.7
Art gallery	1969.4	5787.8	25.4	917.4	3420.8	21.1	2886.8	9208.7	23.9
Museum	2470.0	5287.3	31.8	1163.0	3175.2	26.8	3632.9	8462.5	30.0
Popular music concert	2261.4	5495.8	29.2	1195.0	3143.3	27.5	3456.4	8639.0	28.6
Dance performance	947.7	6809.6	12.2	401.7	3936.5	9.3	1349.4	10 746.0	11.2
Musical theatre	1746.9	6010.3	22.5	680.5	3657.7	15.7	2427.4	9668.0	20.1
Other theatre performance	1545.3	6211.9	19.9	606.0	3732.2	14.0	2151.3	9944.1	17.8
Classical music concert	743.2	7014.0	9.6	242.7	4095.5	5.6	985.9	11 109.5	8.2

Source: Australian Bureau of Statistics, June 1991, Attendance at Selected Cultural Venues, Australia, 4114.0

Ex-smokers of packet cigarettes: Age last quit smoking by reasons for quitting smoking, Australia, 1989–90 ('000)

Age group (years)	18–24	25–34	35–44	45–54	55–64	65–74	75 and over	Total
Smoking harmful to health/cancer/lung disease/heart disease	80.5	228.9	250.3	194.2	165.4	156.1	64.9	1140.3
Cough/sore throat	7.7	29.8	37.2	34.3	44.1	35.2	17.8	206.0
Reduces fitness/restricts activity	36.5	79.6	63.0	38.7	22.0	20.0	*4.5	264.4
Other health reasons	25.1	95.6	74.7	42.2	55.8	38.9	14.1	346.4
Offensive to others	26.6	61.4	55.8	36.0	24.9	18.5	8.0	231.2
Expense	17.9	51.3	54.7	49.4	38.4	34.8	14.1	260.7
Lost interest/didn't feel like it anymore	58.9	114.5	121.8	102.7	76.0	70.3	34.2	578.5
Other reasons	18.4	59.3	65.7	55.1	42.8	37.0	12.7	291.0
Total[a]	195.2	521.3	554.4	430.8	376.0	334.2	146.8	2558.7

[a] Each person may have reported more than one reason for quitting smoking, and therefore components do not add to totals.
* Figures too small to be published

Source: Australian Bureau of Statistics, 1989–90 National Health Survey Risk Factors, Australia, Table 23, 4380.0

SELECTED AUSTRALIAN STATISTICS 283

The Australian All Ordinaries Index Companies Handbook 1990–91

Corporate profiles

The Australian All Ordinaries Index is the official and most widely recognised measure of Australian Stockmarket performance—on an historical basis, and in providing for comparison against other stockmarkets around the world. This is the first time that the Australian Stock Exchange has produced a handbook specifically written about the companies which comprise the All Ordinaries Index. The handbook is a valuable addition to the wide range of publications available from the Exchange. The following four detailed corporate profiles have been selected from the Index to complement readings and case studies used in this book.

Elders IXL Limited

Head Office: 1 Garden Street, South Yarra Vic 3141.
Telephone: (03) 828 2424   *Fax*: (03) 826 9310.
Directors: J. D. Elliott (Chairman), A. G. McGregor (Deputy Chairman), P. T. Bartels, K. R. Biggins, E. A. Burton, D. I. Darling, O. R. Gunn, G. F. Ford, S. B. Myer, R. F. Wiesener, Sir Edward Williams.
Management: P. T. Bartels (Chief Executive), *Group Chief Executives*: P. T. Bartels (Brewing Group), K. E. Lawson (Elders Agribusiness Group), A. D. Cummins (Investment), C. R. Faggotter (Secretary)
Holding Company: Harlin Holdings Pty Ltd (55%)
Associated Companies: Not applicable.

Corporate profile

The company (Elders) represents the merger (since 1982) of Elder Smith Goldsbrough Mort Ltd and Henry Jones (IXL) Ltd. Subsequent to the merger, the company has taken over Carlton and United Breweries Ltd, Courage Ltd (U.K.) and Carling O'Keefe Breweries of Canada Ltd plus a number of other businesses predominantly outside Australia. Elders is Australia's largest wool selling broker, handling about one-third of Australia's wool clip. The company was the subject of a take-over bid launched by Harlin Securities Pty Ltd and Wickliffe Pty Ltd (companies associated with J. D. Elliot and other Elder's executives) during 1989. This offer closed on 2 October 1989, at which point the Harlin/Wickliffe held 55%. In March 1990, the company announced a major reconstruction of the group to create independent corporate entities focusing on single businesses, and to return the proceeds of disinvestments to shareholders. The key elements of the reconstruction are: Elders IXL will become Foster's Brewing Group Ltd, all non-brewing assets including Elders Finance and Elder Resources NZFP will be sold and surplus proceeds distributed to shareholders. On 12 March 1990, the company's wholly owned subsidiary Courage Ltd signed agreements with Grand Metropolitan Plc to acquire Grandmet's United

Kingdom brewing and brands interest, in return for contributing 4940 Courage pubs to an equally owned joint venture company, Inntrepreneur Estates. The agreement remains conditional upon relevant government clearances. In June 1990, the company sold its 52.7% interest in Elders Resources NZFP Ltd to New Zealand natural resources group Carter Hold Harvey Ltd for approximately A$623 million. The final consideration is contingent on the sale price of resource assets which the purchaser intends to sell. In September 1990 Harlin Holdings Pty Ltd announced its intention to sell 19.9% of its shareholding in Elders to Asahi Breweries of Japan. The sale would inject approximately $960 million into Harlin, and is subject to approval from the Australian and Japanese government authorities.

Elders Brewing Group: The seventh largest brewer in the world comprising an integrated international brewing organisation with businesses in three continents—Carlton in Australia, 50% of Molson Breweries in Canada, and Courage Breweries in the United Kingdom. The brewing group has acquired strategic interests in the United Kingdom breweries Scottish & Newcastle Breweries Plc and Green King & Sons Plc. In October 1988, the company announced a take-over offer for Scottish & Newcastle Breweries Plc valuing the company at £1.6 billion. The company abandoned the take-over when the British Government's Monopolies & Merger Commission blocked its bid and has since disposed of its interest in both Scottish & Newcastle and Green King. The Courage Pub Company, an associated company, owns the freehold to 5000 Courage Pubs. The company operates a dividend reinvestment plan.

Financial statistics (in $'000)

For year ended	85/06/30	86/06/30	87/06/30	88/06/30	89/06/30	Period to 89/12/31
Sales revenue	6 994 820	7 658 660	10 560 300	15 350 300	17 647 100	9 034 950
Other income	261 451	516 002	569 995	700 938	988 992	52 365
Interest paid	360 487	522 615	742 859	848 817	976 918	572 370
Depreciation	51 227	51 009	112 743	147 853	150 914	64 556
Taxation	24 880	27 577	41 572	176 652	80 077	46 716
Cons. net profit	108 569	209 272	355 205	792 124	659 617	172 726
Extraordinaries	4781	-2436	-3706	0	0	0
Total assets	2 147 220	4 795 390	9 663 730	9 198 290	9 907 630	n/a
NTA adj. ($)	0.72	0.89	1.49	1.67	1.73	n/a
EPS hist. (cents)	51.95	47.60	28.44	38.07	29.78	7.23
EPS adj. (cents)	15.42	17.66	16.35	27.30	25.69	7.23
DPS hist. (cents)	20.00	18.00	19.00	19.00	20.50	8.50
DPS adj. (cents)	5.43	6.67	10.29	13.62	17.68	8.50
Debit/sales (%)	7.06	9.92	10.79	11.84	9.73	10.01
Interest cover (X)	1.37	1.45	1.53	2.14	1.76	1.58
Dividend cover (X)	2.14	2.84	3.41	3.48	2.24	0.81

Capital as at 31 August 1990: $2 241 271 934 in 2 233 095 563 $1 ord. shares; 69 069 739 $1 shares paid to 1c and 74 856 744 1985 10c 9% red. pref. shares redeembable at $1.00 by 30/06/92.

Options: 537 343 560 exercisable by 14/04/93 at an initial issue price of $1.972 per share, rising progressively to $2.186 in 1993.

Multiple Currency Bonds: 115 814 691 at 5% maturing 1997.

Recent Issues:
1987 1 for 3 Cash at $3.50 prem. (Mar.).
1988 1 for 4 Bonus (Apr.).
1988 1 for 5 Bonus (Nov.).
1989 1 for 6 Bonus (Nov.).

(Australian Stock Exchange Ltd, *All Ordinaries Index Companies Handbook* (1st edn), 1990–91, Sydney).

National Australia Bank Ltd

Head Office: 24th Floor, 500 Bourke Street, Melbourne Vic. 3000.
Telephone: (03) 641 3500 *Fax*: (03) 641 4927.
Directors: Sir Rupert Clarke (Chairman), Sir Peter Finley (Vice-Chairman), D. R. Argus (Managing), N. R. Clark (Managing), D. R. Argus, P. J. W. Cottrell, D. A. T. Dickens, W. R. M. Irvine, B. T. Loton, D. K. McFarlane, R. N. Millar, M. R. Rayner, J. C. Trethowan, Sir Bruce Watson, Sir Eric Yarrow.
Management: N. R. Clarke (Joint Man. Dir.), D. R. Argus (Joint Man. Dir & Exec. Dir-Banking). *Chief Gen. Mgrs*: J. F. Astbury, C. W. Breeze, R. B. Miller. *Gen. Mgrs*: M. L. Browne, F. J. Cicutto, F. J. Davis, R. M. C. Prowse, I. Reed, L. R. Ryan, J. H. Seymour, G. C. Upton, G. J. Wheaton, B. V. Woods, R. J. Barnier (Secretary).
Substantial Shareholder: Not applicable.
Associated Companies: The Scottish Agricultural Securities Corporation Plc (33.3%), Australian Resources Development Bank Ltd (25%), Wilton Securities Ltd (25%).

Bank profile

National Australia Bank Ltd (NAB) is the outcome of a merger in 1981 of the National Bank of Australasia Ltd and the Commercial Banking Company of Sydney Ltd. This was subsequently effected on 31 December 1982 when legislation was enacted by Parliament. The merger formed the National Commercial Banking Corporation of Australia and expanded consistently by way of mergers of interests with similar institutions including: The Colonial Bank of Australiasia Ltd (1918), The Bank of Queensland Ltd (1922), The Queensland National Bank (1945), The Ballarat Banking Company Ltd (1955) and Commercial Banking Company of Sydney Ltd (1981). The bank began savings operations in 1962 and set up the Bank of South Pacific Ltd in 1974 to handle business in Papua New Guinea. Between 1954 and 1973, the bank diversified into non-bank financial areas. Purchases included: the finance company, Custom Credit Holdings Ltd and its insurance subsidiary; and

National & General Insurance Company Ltd (sold in July 1987, with the bank continuing to sell its products as an agent). In 1969, the bank bought a 75% interest in Carrington Confirmers Pty Ltd, trade finance house (an interest that increased to 97.5% in 1987). In October 1984, NAB purchased the outstanding stock in the merchant bank First National Limited, and a 50% interest in the stockbroker A.C. Goode & Co.Ltd, increasing this holding to 100%, this interest was sold in June 1990. Also in 1987, the bank established a major presence in the British Isles through the purchase of Clydesdale Bank Plc (founded 1838), Northern Bank Ltd (founded 1824) and National Irish Bank Ltd, with branch chains in Scotland, Northern Ireland and the Republic of Ireland. In the same year NAB began operating in New Zealand and today holds a 74% interest in National Australia Bank (NZ) Ltd. In September 1988, the bank pioneered the bond market in Australia with a $250 million issue of ten-year subordinated bonds. In October 1989, the group increased its interest in Australia Resources Development Bank Ltd to 100%. In January 1990, the bank acquired the whole of the issued capital of Yorkshire Bank Plc (Yorkshire) for a total of A$2031 million. Yorkshire Bank has approximately 250 branches primarily located in the north of Engalnd and the Midlands and the acquisitons will complement the market positions of the bank's subsidiaries in the United Kingdom and Ireland. In June 1990, NAB substantial shareholder the Adelaide Steamship Co. Ltd diluted its interest (held by associate David Jones Ltd) to non-significant levels. NAB offers trustee services through National Australia Trustees Ltd. Under a dividend package introduced in 1987, the bank offers a dividend reinvestment scheme, a dividend scrip plan and a bonus share plan, as well as a staff share scheme. Throughout the world, NAB employs nearly 38 000 people.

Financial statistics (in $000)

For year ended	85/09/30	86/09/30	87/09/30	88/09/30	89/09/30	Period to 90/03/31
Sales revenue	0	0	0	0	0	0
Other income	4 044 210	5 253 350	5 976 700	7 459 300	9 248 400	5 957 700
Interest paid	2 496 290	3 505 500	3 872 200	4 083 100	5 487 500	3 769 200
Depreciation	57 466	94 356	121 900	54 500	35 800	67 500
Taxation	189 181	195 579	276 400	479 200	540 100	274 600
Cons. net profit	302 108	303 976	328 900	530 400	781 800	440 000
Extraordinaries	30 418	-10 796	-6300	38 000	8900	0
Total assets	35 357 600	42 574 800	47 060 000	63 899 200	76 143 104	n/a
NTA adj. ($)	4.21	4.87	5.28	5.69	6.06	n/a
EPS hist. (cents)	80.54	78.25	61.97	76.49	96.12	47.75
EPS adj. (cents)	61.89	60.13	59.33	76.31	96.12	47.75
DPS hist. (cents)	27.50	28.50	24.75	60.00	60.00	26.00
DPS adj. (cents)	21.13	22.28	23.26	59.20	60.00	26.00
Debit/sales (%)	0.00	0.00	0.00	0.00	0.00	0.00
Interest cover (X)	1.20	1.14	1.16	1.25	1.24	1.19
Dividend cover (X)	3.27	3.01	2.83	1.26	1.57	1.80

Capital as at 31 August 1990: $962 336 352 in 961 088 619 $1 ord. shares; 3 982 287 $1 ord. shares paid to 25c and 365 450 $1 ord. shares paid to 69c.

Convertible notes: 4 446 688 $3.40 10% conv. unsec. notes, convertible by 30/09/93 & 427 586 $5.60 8% conv. unsec. notes undated.

Recent Issues:
1983 1 for 4 Cash at $1 prem. (Sept.).
1984 1 for 8 Issue of $3.40 10% conv. unsec. notes. (June).
1987 1 for 5 Bonus (May).
1987 1 for 5 Cash at $3 prem. (Aug.).
1988 1 for 5 Cash at $3.60 prem. (June).

(Australian Stock Exchange Ltd, *All Ordinaries Index Companies Handbook* (1st edn), 1990–91, Sydney).

W.D. & H.O. Wills Holdings Ltd

Head Office: 6th Floor, 71 Macquarie Street, Sydney NSW 2000.
Telephone: (02) 259 6333 *Fax*: (02) 259 6622.
Directors: B. D. Bramley (Chairman), W. R. McComas (Deputy Chairman), G. H. D. Watson, J. F. Bone, P. V. Smith, S. J. Walker
Management: G. H. D. Watson (Chief Exec.), M. Harrison (Asst Secretary), F. J. Gulson (Secretary).
Holding company: B.A.T. Australia Pty Ltd (67.32%)
Associated companies: Not applicable.

Corporate profile

The company was formed in 1989 to acquire W.D. & H.O. Wills (Australia) Ltd (Wills), the tobacco manufacturing subsidiary of Amatil Ltd (now Coca-Cola Amatil Ltd), which was rationalising its activities so that its main line of business was as an operator of Coca-Cola franchises and a manufacturer of snack foods. The company was to purchase Wills from Amatil for $350 million by way of a public issue of ordinary shares to Amatil shareholders on a one for one basis at $2.27 per share to raise $299.6 million, and the remainder by long-term bank borrowings. The June 1989 issue was underwritten by B.A.T. Industries (Australia) Pty Ltd (now B.A.T. Australia Pty Ltd) a wholly-owned subsidiary of the United Kingdom conglomerate B.A.T. Industries Plc. whose main line of business is tobacco manufacturing. Prior to the restructure, B.A.T. Industries had been Amatil's major shareholder with a 41% interest. Under the terms of the formation of the company, B.A.T. Industries had issued the right to acquire a minimum 51% holding in the company. At listing of the company on the Australian Stock Exchange Limited on 24 August 1989, B.A.T. Industries held a 67.32% interest. The company manufactures and markets various well-known cigarette brands such as Benson and Hedges, Sterling, Stradbroke, Freeport, John Player Special, Kent, Escort and Wills Super Mild which are amongst the top 20 cigarette brands by sales. The company is the largest Australian manufacturer of tobacco, marketing such brands as Capstan, Champion, Port Royal, Haveloch and Log Cabin it also manufactures cigars including Statesman and Monopoles and maintains a 30% market share of the Australian cigarette industry, behind Rothmans (37%) and Philip Morris (32%). The company markets primarily to Australian consumers but also has distribution operations in Papua New Guinea, Fiji and the Solomon Islands. The company's manufacturing and packaging operations are based at Pagewood in eastern Sydney, at recently completed premises covering 6.4ha built at a cost of $100 million. Branch distribution points are located in every other Australian capital city, and major depots in several country areas with distribution activites undertaken through TPD Distributors in all states except Victoria, where distribution is undertaken by LH&P Distributors. Ultimately, the company's products are sold from in excess of 55 000 retail outlets. In its first five month operation to 31 December 1989 turnover was $480.3 million with a pre-tax profit of $21.6 million and after tax profit of $12.97 million. The company's total assets are presently valued at $449 million. The position (as a percentage) of the major companies in the Australian cigarette market is:

	1984	1985	1986	1987	1988	1989
Wills	31	31	29	29	30	30
Rothmans	38	37	37	37	37	37
Philip Morris	30	30	32	33	32	32
Others	1	2	2	1	1	1
Total	100	100	100	100	100	100

Financial statistics (in $000)

For year ended	89/12/31
Sales revenue	480 272
Other income	3736
Interest paid	3802
Depreciation	7725
Taxation	8614
Cons. net profit	12 968
Extraordinaries	0
Total assets	449 466
NTA adj. ($)	2.28
EPS hist. (cents)	9.82
EPS adj. (cents)	9.82
DPS hist. (cents)	0.00
DPS adj. (cents)	0.00
Debit/sales (%)	5.29
Interest cover (X)	6.68
Dividend cover (X)	0.00

Capital as at 31 August 1990: $132 002 789 in 132 002 789 $1 ord. shares.

Recent Issues: 1989 1 for 1 Entitlement to shareholders of Coca-Cola Amatil Ltd at $2.27 (July). *Listed (ASX)*: 24/08/89.

(Australian Stock Exchange Ltd, *All Ordinaries Index Companies Handbook* (1st edn), 1990–91, Sydney).

Foodland Associated Ltd

Head office: 18 Miles Road, Kewdale WA 6105.
Telephone: (09) 350 2400   *Fax*: (09) 353 2624.
Directors: P. R. Burnett (Chairman), P. G. Flavel (Deputy), D. R. Fawcett (Managing), R. S. Finn, N. A. Gale, J. R. McGillvray, E. Samec. *Assoc. Dirs*: P. T. Colleran, W. Treloar.
Management: D. R. Fawcett (Man. Dir.), P. T. Colleran (Mktg), G. T. Clifford (Finance & Secretary).
Substantial shareholder: Davids Supermarkets Pty Ltd (16%).
Associated companies: Action Holdings Ltd (37%), Tactix Clothing Company (25%), Carbarns Pty Ltd (30%).

Corporate profile

The present company was formed in Western Australia in 1972 by the merger of Associated Grocers Ltd and Foodland Co-operative Ltd. In 1981 the grocery wholesale division of D. & J. Fowler Ltd was acquired followed by the Action Food Barns (Action) chain in 1985. The holding company of Action was listed on the Australian Stock Exchange in November 1986. In May 1988, the company acquired the Charlie Carter chain, which was then sold by tender. Foodland purchased the remaining 50% interest in the Merifield Cooksey Unit Trust (a 50% interest had been acquired in 1987) and the trust's name was changed to Foodland Property Holdings Pty Ltd. It specialises in retail property acquisition and development. The group is the largest wholesaler of grocery and associated merchandise in Western Australia and distributes in excess of 50% of the groceries sold in Western Australia. Distribution is through a network of four main warehouses located at Canning Vale, Osborne Park and two at Kewdale. There are also three Cash & Carry warehouses located at Balcatta, Canning Vale and Kalgoorlie where members purchase and take delivery of goods direct. The principal activities of the company are: *Wholesale Grocery and General Merchandise*.

Grocery: This is the largest division accounting for approximately 60% of turnover with annual sales revenue of $394 million. It sells goods to approximately 365 franchisees including over 290 in Foodland's banner groups: Foodland, Four Square, Supa Valu, Cheap Foods, Bi-Lo, and Quick Stop.

Cold stores: The chilled and frozen warehouse operations are principally carried out at the Canning Vale complex.

General merchandise: New generation Action Stores and large franchised stores (e.g Bi-Lo) designed to carry substantial ranges of general merchandise have been operating since 1986. These stores have contributed to the increased turnover of the general merchandise division which in the year ended 31 October 1989 amounted to approximately $22 million.

Australian Liquor Marketers (WA): In December 1989, the company acquired the trading assets of the liquor distributors Westel Pty Ltd. Subsequently, Davids Holdings Pty Ltd acquired a 50% interest in the enlarged liquor distribution company and operations now trade in Western Australia as Australian Liquor Marketers (WA). The operation services 143 outlets within its franchise groups such as Cheap Liquor Hallmark Cellars and Pubmart as well as 87 main independent outlets.

Cash & Carry Division: Specifically designed to enable smaller businesses to obtain their stock at prices generally equivalent to those at the main warehouse. Through the Cash & Carry outlets Foodland distributes a wide range of groceries and general merchandise.

Investments:
Tactix Clothing Company (25%): Acquired in January 1989, it is based in Western Australia and manufactures high quality, low cost, basic clothing such as track suits, T-shirts and mens shorts in large quantities. The company supplies independent wholesalers throughout Australia for distribution to their members.

Action Holdings Ltd (37%): The holding company of the Action Food Barn chain.

Foodland Property Holdings Pty Ltd: This is a trust specialising in retail property acquisition and development.

Carbarns Pty Ltd (30%): Acquired in November 1988, the company is a potato merchant and distributor.

Capital as at 31 August 1990: $20 084 153 in 20 084 153 $1 ord. shares.

Recent Issues:
1989 4 for 5 Bonus
1990 Listed (ASX): 29/03/90

(Australian Stock Exchange Ltd, *All Ordinaries Index Companies Handbook* (1st edn), 1990–91, Sydney).

Part D

CRITICAL ESSAYS

Competitive strategy: A critique of Porter's analysis

by John Forster

Introduction and overview

Arguably the most influential text in the study of strategic management is 'Competitive Strategy: *Techniques for Analyzing Industries and Competitors*' by M. E. Porter. Published in 1980 it remains standard fare in marketing and management courses of all levels and descriptions. But, despite a number of both laudatory and critical papers, including Hendry (1990), Sharp (1991), Speed (1989), Stiles (1992) and Wright and Parsina (1988), surprisingly little has been written that can serve as a critique of the book as a whole. This paper is an attempt to present such a critique.

One critical analysis that does stand out, however, is contained in the work of Mintzberg (1990). Even here the critique was of what Mintzberg terms the 'positioning school' as a whole, with Porter's 'competitive strategy' discussed only in as much as it is the seminal text of that school. Nevertheless Mintzberg's work will be seen to play an important role in the present discussion.

This paper proceeds in several stages. First a description of the major ideas of Porter's work is presented. This description is presented in as neutral a manner as is possible. To further this aim Porter is quoted extensively in order to allow him to speak for himself, although it must be accepted that the very selection of the quotations involves breaking that neutrality to a greater or lesser degree. Two other steps have been taken to try to preserve neutrality. One is that no critique is offered during this initial description. The other is that any statement of the theoretical and empirical implications of Porter is avoided at this stage, unless they have been stated explicitly in the 1980 text. Having said this, it is admitted that a few comments on the work have been allowed to stay in this section. Furthermore, because of its singular importance the description and the critique are restricted solely to 'Competitive Strategy', while Porter's later works, notably *The Competitive Advantage of Nations*, are deliberately ignored, although, interestingly it appears from his later works that Porter's views and ideas have remained very close to those of 'competitive strategy' (Porter 1990, 1991).

The second stage consists of a summary, description and commentary on Mintzberg's critique of the positioning school. Here, as with Porter, considerable use is made of Mintzberg's own words, but no attempt is made to remain neutral. Overall Mintzberg's critique of Porter is one which is consistent with and complementary to the present critique. Where there is any difference with the present discussion, or where it appears Mintzberg's critique is either incorrect or arguable, then some comment is made. One basic disagreement with Mintzberg is worth mentioning at this point. Mintzberg argues that Porter, and the positioning school as a whole, belong to the prescriptive side of strategy formation. It is very strongly argued here that Porter's work is very badly misrepresented if it is seen solely in this light.

The third and major part of this paper considers the work of Porter under a series of specific topics, although it is not suggested that these are the only topics that are either possible or important. It is suggested, however, that they do go to the heart of some of Porter's major ideas. The topics covered are: (i) generic strategies; (ii) markets and industries; and the problem of (iii) internal versus external strategy of the enterprise. Two other problems which are related to these, and which are broached, are Porter's argument that competitive strategy determines and should determine organisational structure and the implicit and traditional concept of a commodity (and service) that is apparent in his work. In addition the concept of a strategic group is examined as part of an overall conclusion which attempts to assess why Porter's work has gained such pre-eminence. It will be argued that despite its flaws, and despite the possibility that much of his work is now superseded, this success was deserved.

Porter's analysis

Porter claims his work is concerned with the competitive strategy of an enterprise, and the analytic approach that can and should underlie the selection of an appropriate competitive strategy.

> Competitive strategy is an area of primary concern to managers, depending critically on a subtle understanding of industries and competitors. Yet the strategy field has offered few analytical techniques for gaining this understanding, and those that have emerged lack breadth and comprehensiveness.
>
> (Porter 1980, p. ix)

Here Porter indicates quite explicitly the primacy he affords to competitive strategy, the primacy it has with management, as well as the primacy it should but does not have in the *analysis and study* of strategy. His concern is very much with the competitive position of the enterprise with respect to other enterprises and with its external business environment as a whole. Significantly Porter begins his first chapter with the very forthright statement that: 'the essence of formulating competitive strategy is relating a company to its environment.' (Porter 1980, p. 3.) In explanation and support of this Porter says, 'the key aspect of the firm's environment is the industry or industries in which it competes.' (Porter 1980, p. 3.)

For Porter the key to the success or failure of an enterprise is its standing in relation to its competitors. Porter defines *competitive strategy* thus:

> competitive strategy as taking offensive or defensive actions to create a defendable position in an industry, to cope successfully with the five competitive forces and thereby yield a superior return on investment for the firm.
>
> (Porter 1980, p. 34)

To emphasise the importance of this Porter repeats what he said a little earlier, that an 'effective competitive strategy takes offensive or defensive action in order to create a defendable position against the five competitive forces.' (Porter 1980, p. 29.)

But with the firm now concentrating on competitive strategy it must clearly understand the nature of competition. At the crux of this understanding are the 'five competitive forces', and it is understanding these forces that Porter sees as requiring a highly analytical approach.

> The collective strength of these forces determines the ultimate profit potential in the industry, where profit potential is measured in terms of long-run return on invested capital.
> (Porter 1980, p. 3)

The five competitive forces are:

1. Threat of entry.
2. Threat of substitution.
3. Bargaining power of buyers.
4. Bargaining power of suppliers.
5. Rivalry among current competitors.

Porter distinguishes these 'structured' forces from the:

> many short-run factors that can affect competition and profitability in a transient way. For example, fluctuations in economic conditions over the business cycle influence the short-run profitability of nearly all firms in many industries, as can material shortages, strikes, spurts in demand and the like.
> (Porter 1980, p. 6)

He then goes on to argue that analysis for competitive strategy is concerned with the structural rather than the transient: 'understanding industry structure must be the starting point for strategic analysis' (Porter 1980, p. 7).

Porter summarises these forces in his Figure D1.1 (Porter 1980, p. 4) which is reproduced here and his first chapter is largely devoted to considering each of the forces in more detail; and in such a way that he provides tools for industry analysis and the possible means of competitive strategy in altering these forces to advantage. Porter argues for the primacy of competitive strategy for management, and that competitive strategy is designed to cope with, alter and utilise the five competitive forces for the long-run profit of the firm. Turning to strategy itself, Porter argues that:

> there are three potentially successful generic strategic approaches to outperforming other firms in an industry:
> 1. overall cost leadership;
> 2. differentiation;
> 3. focus differentiation.
> (Porter 1980, p. 35)

```
                    ┌─────────────────────────┐
                    │   POTENTIAL ENTRANTS    │
                    └─────────────────────────┘
                                              Threat of New Entrants
                                    │
                                    ▼
  Bargaining Power          ┌───────────────┐          Bargaining Power
  of Suppliers              │   INDUSTRY    │          of Buyers
                            │  COMPETITORS  │
  ┌───────────┐             └───────────────┘             ┌─────────┐
  │ SUPPLIERS │────────▶                        ◀─────────│ BUYERS  │
  └───────────┘             RIVALRY AMONG                 └─────────┘
                            EXISTING FIRMS
                                    ▲
  Threat of Substitiute             │
  Products or Services              │
                            ┌───────────────┐
                            │  SUBSTITUTES  │
                            └───────────────┘
```

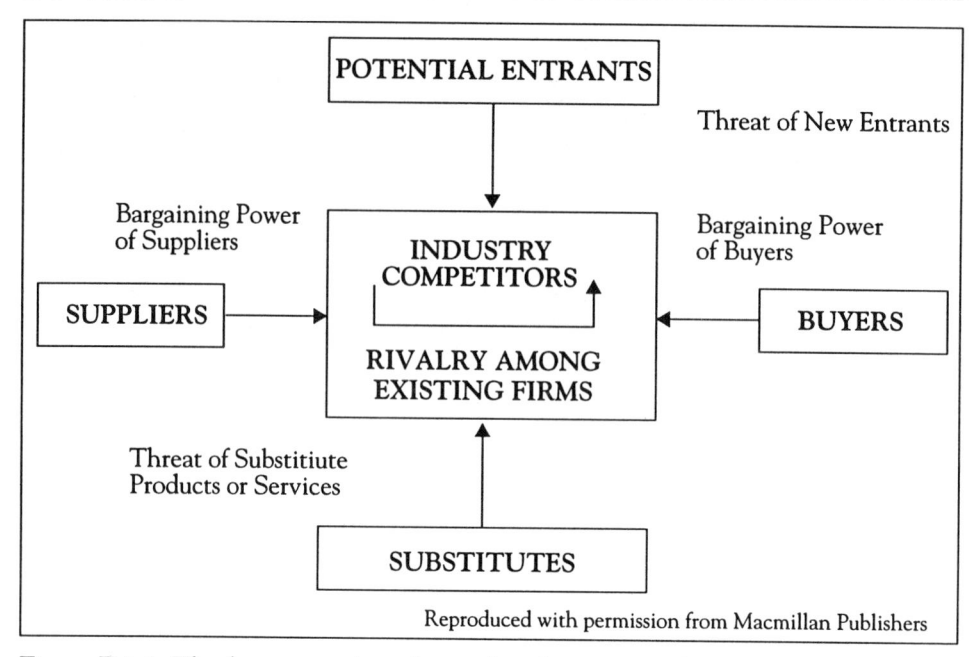

Reproduced with permission from Macmillan Publishers

Figure D1.1 The five competitive forces that determine industry profitability

Before turning to these generic strategies individually, it is worth considering Porter's statement in more detail. First, strategy is again seen entirely in terms relating to other firms; that is, outperforming them. Second, strategies are not necessarily, but only potentially, successful; and third, they are *generic*. The use of the term, *generic*, with its taxonomic overtones, implies a hierarchy of strategies, with all competitive strategies necessarily belonging to one of these three basic types.

As a strategy overall cost leadership is largely self-explanatory. Pursuing this strategy implies rigorous cost-cutting and minimisation in all functional areas of the enterprise's activity, including: 'R & D, service, sales force, advertising and so on', promoting low-cost relative to competitors' (Porter 1980, p. 35).

The second generic strategy, differentiation, implies that the product offered by the firm is distinguishable in some way, from all other products in the industry. There are a variety of ways in which products, or their marketing and other dimensions such as repair networks, guarantees and durability, can be differentiated. The purpose is to provide a brand loyalty that reduces the potential impacts of the five competitive forces. The third generic strategy, focus, implies concentrating upon 'a particular buyer group, segment of the product line, or geographic markets' (Porter 1980, p. 38).

The success or otherwise of this strategy depends upon the ability of the firm to service a narrowed strategic target more effectively than competitors who are competing industry-wide. 'Even though the focus strategy does not achieve low cost or differentiation from the perspective of the market as a whole, it does achieve one or both of these positions vis-à-vis its narrow market target.' (Porter 1980, pp. 38–39).

Porter, however, goes much further than just saying these strategies are potentially successful; he also says that:

(a) they are alternatives, that is, they are mutually exclusive, under most circumstances, and consequently only one can be pursued by any company at any one time with any possibility of success; (Porter 1980,p. 41)
(b) firms who do not follow them are 'almost guaranteed low profitability' (Porter 1980, p. 41). These are firms who are 'stuck in the middle'; (Porter 1980, p. 42)
(c) no other strategies exist that cannot be fitted into one of these three generic categories. This argument is woven through the second chapter of Porter.

These three generic strategies then are inclusive of all competitive strategies. Despite the epistemological and practical significance of this claim Porter makes little use of the generic strategies in the rest of his text. Generic strategies only reappear in any substantive manner in Chapter 7, where he analyses strategic groups within industries.

A *strategic group* is a group of firms within an industry, which are following the same competitive strategy. As such the group is an intermediate stage between the industry as a whole and individual firms. Within any industry there may be just one strategic group, if all firms are pursuing the same strategy. At the other extreme there may be a strategic group for each firm if they are all pursuing different strategies. Judging from his text it would appear that Porter regards strategic groups as both an objective reality and as a conceptual tool of analysis. In either case the significance of the concept of the strategic group is that it can allow the enterprise to understand better where it may position itself. One of Porter's most original and useful ideas is that barriers to entry are about entry to a strategic group rather than to an industry as a whole. This also allows him to formulate an important idea of significance to market economics as well as to management studies: this is that industry structure is determined by the behaviour of the enterprises within it. This is very different from the prevalent idea that industry and/or market structure is to be seen as determined by factors, such as technology and consumer behaviour, over which the firm has little or no control and that, consequently, industry/market structure determined behaviour and conduct of the firm. Porter does not deny that there are elements of truth in this but a major argument of his is that the firm can determine its own conduct, within quite wide parameters, and still survive and succeed.

It is earlier in the book that Porter argues that for such strategic behaviour to be successful, it must be based on sound information:

> Competitive strategy involves positioning a business to maximise the value of the capabilities that distinguish it from its competitors. It follows that a central aspect of strategy formulation is perceptive competitor analysis.
> (Porter 1980, p. 47)

Porter goes on to say:

> Despite the clear need for sophisticated competition analysis in strategy formulation, such analysis is sometimes not done explicitly or comprehensively in practice.
> (Porter 1980, p. 47)

This is a major component of Porter's epistemology, that such analysis is required for successful competitive strategy. However, the effort that Porter indicates must go into such analysis is not feasible except for very large and well-resourced companies. In this section of the book Porter outlines an intelligence process that is linear and rationalist, but little is said about the potential problems and failures of such intelligence systems. It is not made clear if any companies may have ever operated such a comprehensive system.

The rest of Porter's text is not as central to his main themes. It is largely an attempt to apply these concepts, an attempt that is achieved with mixed success. The discussion of industry evolution, for example, which follows that on strategic groups contains little that is new. The following section of the book is entitled 'Generic industry environment' and its five chapters comprise just under a third of the text. The generic industries are termed the 'fragmented', 'emerging', 'transition-to-mature', 'declining' and 'global'. Surprisingly, little use is made of the generic strategy concept within this section. The third and final section of the book deals with the strategic analysis of vertical integration, of capacity expansion and of entry in new businesses. Again there is little that is particularly new in these chapters when compared with other work of the period. A surprising omission is that there is no concluding chapter with which Porter could pull the entire set of his ideas together. This almost certainly has some effect on the ability of readers to treat the book as a whole.

Mintzberg's critique of Porter

The main critique of Porter's work to date is that of Mintzberg (1990). Indeed this is one of very few overall critiques and because of this alone, it would deserve mention here. Mintzberg's work, however, is more important than this, having importance in its own right, quite apart from references to Porter. Because of this, and because Mintzberg takes lines which are arguable, Mintzberg will be quoted in detail.

Mintzberg places Porter's work in context, arguing that Porter is of the positioning school of strategic management. This school Mintzberg also subtitles as 'strategy formation as an analytic process'. He considers and delineates 'ten schools of thought on strategy formation' (Mintzberg, p. 107). Following Mintzberg these ten schools are taken as:

- The design school: strategy formation as a conceptual process.
- The planning school: strategy formation as a formal process.
- The positioning school: strategy formation as an analytical process.
- The entrepreneurial school: strategy formation as a visionary process.
- The cognitive school: strategy formation as a mental process.
- The learning school: strategy formation as an emergent process.
- The political school: strategy formation as a power process.
- The cultural school: strategy formation as an ideological process.
- The environmental school: strategy formation as a passive process.
- The configurational school: strategy formation as an episodic process.

(Mintzberg 1990, p. 108)

Mintzberg then immediately goes on to describe the first three schools including Porter's work by implication, as prescriptive. The following six schools are argued to concentrate on the specific part of the strategy formation process implied by each of their names and 'are concerned less with prescribing ideal strategic behaviour than with describing how strategies do, in fact, get made.' (Mintzberg, p 108.) The third group contains only the configurational school which Mintzberg describes as integrative of all other schools (Mintzberg, pp. 182–83).

Returning to the positioning school, Mintzberg argues that, in common with the design and the planning schools, the strategy formation process is a 'controlled, conscious process of thought that produced full-blown strategies' (Mintzberg, p. 126). These strategies were only transformed into actions after they were made explicit strategies within the organisation. 'Again, the chief executive was the strategist in principle, with the planner the power behind the throne, except that the positioning school elevated the planner's importance another notch. Now that person became an analyst, a numbers-oriented technical person who amassed and studied means of hard data to recommend optimal strategies. And most notably, the old design school premise of strategies being unique was discarded. To the positioning school, strategies became generic; in other words, they were clearly delineated categories—well-defined positions in the economic market-place' (Mintzberg, p. 127.).

In relation to Porter's work Mintzberg probably places too much emphasis on the planner being a technical number-cruncher. Porter certainly emphasises analysis as a precursor to sensible strategy formation, but analytical skill rather than technique or data collection and manipulation. In a sense Porter had relegated technique to the two very elementary appendices found at the end of his book. This is all despite the subtitle of Porter's 1980 book, which is *Techniques for Analyzing Industries and Competitors*. Similarly it is difficult to understand why Mintzberg uses the term 'optimal strategies' in relation to Porter. In fact, Mintzberg's next two sentences after his reference to 'optimal strategies' indicate very clearly that optimisation was not what was being considered by Porter.

Certainly little in *Competitive Strategy* appears to refer to optimality or optimisation techniques. The only mention of 'optimal' in Porter appears to be in the term 'optimal competitive strategy' (Porter 1980, p. xix). On one major related point, however, it is possible to agree with Mintzberg's interpretation of Porter. This is the point where he states, immediately after the previous long quotation, 'In effect, the analyst did not design strategies (indeed, did not even formulate them) so much as select them.' (Mintzberg, p. 127) In fact, Porter's use of the generic strategy concept involves the analyst in hierarchical decision-making from the suite of strategies 'identified' by Porter. (Porter 1980, p. 34). Thus, depending upon its circumstances the enterprise chooses between:

1. overall cost leadership;
2. differentiation;
3. focus.

(Porter 1980, p. 35)

Depending upon which of these is chosen, the enterprise makes a further choice within the generic strategy, again depending upon its circumstances. If this is the conceptual framework it is going to use, for the economic and financial well-being of the enterprise embarking upon such strategies, Porter has to have correctly identified the circumstances, the strategies and their hierarchy, and the relationship between circumstances and appropriate strategy. Thus, as Mintzberg seems to recognise, Porter has established himself as the arbiter of all business strategies. This is fundamental in that this places Porter's subtitle in context: the enterprise must be able to correctly analyse its industrial situation, as well as the nature of its competitors, if it is to have any hope of being successful.

Mintzberg sees clearly the weaknesses of such an approach which are:

(i) The strategic and analytical focus is narrow, concentrating on economic as opposed to the social and political, (Mintzberg, p. 131). Mintzberg also emphasises the quantitative as opposed to non-quantitative aspects of Porter at this point, but it is also possible to interpret Porter's text as the antithesis of quantitative economic thinking of neoclassical economics.

(ii) The context is narrow, concentrating on traditional industries and big businesses rather than the newer and smaller (Mintzberg, p. 132). Mintzberg's analysis here is very telling and emphasises the partial (in more than one sense of the word) nature of Porter's analysis. In this section (pp. 132–3) Mintzberg has much to say in detail that is interesting, but it should be pointed out that Mintzberg is in fact speaking about the positioning school as a whole rather than Porter alone.

(iii) The (strategic) process is narrow. 'Its message is not to get out there and learn but to stay home and calculate' (Mintzberg, p. 134). Again this is Mintzberg looking at the school as a whole and again it is an interpretation rather than a testable hypothesis. Consequently one can imagine Porter begging to differ, arguing that his analysis is about learning about one's industry and competitors in the market-place.

(iv) Strategy is narrow in that a prescribed list is given; what Mintzberg terms a 'restricted list', (Mintzberg, p. 135), in that many alternatives are omitted. Strategy is in many ways constructed rather than chosen. In other words strategy is not envisaged in terms of creativity.

This leads naturally into Mintzberg's summing up of the positioning school and, by implication, Porter's contribution:

> The process of strategy formation is messy and dynamic; strategic analysis, in contrast, is orderly and static. Thus, its job is to support that process, not to be it.
>
> (Mintzberg, p. 136)

Critique of Porter

Introduction

This critique of Porter is broken into several sections, each section dealing with a perceived problem in Porter's work. Where this critique coincides with Mintzberg that particular point is not re-examined unless, either it is important in an argument presented here or a rather different interpretation of Mintzberg's is to be made.

Generic strategies

The concept of a generic strategy would, at first sight, appear to be central to Porter's text but, in reality, this seems far from clear. Porter certainly pays this concept a great deal of attention in the early stages of his text, but the lack of attention in later chapters is a warning signal. That signal appears to be that Porter is himself not clear on how to apply the concept. A clue to the reasons for this comes at the beginning of the chapter (Chapter 2) entitled 'generic competitive strategies'. There Porter states:

> the best strategy for a given firm is ultimately a unique construction reflecting its particular circumstances. However, at the broadest level we can identify three internally consistent generic strategies.
> (Porter 1980, p. 35)

If each of the situations that Porter has to deal with is a unique construction there would then seem to be little need for the concept of generic strategies, at least at the applied level. A strategic manager would not be concerned with the category a strategy to be used fitted into but rather the ability to construct and implement a strategy which was effective. Nevertheless, despite his claim to be addressing the book to practitioners, there could also be a legitimate analytical/theoretical rationale for the concept. Unfortunately no such rationale appear in Porter's text. At this level one of the difficulties in coming to grips with Porter's ideas, whether in an applied or theoretical framework, is the absence of definitions or references for the meaning of his terms. This leaves us without any definition of the term strategy and the term, generic. Whilst what he means by strategy remains unclear, by generic Porter appears to mean that all of the individual and uniquely constructed strategies can be classified under the heading of either one of the three generic strategies or a mixture of the three. His discussion leaves little doubt, however, that to try to pursue a strategy that is a combination of the three is highly likely to lead to failure. Porter states:

> Effectively implementing any of these generic strategies usually requires total commitment and supporting organisational arrangements that are diluted if there is more than one primary target.
> (Porter 1980, p. 35)

So, to this point, Porter has introduced the concept of generic strategy and, from my interpretation of the text:

(i) claimed there are three types, but has done this without either demonstrating that there are only three or indicating the methodology he used to arrive at the conclusion there are only three;

(ii) claimed that he has identified internally consistent generic strategies, without pointing out what he means by internal consistency;

(iii) claimed that the three types are overall cost leadership, differentiation and focus as opposed to any other possible types; and, furthermore,

302 PART D

(iv) claimed that successful strategy requires simple-minded pursuit of one and only one of these, without demonstrating that this is the case. All of these claims, either implicitly or explicitly, appear in his second chapter.

One of the major problems then, at least for generic strategies, is that strong claims are made but not supported, by either empirical evidence or theoretical argument. Of less importance, but interwoven with and compounding the problem, is the use of terms without adequately explaining what is meant by them. This means that in attempting to solve the problems of the claims, concepts have to be used which may or may not correspond to Porter's terms. In the case of generic and strategy this may not be too difficult as accepted definitions are available elsewhere. Nevertheless Porter's text offers clues that his use of the terms can be idiosyncratic or, at least, rather specialised. See, for example, the definition of competitive strategy (Porter 1980, pp. 29–30). One term that is especially problematic is internally consistent: the context does not directly reveal what this means. The position taken here is that internally consistent refers to logical consistency of the argument or theory in that: (a) there are no logical contradictions inherent in the argument: (b) the base categories are mutually exclusive (i.e. they do not overlap) and elemental (i.e. they cannot be composed from other hidden and more basic units); and (c) the base categories are universally inclusive (i.e. all other categories can be obtained from them). The specific application of the rules outlined here are especially apposite for the construction of a global taxonomy (of competitive strategies), and it would appear that although Porter does not use the term taxonomy, it is what he is attempting to construct.

Given Porter provides little clue as to his means of arriving at these three strategies as being the three generic strategies, how is it possible to examine them? At various points, however, especially in the Preface, (pp. ix–x), there are clues that the three were arrived at in an inductive fashion. Porter does not, at any point in the text, indicate a theoretical line of argument that led him to the three. Having said this, and given the claims that have been interpreted as being made, how can analysis of his concept proceed? One might either ask whether or not the categorisation is empirically falsifiable and then, if it is, attempt the falsification in a Popperian sense or subject the concepts to tests for internal logical consistency, for complete inclusivity and/or mutual exclusivity of the three base categories. By Porter's own admission it is arguable that the last of these tests, mutual exclusivity, produces a failure of the three to constitute all generic strategies, if not the concept itself. The focus strategy he argues can be either differentiation or cost leadership aimed at 'one or both of these positions vis-à-vis its narrow target market.' (Porter 1980, p. 39). In this sense the categories are not basic categories but, in the case of focus, a combination of other strategies. Porter himself states explicitly that this is a combination strategy (Porter 1980, p. 41). It is also possible to provide counter-examples of strategies that do not fit under any of the three generic strategies. Counter-examples include buying out the opposition to create a monopoly position. This is clearly none of the three.

Vertical integration, dealt with by Porter in his Chapter 14, does not mix happily with the three generic strategies. It may combine one or two or even all three generic strategies but there are other reasons which do not fit with those three. One of the most vital of these is the reduction of risk or uncertainty of demand or supply. It is certainly not a focus or differentiation strategy, assuming as we may that the original product stays the same. It would also be a massive sleight of hand to describe it as cost leadership: costs, in fact, can be raised by such integration. The benefit and therefore the strategy is something different. This could easily be to ensure that in crucial periods, the firm never loses either market or supply. It is, therefore, a survival strategy which yields the massive competitive advantage of staying afloat in lean times, to reap the rewards in the good times. Another alternative strategy which does not fit easily with the three is that of the enterprise that models itself for rapid adjustments within the market. This enterprise will treat the market as continually in disequilibrium and, therefore, constantly change. Its strategy will be to always have the ability to be the first to recover in terms of the opportunities and problems presenting themselves. Thus, if there is a sudden expansion in the market, be it temporary or permanent, this enterprise will be first there if it is profitable. Again this strategy is incompatible with cost leadership: it will need resources that are underutilised, that is, in reserve, to pursue such a strategy. Nor is the enterprise focusing on specific segments as, by definition, this strategy is quick response either across the whole market or in any specific segment. Product differentiation is one possibility, if it is allowed that rapidity of availability in special circumstances is differentiation. There are two problems with the attempt to interpret rapid availability as differentiation. First, availability seems far more fundamental than mere differentiation and, second, differentiation is a static concept compared to the dynamism implied by the opportunistic strategy.

In broad terms so far it has been argued that there are problems with Porter's representation and development of the generic strategy concept. It has also been argued that the three generic strategies chosen fail tests that would establish them as such. What has not been argued is that the generic strategy concept itself is necessarily invalidated. If the concept of generic strategy is taxonomic then it almost certainly can be constructed, at least in principle. The two unanswered questions to date are; first, whether or not such a classification is useful in developing practice and theory; and, second, whether or not the dimensions for such a classification can be uncovered.

Markets and industries

Porter places much emphasis on industry analysis, which he regards as a *sine qua non* of successful strategy formulation. If this is correct than it is important that the concept of industry be clearly and correctly formulated. The argument of this section is that Porter has not done this and, in common with many industrial organisation theorists, what is really being utilised is market theory.

To establish this it is possible to turn to Porter's analysis of an industry and the five competitive forces in his first chapter. His five competitive forces are: (i) threat of new entrants; (ii) threat of substitute products or services; (iii) bargaining power of buyers; (iv) bargaining power of suppliers; and (v) rivalry among existing firms. This, and his corresponding diagram (Figure D1.1, Porter 1980, p. 4: also reproduced earlier in this chapter) establish the framework of a market rather than an industry. Indeed one recent paper described Porter's view of industry as a set of vertical markets (Stiles 1992). While Porter's view of an industry may have usefulness it is severely limited in several respects. These limitations include:

(i) markets deal only in exchange whereas industries also deal in production;
(ii) not all transactions within an industry necessarily take place within a market;
(iii) an industry can contain many vertically and horizontally linked markets (as well as the non-market transactions).

The first of these comments is largely self-explanatory in that market theory does not deal in production and then exchange, but solely in the exchange process. Thus the terms supply and demand do not indicate any production on the part of suppliers: they merely sell property rights in commodities, which rights they hold at the time. Thus the suppliers can be a pure *rentier* class. One of the major implications of this for Porter's work is that he says very little about production in industries and production strategies within competitive strategies. The nearest approach to this is his inclusion of cost leadership within his set of generic strategies. But here his analysis is very similar to the traditional economics approach. One apparent departure from that tradition is that enterprises can, at least to some degree, control their costs but this is not explained in any great detail. But it would appear that it is non-production costs that are reduced. The manner in which he treats cost-curves, and costs as a smooth function of output levels, is a very traditional format, especially in that he appears to treat firms as one-product entities.

This seems to be a common failing in strategic management analyses; that very little attention, as yet, is paid to production management. While there are many strategic marketing texts, there are few, if any 'strategic' production management texts. Given that the vast majority of resources in most enterprises are devoted to either production or production and administration together, rather than externally oriented activities this is strange. One of the major failings of neoclassical economics and Porter's text, which follows that treatment, is that production when it is considered is treated in very simplistic terms. As with the cost-curve analysis, production is treated in a black-box fashion, with output taken as a mathematical function of the inputs. Implicitly this assumes an optimisation approach allied with best-practice technology. In the real world this is clearly not the case. Production takes considerable managerial input and is usually far less determined by technology than by human factors such as the organisation and morale of the workforce. One other major element that Porter completely ignores in this respect, and in many others, is the element of time. No matter how efficiently organised, production is a time-consuming practice. The normal and maximum rates of production, that is, units per period, and the speed with which production rates can be altered, and product specifications are not touched upon by Porter. But they are one of the most vital elements in industry. Vertical integration is often about productionary speed and flexibility rather than unit costs. Similarly Porter's concept of strategic groups completely ignores this dimension along which groups could be defined.

All of this, it is argued here, is because markets, as opposed to industries, emphasise exchange of property rights in commodities rather than the production of those commodities.

Turning to transactions as the second of the differentiating factors between markets and industries it is clear that Porter is aware of this area of analysis. This comes in his Chapter 14 where vertical integration as a strategy is considered. Porter argues, vertical integration 'represents a decision by the firm to utilise internal or administrative transactions rather than market transactions to accomplish its economic purposes' (Porter1980, p. 300).

Porter clearly recognises that a choice can sometimes be made between organising the firm so that transactions occur within it rather than between the firm and some other firm. But here there are several issues that can be raised with respect to the vital market-industry distinction. One is that Porter treats the decision as a strategic binary-structural one whereas, in many industrial situations, it is a matter of choice in each situation. Thus many firms, rather than make a structural and, therefore, strategic decision to place all of a certain type of transaction entirely within (or outside) the enterprise, will choose a structure that allows them to make the internal versus external decision as each situation demands. It then becomes a situational or tactical decision rather than a strategic and structural one. This helps determine the structure of the industry, including production capabilities, as well as being influenced by industry structure. As an aside it is well worth noting that Porter has little if anything to say about the distinction between tactics and strategies.

Implicit in all of this discussion is the notion that all transactions are of the exchange variety. This might be the case, but it is by no means certain that it is. In addition not all exchanges which are external to the firm, let alone those that are internal, are made via the market. On the first point, within an industry enterprises very often make requests of each other, even competitors. These requests, most often for information, or help when a firm faces a tight schedule, are more often acceded to than not. The question then is, why should an enterprise undertake a transaction with another enterprise when, (a) it will get no immediate reward and (b) it is helping a competitor? The answer is relatively easy, the avoidance of cut-throat competition which could threaten the survival of both, the promotion of a co-operative spirit which helps to create barriers to entry to other firms, and an insurance against the firm being attacked when it is most vulnerable.

In addition to these sorts of transactions, which are particularly important within the firm, where co-operation not competition must be the hallmark, there are exchange transactions outside the firm which are non-market. This point, however, depends to some degree on the market. Here a fairly strict view of the market is taken in which it is the market as a whole which sets the price rather than individual buyers and sellers. This means that bilateral exchange transactions, such as those between a monopolist and a monopsonist, should not be treated lightly as a market. Similarly there are firms which have long-term relationships, both informal and formally contracted, where prices and quantities are determined by mechanisms other than the market. This will be by negotiation rather than market price, internal administrative fiat or even market power. It will be in the long-run perspective, to facilitate the negotiations and avoid injury to the other party even at their own short-run expense.

The final point in relation to industries, as opposed to markets, is that industries will usually contain a series of vertically and horizontally related markets. Indeed Stiles (1992) argues that Porter's view of an industry is as a series of vertically related markets. This is insufficient, however, even if it were generalised to a series of vertically related transactions. It ignores the multiplicity of relationships that exist horizontally as well as vertically. It also implies a linear view of the production process from raw material to the consumer, and is a concept most closely akin to minerals industries. However even in those industries there are numerous alternative vertical paths for the material to take. Each of these will have their own market/transaction structure and each will usually involve substitute commodities being available. This massively increases the scope of an industry beyond a narrow, linear vertical arrangement of markets. When service industries such as banking or transport are considered the concept of a vertical arrangement dies away almost completely. It is, for example, impossible to prevent the finance industry, or its subspecies the banking industry, from integrating in any meaningful vertical manner.

As a consequence of all of these comments it would appear that Porter misconceives the meaning of an industry as a market. However, this is not just a semantic or contextual problem; it is an epistemological one with potentially huge practical implications.

External and internal strategy

A distinct view of strategy is presented by Porter, and part of that view is that business strategy is almost entirely, if not entirely concerned with the rivalry between firms. This is the embodiment of what Mintzberg and others have called the positioning school: the firm positions itself in its industry or market in relation to its opposition. The opposition here are in fact, summed up by the five competitive forces. Each of these forces, however, only exists as the actions or potential actions of other enterprises. Again the emphasis on the rivalry between firms is marked.

All the major actions that any firm can take are subsumed under the three generic strategies, which we have already examined. In each of these cost leadership, differentiation and focus, the emphasis is upon the firm in relation to other firms. Differentiation and focus are clearly about the external relationships of the firm, each involving the firm in distancing itself from the others within the market. The cost-leadership strategy is, however, somewhat separate from the other two as it seemingly implies emphasis on the internal actions of the firm. As we shall now demonstrate this is not the case, but another variant of the external rivalry orientation of the strategy of the firm.

Part of this argument has already been covered: that the cost-leadership approach of Porters is formalistic, technological and inherited from neoclassical economics. Consequently he is saying little about the enterprise, but about the production technology. In particular he is assuming best practice technology. Porter says little or nothing about the internal organisation of the firm that has to go with production of any sort, let alone best practice technology which is virtually a *sine qua non* for cost leadership. In addition to this Porter also argues quite explicitly that cost leadership is a means to an end in terms of positioning: that is creating a defensible position in an industry. Strangely it is never seen in perhaps the most obvious way, as a direct means of creating greater total profits and unit profits, by cutting costs at any level of output. Thus it is not a direct means of obtaining what Porter sees as the goal of the firm, greater long-run profits, but as a contribution to positioning, which then implies those greater long-term profits.

Another very strong piece of evidence of the way in which Porter views any strategy other than competitive strategy is an argument that occurs in several places in the text. This is the argument that internal organisation is subordinate to external strategy. Porter states: 'The generic strategies also imply differing organisational arrangements, control procedures, and inventive systems' (Porter 1980, p. 40). On the following page he argues 'The generic strategies may also require different styles of leadership and can translate into very different corporate cultures and atmospheres. Different sorts of people will be attracted' (Porter 1980, p. 41).

Now what we have is essentially a prescriptive argument: that if a competitive, (that is, external), strategy is to be successful then the firm must try to base its organisational structure on that strategy. Given the manner in which Porter compiled the evidence for this work, upon his own personal experience in consulting and so on (Porter 1980, pp. ix–x, xvi) then it can also be argued that some firms, successful ones at least, do operate in this manner. The main point here, however, is not whether Porter is being prescriptive or analytical, and not even if his approach is inductive or otherwise. The main point is the subordination of the internal elements of the enterprise to the external in Porter's work. It is worth noticing that Porter refers to competitive strategy but only to internal organisation, that is (a) he does not perceive any need for internal strategy and (b) what occurs within the firm is purely operational and subordinate.

Note that these two points, although closely related, are rather different. It could, for example, be argued that there is a need for internal strategy, but that it is not subordinate to competitive strategy. Conversely it could be argued that not only does internal strategy form a significant part of a firm's arsenal but also that it dominates or determines external policy. There is at least one *a priori* reason for suggesting this is the case. This is that while external strategy can be changed relatively rapidly and relatively inexpensively, the same is not true of internal strategy. Significantly internal strategic changes require disruption of the whole firm, but external strategy changes do not necessarily require the same degree of upheaval.

An analogy may help make it clearer why internal strategy is so significant when it might still be argued that 'beating' its rivals is absolutely vital for the company. Consider a middle-distance race, perhaps 1500 or 5000 metres, where the objective is to win (i.e. directly beat one's rivals). Once on the track and the race has begun it is a matter of strategy and tactics that can decide the winner. This is the external or competitive strategy with the runner representing the firm. But how do firms and runners spend most of their time, effort and resources? In the case of the enterprise it is in its own internal transactions, especially if the firm is very large. In the case of the athlete much more time and effort and other resources is spent on training and raising one's fitness level for competition. To maintain a peak the athlete must be continually training. So it is with the firm. If it is to be successful then internal strategies designed to increase its general and specific competitive skills are continually being utilised. Indeed, much recent literature has argued that it is the nature of the firm, rather than the overt competitive manoeuvres that explains the success of the Japanese firm (Aoki 1988, pp. 2–3, 11–16). In Aoki's analysis, for example, he compares the A-firm to the J-firm, where the A and J denote the American and Japanese-style firms. In the A-firm workers are highly specialised and very cost-efficient in a small range of expertise. These workers are controlled hierarchically, and gain promotion by competing against each other for the jobs that become available in the hierarchy. In the J-firm workers are far less specialised and gain rank by achievement, seniority and competition rather than solely by competition with their fellow workers. The company, as a consequence, is less rigidly hierarchical. Workers are more flexible and, because they are not so much in competition, are much more willing to co-operate with the firm as a whole and other individual workers. These are two very different strategies, but both are internal rather than external ones. They represent very different philosophies of competition and production. Whichever one is superior may depend upon the external environment but the A-firm most closely corresponds to the tight manner in which Porter regards cost-efficiency. Even for mass-production and simple commodities this may no longer be the appropriate strategy for a dynamic environment. The J-firm can adopt different external/competitive strategies more readily than the A-firm can change its internal fitness strategy.

Conclusion

An argument has been made that Porter's work contains many debatable assertions rather than uncontestable and rigorously derived conclusions, contains many points which can be given different interpretations to those he gave and, which, in many cases, are also theoretically and empirically flawed. In fact, not all of the potential criticisms of Porter's work have been made. It is more than arguable, for example, that Porter has a very limited and simple view of what constitutes a commodity (or service). Mintzberg has also put forward this view. Allied with this is a relatively simplistic view of what constitutes an industry. Similarly there is little that is said about the retail consumer. And in as far as it follows Porter, many of these and other faults could be regarded as being shared by the positioning school as a whole. But here a crucial question arises: is the text deserving of the success it has obtained? The answer to this might be as follows.

Porter's book was a major step forward not only in the limited sense of defining the positioning school, but for strategic management thought in general. It seems likely that the positioning school will endure a steady decline, but Porter's work will remain. The reason for this would appear to stem, at least in part from its presentation, readability and understandablity. But, in substantive terms there was also an unequalled attempt, for that time, to create an analysis of the strategic problem as a whole, although seen almost entirely in a competitive framework.

Given this influence, one of the thoughts that is most intriguing is how far different and how much less influential such a text would have been if written from outside the North American sphere? And, given the burgeoning success of several other nations during the seventies and eighties, it is also possible to wonder if the competitive habits of the American firms, and the economic theory of markets upon which Porter based his work, were not already dated.

References

Aoki, M. (1988), *Information, Incentives and Bargaining in the Japanese Economy*, Cambridge University Press, Cambridge.

Hendry, J. (1990), 'The Problem with Porter's Generic Strategies', *European Management Journal*, 8, pp. 443–450.

Mintzberg, H. (1990), 'Strategy Formation: Schools of Thought', in *Perspectives on Strategic Management*, Harper Business, New York, Chapter 5, pp. 105–235.

Montgomery, C. A. and Porter, M. E. (eds) (1991), *Strategy: Seeking and Securing Competitive Advantage*, Harvard Business School Press, Boston.

Porter, M. E. (1980), *Competitive Strategy: Techniques for Analyzing Industries and Competitors*, Free Press, New York.

Porter, M. E. (1990), *The Competitive Advantage of Nations*, Macmillan, London.

Sharp, B. M. (1991), 'Competitive Marketing Strategy: Porter Revisited', *Marketing Intelligence and Planning*, 9, pp. 4–10.

Speed, R. J. (1989), 'Oh Mr Porter! A Re-appraisal of Competive Strategy', *Marketing Intelligence and Planning*, 7, pp. 8–11.

Stiles, C. H. (1992), 'The Influence of Secondary Production on Industry Definition in the Extended Vertical Market Model', *Strategic Management Journal*, 13, pp. 171–187.

Wright, P. and Parsina, A. (1988), 'Porter's Synthesis of Generic Business Strategies', *Industrial Management*, 30, pp. 20–23.

Marketing, strategic management and models of strategy formation

by Michael Browne

Introduction

To either the practitioner or student of management, both management academia and the consulting industry offer a diverse and confusing array of advice and opinions on how the business enterprise should best be managed. Programme budgeting, quality control, project management, total quality management, strategic planning, workshops on leadership, multiskilling, the application of new technologies and the construction of executive information systems are just a few of the prescriptions on offer. In their more enthusiastic moments, peddlers of such prescriptions often purport to hold 'the key to success' whether that key is focusing on the consumer, better information, or a 'commitment to excellence' or 'quality'. Management education also presents a diverse range of perspectives on the problems of management generally. Human resource management, management accounting, finance, informatics and marketing have all emerged as important specialist disciplines. But the specialist disciplines tend to present a neat self-sufficiency which belies the diffuse origins (from practice as well as theory) from which they have made an untidy emergence. As Bartels noted some thirty years ago with respect to marketing 'the development of marketing thought is not only the product of ideas developed by students of marketing . . . one must be conversant with other intellectual findings' (1962, p. 205). More importantly, perhaps, the neat self-sufficiency of the specialist disciplines masks the interdependence in practice of the issues with which they deal. Although there can be no doubt that specialisation has engendered greater sophistication, there is a risk that a Balkanisation of the management disciplines might lead to an uncritical acceptance of narrow orthodoxies. Thus as Firat et al. claim for marketing, what is required is 'a spirit of free inquiry which transcends conventional boundaries, confronts established paradigms and questions received wisdom' (1987, p. 379). Because of their divergent perspectives, the opportunity is now afforded to compare and contrast established paradigms across specialist disciplines where the specific interests intersect. It is with the interdependence of the specialist functions that the generalist field of strategic management is concerned, and it is across the foundations of the specialist disciplines that a coherent theoretical synthesis has long been advocated but is yet to be constructed (Brunsson 1982; Jaunch & Osborn 1981; Jemison 1981; Ruekert et al. 1985; Simon 1978).

This paper addresses one issue at the intersection of marketing and strategic management. These two disciplines have long shared common prescriptive models of strategy formulation. In reviewing their recent literatures, however, it has become apparent that theoretical developments in the two fields have not kept apace. Models of strategy formulation in marketing appear to have been relatively immune from the new critical ideas which have emerged in the strategic management literature.

In this paper, the common models of strategy formulation are traced to the common origins of marketing and strategic management. A sample of popular teaching texts in marketing are surveyed and the critical themes emergent in the strategic management literature used to construct a critique of the model of strategy formulation on which they are based. It is argued that these models of strategy formulation are both simplistic and unrealistic, misrepresenting both the nature and context of strategic marketing decisions with important implications for its practical application. The paper concludes that greater research emphasis needs to be placed on descriptive empirical research and analysis of strategic management in practice in order to provide more robust and realistic axioms on which to construct theory and from which to deduce prescriptions for marketing strategy formulation.

Common origins

The significance of the present opportunity to construct a cross-disciplinary critique can best be appreciated in the light of the common origins and divergent histories of marketing and strategic management.

Marketing has a longer history in management education than strategic management. The first courses in marketing have been dated from the turn of the century (Converse 1945, p. 14), while strategic management has been dated from the simultaneous publication in 1965 of Ansoff's *Corporate Strategy* and the text *Business Policy: Text and Cases* by the Harvard team of Learned, Christensen, Andrews and Guth. Indeed, the current term 'strategic management' did not succeed the earlier term 'business policy' until 1977 (Clutterbuck & Crainer 1990, p. 152; Bartlett & Ghoshal 1991, p. 7). Although the fields of marketing and strategic management have both developed from diffuse origins, to some extent strategic management is historically a tributary of marketing. Accounts of the early development of marketing point to its origins in economics and the subsequent development, particularly at Harvard, of a strong inductive tradition, case-study based, and focused on the managerial problems of formulating marketing policies for the business enterprise (Bartels 1951, p. 17; Jones & Monieson 1990, p. 111). It was from this Harvard tradition that the Learned et al. text was to emanate in 1965, marking the beginning of strategic management as a complimentary but distinct subject in management education.

What marketing and strategic management shared from this common tradition was a managerialist approach concerned with developing practical prescriptions for marketing management or business policy more generally. They also shared a common inductive methodology—the process of distilling general principles from a large collection of specific cases. They shared in addition a large commonality of interest, in particular a concern with the business enterprise's environment—the needs of consumers and the behaviour of rivals in a competitive market context (Biggadike 1981, p. 621).

Where the two disciplines diverged was in the broader focus adopted in strategic management. It could be argued that with the conception of strategic management established in Learned et al. (1965)—later to be termed the 'design school' by Mintzberg—the first foundations were laid to build a bridge across the gulf that existed (and to a large extent still persists) in management education between those disciplines concerned with internal management and those concerned with the management of the external relations of the business enterprise. Whereas marketing was, and is, concerned predominantly with the enterprise's relationship with consumers in the context of competitive markets, the design school conception of strategic management was concerned with 'the process by which general managers of complex organisations develop and utilise a strategy to coalign their organisation's competences with the opportunities and constraints present in their environment' (Jemison 1981, p. 601) Thus this more general focus subsumed the specialist foci not only of marketing but also of other specialist domains such as human resource management, finance and to some extent technology and manufacturing. The integration of human resource management within the strategic management framework, however, was not to emerge as a distinct project of scholarship until the 1980s. In the early stages of its development, therefore, the conception of strategic management associated with Harvard shared with marketing a large degree of commonality in origins, focus and methodology and further elaborations of the design school tended to be incorporated equally into these highly complementary disciplines. The common conception of strategy formation Mintzberg has since termed the 'design school' (1990a, p. 111).

The design school model

The 'design school' model of strategy formation has been described by Mintzberg as the most entrenched view of the strategy formation process (1990b, p. 171). It will also be immediately familiar to students of marketing. At the core of the design school model lies SWOT, the commonplace acronym for the approach to strategy formulation which prescribes an analysis of the internal strengths and weaknesses of the business enterprise and the opportunities and threats of its external environment as the essential first step in the process of designing a strategy which coaligns the enterprise's distinctive capabilities with its market opportunities (Mintzberg 1990a, p. 111). The fundamental character of the design school is its prescriptive nature. A fundamental distinction in social science, but one notable by its absence from the marketing texts, is that between *normative* theories (theories which *prescribe* what should be done) and *positive* theories (those which *describe* or explain what is in fact done). The design school conception of strategy is a normative one. It prescribes how strategies should be formulated rather than how they are formulated in practice.

The origins of the design school model have been the subject of Mintzberg's intellectual archaeology. Although he takes care to show that the Harvard school can not take credit for the invention, Mintzberg himself nevertheless takes the statement of the model contained in Learned et al. to be a classical one (1990b, p. 172) The text material which describes what Mintzberg has since termed the design school model is attributed to Professor Andrew's in the Preface to the Learned et al. text (1969, p. ix).

One of the rewards of intellectual archaeology is the rediscovery of the force and richness of original ideas. And there is much to be gained from revisiting Andrew's original text. Andrews presented the SWOT framework more tentatively than it has been repeated by his more recent imitators. His prose is redolent with insights from business practice and his qualifications anticipate many of the criticisms which the more recent and more simplistic reductions have since attracted. Andrews insists, for example, that the concept of strategy he describes is neither a 'theory', a 'model', nor 'a manual for policy makers or a how-to-do-it checklist for corporate planners'(1969: 10–11). It was instead 'a simple practitioner's theory, a kind of everyman's conceptual scheme' (1969:vii). Andrews did not consider he had discovered the acme of strategic decision making:

> But in lieu of a better theory or a more precise model, it will serve as an informing idea to which we can return again and again with increasing understanding after dealing with one unique case after another.
> (Learned et al. 1969, p. 11)

In the many texts in both strategic management and marketing which have adopted the SWOT framework, Andrew's qualifications have been forgotten or ignored. And it would appear that his 'informing idea' has been returned to again and again with *decreasing* understanding—indeed until it has been reduced to the irreducible four-letter acronym SWOT.

Eight of the nine marketing texts surveyed subscribe broadly to the design school model (Berkowitz 1986, pp. 520–525; Busch & Houston 1985, p. 43; Gross & Peterson 1987, p. 24; Kotler et al. 1989, p. 64; Lazer & Culley 1983; McCarthy & Perrault 1990, p. 114; McColl-Kennedy et al. 1992, p. 47). Some of these treat the design school model more centrally than others. Busch and Houston, for example, describe the matching of a firm's competencies to its environment as the 'essential first step in the formulation of strategy' (1985, p. 79). Kotler et al., McColl-Kennedy et al., and Schewe are similarly committed to the design school model. McCarthy and Perrault refer to the design school model only as depicting the corporate strategy context within which they then emphasise the marketing function as a specialist subroutine. In Berkowitz, as in Gross and Peterson, the SWOT elements of the design school model are not described explicitly but various elements are implicitly discernible. It also should be noted that in these marketing texts the design school characteristics are not undiluted. They are also heavily influenced by what Mintzberg has elsewhere described as the 'planning' and 'positioning' school of strategy formation (1990a, p. 117).

A critical distinction must be made between two dimensions inherent in this model, a distinction emphasised by Jemison:

> A distinction can be made between the study of what should be done (the *content* of a firm's strategy) and how it is accomplished (the *processes* of strategy formulation and implementation).
> (1981, p. 602)

The design school model prescribes, in the very broadest of terms, the *content* of the analysis required for the design of strategies: both the internal and external circumstances must be considered. Often these are subsumed under the general heading of 'situation analysis'. Additionally, the model locates this content of strategic analysis within a *process* of deliberation, design and decision-making.

The content of the design school model

In its fundamental form the design school or SWOT model of strategy formulation provides little more than a bare skeleton with which to frame strategic deliberations. Ironically, whereas marketing was to incorporate the design school framework, it was marketing that was to provide the model with much needed substance.

The external dimension: Consumers

Marketing provided analytical content for the external analysis prescribed in the SWOT model. Its distinctive contribution was the consumer focus by which the discipline is invariably defined—the notion that the key to achieving organisational goals is determining the needs and wants of target markets and delivering the desired satisfactions more effectively and efficiently than competitors (Kotler 1989, p. 15). It is on this premise that marketing's main analytical techniques have been constructed:

> Marketing concepts and techniques such as market segmentation, positioning, and perceptual mapping help define the environment and frame strategic choices in customer terms . . . Essentially, marketing sees strategic management as being market-driven, and provides aids for hypothesising about customer needs and competitor behaviour.
>
> (Biggadike 1981, p. 621)

The flourishing field of consumer behaviour illustrates well the powerful influence of applied psychology in constructing and testing hypotheses about consumer needs and behaviour. Not only has psychology provided ways of understanding consumer behaviour, psychology has also lent marketing strong empirical research techniques with which to operationalise analyses such as segmentation and positioning. In contrast to standard micro-economic models which typically treat consumers homogeneously, segmentation provides an analysis based on differential hypotheses as to the determinants of consumer behaviour. Positioning complements this approach by investigating cognitive aspects of consumer choice and purchase behaviours. These in turn Biggadike ranks as 'marketing's most important contributions to strategic management' (1981, p. 624).

The external dimension: Competition

In contrast, the appreciation of the competitive market or industry environment was less well developed in marketing. A very limited appreciation was constructed rather clumsily on the basis of an eclectic collection of models which emanated in the 1970s from the realms of business practice and the consulting industry. This eclecticism, which as Firat et al. complain 'gnaws at the self-confidence of struggling dissertation writers in marketing' is still evident in the disjointed recitation of simplistic and partial models. These include the notion of the experience curve, the Boston Consulting Group's portfolio matrix, the McKinsey/General Electric industry attractiveness matrix, the enormous empirical project the Profit Impact of Marketing

Strategies (PIMS) and the ubiquitous product life cycle. The matrix approaches are distinguished by their simplicity and the very limited range of variables they consider. Thus they contribute only very partial insights into the complex problems of strategic management and even less to the concerns of marketing as a specialist discipline. Yet these constructions have become entrenched as part of the orthodoxy of marketing texts (Berkowitz et al. 1986, pp. 530–533; Busch & Houston 1985, pp. 57–61; Lazer & Culley pp. 151–153; Kotler et al. 1989, pp. 67–72; McCarthy & Perrault 1990, p. 117; McColl-Kennedy et al. 1992, pp. 63–64; Schewe 1987, pp. 45–48; Stanton et al. 1991, pp. 55*ff*). And, typically, they are made to pass for analysis without any debate of their logical construction, appropriate context or inherent limitations. Lazer and Culley (1983) provide an exception with a short summary of limitations (p. 156). Their main value lies in the deceptive relief they may bring as simple solutions for managers facing complex problems. Greenley's survey of strategy concepts in the marketing literature struggled with this eclecticism and, disappointed, reached the conclusion that 'a true understanding and application of strategy within marketing can become confused by the very body of knowledge which is attempting to clarify it' (1989, p. 57).

A more sophisticated approach to competitive strategy was developed, again at Harvard, by Porter whose *Competitive Strategy: Techniques for Analyzing Industries and Competitors* published in 1980 applied the market structure, conduct and performance paradigm from neoclassical economics to the problem. Porter adapted the framework to provide a more active role for the enterprise in adopting strategies which would influence both market structure and performance. Porter's work revolutionised the conception of competitive strategy:

> Porter formulated a piece of marketing theory, his analysis of industry structure was certainly economic work, but its outcome—competitive strategy—is theory which describes marketing decisions, a fact which was quickly appreciated by marketing academics and practitioners worldwide.
> (Sharp 1991, p. 4)

In spite of this claim, Porter's work has found its way into only a few of the marketing texts reviewed and in only a very reduced form (Busch & Houston 1985, p. 91; Kotler et al. 1989, p. 609; McColl-Kennedy et al. 1992, p. 32; Stanton et al. 1991, pp. 29, 54). Like Andrews before him, the force of Porter's ideas have been lost in the very much reduced and simplistic recitation it receives as yet another model added to the eclectic collection in the marketing texts.

The content of external environmental analysis is not limited of course to the consideration of consumers and rivals in the context of competitive markets. Indeed, Dickson warns that an overemphasis on these dimensions may be the result of conceptual biases inherent in the frame of reference adopted—other pertinent considerations might by neglected (1992, p. 75). The possible breadth of scope in environmental analysis was defined by Andrews to include the technological, economic, social and political (Learned et al. 1969, p. 172). Similar and occasionally more extensive categories are recited in all the marketing texts reviewed and can be exemplified by Kotler's catalogue which lists demographic, economic, natural, technological, political and cultural dimensions of the enterprise's 'macroenvironment' (1989, p. 150). These dimensions provide ample scope for contributions from academic disciplines as diffuse as anthropology, sociology, and politics and the natural sciences. However, unless the practising marketing manager is a polymath of extraordinary capacity, these various dimensions can not expect to receive more than the scant attention given to them in the marketing texts. They provide a genuflection to an apparent but illusory and impossible ideal of comprehensiveness in strategic environmental analysis.

The internal dimension

Although, as we have seen, SWOT has become entrenched in the orthodoxy of the marketing texts, the analysis of the internal dimensions of an enterprise's comparative strengths and weaknesses has remained undeveloped:

> In recent years, only a few articles, either conceptual or empirical, have addressed organisational issues in the marketing literature ... there is little in terms of conceptual development or empirical evidence that gives insight to marketing managers in developing appropriate organisational structures
>
> (Ruekert et al. 1985, p. 13)

Ruekert's conclusion is not contradicted by the nine marketing texts reviewed for the current exercise. Organisational analysis is typically restricted to prescriptions for organising the implementation of management strategies only after the fact of strategy design (Berkowitz 1986, p. 554; McCarthy 1990, p. 541; McColl-Kennedy 1992, p. 65). Little *conceptual* basis is provided for the analysis of an organisations strengths and weaknesses as part of the process of strategy formulation.

In contrast, however, during the 1980s the field of strategic management burgeoned and a range of new influences contributed to the development of the field. Whereas Porter had advanced dramatically the treatment of the external focus in strategic management, the emphasis shifted towards the internal focus. Organisational structures, behaviour, politics and culture became the ascendant topics in the field with contributions from management, psychology, sociology and politics. The scope of strategic management also broadened to include public and voluntary sector organisations. Most notably, the 1980s witnessed the specialist discipline of personnel management reconceptualised in strategic terms as human resource management. By 1990 the field had so expanded that Mintzberg was able to identify ten distinct schools of thought in the management strategy literature (Mintzberg 1990a). With the contributions of these new perspectives, the fields of strategic management and marketing became more clearly differentiated not only in terms of their scope and emphasis, but also in terms of their theoretical foundations. In particular the new perspectives in strategic management challenged the presumptions of the prescriptive managerialist models that characterised the 'design school' conceptions that strategic management and marketing had hitherto shared. It is from this challenge that the notions of strategy formulation in marketing has been relatively immune.

Apart from the content of internal strategic analysis, however, this influx of ideas was to challenge the process dimensions of the design school model of strategy formulation.

The process of strategy formulation

Not only has the content of the design school model been elaborated in greater detail by the accretion of various analytical perspectives onto the basic skeleton of SWOT, but the process dimension of the model has also become elaborated. Considerable variation is evident between the marketing texts surveyed, however the basic SWOT model is typically located within a more extended framework. The clarification of a mission statement and the articulation of organisational objectives are prescribed as prior steps in the process while implementation is extended to be succeeded by monitoring, evaluation and control procedures.

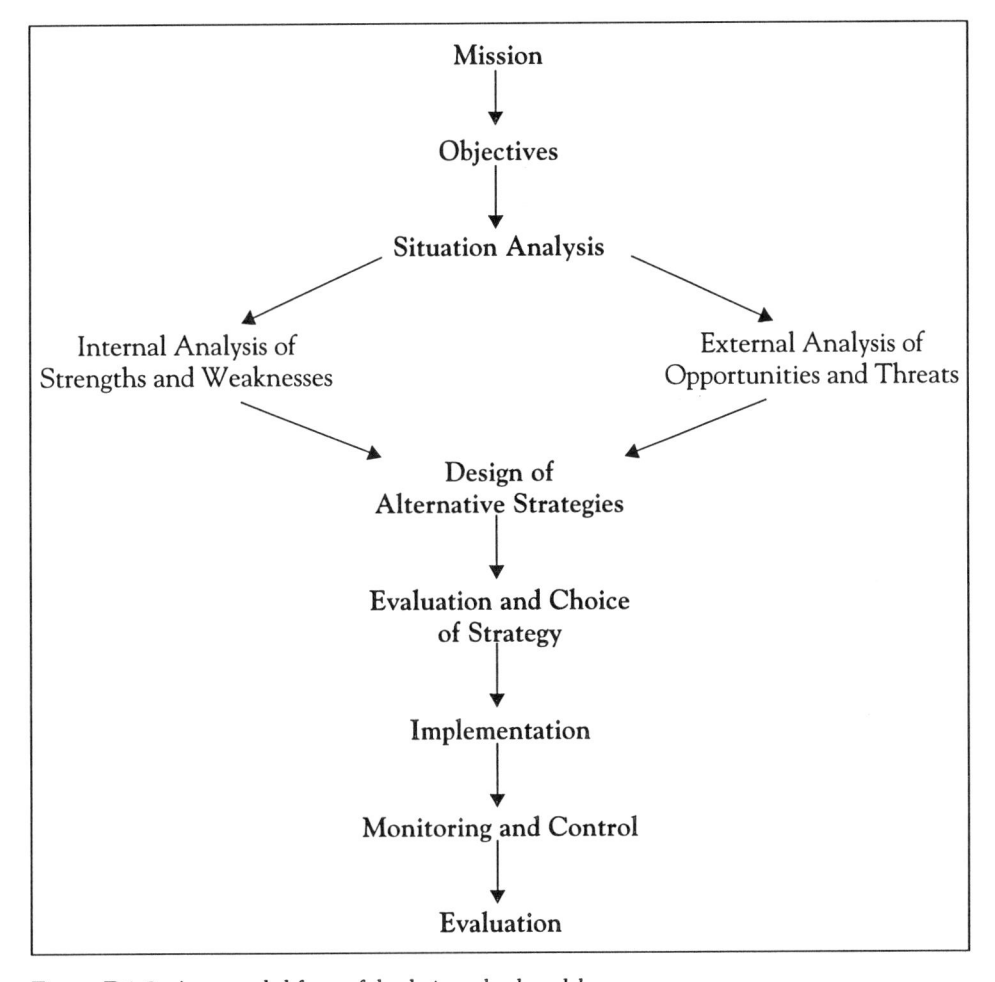

Figure D1.2 *An extended form of the design school model*

In spite of the accretions and extensions to the content and process dimensions, the fundamental structure and features of the design school model remains intact. What has emerged, however, is a more extensive model than that first skeleton prescribed by Learned et al. To the practical marketing manager the prescriptions of the design school model have the ring of sound advice. As McDonald describes it, the model is 'simply a series of activities in a logical sequence leading to the setting of marketing objectives and the formulation of plans for achieving them' (1992, p. 6). The prescriptive and serial nature of the model gives it the characteristics of a recipe. Practical advice for the students of marketing and prospective and practicing marketing managers, it has indeed become a 'how-to-do-it checklist for corporate planners'. It is interesting to note, however, that the practical appeal of the model endures in spite of the fact that it is derived not from practice but from theory. The model is based not on how marketing management is practiced, but on a rational calculation of how marketing management *should* happen in theory. And Andrews' qualifications, greatly informed by practice, have ebbed away.

In mounting a critique of the model, it is the rational basis of the model that must be critically re-examined. As Piercy has noted 'the prescriptively-based literature of marketing relies on the notion of "rational" management decision making'. And it is this 'rationality' that accounts for the model's perennial appeal. But what is the basis of this rationality?

Herbert Simon distinguishes between two conceptions of rationality: *substantive rationality* which refers to 'the extent to which appropriate courses of action are chosen', and *procedural rationality*—'the effectiveness . . . and limitation of the *procedures* used to choose actions'. These two different conceptions of rationality are particularly instructive in the present case as they correspond to the content and process dimensions of the design school model we have described.

The substantive rationality of the model

Simon defines substantive rationality in the following terms:

> Behaviour is substantively rational when it is appropriate to the achievement of given goals within the limits imposed by given conditions and constraints... Given these goals, the rational behaviour is determined entirely by the characteristics of the environment in which it takes place.
>
> (1976, p. 130)

The correspondence of this definition of substantive rationality to the extended form of the design school model (Figure D1.2 above) should be immediately evident. In the extended design school model the mission and objectives of the enterprise are established prior to the analysis of the external and internal analysis, and strategy is determined by the optimal matching of the enterprise's internal strengths to its environmental opportunities.

Goals

One of the assumptions of the design school model relates to the goals of the enterprise. As Narayanan and Fahey point out, within the rational model 'the microeconomic assumption of a unitary voice within the firm has predominated: organisational preferences are assumed to be known and consistent' (1982, p. 25). This assumption is echoed by Mintzberg who noted that strategy formulation is the responsibility of the chief executive officer: 'that person is the strategist' (1990a, p. 113). Thus the design school model tends to treat the determination of the mission of the enterprise and its objectives as unproblematic and consensual.

In contrast in the original text Andrews remarks are qualified by the observation that: 'The purpose of organised effort, in business as elsewhere, are usually neither clear, fixed nor unchanging' (Learned et al. 1969, p. 4).

But Andrews does not explore the purely logical implications of this admission. The substantive rationality of the model, however, depends upon an agreed set of objectives as a prior and necessary condition. Without goal consensus, no substantively rational strategy can be designed.

The notion that decisions regarding goals precede the choice of strategies by which they might be achieved is also not uncontroversial. Tversky and Tahneman have demonstrated experimentally that preferences and frames of reference by which alternatives are constructed and evaluated are not independent (1981, p. 453). Andrews anticipated this too. He recognised that 'the choice of goals and the formulation of policy cannot in any case be separate decisions' (Learned et al. 1969, p. 17).

The robustness of the treatment of goals within the model will be further tested below when we consider the implications of dissensus for the *procedural* rationality of the model.

Substance

As we have already noted, the basic design school model provides only the barest skeleton of the content dimensions of strategy deliberations and marketing has provided much of the substance of external environmental analysis which has so enriched the model. This alone highlights the fact that the basic model itself does not provide any analytical content on which to claim any substantive rationality whatsoever. Such substantive rationality as may exist depends upon the analytical capabilities of managers and their deduction of implications on the basis of their particular understanding of the specific environment in which they find themselves. At a theoretical level, substantive analysis in support of the design school model has been borrowed from psychology via consumer behaviour, from marketing and from economics courtesy of Porter's *Competitive Strategy* (1980). And, as we have already seen, large gaps in marketing's appreciation of the internal context of strategy formulation and implementation persist.

Bounded rationality

To the extent that the substantive rationality of the design school model depends upon the rational capacities of the particular decision maker, the model assumes that the conditions and constraints of the circumstances are not so complex as to overwhelm the decision maker's capacities. In common with rationalist models in economics, the design school model tacitly presumes perfect or unbounded rationality on the part of decision makers. This is, of course, a theoretical fiction. 'Bounded rationality' is the renowned term given by Simon to the alternative theorem that the information-processing capacities of human beings are in fact limited:

> For most procedures that man encounters in the real world, no procedure that he can carry out with his information-processing equipment will enable him to discover the optimal solution . . . There is no logical reason why this need be so; it is simply a rather obvious empirical fact about the world we live in—a fact about the relation between the enormous complexity of that world and the modest information-processing capacities with which man is endowed.
>
> (Simon 1976, p. 135)

Whereas contemporary expositions of the design school model are typically silent on this problem, Andrews was not. He too noted that 'to design a strategy that is optimal is a challenge to insight and intelligence which simply lies beyond the capacity of many an effective operator' (Learned et al. 1969, p. 21). But again while Andrews' informing idea has had an eminent career, the implications of his own qualifications have not survived.

Selectivity

The complexity of the environment in which strategies are formulated and the boundedness of our information-processing capacity suggests a further characteristic of the way in which practical marketing managers must deal with this complexity. Simon has repeatedly made the point that there is inevitably a considerable difference between 'the world as God or some other omniscient observer sees it' and the environment as it may be perceived by the decision maker (1978, p. 8; 1955, p. 114). One of the perennial problems facing practicing marketing managers is to select the information critical to their strategic deliberations. Practical decision makers have no choice but to deal with a simplified model of the environment rather than with the complex world in its entirety. There can be little surprise then that different perceptions of the world and different judgments as to which are the critical features persist. Thus managers at different levels of the enterprise and in different specialist functions are likely to construct different simplified models in their attempt to grapple with a complex environment. As Piercy has noted, the corporate environment underpins perceptions of the marketing environment and introduces 'problems of bias and selectivity in strategic thinking' (1990, p. 27).

It is worth noting that the problem of identifying the critical variables on which to focus in an environment is one of the primary functions of theory in both marketing and strategic management. The selectivity involved in determining the appropriate critical variables on which to focus also explains how different models can be constructed for different purposes to explain the same phenomena:

> A characteristic of social science is the multitude of perspectives used by different researchers. The significant differences between research fields lie less often in what is described than how it is described.
>
> (Brunnson 1982, p. 29)

Thus what we see in the real world depends to an important extent on what we are looking for, and the significance we attach to our observations depends similarly on our understanding of how the world works. Teachers of marketing and economics theory often despair of students who, professing a practical bias, naively prefer the complexity of the real world to the relative simplicity of theoretical models which might help them understand it. In fact their preference is not for the complexity of the real world, but for their own more simplistic misunderstandings of it.

Yet, in spite of this complexity, the design school model glibly prescribes an analysis of the environment and presents this as unproblematic. It fails to recognise that even within its own constraints, the selectivity we apply in making the world intelligible implies that not only is there no absolute rationality, that there is likely to exist several competing partial rationalities with which people interpret and understand their world and on which they base their decision.

Uncertainty

Notwithstanding the enormous increases in information-processing capacity achieved by modern information technologies (Simon rates their historical importance along with the invention of writing and the printing press) there is a further intractable limitation to the rational capacities of human beings which frustrates rational decision making. Since strategies involve decisions to guide actions in the expectation of future consequences, strategy formulation inevitably occurs under circumstances of uncertainty. Again Andrews was aware of the problem, but did not explore the implications:

> . . . it is of course, impossible for us to describe or even to know for all business the relevant characteristics of today's world, to say nothing of tomorrow's.
>
> (Learned et al. 1969, p. 173)

Where the consequences of actions cannot be predicted with accuracy, no substantively rational solution to the problem of choice of strategies can be established (Simon 1976, p. 142). Shackle provided a succinct but characteristically pessimistic statement of the problem of uncertainty:

> . . . we can choose only among imaginations and figments. Imagined actions and policies can only have imagined consequences, and it follows that we can choose only an action whose consequences we cannot directly know since we cannot be eyewitnesses of them.
>
> (Shackle as cited in Savitt 1987, pp. 312–13)

On this very pessimistic view, there could be no substantively rational basis for any decision whatsoever. Clearly this is not always the case.

The corollary to absolute uncertainty in the relationship between an action and its consequences is the condition of certainty. Such certainty implies the notion of causality. Narayanan and Fahey have argued explicitly that the rationalist model must assume that cause and effect relationships are 'fairly well understood' (1982, p. 25). Of course, a staunch rationalist would require that they are understood absolutely! The point is, however, that our understanding of causal relationships within the market context, or for that matter within the organisational context, is far from absolute. An intractable problem in neo-classical economics has been the problem of oligopoly—the uncertainty which is endemic to a situation where the outcome of any decision is determined not only by the strategy adopted but also by a rival's reaction to it. And the reaction of competitors is only one source of uncertainty which faces the practicing marketing manager. Interestingly, the limitations of our tools of substantive analysis has been the subject of empirical research which has observed:

> "analyser" firms outperform other organisation types in mildly volatile markets but do not exhibit superior performance in highly volatile markets ... In such a world, success depends more on luck than on the ability to analyse and plan.
>
> (Dickson 1992, p. 75)

The design school model provides no substantively rational solution to the problem of uncertainty in marketing strategy formulation.

Implications

Thus even though the apparent rationality of the design school model recommends itself to the practising marketing manager, the substantive rationality of the model can be demonstrated to be entirely spurious. Even if we assume that a set of specific organisational goals can be determined in advance (and we will re-examine this assumption shortly) the substantive rationality of the model is frustrated by the complexity of the real world, the limits of our cognitive capacities, the selectivity and simplicity with which we deal with complex realities, the incompleteness of our understanding of causal relationships and consequently our uncertainty of the outcomes of proposed actions.

A caveat needs to be added. This deconstruction of the design school model, however, depends on the application of the particularly strong form of rationality. It may be claimed, with some justification, that the Aristotelian logic which underpins the notion of substantive rationality is inappropriately applied to questions of strategy. Aristotelian logic applies reason in the search for truth. In the narrow technical sense, it examines the logical relationship between a premise and a conclusion. Questions of strategy, however, are concerned with reason aimed toward action where the relevant logical relationship lies between an action and its expected consequences. Since in a complex world our actions are not the only determinants of outcomes, we can never 'prove' logically that one course of action is appropriate in any absolute sense. If we were to insist on this degree of proof, no action could be sanctioned as rational. For the perfectly rational marketing manager, the result would be 'paralysis by analysis'.

The procedural rationality of the model

In spite of these problems of the substantive rationality of the design school model, there is another dimension that needs to be explored. While as we have seen the content of the model provides little more than the very broad general headings of internal and external environmental analysis, the structure of the model provides a process of decision making. Indeed the substantive content of the model, such as it is, implies a procedural rationality in its application. The viability of the basic design school rests strongly on the process dimension. Simon provides this definition of procedural rationality:

> Behaviour is procedurally rational when it is the outcome of appropriate deliberation. Its procedural rationality depends on the process that generated it.
>
> (1976, p. 131)

The notion of procedural rationality, as Simon describes it, has emerged from psychology. Whereas economists, for example, might be concerned with the substantive rationality of a decision or a policy given the specific economic goals and an analysis of the pertinent circumstances, psychologists have been typically interested in the rationality of the processes involved in problem-solving behaviour. Typically psychologists seek to describe and explain observed individual behaviour (Simon 1976, pp. 131–32). But the process dimension of the design school model differs from this in two fundamental respects. Firstly, except in a limited set of cases, the model is concerned with organisational rather than individual behaviours. Secondly the model is concerned with *prescribing* rather than *describing* a decision process.

For evaluating the procedural rationality of such a model, however, Simon offers little advice as to the logical criteria which might apply. 'Appropriate deliberation' is a much more vague criterion than that of the Aristotelian logic which was applied to the substantive rationality of the model. Nevertheless one measure of 'appropriateness' of the model might be the extent to which it is appropriate to the context in which it is applied. As Piercy has remarked, this has become the matter of some debate:

> ... one theme emerging from the literature is that the received marketing literature has tended to portray management decision making as something isolated from, and independent of, the organisational context in which organisational decisions are made.
>
> (1990, p. 25)

Examining the context of organisational decision making, we return to investigate organisational goals and the processes by which they and the strategies designed to achieve them are formulated.

Organisational goals

As we have noted above a set of explicit, internally consistent and stable set of objectives must be articulated as a prior and necessary condition of substantive rationality in strategy formulation. In practice this is a very demanding condition. The design school model carries what Narayanan and Fahey describe as the 'microeconomic assumption of a unitary voice within the firm' (1982, p. 25). Mintzberg's observation that responsibility for strategy formulation rests with the chief executive officer supports this contention and simply identifies whose voice in particular carries the unitary authority for determining or expressing the objectives of the enterprise. This unitarist conception of the firm is a prescriptive one which derives its force from a managerial ideology which holds that there is only one set of legitimate interests within an organisation and these are derived from the ownership of the enterprise and implemented by management.

One alternative conception to unitarism is the pluralist view of organisations. This view recognises that organisations are in fact characterised by a diversity of interests. It either recognises each of these as legitimate, or alternatively, recognises diversity only as a matter of fact and does not enter into an ideological judgment regarding their legitimacy. For example, the pluralist view recognises the fact of the aspirations and interests of employees, including collective associations among employees such as trade unions, as well as those of shareholders and management.

Pluralities of interests, or 'multiple stakeholders' as they are described, are nevertheless represented in some marketing texts as constituting part of the external context with which strategy formulation must be concerned. But multiple stakeholders are treated only as a factor to be taken into account in the analysis of the *content* of strategy formulation. The affect of multiple stakeholders on the process of strategy formulation is entirely ignored. Once we admit, however, that multiple stakeholders can influence the process of strategy formulation as well as its content, we must admit that the unitarist assumption governing the single set of explicit, internally consistent and stable set of organisational objectives becomes increasingly untenable.

The design school model, however, presumes the unitarist perspective and takes no account of the implications in practice of the likely existence of dissensus and conflict in the determination either of the enterprise's objectives or its strategies. Again Andrews' lost qualifications are instructive:

> . . . the concept of strategy is no panacea in the inevitability of conflict between corporate and departmental goals and between organisational and personal goals.
>
> (Learned et al. 1969, p. 21)

Andrews' qualifications having been lost, the design school model accepts implictly or uncritically the unitarist conception of the firm.

Organisational decision making

Except in the limited cases of the elementary own person enterprise, and organisations characterised either by absolute consensus or absolute management control, the reconciliation of diverse opinions and the dispersion of power throughout an organisation can only be achieved by political processes.

Piercy found that this political perspective had clear relevance to processes of marketing decision making:

> ... the contingencies typically surrounding marketing decision making were frequently those favouring political behaviour—primarily goal and technology dissensus—and that where those contingencies exist the use of power and politics is inevitably to resolve the conflict implied by the pluralism of interests in organisations.
>
> (1990, p. 30)

There is a marked deficiency of empirical studies investigating processes of marketing decision making in practice. As McDonald found, the marketing literature is dominated by prescriptive rather than descriptive accounts. His conclusion, however, is a telling one:

> A recent study of marketing planning identified only seven UK empirically based studies into the marketing planning practices of commercial organisations, the remaining mass of published materials are largely prescriptive and amount to little more than logically deduced theories based on ungrounded assumptions. Most of the empirical studies concluded that few companies actually practice the theory of marketing planning so prolifically written about.
>
> (McDonald 1992, p. 6)

That the processes of decision making within the organisational context are likely to be characterised by political rather than the comprehensive-rational processes prescribed in the design school model is a conclusion shared by Brunsson (1982, p. 30), Narayan and Fahey (1982, p. 27), Jemison (1981, p. 604), Piercy (1990, p. 27) and Anderson (1988, p. 87).

Alternative models of strategy formation

Political science has informed much debate in the strategic management literature. Indeed the 'political school of strategy formation' constitutes one of the ten schools of strategy formation described by Mintzberg (1990a). The origins of the political perspective can be found in the ideas of Charles Lindblom whose article 'The Science of "Muddling Through"' (1959) challenged the presuppositions of rational models of public policy formulation and implementation. Lindblom described policy formation as emerging from a highly disjointed process in the political context of multiple and competing interest groups, explicitly recognising the impact of multiple stakeholders on the process of policy formation as well as its content. Significantly, emerging policies were seen as the result of compromise between competing positions not only during the deliberative stages of policy formulation but during implementation as well.

To this extent Lindblom's incrementalist model constitutes a positive or descriptive theory of policy formation. But on this understanding he also constructed a normative or prescriptive theory of strategy formation by which he proposed a method of 'successive limited comparisons'. The exigencies of environmental uncertainty and a diversity of competing interests suggests that decision makers should 'move cautiously in small incremental steps, edging forward from historically determined precedents' (Astley et al. 1982, p. 358). This approach has been further developed by Quinn who has prescribed 'logical incrementalism', an alternative model of strategy formation which combines environmental analysis, the recognition of the limits of both analysis and cognitive capacity, and an experimental, learning approach. Organisations 'learn' from formulating and testing incremental changes to strategy.

The model of logical incrementalism may also better describe the nature of marketing management in practice. The design and implementation of grand strategy is likely to be an inaccurate description of marketing practice generally. More typically marketing decisions will relate to incremental changes to strategies already in place. Most decisions will be taken at the margins—discounting in the face of excess stocks, increased advertising, the renegotiation of distribution contracts—rather than the wholesale design *ab initio* of a complete marketing strategy. Even in those circumstances where grand strategy design is appropriate, as in the launching of new products—a new airline or brewery, the practical contingencies of implementation and the pressures of a dynamic environment will mandate incremental changes to the grand design. As Andrews remarked:

> New opportunities, unexpected innovations, sudden emergencies, competitive pressures, and incomplete programming of actions required by the strategy selected all constitute real problems in adhering to a plan once it has been initiated.
>
> (Learned et al. 1969, p. 22)

Logical incrementalism provides an alternative model of strategy formation based on more realistic axioms and a clearer appreciation of the changing environmental and organisational context of strategic decision making. For the marketing discipline it offers the possibility of grafting the valuable content of environmental analysis which marketing has established onto a more realistic and more useful model of the process of strategy formulation. A great deal of work remains to be done, not only in constucting a coherent synthesis but also in the empirical work describing the practice of marketing decision making which is essential to testing the axioms, appropriateness and the practical utility of the model.

Conclusion

Economists are familiar enough with the common complaint, levelled as often as not by practical marketing and strategic management academics, that their theoretical models are based on unrealistic assumptions regarding, for example, the rationality of agents or the nature of competition. Less often, however, do we examine the assumptions on which our own models and prescriptions are based. This is because unlike the economic models, the assumptions of the design school model are tacit ones. Since they have not been articulated in any systematic form they have not been as subject to scrutiny and critique.

In this paper we explored the presumptions and assumptions of the design school model which has informed notions of strategy formulation in marketing for a quarter of a century. A complete understanding of these assumptions is only beginning to emerge in the literature. And for our enlightenment we are indebted to the massive influx of critical ideas from public policy, the decision-sciences, and psychology which has been challenging the prescriptive foundations of strategic management over the last decade.

This critique argues that the design school model is fundamentally flawed with regard to both its substantive and procedural rationality. It takes insufficient account of the limits of our capacity for strategic analysis in the face of a complex and uncertain environment. It prescribes a process of appropriate deliberation which takes no account of goal dissensus and the political processes by which divergence of opinions regarding goals and strategies are reconciled by political rather than 'rational' processes. Any application of the model, therefore, must take into account, as Andrews did, its inherent limitations and the appropriateness of the context of its application. Without such considerations, adherents to the design school can be expected to complain that organisational politics frustrates rational decision making. However, as Simon has remarked:

> an empirical science cannot remake the world to its fancy: it can only describe and explain the world as it is.'
>
> (Simon 1976, p. 146)

References

Anderson, Paul F. (1988), 'Marketing, Strategic Planning and the Theory of the Firm', in Ennis and Cox (eds) *Marketing Classics* (6th edn).

Ansoff, H. Igor (1991), 'Critique of Henry Mintzberg's "The Design School: Reconsidering the Basic Premises of Strategic Management", *Strategic Management Journal*, 12, pp. 449–61.

Astley, W. G., Axelsson, R., Butler, R. J., Hickson, D. and Wilson, D. C. (1982), 'Complexity and Cleavage: Dual Explanations of Strategic Decision-making', *Journal of Management Studies*, 19 (4), pp. 357–75.

Bartels, Robert (1951), 'Influences on the Development of Marketing Thought, 1900–1923, *The Journal of Marketing*, XVI (1) (July), pp. 1–17.

Bartels, Robert (1962), *The Development of Marketing Thought*, Richard D. Irwin Inc, Homewood, Illinois.

Berkowitz, E. N., Kerin, R. A. and Rudelius, W. (1986), *Marketing*, Times Mirror/ Mosby College publishing, St Louis Missouri.

Biggadike, E. Ralph (1981), 'The Contributions of Marketing to Strategic Management', *Academy of Management Review*, **6** (4), pp. 621–32.

Brunnson, Nils (1982), 'The irrationality of Action and Action Rationality: Decisions, Ideologies and Organizational Actions', *Journal of Management Studies*, **19** (1), pp. 29–44.

Busch, P. S. and Houston, M. J. (1985), *Marketing: Strategic Foundations*, Richard D. Irwin, Homewood, Illinois.

Converse, Paul D. (1945), 'The Development of the Science of Marketing—An Exploratory Survey', *The Journal of Marketing*, **10** (July), pp. 14–25

Dickson, Peter Reid (1992), 'Toward a General Theory of Competitive Rationality', *Journal of Marketing*, **56** (January), pp. 69–83.

Firat, A. F., Dholakia, N. and Bagozzi, R. P. (1987), *Philosophical and Radical Thought in Marketing*, Lexington Books, Lexington, Massachusetts.

Fullerton, Ronald A. (1987), 'The Poverty of Ahistorical Analysis: Present Weakness and Future Cure in U.S. Marketing Thought' in *Philosophical and Radical Thought in Marketing*, Firat, Dholakia and Bagozzi (eds), Lexington Books, Lexington, Massachusetts.

Fullerton, Ronald A. (1988), 'Modern Western Marketing as a Historical Phenomenon: Theory and Illustration' in *Historical Perspectives in Marketing*, Nevett and Fullerton (eds) Lexington Books, Lexington, Massachusetts.

Greenley, Gordon E. (1989), 'An Understanding of Marketing Strategy', *European Journal of Marketing*, **23** (8), p. 45.

Gross, C. W. and Peterson, R. (1987), *Marketing Concepts and Decision-making*, West Publishing Company, St Paul, Minnesota.

Jauch, Lawrence R. and Osborn, Richard N. (1981), 'Toward an Integrated Theory of Strategy', *Academy of Management Review*, **6** (3), pp. 491–98.

Jemison, David B. (1981), 'The Importance of an Integrative Approach to Strategic Management Research', *Academy of Management Review*, **6** (4), 601–08.

Jones, D. G. and Monieson, D. D. (1990), 'Early Development of the Philosophy of Marketing Thought', *Journal of Marketing*, **54** (January), pp. 102–13.

Kotler, P., Chandler, P., Gibbs, R. and McColl, R. (1989), *Marketing in Australia* (2nd edn), Prentice Hall, Sydney, Australia.

Lazer, W. and Culley, J. D. (1983), *Marketing Management: Foundations and Practices*, Houghton Mifflin Company, Boston.

Learned, E. P., Christensen, C. R., Andrews, K. R., and Guth, W. D. (1969), *Business Policy: Text and Cases*, (revised edn), Richard D. Irwin Inc, Homewood Illinois, (First edition published 1965).

Lindblom, Charles E. (1959), 'The Science of "Muddling Through"', *Public Administration Review*, **19** (2), pp. 79–88.

McCarthy, E. J. and Perrault, J. R. (1990), *Basic Marketing*, Irwin, Homewood, Illinois.

McColl-Kennedy, J. R., Keil, G., Lusch, R. F. and Lusch, V. N. (1992), *Marketing Concepts and Strategies*, Nelson, South Melbourne, Australia.

McDonald, Malcolm H. B. (1992), 'Ten Barriers to Marketing Planning', *Journal of Business and International Management*, **7** (1) (Winter), pp. 5–18.

Mintzberg, Henry (1990a), 'Strategy Formation: Schools of Thought', in J. W. Frederickson (ed.) *Perspectives on Strategic Management*, Harper Business, New York.

Mintzberg, Henry (1990b), 'The Design School: Reconsidering the Basic Premises of Strategic Management', *Strategic Management Journal*, 11, pp. 171–95.

Narayanan, V. K. and Fahey, L. (1982), 'The Micro-Politics of Strategy Formulation', *Academy of Management Review*, 7 (1), pp. 25–34.

Nevett, Terence (1991), 'Historical Investigation and the Practice of Marketing', *Journal of Marketing*, 55 (July), pp. 13–23.

Piercy, Nigel F. (1989), 'The Power and Politics of Sales Forecasting: Uncertainty Absorption and the Power of the Marketing Department', *Academy of Marketing Science*, 17 (2) (Spring), pp. 109–20.

Piercy, Nigel (1990), 'Marketing Concepts and Actions: Implementing Marketing-led Strategic Change', *European Journal of Marketing*, 24 (2), pp. 24–42.

Ruekert, R. W., Walker, O. C. and Roering, K. J. (1985), 'The Organisation of Marketing Activities: A Contingency Theory of Structure and Performance', *Journal of Marketing*, 49 (Winter), pp. 13–25.

Rumelt, Richard D., Schendel, Dan and Teece, David (1991), 'Strategic Management and Economics', *Strategic Management Journal*, 12, pp, 5–29.

Savitt, Ronald (1987), 'Entrepreneurial Behavior and Marketing Strategy', *Philosophical and Radical Thought in Marketing*, Firat, Dholakia and Bagozzi (eds) Lexington Books, Lexington, Massachusetts..

Schewe, Charles D. (1987), *Marketing Principles and Strategies*, Random House, New York.

Sharp, Byron (1991), 'Competitive Marketing Strategy: Porter Revisited', *Marketing Intelligence and Planning*, 9 (1), 1991, pp. 4–10

Simon, Herbert A. (1955), 'A Behavioural Model of Rational Choice', *Quarterly Journal of Economics*, 6 (4), pp. 99–118.

Simon, Herbert A. (1976), 'From Substantive to Procedural Rationality', in *Method and Appraisal in Economics*, Spiro J. Latsis (ed.), Cambridge University Press, pp. 129–48.

Simon, Herbert A. (1978), 'Rationality as Process and as Product of Thought' *American Economic Review*, 68 (May), pp. 1–16.

Simon, Herbert A. (1979), 'Rational Decision Making in Business Organisations', *American Economic Review*, 69 (September), pp. 493–512.

Stanton, W. J., Miller, K. E. and Layton, R. (1991), *Fundamentals of Marketing* (2nd Australian edn), McGraw-Hill Book Company, Sydney, Australia.

Turnbull, Peter W. (1990), 'A Review of Portfolio Planning Models for Industrial Marketing and Purchasing Management', *European Journal of Marketing*, 24 (3), pp. 7–22.

Tversky, A. and Kahneman, D. (1974), 'Judgement Under Uncertainty: Heuristics and Biases', *Science*, 185, 27 September, 1974.

Tversky, A. and Kahneman, D. (1981), 'The Framing of Decision and the Psychology of Choice', *Science*, 211, 30 January 1981.

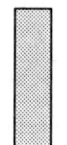

Marketing's domain: A critical review of the development of the marketing concept

by Peter Graham

Abstract

The development of the marketing concept is critically reviewed. Marketing as a discipline is traced from its origins as a business activity to its contemporary position as a generic activity applying to all types of organisations and exchange transactions. In such a broadened domain, the centrality of the customer is questioned as is the nature and extent of the exchange process that takes place. The paper concludes that if the problems addressed by marketing are so universal, if the discipline is now to be seen as so generic, then it may well lose its separate identity.

Introduction

This paper begins with looking to changes in the definition of marketing. It traces marketing's expansion from a discipline concerned with business transactions in an economic market-place, through a discipline concerned with any organisation that can be said to have customers, to a discipline concerned with all organisations in their relationships with all their publics, not just their customers.

Difficulties with this broadened domain of marketing are then reviewed with particular emphasis on the nature and extent of the exchange process which is implicit in the broadened concept of the discipline.

Definitions of marketing

The modern shape of marketing has the exchange process and the transactions that make up that process as its focus (Alderson 1957, p. 15; Bagozzi 1975, p. 39; Kotler 1984, p. 4). Kotler states that exchange is the defining concept underlying marketing. He defines exchange as 'the art of obtaining a desired product from someone by offering something in return' (1988, p. 6). For exchange to take place Kotler believes five conditions must be satisfied:

1. There are at least two parties.
2. Each party has something that might be of value to the other party.
3. Each party is capable of communication and delivery.
4. Each party is free to accept or reject the offer.
5. Each party believes it is appropriate or desirable to deal with the other party.

(Kotler 1988, p. 6).

Marketing therefore comprises the set of activities that facilitate transactions in an exchange economy. The nature and extent of what is understood to be *exchange* is therefore fundamental to understanding the domain of marketing.

The American Marketing Association (AMA) seems to be the self-appointed arbiter of the definition of *marketing*. Certainly in Australia and New Zealand, American texts and definitions dominate study of the discipline in academia. Currently the AMA defines marketing as, 'The process of planning and executing the conception, pricing, promotion and distribution of ideas goods and services to create exchange and satisfy individual and organisational objectives' (*Marketing News*, 1985, p. 1). In this definition, the lack of specificity surrounding both the word *exchange* and the phrase *individual and organisational* is clearly deliberate as it contrasts markedly with the AMA's much narrower 1960 definition. The 1960 definition stated that marketing was, 'The performance of business activities that direct the flow of goods and services from producer to consumer or user' (Committee of Definitions 1960, p. 15). This was not very different from the earlier 1948 definition: 'The performance of business activities directed toward, and incident to, the flow of goods and services from producer to consumer or user' (American Marketing Association 1948).

The 1948 and 1960 definitions reflected marketing's experience, history and origins. Until only a little over 20 years ago, journals, magazines and texts reflected marketing's view of itself as a management technology applicable to the commercially oriented business environment. There were some exceptions to this perspective. For example, in 1931 Breyer devoted a chapter in his marketing textbook to studying public utilities as a market commodity. In 1951 Wiebe had presented provocative ideas and examples of merchandising public issues using marketing communications. In 1967 Beckman and Davidson spoke of the increasing emphasis in the 1960s on marketing as a social process.

Broadening the domain of marketing

In 1969 a wider definition of marketing was articulated (Kotler & Levy 1969) and this was further extended by Kotler in 1972. Kotler and Levy argued for a dramatically broadened conceptual domain for marketing from the business activity it had hitherto been, to 'a pervasive societal activity that goes considerably beyond the selling of toothpaste, soap and steel' (Kotler & Levy 1969, p. 10). Kotler and Levy felt the business heritage of marketing provided a useful set of concepts for guiding all organisations whether profit-oriented or not and whether involved in marketing toothpaste or persons and ideas. In fact they felt the choice facing managers in non-business organisations was not whether to use marketing or not but whether to use it 'well or poorly' (Kotler & Levy 1969, p. 15).

In support of this all-inclusive view of marketing, Kotler and Levy used examples of a police department developing a campaign to 'win friends and influence people'; a museum director sponsoring contemporary art shows and 'happenings' to broaden the museum's appeal; a public school system using television to dramatise its work in order to increase support for what it was doing to fight the high school drop-out problem, to develop new teaching techniques and to enrich the children; the junta of

Greek Colonels who seized power in Greece in 1967 hiring a major New York public relations firm to arrange for newspapers to carry full page advertisements proclaiming, 'Greece was saved from Communism', and detailing in small print why the take-over was necessary for the stability of Greece and the world; and the anti-cigarette group in Canada who came up with innovative ways to use their limited funds (Kotler & Levy 1969, p. 11).

Using these examples and broadened conceptual boundaries, the authors proudly proclaimed that 'marketing has taken a new lease on life and tied its economic activity to a higher social purpose' (Kotler & Levy 1969, p. 15). One eminent marketing academic was quick to attempt to temper such ambitious claims. He was concerned that when views were propounded by such prominent authors as Kotler and Levy their uncritical acceptance seemed likely, so contrary opinions needed a vigorous voice (Luck 1969). Luck's contention was that whilst Kotler and Levy were implicitly asking for a redefinition of marketing, they did not explicitly offer one. Indeed Luck maintained that if a definition were framed to meet Kotler and Levy's contentions:

> marketing no longer would be bounded in terms of either institutions or the ultimate purpose of its activities. If a task is performed, anywhere by anybody, that has some resemblance to a task performed in marketing, that would be marketing.
>
> (Luck 1969, p. 53).

Apart from marketers self-image being 'pleasurably inflated', Luck saw little to be gained from such reasoning. However, his attempt to be a vigorous voice of dissent did not prove successful. In hindsight it is embarrassing to observe the uncritical haste with which marketing academics embraced this radically new conceptualisation of their discipline. The 1970 Autumn Conference of the American Marketing Association was given over to discussing marketing's new-found role and social purpose. The *Journal of Marketing* issue of July 1971 was devoted exclusively to 'Marketing's Changing Social/Environmental Role', with no published article voicing significant dissent from Kotler and Levy's proposition.

One of the articles in that 1971 edition of the *Journal of Marketing* specifically examined how marketing concepts and techniques could be effectively applied to the promotion of social objectives such as brotherhood, safe driving and family planning (Kotler & Zaltman 1971). The authors claimed to show how social causes could be advanced more successfully through applying principles of marketing analysis, planning and control to problems of social change. The question Wiebe raised in 1952, 'Why can't you sell brotherhood like you sell soap?' (Wiebe, 1951–52, p. 679), was simplistically answered, *you can*. This further extended the domain of marketing to include not only non-business and non-profit organisations involved in bilateral exchange processes, but organisations involved in planning and implementing social change.

The irony here is that this further extension, whilst perhaps pandering to the needs of those who feel that marketing cannot be socially useful if it confines itself to business activities, violates the fundamental premise of the *marketing concept* which had emerged in the 1950s with a *consumer* orientation as its base. The marketing concept contrasted with the *selling* orientation that had preceded it and the *production* orientation that is said to have been the 1930s model of marketing. In the terms of the *marketing concept*, the customer is central and organisations meet their objectives by discovering and staying in touch with their potential customers needs and wants and then satisfying them by producing an appropriate product.

However, in programmes of planned social change, it is very rarely the *customers* or target market(s) whose views on their needs and wants are sought. It is usually the views of those in positions of power, influence and sometimes knowledge, who *know what is best* for the target market, or what the target market really needs or wants, or ought to want. In such programmes, products are not modified to make them acceptable to the target market, as happens in the economic exchanges of the business market, but efforts are redoubled to make the target market better understand what is good or best for them. In writing a text on *Strategic Marketing for Not-for-Profit Organisations*, Lauffer gives specific examples from his own experience as a social worker to support this view (Lauffer 1984). He points out that many social workers begin with the assumption that their products, the services provided, are in the best interests of the public. They assume that there is a need (even if sometimes there is no demand) for the services provided, simply because they are convinced that they are good for people (Lauffer 1984, p. xii).

> I remember working for a family service agency in which everyone's problems were defined in psycho-analytic terms the moment the client walked through the front door. It didn't matter what clients asked for—housing, guidance in coping with an ageing parent, or help with a child who suffered from a learning disability. The agency's "products", its analytically oriented counselling services, were considered by the staff to be just what the client needed. Staff then set about shaping the client's perceptions about his or her needs according to the agency's definition of its services, and educating the client to make effective use of those services.
> (Lauffer 1984, pp. xii–xiii)

Many other contemporary examples spring to mind such as economical driving, safe sex and self-examination for cancerous growths. The needs and wants of those who enjoy accelerating away from traffic lights, or who wish to continue what are considered by some to be promiscuous or deviant sexual practices, or who do not wish to know they have a malignant tumour, are *not* central to the relevant programme of social change. The needs and wants of such persons may well need to be modified for the greater good of society or some other social, moral or economic purpose. Whatever justification for such activity, it is not an arena where the marketing concept is applied.

However, 20 years ago such reasoning did not impede the rush to accept the proposed extensions to marketing's domain. Following the conference of the American Marketing Association in 1970 and the 1971 *Journal of Marketing* devoted to the expansion theme, one of the original authors of the article that started it all published a further paper arguing that the 1969 broadening proposal's main weakness was not that it went too far but that it did not go far enough (Kotler 1972). Kotler claimed that marketing should be expanded to include the transactions between any organisation and all its publics. This was a significant extension from the 1969 view that marketing was a relevant discipline for all organisations that have customers and products (Kotler & Levy 1969).

Kotler described marketing in three stages of consciousness. Consciousness One related to the pre-1969 articulation of marketing being essentially a business subject composed of market transactions. Consciousness Two was really the 1969 articulation of marketing being appropriate for all organisations that have customers, and comprised organisation-client transactions. Consciousness Three is the generic and now conventional view of marketing being appropriate for all organisations in their relations not only with their customers but with all their publics. The core concept in Consciousness Three is *transactions* and therefore marketing is said to apply to any social unit seeking to exchange values with other social units (Kotler, 1972).

Some concerns with the broadened concept

Other concerns were voiced at this broadened concept in addition to Luck's immediate response to Kotler's 1969 article referred to earlier in this article. Enis (1973) also responded to Kotler's argument for further expansion with a wish to *deepen* rather than *broaden* the concept of marketing. He listed the following activities, which Kotler and Levy might argue are activities within the scope of marketing and which Luck would probably maintain are beyond marketing's proper domain:

- A financial vice-president seeks a loan from a bank.
- A merchant bribes a government official.
- A graduate student seeks a fellowship.
- A man endeavours to win a woman's heart.
- Reverend Billy Graham holds a revival.
- An insurance agent is active in his church or civic club.

(Enis 1973, p. 57)

In his analysis, Enis points out that marketing has traditionally connoted an exchange relationship between buyers and sellers of economic goods and services. Kotler and Levy emphasise that it is the notion of *exchange* rather than the economic basis for the relationship that is central to the concept of marketing. Exchange is the process of satisfying human wants *via trade* (barter, swap, purchase, lease and so on) as opposed to other methods of want satisfaction, such as origination, force or gift (Enis, 1973).

Enis goes on to summarise the counter-arguments to the generic concept of marketing which he sees as threefold. First, that marketing, like any other discipline, has a traditional domain, the boundaries of which should be respected. Thus, studies of the bribery of public officials belong to the discipline of political science, and loan procurement is the province of finance. Second, that activities should be studied from the perspective of their primary function. In this view, the purposes of the graduate student and the suitor are not primarily economic. Although market transactions may be involved in such activities, they are incidental to the primary function of the activity. Third, that transactions where the exchange cannot be accurately determined should be excluded from the domain of marketing. Thus Billy Graham's requests for donations or the insurance agent's services to his church or club lack a specific, determinable return (Enis, 1973).

Whilst *broadening the concept of marketing* was seen by Enis as a significant contribution to the development of the discipline, he did not see it as straightforward as it first appeared. Rather he saw it as multidimensional. Broadening the nature of the *product* exchanged from economic goods and services to anything of value; broadening the *objective* of the exchange from profit to any type of payoff; and broadening the *target audience* of the exchange from consumer to any 'public' that relates to an organisation (Enis 1973, p. 59). Enis did not object to the broadened concept of marketing *per-se*, but felt that to be meaningful and useful it would have to be more comprehensive, better integrated, and communicated with greater clarity. This he called deepening (Enis 1973, p. 62).

Bartels (1974) traced the evolution of marketing through various distinct phases since the turn of the century. He saw marketing as originally concerned with the distribution of products and wondered if marketing was now to be regarded as so broad that perhaps marketing as originally conceived would ultimately reappear under another name, possibly *logistics* or *physical distribution*. Specifically, Bartels saw the following disadvantages to broadening the concept of marketing:

- At a time when many problems of physical distribution are calling for solution, the broadened concept has turned attention away from these problems to non-business interests.
- Methodology has to some extent replaced substance as the content of marketing knowledge.
- Forms of decision making have become more important than knowledge of the subject about which decisions are made.
- Literature has become increasingly esoteric, abstract, and unintelligible to many business practitioners.
- Graduate marketing education has excluded, presuming foreknowledge, much factual content concerning markets and product marketing.
- Undergraduate programmes, as provided for by numerous textbooks, have become managerial, behavioural and quantitative.

(Bartels 1974, p. 76)

In addressing what he called 'the proper conceptual domain of marketing', Hunt (1991) commented on this broadening of the concept of marketing. Whilst agreeing that the advocates of extending the notion of marketing had won the semantic battle, he felt their efforts had not been victimless (Hunt 1991, p. 8). In support he cites Carman (1973, p. 14) as noting that the definition of marketing plays a significant role in directing the research efforts of marketers. Carman believes that many processes, for example political processes, do not involve an exchange of values and that marketing should not take such processes under its 'disciplinary wing' (Hunt 1991, p. 8).

Tucker (1974) explicitly attacked Kotler's generic concept as a foundation for theory. Whilst he felt that there was little harm involved in thinking of a churchgoer as a consumer of religion or a teacher as a salesman of mathematics, he considered it sensible to ask what marketing theory could derive from an intensive study of religious practices or educational efforts.

> Marketing is heavily concerned with economic rationality in terms of store location, advertising effectiveness, merchandise assortments, pricing policies, inventory management, sales territories, and the like. Relatively prompt and specific consumer satisfaction characterizes the great majority of transactions.
>
> (Tucker 1974, p. 32)

Despite these comments, the broadened conceptual domain that constitutes the *generic concept of marketing* has become the dominant paradigm in the marketing discipline. As early as 1974 a survey of randomly selected professors of marketing showed an overwhelming acceptance, over 92%, of the proposition that the concept of marketing should be expanded to include the marketing of schools, charities, politicians and other non-business activities (Nickels 1974). The survey also showed that marketing professors wanted a broader definition than *market transactions*. Specifically the professors wanted emphasis placed in introductory marketing classes on transactions that further the goals of churches, schools, charities and other social causes (Nickels 1974, p. 141).

> More than 90% of the responding professors agreed that the marketing concept should be broadened to include the efforts of non-business organisations to satisfy society's needs.
>
> (Nickels 1974, p. 142)

Some authors went further and asserted that marketing would have to become vitally concerned with human welfare rather than economic gain, and with the broader needs, aspirations, and potentialities of society rather than merely with the problems of competition, sales volume and profit (Shuptrine et al, 1975, p. 65).

Foxall acknowledges the dominance of the generic concept of marketing but is critical of the usefulness of the concept as it is based on the notion of *exchange*. He believes that:

> the concept of marketing as a process of matching—of aligning the relationships between organisations and/or individuals—may provide a more coherent framework for any extended concept of the marketing function and marketing oriented management.
>
> (Foxall 1989, p. 8–9)

Although marketing academics have accepted the broadened and socially useful concept of marketing, the literature acknowledges that 'it is more difficult to sell brotherhood than soap' (Rothschild 1979; Bloom & Novelli 1981; Barach 1984).

This is an acknowledgement that the extension of marketing's domain may not be without difficulties.

The mainstream of marketing literature is not concerning itself with whether it is appropriate or useful to extend the marketing concept but with trying to identify why, when marketing is extended beyond its traditional domain, it seems to be more difficult to implement. A noticeable exception is in Part I of the volume edited by Mokwa and Permut where at least an attempt was made to raise the conceptual question of whether a more conscious marketing perspective is truly appropriate for government (Mokwa & Permut, 1981, p. xiv). However, the question normally addressed is why is it harder to sell brotherhood than soap?

> As marketing has formally extended the boundaries of its discipline to encompass the public and third sectors, tools and techniques of market programming and research and the impediments to their imple-mentation have been the overwhelming concerns.
> (Mokwa & Permut 1981, p. 17)

The implicit assumption underpinning the generic concept of marketing is that it applies to exchanges of all kinds not just economic exchanges in a market-place.

Marketing as exchange

The core concept of marketing is the exchange process (Bagozzi 1975, p. 32; Kotler 1988, p. 6). On this there is little contention. However, there has been debate about the nature and extent of the exchange process that is in consonance with marketing. Kotler, concomitant with his generic concept of marketing, gives a broad interpretation as to what constitutes an exchange process to which the marketing discipline applies. He specifically includes as market transactions such examples as a church providing religious services for its members and a donor providing money or service to a charity (Kotler 1988, p. 8). Bagozzi supports Kotler's broad interpretation and describes three types of exchanges; restricted, generalised and complex (Bagozzi 1975, p. 32). *Restricted exchange* is defined as two party reciprocal relationships:

> Most treatments of, and references to, exchanges in the marketing literature have implicitly dealt with restricted exchanges; that is they have dealt with customer-salesman, wholesaler-retailer, or such other dyadic exchanges.
> (Bagozzi 1975, p. 32)

Generalised exchange is defined by Bagozzi as univocal, reciprocal relationships among at least three actors in an exchange relationship. To illustrate his definition, he uses the example of a public bus company asking a local department store to give a number of benches to the bus company to be placed at bus stops for the convenience of its passengers. Advertisements placed on the benches by the department store persuade the passengers to patronise the store (Bagozzi 1975, p. 33). *Complex exchange* is defined by Bagozzi as a system of mutual relationships between at least three parties. To illustrate this exchange he refers to a distribution channel consisting of a manufacturer, a retailer and a consumer. The three together form an exchange system but individually the manufacturer *exchanges* with the retailer who *exchanges* with the customer (Bagozzi 1975, p. 33).

Bagozzi goes on to argue that each type of exchange can have one of three classes of meanings; utilitarian, symbolic or mixed (Bagozzi 1975, p. 35). *Utilitarian exchange* is more usually referred to as economic exchange where goods are given in return for money or other goods and is the traditional domain of marketing. *Symbolic exchange* extends to the mutual transfer of psychological, social, or other intangible entities. A *mixed exchange* involves aspects of both utilitarian and symbolic transfers.

Bagozzi is quite explicit in including social relationships, as opposed to economic relationships, within the ambit of marketing. He sees social marketing as a subset of the generic concept of marketing, addressing how exchanges are created and resolved in social relationships such as family planning agent—client; welfare agent—indigent, social worker—poor person, and so on (Bagozzi 1975, p. 36). He is emphatic that exchanges exist in social marketing relationships but suggests that such exchanges are usually generalised or complex exchanges rather than the simple *quid pro quo* notion characteristic of most economic exchanges. Bagozzi then goes further and asserts the universal applicability of marketing as the discipline of exchange behaviour:

> It is not so much that the subject matter of marketing overlaps with that of other disciplines as it is that the problems of marketing are universal.
> (Bagozzi 1975, p. 38)

Laczniak and Michie point out some of the problems with such a universal territory claim, calling it, 'the ultimate illustration of empire building' (1979, p. 228). They maintain that the widespread acceptance and practice of broadened marketing has the potential to damage the reputation of the marketing discipline as the discipline is unlikely to be able to sustain playing, 'the role of a symbolic Atlas with the weight of the world upon its theoretical shoulders' (1979, p. 226). If marketing embraces all kinds of exchanges, then everyone is a 'marketer' because virtually everyone engages in some social exchanges.

Foxall also takes issue with this broad interpretation of a market exchange. He argues that, 'Social marketing, which confuses relationships with exchanges, renders the market-place redundant; it has no place for consumers' choice or for the functions of a market mechanism' (Foxall 1989, p. 19).

Luck has a much narrower definition than Kotler or Bagozzi of the scope of exchanges that are properly within marketing's domain. For example, Luck could not be expected to accept Bagozzi's assertion that marketing exchanges take place in social relationships 'where there is no established price or terms of sale and no specific *quid pro quo*' (Luck 1969, p. 54). In fact Luck was quite specific in stating that marketing was only appropriate where the exchange process result is a *market transaction* (Luck 1969, p. 54). Attenuating the definition of marketing to make it almost universal would, Luck argued, result in marketing losing its identity.

This debate on trying to limit the nature of exchanges that are properly within the domain of marketing has also been won by the expansionists in the discipline. The generic concept of marketing applying to all types of organisations and all types of exchanges is now uncritically portrayed in all the popular marketing texts used to introduce study of the subject. Even its critics acknowledge that: 'the extended concept of marketing has clearly emerged over the last 15 years as an idea whose time has come' (Foxall 1989, p. 9).

Summary

This paper has highlighted the almost embarassing haste with which marketing academics rushed to embrace the dramatic extensions to the discipline's domain articulated by Kotler and others just over 20 years ago. Some key problems have been reviewed, particularly difficulties with the central role of the customer and the nature and extent of the exchange process which the broadened concept implies.

Perhaps more fundamental than the problems traversed here is the confusion and difficulty caused to the development of the discipline's theory by such significant territory claims. As a relatively young academic discipline marketing has a long way to go in developing a sound and coherent theoretical framework. It does not help to claim that marketing is everything, because then it is nothing. If marketing is as generic as its contemporary literature suggests, then it may well lose its separate and specific identity.

References

Alderson, W. (1957), *Marketing Behaviour and Executive Action*, Irwin, Homewood, Illinois.
American Marketing Association (1948), 'Report of the Definitions Committee,' *Journal of Marketing*, 13 (October), pp. 202–10.
Bagozzi, R. P. (1975), 'Marketing as Exchange', *Journal of Marketing*, 39 (October), pp. 32–39.
Barach, J. B. (1984), 'Applying Marketing Principles to Social Causes', *Business Horizons*, July/August, pp. 65–69.
Bartels, R. (1974), 'The Identity Crisis in Marketing', *Journal of Marketing*, 38 (October), pp. 73–76.
Beckman, T. N. and Davidson, W. R. (1967), *Marketing*, Ronald Press Co., New York.
Bloom, P. and Novelli, W. (1981), 'Problems and Challenges in Social Marketing', *Journal of Marketing*, 45 (Spring), pp. 79–88.
Breyer, R. F. (1931), *Commodity Marketing*, McGraw-Hill, New York.
Carman, J. M. (1973), 'On the Universality of Marketing', *Journal of Contemporary Business*, 2 (Autumn), pp. 1–16.
Committee on Definitions (1960), *Marketing Definitions: A Glossary of Marketing Terms*, American Marketing Association, Chicago.

Enis, B.M. (1973), 'Deepening the Concept of Marketing', *Journal of Marketing*, 37, pp. 57–62.

Foxall, G. (1989), 'Marketing's Domain', *European Journal of Marketing*, 23 (8), pp. 7–22.

Hunt, S. D. (1991), *Modern Marketing Theory*, South Western Publishing Co., Ohio.

Kotler, P. (1972), 'A Generic Concept of Marketing', *Journal of Marketing*, 36 (April), pp. 46–54.

Kotler, P. (1984), *Marketing Management: Analysis, Planning and Control*, Prentice Hall, New Jersey.

Kotler, P. (1988), *Marketing Management: Analysis, Planning, Implementation and Control*, Prentice Hall, New Jersey.

Kotler, P. and Levy, S. J. (1969), 'Broadening the Concept of Marketing', *Journal of Marketing*, 33 (January), pp. 10–15.

Kotler, P. and Roberto, E. L. (1989), *Social Marketing: Strategies for Changing Public Behaviour*, The Free Press, New York.

Kotler, P. and Zaltman, G. (1971) 'Social Marketing: An Approach to Planned Social Change', *Journal of Marketing*, 35 (July), pp. 3–12.

Laczniak, G. R. and Michie, D. A. (1979), 'The Social Disorder of the Broadened Concept of Marketing', *Journal of Academy of Marketing Science*, 7 (3) (Summer), pp. 214–232.

Lauffer, A. (1984), *Strategic Marketing for Not-for-profit Organisations*, The Free Press, New York.

Luck, D. J. (1969), 'Broadening the Concept of Marketing—Too Far', *Journal of Marketing*, 33 (July), pp. 53–55.

Marketing News (1985), 'AMA Board Approves New Marketing Definition', No. 5, 1st March.

McKenna, R. (1991), 'Marketing is Everything', *Harvard Business Review*, January–February, pp. 65–79.

Mokwa, M. P. (1981), 'Government Marketing: An Inquiry Into Theory, Process, and Perspective', in Mockwa, M. P. and Permut, S. E. (eds), (1981), *Government Marketing: Theory and Practice*, Praeger Publishing, New York, pp. 17–35.

Mockwa, M. P. and Permut, S. E. (Eds), (1981), *Government Marketing: Theory and Practice*, Praeger Publishing, New York.

Nickels, W. G. (1974), 'Conceptual Conflicts in Marketing', *Journal of Economics and Business*, 27 (Winter), pp. 140–143.

O'Faircheallaigh, C., Graham, P. and Warburton, J. (1991), *Service Delivery and Public Sector Marketing*, McMillan & Co., Sydney.

Rothschild, M. L. (1979), 'Marketing Communications in Nonbusiness Situations, or Why It's so Hard to Sell Brotherhood Like Soap', *Journal of Marketing*, 43 (Spring), pp. 11–20.

Shuptrine, F. K. and Osmanski, F. A. (1975), 'Marketing's Changing Role: Expanding or Contracting?', *Journal of Marketing*, 39 (April), pp. 58–66.

Wiebe, G. D. (1951–52), 'Merchandising Commodities and Citizenship on Television', *Public Opinion Quarterly*, 15 (Winter), pp. 679–691.

Reproduced with permission from *Marketing Bulletin*, Vol. 4, No. 1, 1993.

Most service quality research is wrong

by Chuck Chakrapani

If a manufacturer sells a product and if a service organisation markets a service, should the principles of research apply equally to both? Why do we need a different set of principles to research service quality?

Product research has two major aspects:

1. Is the product 'good' from an objective point of view?
2. Is the product perceived to be good from a subjective point of view?

The first aspect—is the product objectively good—can be answered by objective tests. It is easy to decide whether a product is delivering what it is supposed to deliver. A car's fuel efficiency can be tested, and so can the cleaning power of a detergent. The second aspect—consumer's perception of the product—can also be tested fairly easily through marketing research. The emotional benefits of some products can be difficult to assess through survey methods. For instance, a person may be reluctant to admit to driving a BMW to impress others. But such benefits are relatively easy to identify through other methods such as qualitative research.

Service quality cannot be assessed by either of the above two methods. First, a service cannot be tested in the same way as a product. How does one measure whether X amount of courtesy and Y amount of flexibility were delivered to the customer? The second aspect—customer perception—often cannot be measured satisfactorily thorough traditional research methods.

Why is this so? There are at least three major reasons why traditional research can be misleading.

1. *Regression towards the mean*: When consumers are presented with no alternatives, they tend to accept what is available as the standard. Customer ratings will be inflated as a result.

If, for instance, customers get poor service from *all* financial institutions, then poor service becomes the norm for the industry. Scores will 'regress to the mean'. Consider a situation in which customers have a choice of several institutions, ranging from mediocre to excellent. On a ten-point scale, mediocre institutions may score an average of about two or three. Excellent institutions may score an average of about seven or eight. But when all institutions offer mediocre service, the scores will cluster around the midpoint of the scale. Institutions that are marginally better may get a score of seven or eight. This commonly observed 'regression towards the mean' phenomenon results in inflated scores of satisfaction.

2. *Artifact of satisfied customers*: Any service industry will automatically generate a segment of satisfied customers. Average customer satisfaction ratings will increase as a result.

All customers do not expect or need the same level of service. The level of service expected by some customers (in most service industries) is so minimal, that they are satisfied with just minimal service. For instance, in rural areas, many people may use their banks once or twice a month. They may not be pressured for time and they may know everyone at the bank well. If they wait 20 minutes, if the staff are not very knowledgeable or if the bank made a mistake—none of these problems may really matter to the customer. The customer doesn't care if the staff is not knowledgeable—he or she does not need their service anyway. Service charges do not matter because they do not apply to this customer. The customer is happy with the service received.

3. *Perception is limited by current framework*: Customers do not normally think outside the current framework when asked what they would ideally like.

It is difficult to find out from customers what would constitute 'service quality'. It is not that customers do not want to tell the researcher, but simply that they do not know. Let us consider a few examples: A few years ago, when customers were asked what they ideally expected from their bank, they seldom mentioned 'flexible hours'. Now many more customers are 'satisfied' with inflexible hours. When customers go into a bank or a trust company, they fill in a deposit or withdrawal slip. The teller repeats this process in the computer. It is not clear why the customer has to fill in the form. Couldn't the teller simply print out a receipt from the computer and ask the customer to sign? The customer will be unlikely to mention this issue, because it is 'given', it is always done. It does not occur to the customer that this process could be a vestige of the pre-computer era. Why should it? The idea had not occurred to the people who operate the system.

The three factors described above may interact to inflate customer satisfaction scores in the following manner:

1. Let's start with service quality which has a 'true' rating of three, on a ten-point scale where ten is high and one is low.
2. Because all institutions in the category offer service quality, the actual ratings 'regress towards the mean'. The average moves up to five.
3. Let us assume that such ratings follow the normal curve. This would mean that a certain proportion of your customers will be very dissatisfied and a certain proportion of your customers will be satisfied, for no specific and identifiable reason. Let us further assume that about 5% of your customers are very satisfied.
4. Let us further assume that 25% of your customers do not need or expect a high quality of service. They will also be 'satisfied customers'.
5. Because customers in (3) and (4) are happy with the institution, they might give it an average rating of eight. Because 40% of the respondents gave a rating of eight, the overall average moves up to about six.
6. If you are marginally better than average, one or two rating points will be added to the average, resulting in an average rating of seven or eight.

An average score of seven or eight might seem high and lead you to believe that customers are very satisfied with your institution. Yet, as we saw, all this might mean is that the institution is mediocre, perhaps marginally better than the competition. The faulty understanding of customer satisfaction obtained through traditional research methods creates weak links in the model management uses to communicate about service quality.

The problems described above do not arise in product testing. Certainly if all products are equally unsatisfactory there will be a regression towards the mean. But the objective qualities of a product can be independently tested and improved without reference to customers. A product can be improved in a laboratory. A service cannot be meaningfully enhanced without reference to customers. Second, poor service is not always transferred to the product. For example, if you like a particular car, but do not like the service you get from the dealer, you can buy the same car from a different dealer. It is different with service. If you are unhappy with a bank, for example, you're unlikely to go to another branch of the same bank. You are more likely to go to a different bank altogether. Third, there are fewer 'moments-of-truth' for a product than for a service. 'Moments-of-truth' is a concept used by Jan Carlzon of the Scandinavian Airline Systems (SAS). Any contact between an employee of an organisation and a customer constitutes a 'moment-of-truth'.

Any of these encounters, however brief, give a customer the opportunity to make up his of her mind about the organisation. These are the 'moments-of-truth'. Such 'moments of truth' may start with insufficient parking spots, and continue with a number of trivial things; pens at the counter that do not write, a dirty office, illogical signs and so on. These 'moments-of-truth' considerations are somewhat less relevant to the marketing of a product. There are many more differences between product and service quality research.

Service quality research, to be effective, should address three problems:

1. The inability of customers to articulate needs that go beyond the current framework.
2. The inability of traditional research to identify impediments to service that arise out of systems that are already in place.
3. The need to overcome the artificially high score on satisfaction measures and to identify the source and nature of service quality problems.

Are there methods that fulfil these conditions? The answer is yes. Yet, paradoxically, the methods are not new. They have all been used in product research in different ways. The only difference is that these methods are chosen and used with specific purposes and in specific ways to overcome the limitations of run-of-the-mill service quality research.

Reproduced with permission from *Marketing*, July 1992, pp. 17–19.

How manipulanda and discriminanda can builda your branda

by Stan Glaser, Michael Halliday and Ross Cameron

What does value-added mean? How do you do it? In this paper academics Stan Glaser, Michael Halliday, and Ross Cameron find the answer in psychological theories from the 1930s.

The Western focus on product differentiation contrasts with the approach of Japanese marketers who have taken literally the notion of value-added. This difference helps to explain differing performance and arises from the lack of framework for understanding how people relate to products.

Both the practice and teaching of marketing are prone to the same fads and fashions found in the markets for consumer goods. A recent vogue has been to focus on the concept of *excellence*, no more than an exhortation that some basic level of competence in business management is to be desired. What was largely ignored however, was how one might actually achieve excellence.

The latest vogue in Australian management circles appears to be the notion of 'value-added'. Here too the procedures whereby one might actually add value are at best dimly discussed as is judgment as to what value is, and how it might actually be added. Anecdotal evidence is generally the total extent of evidence as to marketers' achievements in adding value to products. Marketing educators approach or avoid the problem of providing such evidence by stressing the need for differentiation and the creativity fundamental to achieving this end.

However, this academic perspective neglects a more fundamental issue: is there a framework within which substantive meaning can be given to the push for 'value-added'? This quest is far from trivial: for example, Kotler and Levy (1969) talk about 'ideas marketing'. They instance family planning organisations trying to 'sell the idea of birth control' and temperance groups advocating 'the idea of prohibition'. What 'ideas' represent in a practical, operational sense is not made clear. What Kotler and Levy seem to have said is that 'intangibles' can be marketed, and through some process value can presumably be added to these ideas.

This problem has been addressed, but not in the management literature. Psychologists Tolman and Brunswick (1939) attempted to understand the interaction of people with their environment and answer the question: how are the objects in the environment co-ordinated with an individual's goals or purposes? They used the generic term, *behaviour objects* to refer to any perceived object which affords the possibility of satisfying some consumer need or want.

This view of a behavioural object corresponds to the definition of a product in marketing theory. Later works, such as Lancaster's 'Goods aren't goods', seem to have gone largely unnoticed but were concerned '. . . (with) . . . breaking away from the traditional approach that goods are direct objects of utility and, instead, supposing that it is the *properties or characteristics of the goods from which utility is derived*'.

In considering any behaviour object, such as a product or service, there are three aspects of the object which need to be considered. The first Tolman and Brunswick call the *discriminanda* properties of the object, those aspects of the object which are the direct causes of immediate sensory cues: the object's colour, shape, texture, size and so on, the most visible means by which one differentiates between objects.

Next are the *manipulanda* properties of the object, the properties which make possible and support actual behavioural manipulations. These include the object's grasp-ableness, pick-up-ableness, chew-ableness, sit-on-ableness, run-through-ableness and the like.

The final property identified, similar to the notion of utility in economic theory, embraces the object's *utilitanda*: '. . . the ways in which the object, given its *manipulanda*, or its *manipulanda* and *discriminanda* combined, can be useful as a means of getting further objects and goals . . . a behaviour-object such as a piece of chocolate will have, by virtue of its *manipulanda* character as something chewable, the *utilitanda* character of something that will lead towards a full stomach'.

The 'utilities' Tolman and Brunswick speak of are derived from the interaction of the *manipulanda* and *discriminanda* components. Thus *utilitanda* is in a sense a derived dimension. Further, these dimensions are part of the same set: changes on one dimension impact, to a greater or lesser degree, on the standing that the object has on the other two dimensions.

Conceptually the relationships can be depicted in three-dimensional space as in Figure D1.3.

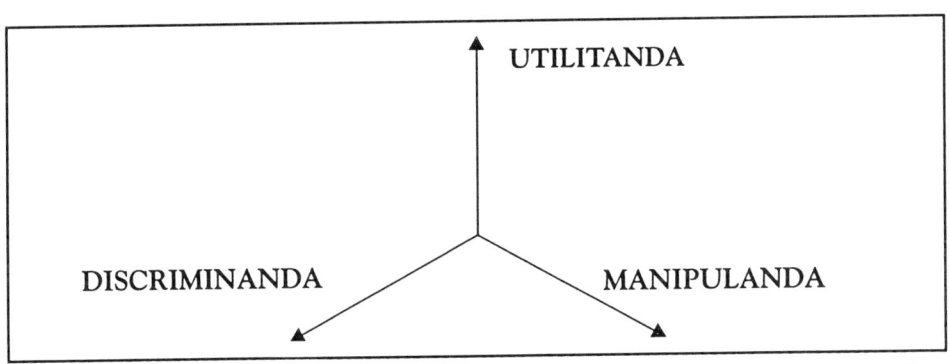

Figure D1.3 *In 1935, psychologists Tolman and Brunswick decided people experience objects along three dimensions: discriminanda (colour, shape, size, etc), manipulanda (feel, taste, smell, etc) and utilitanda (benefits derived from the two other dimensions).*

It is possible to position a good or service within this space. However this perspective goes further than conventional 'positioning' exercises because it reflects the character of the object, such as its rating on attitude scales. Moreover, it reflects the complex relationships between the total perception of the object and the ways in which these perceptions or judgments may be modified.

For instance, flavoured milk has been a familiar and satisfying product to significant numbers of Australians for decades. In recent years milk marketing authorities introduced branded flavoured milk to the Australian market using brand-names such as 'Big-M' and 'Moove'. Prior to these innovations, flavoured milk was low on both the *manipulanda* and *discriminanda* dimensions as depicted in Figure D1.4. To most consumers flavoured milk was simply a commodity or an undifferentiated product. The behaviour of the marketers of this commodity—flavoured milk—suggested they too saw it as an undifferentiated product. Introducing branded milk, and thereby avoiding use of the label 'milk' had marked effects on consumer evaluations of these new products, as shown below.

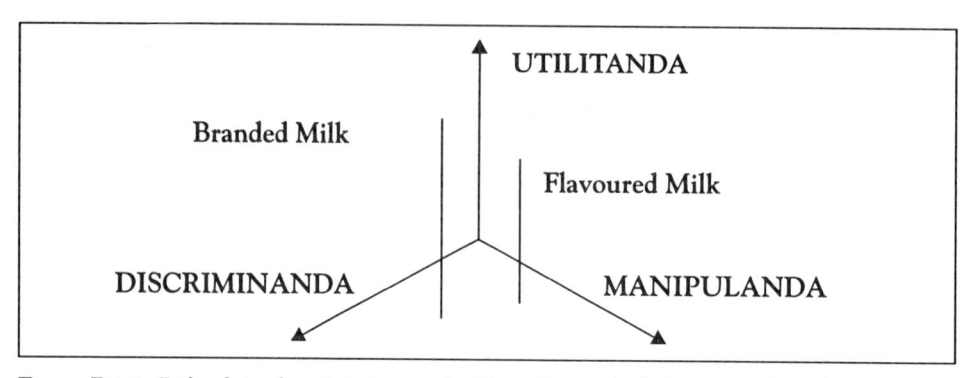

Figure D1.4 *Before being branded, flavoured milk was low on both discriminanda and manipulanda dimensions.*

Despite the fact that all that had been changed with the addition of a brand and promotion and packaging modifications, consumers evaluated 'Big-M' and 'Moove' in interesting novel ways. The taste of these branded products was described as different from flavoured milk although there was, at the earliest stages of their introduction, no change in the formulation at all. Promotion efforts had been directed at placing these branded milk products in an outdoors, active lifestyle context, positioning them against Coca-Cola. Moove in early 1991 enjoys a beverages market share second only to Coca-Cola.

In the process of these changes taking place, branding had imparted greater *utilitanda* to flavoured milk for largely psychological, rather than substantive reasons. It can be argued that consumers saw Big M and Moove as being more compatible with their 'ideal' selves and this increased their propensity to buy and consume these brands.

Value was added cosmetically, synthetically, through branding, packaging and advertising. This encapsulates the Western perspective on marketing strategy. In this view, marketing is concerned with changing the meaning of objects, with modifying perceptions or repositioning products and services. Value-addition flows from changing cognitions about products, rather than changing the reality of the product offer.

In Tolman and Brunswick's terms, much of modern marketing effort focuses on movement along the *discriminanda* dimension. Such a perspective is in stark contrast to that in Japan. There, value-adding is more likely to be seen to flow from value analysis and value engineering. This is most notable in Japanese efforts at miniaturisation in manufactured goods, which represents considerable emphasis on the *manipulanda* dimension. The problems Honda motor vehicles have recently experienced in the Japanese market have been attributed to what Japanese consumers presumably see as excessive concern with appearances with little or no functional improvement.

Returning to Kotler and Levy's argument about the marketing of ideas, we can now address the notion of what an idea represents within the framework above. By their nature, ideas are in the minds of the market and represent aspects of the *utilitanda* dimension. However, the reality of the physical world such that there must be some physical manifestation of an idea for it to have both *manipulanda* and *discriminanda* properties. Lacking these, an idea cannot be meaningfully marketed. It is a matter of strategic choice to attempt to stress the *utilitanda* property rather than the other two dimensions.

This can be illustrated by different approaches to encouraging birth control and safe-sex practices: on the one hand telling people of the necessity and desirability of birth control and safe sex, and on the other showing people how they can practise birth control and safe sex. An Australian AIDS awareness campaign used advertisements featuring the Grim Reaper bowling people over with a bowling ball— men, women and children, homosexual and heterosexual alike. The campaign, short-lived as it was, basically terrified people about the risk of AIDS. But this approach failed to effect sexual behaviour in the direction sought, In advertising parlance the message was 'all push, but no direction'. European approaches to achieving the same behavioural objective have taken vastly different forms, and have variously featured very explicit advertisements about the practice of buying, fitting and using condoms.

The more fundamental issue of value-adding has not been fully explored.

A more substantive way of adding value is to move along the *manipulanda* dimension. Movement along the *discriminanda* dimension is more likely to be construed as simply cosmetic. As King has suggested in a recent forecast of marketing in the present decade: 'People will still be looking for high quality and personal added values, variants, style and fashion changes. But their interpretation of quality seems to be changing quite fast. It's increasingly based on what they feel are *real values*—not superficial styling.'

We are advocating a return to the more classical interpretation and appreciation of the marketing concept. The notion of consumer orientation is captured by the *utilitanda* dimension, and the 'satisfaction function' is the time-honoured starting point. 'Value-added' then becomes a question of how the *manipulanda* and *discriminanda* properties of the object are 'bundled' in order to deliver these satisfactions. In short, the plea is not for product differentiation or positioning, but for genuine innovation.

This may simply be a restatement of conventional positions, but such that correction is necessary because many businesses appear to have actually lost their way. IBM has for example realised that it is no longer enough to continually assert that 'Big Blue is Best' in order to retain a unique position in the market. The difference has to be found in the reality of the market offer.

Sloganeering has led to the organisation's effective crippling over the past decade. There are but two dimensions along which products are differentiated—*discriminanda* and *manipulanda*. These dimensions can be meaningfully described and measured, and the marketing practitioner can then use such measures as a basis for making strategic choices amongst alternative ways of presenting offers to markets.

Reproduced with permission from *Marketing*, December/January 1992, pp. 32–34.

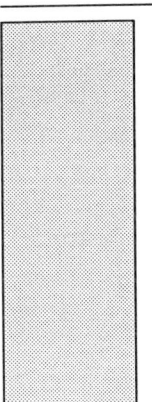

COMPANY INDEX

A C Goode & Co Ltd 286
Action Food Barns 289
Adelaide Steamship Co Ltd 286
Adidas 90
Advance Bank 173, 183
AFP Group PLC 134, 200
AGB McNair 90, 178, 179
Air New Zealand 124–27
AIS Media 266
A Kebab 207
Allied-Lyons PLC 136–37
American Airlines 124–27
American Express Travel Centres 91
Ameritech 229
AMP 172, 181
Ampol 93
AMR Quantum Market Research 64, 90
Andersen Consulting 238
Anheuser-Busch 137
Ansett 53
Ansett Transport Industries 207
Ansvar Insurance Company 148
ANZ 172, 173, 181, 183, 198, 200
Arby's 206
Arnotts Ltd 206, 207
Art Gallery of NSW 91
Arthritis Foundation of Western Australia 128
Asahi 201, 202, 284
Asahi Chemical 207
ASK Solutions 41

Associated Grocers Ltd 289
Asthma Foundation of Queensland 128
AT&T 47
Australia Post 47, 217
Australia Resouces Development Bank Ltd 286
Australian Air Force 46
Australian Airlines 46
Australian Army 217
Australian Broadcasting Corporation (ABC) 70, 76, 84
Australian Bureau of Statistics (ABS) 104, 158–60, 263, 265, 276–79
Australian Consolidated Investments 167
Australian Fast Foods 210
Australian Institute of Sport (AIS) 43
Australian Meat Holdings 135
Australian Planning and Systems Co Pty Ltd (APASCO) 262
Australian Posters 3-M 90
Australian Protective Services 47
Australian Stock Exchange 263, 283, 287, 289
Australian Taxation Office 46
Avis (US) 53

Ballarat Banking Co Ltd (1955) 285
Bank of Queensland Ltd (1922) 285
Bank of South Pacific Ltd 285
Bankers Trust Australia 94
Barclays 174

COMPANY INDEX

Barker Gosling   238, 239
BAT Industries (Australia) Pty Ltd   287
Beechams   52
BHP   92, 123, 200
Bi-Lo   102
Big Rooster   210
Black Stump   210
BMW   34, 341
Bob Lapointe   208, 210
Bond Brewing   167
Bond Corporation   137
BP   93
Brian Sweeney Research   68, 234–37
British Airways   46
Budget Rent A Car   209
Business Planning and Research Ltd   67
BWN Pty Ltd   238

Cadbury Schweppes Australia   97
Caltex   93
Cantinas International   207
Capita   172
Carling O'Keefe Breweries of Canada Ltd   283
Carlton and United Breweries (CUB)   132–46, 153, 165–70, 203, 283
Carrington Confirmers Pty Ltd   286
Carter Hold Harvey Ltd   284
Castlemaine Perkins   167
Castlemaine Tooheys   201
CCA   90
Cellabs   238
Charlie Carter   289
Charlton Media   92
Chase/AMP   174, 182, 183
Chicken Treat   210
Christou Family   210
Circle K   205
Citibank   174, 175, 202
Claude Neon   90
Clemenger   236
Clydesdale Bank Plc   286
Coates Signco   93
Coca-Cola   52, 346
Coca-Cola Amatil Ltd   287
Coles Myer   47, 93, 94, 101–8, 159, 188, 194–99, 200, 203, 210, 235
Collins Foods   206, 208, 210
Colonial Bank of Australasia Ltd (1918)   285
Commercial Banking Company of Sydney Ltd   285

Commercial Economic Advisory Service of Australia (CEASA)   262
Commonwealth Bank   161–65, 174, 178–86
Compadres   207
Compass Airlines   46
Competitive Foods   204, 209, 210
Continental Airlines   124–27
Courage   132–46, 283
CRA   123
Creative Connection   124–27
CSIRO   46
Custom Credit Holdings Ltd   285

D & J Fowler Ltd   289
Dairy Farms International   195
Dancer Fitzgerald Sample Advertising Agency   53
Darling Harbour Amusements   91
David Jones Ltd   286
Davids Holdings   94, 100–8, 290
Delawood Pty Ltd   238, 239
Dennys   207
Diners Club   92
Dow Corning   257–58
Doyle Dane Berbnach Advertising   53
Drug Arm   120, 146–51, 218
Du Pont   35

El Pollo Loco   206
Elders IXL   132–46, 283–85
Esso   243

FAI   92
First National Ltd   286
Foodland Associated   93–95, 289–90
Foodland Co-operative Ltd   289
Foodland Property Holdings Pty Ltd   289
Ford   33, 34
Fosters Brewing   90, 120, 132–46, 165–70, 188, 199–203, 283
Franklins   100–8, 159, 196–99

Gas and Fuel Corp of Victoria   46
General Motors   35, 38
George Patterson   205
Gold Coast Visitors and Convention Bureau   189–93
Grace Bros   197
Grand Metropolitan   132–46, 200, 283
Grandy's   207

COMPANY INDEX

Greene King & Sons Plc   138, 284
Grey Advertising   234–37
Gulliver's   208

Hans Continental Smallgoods Co   207
Hanson Trust   137
Harley Davidson   52
Harlin Securities Pty Ltd   283, 284
Hawaiian Airlines   124–27
Heritage Building Society   181, 183
Hong Kong and Shanghai Bank   202
HongkongBank   174
Hudson Conway   138
Hungry Jacks   204–10

IBM   37, 97, 153, 154–57, 243, 256–57
Independent Holdings Ltd   94
International Brewing Holdings (IBH)   199–203
Ipswich and West Moreton Building Society   181, 183

Jack the Slasher   100–8
Japan Airlines   124–27
Jardine Matheson Group   195, 208, 210
Jetabout Tours   91
John Singleton Advertising   207

Kaasen Ltd   206
Keg Restaurants   205, 207, 210
Kentucky Fried Chicken (KFC)   46, 93, 204–10
K mart   79, 196–99
Kodak   39, 91

L & K Rexona   69
Lang Corporation   200
Lever and Kitchen   90
Lifeline   218
Lion Nathan   165–70, 203

Magic Menu Systems   207
Magnum Corporation   94
Matchbox Toys   125
Matilda Bay Brewing Company   134
MBFI Australia   207
McDonald's   46, 93, 204–10, 240
McKinsey & Co   53, 121
Medical Benefit Fund (MBF)   250
Mercedes   34
Metromedia Technologies   92

Metropolitan Permanent Building Society   173
Metway Bank   173, 178, 179, 181, 183
Meyers Strategy Group   205
Michelin   90
Minter Ellison   239
Molson Companies   132–46, 199, 200, 201, 284
MORI   242
Mount Isa Mines (MIM)   121
Mr Chow Chinese   206

National and General Insurance Co Ltd   286
National Australia Bank (NAB)   161–65, 173, 176–86, 285–87
National Australia Bank (NZ) Ltd   286
National Australia Trustees Ltd   286
National Bank of Australasia Ltd   285
National Brewing Holdings   167
National Car Parks (NCP)   34
National Commercial Banking Corporation of Australia   285
National Irish Bank Ltd   286
National Mutual Royal Bank   183
NatWest   174
Nestlé   97
Nettlefold Outdoor Advertising   89
NML   172, 200
Northern Bank Ltd   286
Northwest Airlines   120, 124–27
NRMA   94
NSW Building Society   173

Outdoor Network Australia   90

Pancakes Australia   205
Parsonage Meats   210
Pearl and Dean   90
Penfolds Wines Pty Ltd   97
PepsiCo   204, 210
Phillip Morris   137
Pick-N-Pay Hypermarket   100
Pickfords   90
Pirelli Tyres   125
Pizza Haven   209, 210
Pizza Hut   93, 204–10
Polaroid   39
Potter Warburg   199, 201
PRD Realty   189
Prudential   92

COMPANY INDEX

Prudential Bache and McIntosh   200
Prudential Insurance Company (Canada)   35
PubCo   137–38, 168

Qantas   122, 124–27, 191
Queensland Art Gallery   188, 211–16
Queensland Independent Wholesalers   100–8
Queensland National Bank (1945)   285
Queensland Permanent Building Societies Association   179
Queensland Temperance League (QTL)   148
Queensland Tourist and Travel Corporation   190–93

R & I Property Trust   94
Red Rooster   210
Reuben's Hot Dogs   205
Rider Hunt   190, 192
RSPCA   222

SA Brewing   169, 199–203
Safeway   102, 169
Salvation Army   218
Samsonite   255
Sanitarium Health Food Company   63
SBS   70
Scandinavian Airline Systems (SAS)   46, 343
Scottish & Newcastle Breweries PLC   132–46, 284
Sears   33
Secton Pty Ltd   238, 239
Shell   205
Sizzler   206, 208, 210
South African Butter Board   52
St George Building Society   173, 176–86
Standard Chartered   174
State Banks
  NSW   174, 181, 183
  Queensland   174, 178, 181, 183
  South Australia   174
  Tasmania   174
  Victoria   174
  Western Australia   174

State Rail Authority   91
State Transit   91
Stochastic Research   67
Suncorp   181, 182, 183
Swan Brewery   95, 167
Sydney Aquarium   91
Sydney Water Board   46

Taco Den   208
Target   196, 197
Telecom   90, 217
Televidcom   91
Texas Instruments   237, 239
3M   48
TNT   53
Tooheys   91, 93, 153, 165–70
Toucano Char   206
Transport Accident Commission of Victoria (TAC)   234–37

Unilever   69
United Airlines   124–27
USAA   48

Vanders   207
Vox Ltd   93

Wal-Mart   33
Watney, Mann & Truman Ltd   132–46
Wendys   46
Westel Pty Ltd
Western Sizzlin   208
Western Steakout   208
Westpac   162, 171, 172, 173, 179–86
Whitbread Restaurants   205, 207, 210
Wickliffe Pty Ltd   283
Wills, WD & HO, Holdings Ltd   287–89
Wintergarden   47
Wollongong City Council   46
Woolcott Research   124–27
Woolworths   47, 93, 94, 101, 159, 169, 195–99

Xerox Computers   52

Yann Campbell Hoare Wheeler   205
Yorkshire Bank Plc   286

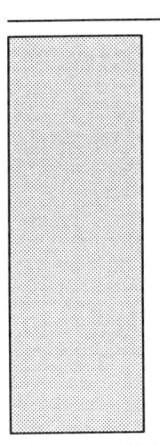

SUBJECT INDEX

Advertising 99, 113–14,
   and fear 234–37
   expenditure 264–66
   retail 158
   'spend' 181
Australian Rugby Union (ARU) 32, 42, 44

Barriers to entry 210
Brand loyalty 98, 99
Buyer behaviour, *see* consumer behaviour

Chain stores 100–8
Client communication technologies 48
Cognitive dissonance 237
Competition 33, 37, 39
   competitive environment 214
   competitive positioning 180–81, 216
   on price 170
Competitive advantage 153
   marketing strategies 153
Competitive strategy 293–309
   a critique of Porter 300–9
   Mintzberg's critique of Porter 298–300
   Porter's analysis 294–98
Consumer behaviour 62, 76, 234
   loyalty 171
Corporate image 242–45
Culture 146, 210, 212
Customer service 85, 112
   measurement systems 154–57
   service quality research 341–43

Deregulation, in banking 171, 176
Design school model 312–29
   content of 314–17
   process of strategy formulation of 317–18
   procedural rationality of 323–26
   substantive rationality of 318–23
Distribution, *see* Place

Effeciency, definitions of, in banking 161–65
   allocative 161
   cost 161
   dynamic 161
Electronic data interchange (EDI) 107, 178
Electronic Funds Transfer at Point-of-Sale (EFTPOS) 178
Environment 64–66, 69, 80, 240
   competitive 214
   external 213
Environmentally friendly 74, 241
Essays 10
Ethical frameworks 252–55
Ethics and marketing 225–33, 241
   and international business 251–58
   contributing factors in business 228–29
   courses of action 229–30
   dealing with problems 226–27
   limitations 230
Exploratory research 80, 81

SUBJECT INDEX

4Ps 73

Harvard Business School 33

Independents 100–8

Just in Time (JIT) 59

Language 7, 8

Market 51
  research 51, 52
  research industry 67–70
  segment 76, 98–100
  segmentation 62, 65–66, 216
    behavioural and attitudinal, of consumers 82–84
  share 156
Marketing 32, 36, 211
  and Bailment 27
  and Contract Law 21
  and *Fair Trading Act* 27
  and *Sale of Goods Act* 22
  and society 224, 245
  and Tort Law 22
  and *Trade Practices Act* 24
  as exchange 337–39
  budget 73
  concept 330–40
  courageous 51–57
  definitions of 330–31
  demand side 149, 221
  global 132–46
  industrial 120
  innovation 104
  international 124–27
  legal aspects of 20
  mission, objectives and goals 214
  mix 88
  non-profit—*see* Non-profit marketing
  plan 58, 199
  planning 188
  profit sector 218
  programmes 188
  research 62, 181
  services 45, 120
  strategic management and models of strategy formation 310–29
  strategies 98, 111, 117, 146
  supply side 148, 220
Me-too 35
Mission statement 212
Monopoly 34

Non-profit marketing 120, 128–31, 146–51, 188, 211–16, 217–22
  non-profit sector marketing 218
  problems facing organisations 222
  publics 131, 213
  stakeholders 131, 243
Not for profit—*see* Non-profit

Oral reports 4
Organisation
  organisational goals 212
  organisational objectives 212
Outdoor advertising 89

Performance indicators 216
Place 73, 250
Plagiarism 19
Presentation 4, 5
Price 73, 95–97, 100, 250
Pricing 88, 97, 107
  of services 182
Product 73, 248–49
  and service development 182
  life-cycle 193
  new 165–70
Promotion 73, 112–13, 249–50
Purchase behaviour 78, 99, 100

Qualitative research 68
  brainstorming 117
  discussion groups 99
Quality service planning 155
  key steps 156
Quality, value, service, perception (QVSP) 48

Retailing 158–60
  food 100–8
  garden centre 109–18
  grocery industry 100–8, 153, 158–60

Selective perception 237
Strengths, weaknesses, opportunities and threats (SWOT) 108
Sur/petition 33–40

Total Quality Management (TQM) 32, 38, 45–49, 157
Tourism 189–93

Value-added 344–48

Wheel of retailing 95, 108